THE GA

T0277332

SEAN CONNOLLY & PHILIP BRIGGS

www.bradtguides.com

Bradt Guides Ltd, UK
The Globe Pequot Press Inc, USA

Bradt GUIDES

TRAVEL TAKEN SERIOUSLY

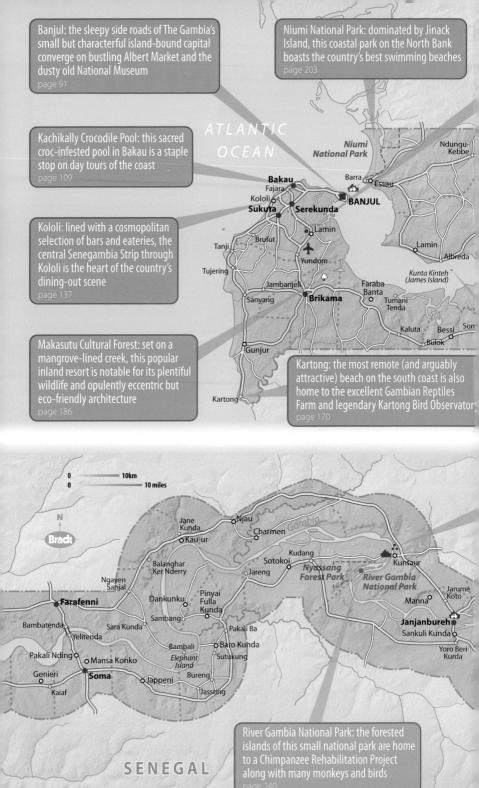

Banjul: the sleepy side roads of The Gambia's small but characterful island-bound capital converge on bustling Albert Market and the dusty old National Museum
page 91

Niumi National Park: dominated by Jinack Island, this coastal park on the North Bank boasts the country's best swimming beaches
page 203

Kachikally Crocodile Pool: this sacred croc-infested pool in Bakau is a staple stop on day tours of the coast
page 109

Kololi: lined with a cosmopolitan selection of bars and eateries, the central Senegambia Strip through Kololi is the heart of the country's dining-out scene
page 137

Makasutu Cultural Forest: set on a mangrove-lined creek, this popular inland resort is notable for its plentiful wildlife and opulently eccentric but eco-friendly architecture
page 186

Kartong: the most remote (and arguably attractive) beach on the south coast is also home to the excellent Gambian Reptiles Farm and legendary Kartong Bird Observatory
page 170

River Gambia National Park: the forested islands of this small national park are home to a Chimpanzee Rehabilitation Project along with many monkeys and birds
page 240

ATLANTIC OCEAN

Niumi National Park

Bakau
Fajara
Kololi
Sukuta
Serekunda
BANJUL
Barra
Essau
Ndungu-Kebbe
Lamin
Tanji
Brufut
Yundum
Lamin
Albreda
Tujering
Jambanjeli
Faraba Banta
Kunta Kinteh (James Island)
Sanyang
Brikama
Tumani Tenda
Kaluta
Bessi
Som
Gunjur
Bulok
Kartong

Bradt

Jane Kunda
Njau
Charmen
Gambia
Kau-ur
Balanghar
Ker Nderry
Sotokoi
Kudang
Kuntaur
Ngayen Sanjal
Jareng
Nyassang Forest Park
River Gambia National Park
Jarume Koto
Farafenni
Dankunku
Pinyai Fulla Kunda
Manna
Bambatenda
Yelitenda
Sambang
Pakali Ba
Janjanbureh
Sankuli Kunda
Pakali Nding
Sara Kunda
Bambali
Baro Kunda
Yoro Beri Kurda
Genieri
Mansa Konko
Elephant Island
Sutukung
Soma
Japperi
Bureng
Kaiaf
Jasseng

0   10km
0   10 miles
N

SENEGAL

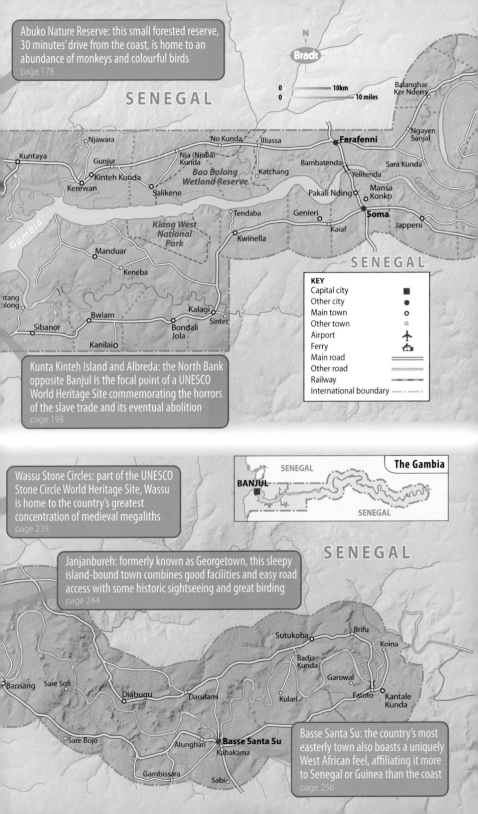

Abuko Nature Reserve: this small forested reserve, 30 minutes' drive from the coast, is home to an abundance of monkeys and colourful birds
page 178

Kunta Kinteh Island and Albreda: the North Bank opposite Banjul Is the focal point of a UNESCO World Heritage Site commemorating the horrors of the slave trade and its eventual abolition
page 198

Wassu Stone Circles: part of the UNESCO Stone Circle World Heritage Site, Wassu is home to the country's greatest concentration of medieval megaliths
page 239

Janjanbureh: formerly known as Georgetown, this sleepy island-bound town combines good facilities and easy road access with some historic sightseeing and great birding
page 244

Basse Santa Su: the country's most easterly town also boasts a uniquely West African feel, affiliating it more to Senegal or Guinea than the coast
page 256

The Gambia

KEY

Capital city	■
Other city	●
Main town	○
Other town	○
Airport	✈
Ferry	⛴
Main road	
Other road	
Railway	
International boundary	

SENEGAL

SENEGAL

SENEGAL

Bradt

N

0   10km
0   10 miles

Balanghar Ker Nderry
Ngayen Sanjal
Njawara
No Kunda
Illiassa
Farafenni
Sara Kunda
Kuntaya
Gunjur
Nja (Njaba) Kunda
Bambatenda
Yelitenda
Kinteh Kunda
Katchang
Mansa Konko
Kerewan
Salikene
Pakali Nding
Bao Bolong Wetland Reserve
Tendaba
Genieri
Soma
Jappeni
Kiang West National Park
Kwinella
Kaiaf
Manduar
Keneba
ntang olong
Bwiam
Kalagi
Sibanor
Bondali Jola
Sintet
Kanilaio

BANJUL
SENEGAL
SENEGAL

Bansang
Sare Sofi
Sutukoba
Brifu
Koina
Badja Kunda
Garowal
Diabugu
Darsilami
Kulari
Fatoto
Kantale Kunda
Sare Bojo
Alunghari
Basse Santa Su
Kabakama
Gambissara
Sabi

THE GAMBIA
DON'T MISS...

WILDLIFE
Wildlife is everywhere in The Gambia, whether it be sparkling dragonflies or colourful butterflies, noisy frogs, scampering lizards or sleepy crocodiles. Pictured here, a chimpanzee in River Gambia National Park PAGE 243
(tm/S)

HISTORY
From old-style Creole architecture to mysterious stone circles (such as Wassu, pictured here), Gambia has a varied and fascinating history PAGE 239
(VZ/S)

BEACHES
The coastline around Greater Banjul is home to some wonderful beaches, including those at Palma Rima and Kotu PAGE 125
(CP/S)

BIRDS
The Gambia is a great destination for first time birders in Africa as birds are a vital part of every habitat; the yellow-crowned gonolek can be spotted without even leaving your resort PAGE 46
(PP/S)

CULTURE
The Gambia is known for its masquerade tradition – there's a festival in Janjanbureh every January PAGE 251
(AVZ)

THE GAMBIA
IN COLOUR

left
(SA/S)

Everything from fruit and veg to beads, fabrics and prints can be found at Albert Market in Banjul
PAGE 101

below
(AVZ)

Street markets are a way of life in The Gambia, but nowhere more so than at Banjul's busy Albert Market
PAGE 101

bottom
(AVZ)

Woodcarvers and other craftsmen are common on the streets of Banjul
PAGE 99

The view over Banjul, one of Africa's smallest capital cities PAGE 91

above
(PPL/S)

Built to honour the previous government, Arch 22 – Banjul's biggest monument – is finding a new role as the Never Again Memorial PAGE 99

right
(e/S)

Despite its small size, Banjul remains an important trading centre, just as it was in the colonial era PAGE 92

below
(SA/S)

AUTHOR

Sean Connolly (◉ @shanboqol; **w** seanconnollytravel. com) first travelled to Africa as a student in 2008 and has been returning to the continent regularly to research, teach or simply soak up the ambiance in Africa's countless little-visited corners ever since. He's been poring over maps since before he could read them, and working with Bradt Guides since 2011. Along with authoring two editions of Bradt's *Senegal*, he's also updated or contributed to the Bradt guides to Somaliland, Malawi, Mozambique, Ghana, Uruguay, Sierra Leone, São Tomé

& Príncipe, two editions of Rwanda and Gabon. When he's not updating guides, leading tours or discussing the many merits of camel meat, you'll find him seeking out a country's funkiest records or otherwise clacking away at a desk in Copenhagen.

Philip Briggs (**e** philip.briggs@bradtguides.com) has been exploring the highways and backwaters of Africa since he first backpacked there in 1986. In the 1990s, he authored pioneering Bradt guidebooks to several destinations then practically uncharted by the travel publishing industry, notably Tanzania, Uganda, Ethiopia, Malawi, Mozambique, Ghana and Rwanda. More recently, he wrote the Bradt guides to Somaliland, Suriname, Sri Lanka and The Gambia. He spends at least four months travelling annually, usually

accompanied by his wife, the photographer Ariadne Van Zandbergen, and spends the rest of his time battering away at a keyboard in the coastal village of Wilderness in South Africa's Western Cape.

CONTRIBUTORS

Craig Emms and **Linda Barnett** are professional ecologists who lived in The Gambia from 1999 to 2006. During this time they worked with the government and were instrumental in the development of a national wildlife conservation organisation called Makasutu Wildlife Trust. They now live in England.

Simon Fenton was a travel writer and photographer who updated the second edition of this guide. He was also a contributor to the Bradt guide to Senegal and published two books chronicling his adventures in the country: *Squirting Milk at Chameleons* and *Chasing Hornbills* (see page 272 for more information). Tragically, he was killed in a car accident in 2017.

Third edition published January 2024
First published 2014
Bradt Guides Ltd
31a High Street, Chesham, Buckinghamshire, HP5 1BW, England
www.bradtguides.com
Print edition published in the USA by The Globe Pequot Press Inc,
PO Box 480, Guilford, Connecticut 06437-0480

Text copyright © 2024 Sean Connolly
Maps copyright © 2024 Bradt Guides Ltd; includes map data © OpenStreetMap
contributors
Photographs copyright © 2024 Individual photographers (see below)
Project Manager: Elspeth Beidas
Cover research: Ian Spick

ISBN: 9781804690611

British Library Cataloguing in Publication Data
A catalogue record for this book is available from the British Library

Photographs Alamy Stock Photos: STOCKFOLIO® (S/A); Shutterstock: Agami
Photo Agency (APA/S), Salvador Aznar (SA/S), Timon Cornelissen (TC/S),
Curioso.photography (CP/S), Jessica Dale (JD/S), evenfh (e/S), matthieu Gallet
(mG/S), David Havel (DH/S), IvetZlin (IZ/S), Dennis Jacobsen (DJ/S), Liz Miller
(LM/S), tony mills (tm/S), Dave Montreuil (DM/S), PhotopankPL (PPL/S), Piotr
Poznan (PP/S), stikstofstudio (s/S), SuxxesPhoto (SP/S), Vladimir Zhoga (VZ/S);
SuperStock (SS); Ariadne Van Zandbergen (www.africaimagelibrary.com) (AVZ)
Front cover Gambian musician playing the Kora (APA/S)
Back cover (left to right) Mangroves around the River Gambia (CP/S); red-throated
bee-eater (PP/S)
Title page (left to right) Traditional woven baskets (SS); boat on Kotu Beach (SS)

Maps David McCutcheon FBCart.S. FRGS

Typeset by Ian Spick, Bradt Guides
Production managed by Jellyfish Print Solutions; printed in India
Digital conversion by www.dataworks.co.in

When I first visited The Gambia in 1999, it immediately came across as West Africa's oddest man out. For one thing, this former British colony is a tiny country, the smallest on the African mainland, only 300km long and nowhere more than 50km wide. Linguistically and politically, it is an incongruous Anglophone enclave surrounded on all terrestrial fronts by French-speaking Senegal. Furthermore, where most of West Africa is typically best suited to hardcore independent travel, The Gambia is an altogether more straightforward prospect, with a package-oriented tourist industry focused on the dense cluster of facilities along the Atlantic coastline immediately south of the capital Banjul.

Despite this, The Gambia has always held a special appeal for me. Coming from almost anywhere else in one of the world's toughest travel regions, it feels strikingly approachable, uncomplicated and well organised, partly due to the innate friendliness of its people and partly due to the superior facilities. It is also a very pretty country, dominated by the contrasting waterscapes of the choppy Atlantic Ocean and more serene River Gambia, and literally teeming with colourful tropical birds and monkeys. For those who find the coastal resorts a little too sanitised for their tastes, a quick sojourn upriver – whether for a few hours or weeks – plunges one straight back into the no-frills travel conditions that typified West Africa back in the 1990s.

KEY TO MAP SYMBOLS

✈ ✛	Airport (international)/airstrip		✕	Restaurant, etc
🛳	Vehicle ferry		⌸	Café
⛴	Small ferry/pirogue		♀	Bar
🚌	Bus station		☆	Nightclub/casino
🚗	Car hire/taxis		℮	Internet café
⛽	Fuel station/garage		⬜	Cemetery
🚲	Cycle hire		†	Church/cathedral
🛈	Tourist information		☾	Mosque
❸	Embassy/consulate/high commission		✿	Garden
♗	Museum/gallery		▶	Golf course
⌗	Important/historic building		⤬	Gate/roadblock
⚲	Statue		◤	Beach
$	Bank/ATM		•	Other point of interest
✉	Post office		🏃	Stadium
⊞	Hospital		≈	Marsh
✚	Pharmacy/clinic		▫	National park/reserve
⌂	Hotel/inn/guesthouse, etc		▨	Market
⚠	Campsite		▦	Urban park

Acknowledgements

Having gotten to know neighbouring Senegal quite well in the process of writing two Bradt guides to the country, I was grateful for the opportunity to discover this little land 'in between' on its own terms, and not simply as an addendum to my work in Senegal. My thanks are therefore firstly due to my predecessors Philip Briggs and the late Simon Fenton, who bequeathed me such a considered and compelling text from which to begin my explorations. Though he is no longer with us, Simon in particular opened doors for me across the length and breadth (ok – mostly length!) of The Gambia, as so many of the people I met instantly remembered his love for the country, his dedicated attention to the previous edition of this guide, and most of all his warm and attentive friendship.

And so in the process of my own explorations in the quite accomplished footsteps of Simon and Philip, I discovered that this 'island' inside Senegal had a distinct charm and flavour all of its own, and one that was eminently worth exploring in its own right. And without the help, companionship, and advice of the following people, I wouldn't have discovered even half of The Gambia's many charms:

Dave Adams (FairPlay Gambia), David and Linda (Footsteps Eco-Lodge and Ethical Travel Portal), Kathrine Roldsgaard Nielsen, Phil Paoletta (Scoot West Africa), Annie Risemberg, Brandon Payne, Yusupha Danso, Lamin Camara, Alikalo, Juliana Peluso, Betty (Suleima Lodge), Rachel (Feel Free), Devon and Amadou (Jinack Lodge), Greg (Evergreen), Diné (Fathala), Amy (Good Vibes), Haddy (White Horse), Sarah (Hibiscus House), Barbara and Bamadi (Kairoh Garden), Abdoul and Carlijn (AbCa's Creek), Silvia (Sambou Kunda), Nikki and Neil (The Folly), Nina (Leo's), George (Georgianna's), Linda (Mandina), Lawrence (Makasutu), Louise Thomas (Gambia Experience), Tombong Sanyang, Khady Mane, and all the many others with whom I shared a bite, a beer or a bus seat.

Back at home, I would like to thank everyone who continues to show me ever so much patience and grace as I endlessly take on more projects than I know what to do with, and often find myself somewhat harried and unhelpful as a result – so a big *mange tak* to Jon Tofteskov and Ellie Taylor for the support on the home front. And an even bigger *qujanaq* is due to my partner Line Riis Christiansen, without whose unfailing encouragement, from both near and far, I would be lost.

And finally my thanks are, of course, also due to my always-superb editors and colleagues at Bradt Guides, in particular Elspeth Beidas, who has made this book shine.

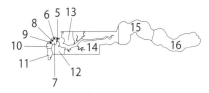

Contents

LIST OF MAPS

Introduction

The Gambia has been called the Gateway to Africa, an assertion with which it is difficult to argue, at least from the perspective of an English-speaker. Closer to Europe than any other Anglophone part of West Africa, this tiny country – the smallest on the African mainland – has become a perennially popular entry point to Africa with sunseekers from Britain and several other northern European countries. During its blissfully sunny dry season, which happens to coincide with the northern midwinter, The Gambia is connected to the UK and Europe by a glut of affordable charter flights. And once there, the coastline is dotted with a vast and varied collection of upmarket resort hotels, quirky eco-lodges and grassroots beach camps offering great value for money on any budget.

Despite its small size, The Gambia offers plenty of variety to tourists. Among the most idiosyncratic legacies of the colonial Scramble for Africa, the country is nowhere more than 50km wide, protruding tendril-like into Francophone Senegal (with which it shares all its terrestrial borders) as it follows the course of the River Gambia inland for 300km. Landscapes and habitats range from lush shady forests festooned with creeping vines to endless expanses of golden sandy beach, from dry Guinean savannah to bounteous seasonal swamps, from brooding mangrove-lined creeks to the broad expanse of the majestic river that gives the country its name.

While most holidaymakers aggregate at the coastal resorts, others succumb to the down-to-earth allure of the interior, where villages of mud-walled grass-roofed round huts dot the muddy banks of the life-sustaining river. Here, cattle and other livestock wander across pot-holed roads where small-wheeled donkey carts plod lethargically alongside battered old bush taxis. Men sit beneath huge shady trees brewing endless pots of green tea, while brightly dressed women walk by, gracefully poised with all manner of bundles, buckets and pots on their heads. People follow traditional pursuits, fishing the protein-rich waters of the river or working the fields using simple hand tools. And while the tradition-soaked tropical ambience of upriver Gambia amounts to more than the sum of its individual attractions, there are highlights aplenty, including the mysterious megaliths of Wassu and the chimps and hippos of River Gambia National Park.

Though beach holidays predominate, The Gambia is also renowned in ornithological circles for providing a superb, and affordable, introduction to Africa's rich birdlife. More so than any other African country we know, birds dominate every niche of the Gambian landscape: spectacularly colourful parrots, rollers, bee-eaters and turacos; comical hornbills and decorous crowned cranes; dozens of eagles and other striking raptors; plus a mind-boggling assemblage of marine and other aquatic species. An astonishing 625 species have been recorded in The Gambia, a country barely half the size of Wales – and fortunately, for first-time visitors to Africa, there's no shortage of knowledgeable local guides to help track down and identify these many avian gems.

In terms of character and facilities, The Gambia is a country of three distinct parts, as reflected in the structure of this guidebook. The first and largest of these covers Greater Banjul and Kololi, the country's main package-tourism hub, extending over less than 1% of its area but accounting for perhaps 95% of hotels and other tourist-related facilities. The second section covers the remainder of the coastal belt, an attractive area dotted with low-key eco-lodges and other isolated getaways that cater to a more independent-minded travel market. The final section covers the untrammelled delights of upriver Gambia, a region that accounts for about 95% of the country's surface area but has very few facilities genuinely oriented to tourists, making it the ideal African taster for the genuinely adventurous. But rest assured on one thing: whichever part of The Gambia you visit, better still all three, it is a wonderfully friendly and enjoyable country; one that has a habit of attracting repeat visitors year after year.

FEEDBACK REQUEST

At Bradt Guides we're aware that guidebooks start to go out of date on the day they're published – and that you, our readers, are out there in the field doing research of your own. You'll find out before us when a fine new family-run hotel opens or a favourite restaurant changes hands and goes downhill. So why not tell us about your experiences? Contact us on ☏ 01753 893444 or e info@bradtguides.com. We will forward emails to the author who may post updates on the Bradt website at w bradtguides.com/updates. Alternatively, you can add a review of the book to Amazon, or share your adventures with us on social:

f BradtGuides & ShanBoqol
X BradtGuides & ShanBoqol
◙ BradtGuides & ShanBoqol

HOW TO USE THIS GUIDE

AUTHORS' FAVOURITES Finding genuinely characterful accommodation or that unmissable off-the-beaten-track café can be difficult, so the authors have chosen a few of their favourite places throughout the country to point you in the right direction. These 'authors' favourites' are marked with a ✳.

PRICES With the exception of some upmarket hotels and car-rental companies, pretty much every price in The Gambia is quoted in the local currency. However, because of the dalasi's ongoing devaluation and comparatively high local inflation rate, we feel that converting dalasi prices to a hard currency equivalent is more likely to provide a reliable medium-term indicator of current prices. As it is clearly the most widely used hard currency in The Gambia, we have opted to use British pound sterling for this purpose and converted October 2023 prices at an approximate exchange rate of D80 to the pound.

PRICE CODES Throughout this guide we have used price codes to indicate the cost of those places to stay and eat listed in the guide. For a key to these price codes, see page 73 for accommodation and page 74 for restaurants.

MAPS

Keys and symbols Maps include alphabetical keys covering the locations of those places to stay, eat or drink that are featured in the guide. Hotels or restaurants that are not listed in the guide (but which might serve as alternative options if required or serve as useful landmarks to aid navigation) are also included on the maps; these are marked with accommodation A, restaurant X, bar V or café W symbols. Note that regional maps may not show all hotels and restaurants in the area: other establishments may be located in towns shown on the map.

Grids and grid references Some maps use gridlines to allow easy location of sites. Map grid references are listed in square brackets after the name of the place or site of interest in the text, with page number followed by grid number, eg: [94 C3].

Part One

GENERAL INFORMATION

Location West Africa

Neighbouring country Bordered by Senegal on all sides except for its short Atlantic coastline

Size 11,295km^2 (4,361 square miles)

Climate Dry mid-October to early June; rainy mid-June to early October

Status Unitary republic

Population 2.47 million (2023 estimate). 2.23% annual growth rate (2023).

Capital Banjul (population approximately 35,000, of 481,000 in Banjul/ Kanifing metro area, 2023)

Economy Major earners are agriculture, trade and tourism

GDP US$7.43 billion (PPP) (2023 estimate)

Gross National Income per capita US$2,308 (2023 estimate)

Language Official language English. Local languages include Mandinka, Wolof, Jola and Fula.

Religion 96% Muslim, 4% Christian, <1% follow traditional religions

Currency Gambian dalasi (100 bututs per dalasi)

Rate of exchange US$1 = D66; £1 = D80; €1 = D69 (October 2023); for up-to-date rates, go to **w** xe.com

International telephone code +220

Time GMT

Electricity Type G, British-style three-pin plug, 220–240 volts

Weights and measures Metric and imperial, as in the UK

Public holidays 1 January, 18 February, 1 May, 25 May, 15 August, 25 December as well as the movable religious holidays including Koriteh, Tobaski, Milad an-Nabi, Good Friday and Easter Monday

Flag Three horizontal stripes – red, blue and green from top to bottom, each colour separated by a narrow white stripe

National anthem 'For The Gambia our Homeland'

National motto 'Progress, Peace and Prosperity'

1

Background Information

GEOGRAPHY

LOCATION AND SIZE The Republic of The Gambia lies on the western coast of tropical Africa, at a latitude almost equidistant from the Equator and the Tropic of Cancer. Shaped like a long, crooked finger extending inland from its Atlantic coastline, it is surrounded on all other sides by the much larger French-speaking country of Senegal. It is nowhere more than 48km from north to south (though the coastline, with its bays and promontories, is longer), but it extends inland from west to east for 325km, roughly following the route of the River Gambia. With a total land area of only 11,295km^2, The Gambia is the smallest country on mainland Africa (the closest contender Swaziland is almost 50% larger). In global terms, it is similar in area to Jamaica or Qatar, and about half the size of Wales or the US state of New Jersey.

THE CAPITAL AND OTHER PRINCIPAL URBAN CENTRES The capital is Banjul (formerly Bathurst), a small island-bound city located at the southern tip of the Gambia River mouth. Unusually for an African city, Banjul has been losing population for years, and the current figure of around 35,000 means that while it remains the country's administrative centre, it is by no means the largest town. That accolade belongs to the vast unplanned sprawl of Serekunda (or more accurately Kanifing Local Government Area, also taking in Bakau, Fajara and other neighbouring suburbs), which is more than 12 times larger, with an estimated population of 450,000, and lies on the mainland only 10km to the east of Banjul. Most of the rest of the population is also concentrated on the coastal belt south of the river mouth, where Brikama, Sukuta and Gunjur all rank along with Banjul and Serekunda among the country's largest towns. Upriver, the largest towns are Farafenni, Soma and Basse Santa Su, none of which has a population much greater than 30,000.

ADMINISTRATIVE REGIONS The Gambia is divided into seven primary administrative sectors. There are two cities/districts, namely the city of Banjul, covering only the island capital, and the much larger Kanifing Local Municipality/ Local Government Area, which incorporates Serekunda and Bakau, as well as five regions (formerly called divisions). The names of the five regions are fairly self-explanatory. The West Coast Region (WCR), located entirely south of the River Gambia, comprises the coastal belt south of Greater Banjul as far inland as the Bintang Bolong (whose natural curves form its eastern boundary), with its capital at Brikama. The North Bank Region (NBR) covers the coastal belt north of the River Gambia, inland through the regional capital Kerewan, past Farafenni, to just beyond the town of Ngayen Sanjal. The Lower River Region (LRR) comprises the

3

South Bank of the river, running east from WCR, via the regional headquarters Mansa Konko and nearby Soma, to the Sofaniama Bolong and the town of Pakali Ba. The Central River Region (CRR), which covers both sides of the river east of the borders with NBR and LRR, contains the larger towns of Kau-ur, Kuntaur and Bansang, but its capital is the small historical town of Janjanbureh on MacCarthy Island. The Upper River Region (URR) comprises the most easterly part of the country and its capital is Basse Sante Su. Each of the administrative regions is further split into smaller districts, of which there are now 42. A chief, known as a *seyfo*, heads each of these districts and the chiefs are elected into their position by the village heads, who are known as *alkalos*.

POPULATION Gambia's population is estimated at 2,468,569 in 2023 (up from 687,817 in 1983). The fertility rate remains high, at around four births per woman, but this is trending downwards year on year, and the latest figures indicate a 2.5% annual population growth. Given The Gambia's small size, the population density is now about 219 people per square kilometre, making it the fourth highest in non-insular Africa, after Rwanda, Burundi and Nigeria.

CLIMATE

The Gambia has a wonderfully warm climate characterised by a long dry season from mid-October to early June, and a short rainy season from mid-June to early October. March and April are the hottest months, with average daytime maximum temperatures of around 34°C on the coast, and even hotter inland. During the rains, known in The Gambia as the 'green season', frequent and magnificent rainstorms cool everything down for a while, before the humidity shoots up to almost 100%. From December to mid-February the average daytime temperature falls to around 24°C, which is fairly comfortable, especially when coming from a cold, wet European or North American winter. After February the days get steadily hotter until the rains come in June. Temperatures are generally slightly lower along the coast, owing to

CLIMATE CHARTS

Banjul

	J	F	M	A	M	J	J	A	S	O	N	D
max°C	32	33	34	33	32	32	31	30	31	32	32	32
min°C	23	16	17	18	19	20	23	24	23	22	19	17
R mm	1	0	0	0	2	63	235	347	255	5	0	0

Janjanbureh

	J	F	M	A	M	J	J	A	S	O	N	D
max°C	35	37	39	40	39	36	32	31	32	34	36	34
min°C	16	18	20	22	24	24	23	23	23	23	19	16
R mm	0	0	0	1	7	92	195	230	205	65	3	1

Basse Santa Su

	J	F	M	A	M	J	J	A	S	O	N	D
max°C	34	36	38	40	39	36	33	32	32	34	35	34
min°C	15	16	21	24	25	25	23	23	23	23	18	15
R mm	0	5	0	5	20	110	210	252	236	65	5	0

cooling offshore winds, but these figures are only averages, and on some days it can be a lot warmer – in the high 30s or more occasionally in the mid 40s. Average rainfall per year is around 1,020mm, but in the west it can be much higher – up to 1,700mm – while in the drier east it can be as low as 800mm. Over the past 40 years or so, a slight warming in average temperatures and a decrease in rainfall has adversely affected the livelihoods of farmers dependent on rain-fed crops.

HISTORY

PREHISTORY There is very little evidence available to tell us when humans first settled West Africa, though it is thought that the earliest settlers were here at least 1.6 million years ago. Before the Stone Age the inhabitants of the region appear to have been nomadic hunter-gatherers who made only temporary settlements before moving on to follow the herds of wild animals that sustained them.

The first actual evidence of people living in the area now called The Gambia comes from Stone Age tools found under the sand dunes at Fajara and Cape Point. These have been dated to around 2000BC. During the Stone Age the lifestyle of the people changed dramatically and they stopped following wild animal herds to settle down and grow vegetable and cereal crops. Cattle were also domesticated during this period. All of this change led to a sudden increase in the size of the human population.

The next major development in West Africa was the coming of the Iron Age (there appears to have been a complete lack of a Bronze Age in the region). The discovery of iron was very significant and heralded the clearance of large areas of forest for agriculture, as iron tools proved to be much more durable than stone tools (and sharper too).

ARAB TRADERS AND THE BEGINNINGS OF ISLAM Trade became increasingly important for West Africans as the whole structure of society slowly changed. Some people gave up being farmers and herdsmen and branched out into other occupations such as traders, smiths, artisans, artists and administrators. Alongside these, of course, came the first soldiers and rulers. During the 1st century AD, another major event began to change the region. This was the introduction of the camel into North Africa from Arabia. The 'ship of the desert', as camels became known, allowed traders to cross the great Saharan desert for the first time in history. This meant that long trade routes were opened up between West Africa and Europe and Asia, via Arabia. Many goods were then transported north across the Sahara, including gold and ivory, as well as enslaved people, which were largely traded in return for rock salt imported from the Amazigh-controlled Saharan salt mines. It appears that by AD500 many settlements were well established in The Gambia. Evidence for their existence is plentiful and can be seen in the form of burial sites, stone circles and shell mounds that are scattered widely across the country.

It was in the early 7th century that one of the most significant events to shape humankind happened in Arabia. This was the birth of the Islamic religion, founded by the Prophet Muhammad. This new religion expanded quickly, and by AD710 all of North Africa was under the control of the Arab Umayyad Caliphate. At first, Islam was the religion of only the wealthy classes and the rulers but its spread southwards into the general population of West Africa was aided by a group of religious teachers who were called *marabouts*. The marabouts were attached to the chiefs as secretaries to their courts. As a reward for good service many of the marabouts received land from the chiefs and were allowed to found their own villages. These villages had Koranic schools, followed Islamic dietary laws and kept fast during the Holy Month of Ramadan, and soon they became 'islands' of Islam among the West African communities that still held traditional beliefs.

Another important event now took place, and this was the sudden growth of the slave trade. Up until this point in time most of the people enslaved in the Arab nations came from the Amazigh people of North Africa. However, the Amazigh people had also converted to the Islamic religion and it was against Islamic laws for one Muslim to enslave another. This meant that a new source of people to enslave had to be found, which was eventually located in sub-Saharan Africa.

THE MANDING (MALI) EMPIRE From the 5th century AD, several major kingdoms arose in West Africa. The three main kingdoms up until the 15th century were Ghana, Manding (known to Arabs and Europeans as Mali) and Kanem Borno. Present-day The Gambia was situated within the Manding Empire, which was at its height known as far away as Baghdad as 'The Land of Gold'. This empire coalesced after the decline and collapse of the Ghana Empire in the 13th century, when founding leader Sundiata Keita led a Malinké force against neighbouring king Sumanguru Kanté at the Battle of Kirina in 1235. This battle is considered the birth of the Manding Empire, and Sundiata's exploits have been passed down by a hereditary caste of historians, storytellers and musicians known as *griots* or *jelis* (page 24) throughout the region for an astonishing eight centuries as *The Epic of Sundiata*.

By the 14th century, the kingdom had grown significantly, now encompassing lands stretching from coastal Gambia and Senegal in the west all the way to what is now Niger in the east. At this time, trade with the Arab nations reached a peak and Mali became very rich and prosperous. Enslaved people were traded for salt, which was in short supply in the region, as well as horses and weapons. Huge armies were raised to protect the trade routes and to further extend the kingdom through conquests.

Overseeing this period of flourishing trade and expansion was Mali's most famous monarch, the ninth *mansa* (king) of Manding, the legendary Mansa Musa – himself the great-nephew of founder Sundiata Keita. A great proponent of Islam, Mansa Musa encouraged the religion's spread in his kingdom during his 25-year reign, building many mosques and eventually undertaking the hajj pilgrimage to Mecca. This was a multi-year affair at the time, not least thanks to the fact he reportedly travelled at the head of an entourage of 60,000 men. These men and their camels carried staggering amounts of gold – perhaps as much as 18,000kg (16 tonnes) – which Mansa Musa famously distributed quite freely all along his route. This generosity was reputed to have crashed the price of gold in Cairo for a decade, and cemented Mali's reputation as 'the land of gold'.

The Manding Empire began to decline in the mid 15th century, and after a series of territorial and successional conflicts it definitively collapsed in the mid 1600s. These territorial conflicts and the loosening of imperial structures saw many groups begin to migrate around the sub-region as the power of the empire receded. The Serer people moved from south of the River Gambia on to the North Bank of the river and created the kingdoms of Siné and Saloum, which remained powerful until the 19th century. A group of Malinké people also migrated south into the Gambia River valley, taking Islam with them, where they encountered the Jola people, who were already present. These migrants settled here and eventually became known as the Mandinka people.

THE KINGDOM OF KAABU The Kingdom of Kaabu started as a westward extension of the Manding Empire, but as the empire declined the Kaabu kingdom gradually took over the reins of power. Stretching from the River Gambia in the north to Guinea in the south, and ruled by Mandinkas, it was a great centre for trade. As time passed, Fula states and kingdoms surrounded Kaabu, and many Fulas, who were nomadic pastoralists, migrated on to Mandinka lands, which were fertile and well watered. By the mid 19th century, the Fula formed the largest single ethnic group in the region. However, they were still governed by the Mandinkas, who ruled with a rod of iron and treated them very harshly. The situation remained the same until after the Soninke–Marabout Wars of the 1880s (page 10) when the marabouts were defeated.

THE ARRIVAL OF EUROPEANS At this time many stories of the untold wealth of West Africa began to reach the ears of the royal houses of Europe. The first nation to strike out for West Africa was Portugal; the Portuguese reached the Cape Verde peninsula (where the city of Dakar was later built) in 1447. Here, explorers heard about the River Gambia and the gold that was reputed to be found in large quantities along its banks. In 1455, Prince Henry of Portugal sent Luiz de Cadamosto and three ships to search for this river. When they eventually found it they managed to sail only a few miles upriver before being attacked by locals in canoes and forced to give up. The next year they returned again to The Gambia and this time managed to sail 60 miles upriver, where they were received warmly by the Mandinka ruler of Baddibu. Along the way one of their crewmen died and was buried on an island in the river that still retains his name to this day: James Island (also known as St Andrew). The Portuguese eventually achieved a foothold in the country amid other European nations who were also becoming interested in the region. Many trading posts were established along the coast, trading brandy, guns and salt for gold, ivory and leather. The incomers also built forts to protect their trading posts from hostile local inhabitants and from marauding pirates.

Unfortunately for them, the Europeans soon found that, despite Mansa Musa's legendary largesse, the West African El Dorado of their imaginations was not to be found on the banks of the River Gambia. They cast about for another source of easily accumulated wealth to be gleaned from these lands and it wasn't long before they realised the vast possibilities of profit that could be gained from the trade in enslaved people.

THE SLAVE TRADE Slavery had existed in West Africa for many years before the Europeans arrived. Already from around the middle of the 7th century, the trans-Saharan slave trade saw thousands of captives taken across the desert to be enslaved in the cities of North Africa and beyond; scholars say between 6 and 10 million people may have been taken from West Africa this way. Within the region, warring groups also often raided each other's villages and took prisoners, who were then enslaved. However, in contrast to the racially codified forms of chattel slavery practised during the Atlantic slave trade period, these individuals were often treated as one of their new master's family and many eventually had a chance to earn their freedom.

When Europeans arrived in West Africa in the middle of the second millennium AD, they were hungry for vast numbers of enslaved people to work in the cotton fields and plantations of their colonies in the New World. Many African kings and chiefs soon realised how much wealth they could accumulate from the sale of enslaved people to the Europeans and set about orchestrating the capture of people needed to supply this growing trade.

It is interesting to note that in 1620 a British explorer, Captain Richard Jobson, was offered some young women as slaves. He refused, saying that these people were 'of his own shape' and should not be enslaved. He went on to write that the English were a people who did not deal in any such commodities; unfortunately, this noble observation was already untrue – Sir John Hawkins had pioneered English involvement in the Atlantic slave trade some 60 years prior, with Queen Elizabeth I's approval – and Britain would go on to become one of the most prolific dealers of enslaved people in West Africa. The Royal African Company, founded by the Duke of York (later King James II), alone would board more than 187,000 captives onto ships bound for English possessions in the Americas between 1672 and 1731.

As the demand for enslaved people began to grow, the entire economic and social structure of the region was profoundly destabilised. Inter-tribal warfare became much more common and attacks on villages more frequent, as this now came with a major economic incentive. Some of the African leaders became very rich by selling their captured enemies into slavery.

For the enslaved people themselves, life was hard and dangerous. Many of them would not survive the voyages taking them to the New World, as the conditions on board the European ships were atrocious (it has often been said that a slave ship could be recognised by its awful smell, even from many miles away). Once they reached their destination, most of the enslaved people would go on to die within the first three years, and very few of them lived as long as ten years. The enslavers soon realised that it was cheaper to work their captives to death and replace them with new ones than to treat them well, let them live longer and bear children. Children would have to be fed for years before they became productive workers and were therefore not economically viable.

The ports of Senegambia were geographically the closest slave-exporting ports to Europe, and though their importance to the trade was eventually surpassed by regions further south (ie: Angola), Africans had been continually abducted from Senegambia since the first days of the Portuguese presence. It is estimated that, regardless of who was controlling the ports, between 200,000 and 500,000 individuals were taken from Senegambia and sold into slavery in the Americas between the years 1600 and 1800. Given that the region as a whole is estimated to have had just over 1 million residents at the time, the scale of the tragedy that occurred here can hardly be overstated. At the height of the slave trade in the 18th century, over 100,000 people were transported from Africa in chains every year. Nobody knows for sure the total number taken from the continent in the four centuries of trade. Estimates as high as 50 million have been floated but most historians agree that at least 12 million individuals were forced from the continent through enslavement between the 15th and 19th centuries.

The Portuguese were the first to develop the slave trade, monopolising it on a massive scale until the mid 16th century, when the English joined in, later followed by the French and the Dutch. The River Gambia became a major route into the interior of West Africa and was strategically very important. Over the time of the slave trade there were lots of skirmishes between traders of different nationalities over ownership of the fortified stations along the river. Fort James, for example, changed hands eight times in violent clashes over a 60-year period before being finally secured by the British. At around the same time the trading station at nearby Albreda became French-controlled.

As would be expected, the loss of so many of the population, and the slave trade's pernicious economic incentive to wage war and kidnap neighbouring peoples, had a profoundly destabilising effect on the regional states. This led to a period of widespread and chronic instability throughout the region, and a shift in the balance of power from inland to the coastal states. The European introduction of firearms into the region predictably only exacerbated these trends.

Islam flourished in the area and the marabouts became very powerful figures. It was believed that many marabouts had divine powers and could communicate directly with Allah. The Fula people were early and devout adherents to the Islamic faith, and could be found living throughout the region. They played an instrumental role in Islam becoming the dominant religion.

In the early 19th century, another major event occurred that would change the world: the Industrial Revolution, which soon took hold of all Europe. Increased mechanisation reduced the need for vast numbers of enslaved people and increased the need for raw materials and markets for the goods that were being manufactured. European countries gradually came to see their colonies both as sources of raw materials and as markets for manufactured goods; and so the relationship between some Europeans and the West Africans changed accordingly.

Slavery was banned by the British in 1807. The Royal Navy became increasingly active in the region, chasing and capturing French slavers and their ships, then releasing the cargoes of enslaved people and resettling them on to the mainland. The captured enslavers were usually hanged. This may make the British seem to be the good guys at this time, but such activity appears to have been carried out primarily for economic reasons: the slave trade was damaging the rest of their trading enterprises. The French eventually followed with their own ban on slavery, but not until 1848.

Such policies did not put an end to the slave trade, however, which carried on upriver of Albreda and Fort James. The trade was perpetuated mainly by Gambians who had found it very profitable and disapproved of the European change in policy; somewhat counterintuitively, the slave trade's abolishment in 1848 may have further destabilised Senegambian regional states, as many of their economies had become so slavery-dependent in the preceding centuries that when the trade disappeared, there was little left to replace it.

In the 1880s, some Muslim leaders in The Gambia were still enslaving people and exporting them, and it was not until new laws were introduced in the late 1890s that this trade became illegal. In 1906, it was declared that the children of enslaved people in The Gambia were to be considered free, as well as enslaved people upon the death of their masters. Still, some slavery carried on in The Gambia until at least 1930, when the institution lost all legal recognition. The social implications of 'domestic' slavery within The Gambia continue to cast a long shadow, however, and discrimination between the descendants of 'noble' and 'slave' castes continues in some parts of the country to this day.

THE COLONIAL PERIOD In 1816, Britain bought the island of Banjul from a local chief, renamed it Bathurst, and built a large fort there to protect their traders and to deny slavers access to the river. Four years later the River Gambia was declared a British Protectorate and in 1826 Fort Bullen was built at Barra Point, on the North Bank of the river mouth opposite Bathurst. In 1828, the British also built another fort upriver at Georgetown (now Janjanbureh). In the early 1830s, there was a short and limited war between the British and the people from the state of Niumi on the North Bank of the river. This resulted in British and French troops retaking Barra Point, which had been captured by the army of Niumi. After a brief and bloody conflict the people of Niumi capitulated to the British.

When the slave trade was officially ended the British and the French found that they needed to establish another source of wealth in West Africa. They decided to introduce groundnuts (peanuts), as there was a huge international market for them. In 1829, large areas along the River Gambia and elsewhere in Senegal were planted with this new crop. However, in the 1870s unforeseen European political and economic events led to increased competition between foreign traders and the growers of groundnuts in West Africa.

This poor state of affairs led to the Berlin Conference of 1884–85. At this conference the major European powers split the whole continent of Africa into a number of colonies to be ruled by them. It was at this time that The Gambia became a colony of Great Britain and its boundaries were set into their present-day position. It is said that the borders of The Gambia, which to a great extent follow the twists and curves of the River Gambia, were set by a British gunboat that sailed the length of the river, firing its gun both north and south, and the border was placed where the shells landed. However, this is just a fanciful, but often-repeated, tale. The maximum range of a British cannon at the time would have been less than 3km – and while The Gambia is narrow, it's not *that* narrow!

THE SONINKE–MARABOUT WARS In the second half of the 19th century the Fula people, led by their marabouts, attempted to overthrow the traditional Mandinka states and their ruling elites by the use of force. The Fula wanted to extend the Islamic faith to displace the traditional faiths and indifferent Islamic beliefs practised by the Soninke, a Mandinka group to which the local rulers and their courts belonged. Sparked by a sense of Islamic revivalism as had been seen in other parts of West Africa (ie: Omar Saidou Tall in Senegal and Usman dan Fodio in Nigeria), much of the fighting in this *jihad* (holy war) took place for reasons of economic and personal ambition as much as for religious zeal.

Regardless, the off-and-on fighting was fierce and bloody, especially near Bathurst, and destabilised the region for decades. The British and French ultimately sought to occupy the Senegambian interior at the close of the 19th century and either defeated the marabouts militarily or forced them into a negotiated peace. Though the marabouts were ultimately defeated, they had still broken the backs of the Mandinka elites and saw most of the Gambian territory convert to Islam under their authority. The early years of the 20th century that followed were largely peaceful.

THE WORLD WARS Thus, The Gambia became just a small colony, with no inherent wealth in the form of mineral resources, so it was of limited interest to the policymakers in London. The main aim of British rule in The Gambia appeared to be to create peace in the area with the minimum of expense. The administration raised enough revenue to run itself but not to provide any social services. Britain's financial policy up to World War II was that its colonies had to be self-supporting, so this resulted in very little attention being paid to the socio-economic development of The Gambia.

During World War II the situation improved slightly as Britain assumed direct responsibility for development in its colonies. However, in spite of a few projects that were set up in The Gambia to try and diversify agricultural production, and a few more resources being directed towards health and education in the country, nothing really changed that much. During both World Wars many Gambian soldiers fought on the side of the Allies, as did hundreds of thousands of other West Africans, and many were killed in action. The brave men who died in the service of their country are remembered in the Fajara War Cemetery (page 120).

INDEPENDENCE It wasn't until the early 1960s that The Gambia again entered the international arena. In 1962, the Gambian parliament – the House of Representatives – was formed. A popular young man by the name of David Jawara, from upcountry, had founded a political party called the People's Progressive Party (PPP) at the start of the decade. This party easily won the elections to form a majority in the House of Representatives. Following this the country gained its independence from British colonial rule in 1965. David Jawara was inaugurated as prime minister, though the Queen of England still remained as titular head of state. Having converted to Christianity in 1955, Jawara returned to Islam later this year and became known as Dawda Kairaba Jawara. Also around this time, Gambia was renamed as *The* Gambia, due in no small part to the fact that it was often getting confused with the African state of Zambia.

From 1965 to 1975, The Gambia prospered. World groundnut prices increased threefold and the tourist industry grew from just 300 visitors during 1966 to over 25,000 ten years later, earning the country the moniker 'The Smiling Coast of Africa'. Initially most of the tourists came from Sweden, but gradually more and more came from the United Kingdom. It was also during this period, after a referendum held in 1970, that The Gambia became a republic, removing Queen Elizabeth II as its titular head of state and turning Prime Minister Jawara into President Jawara. In keeping with The Gambia's symbolic and practical assertion of its independence, the capital city of Bathurst also reverted to its former name of Banjul in 1973.

However, this high couldn't last forever and groundnut prices began to fall sharply in the late 1970s, leaving most Gambians worse off than they had been before independence. In 1981, a group of disillusioned soldiers allied with the banned Gambia Socialist Revolutionary Party (GSRP) staged a coup while Jawara was away in London attending Prince Charles and Lady Diana's wedding. His family were taken as hostages and held prisoner in the Medical Research Council buildings in Fajara. President Jawara sought help from Senegal, along with special forces soldiers from Britain who secured the release of his family. The coup ultimately failed after several days of fighting, causing an estimated 500 deaths and untold economic damage, particularly to the newly important tourism sector.

In 1982, President Jawara announced that The Gambia and Senegal armed forces would be fully integrated and that the two countries would embark upon a path of closer political and economic union: the Senegambia Confederation was formed on 1 February 1982. This policy lacked popular support among the Gambian population, especially with the Mandinka, who saw the coalition as a takeover bid by the Wolof (who are the predominant ethnic group in Senegal), and tensions flared in the country. However, Jawara won the elections of that year, and the following elections in 1987, as he still had a large popular backing. Jawara was widely praised for advancing human rights and for his attempts to improve The Gambia's economy, which led to the African Commission on Human and Peoples' Rights (ACHPR) establishing its secretariat in Banjul in 1989.

However, in the late 1980s things went from bad to worse in The Gambia as groundnut prices continued to fall. At the same time the International Monetary Fund, on whom The Gambia relied heavily, restructured its agricultural subsidies and spending on public services was cut. The remote upcountry areas were hit the hardest and there were cases of malnutrition and even starvation in the poorest areas. There were two more failed coup attempts during this period.

In 1989, relations became strained between Senegal and The Gambia when The Gambia refused to support Senegal in a dispute with Mauritania. The confederation, already struggling with differences of opinion on how much and how quickly integration between the two countries was to proceed, was ultimately dissolved in October. Senegal imposed severe border restrictions between the two countries, but by 1991 things had cooled down and a new treaty of friendship and co-operation was signed between the neighbours. In 1992, the PPP was re-elected for its sixth term in power.

THE JAMMEH YEARS Following his 1992 re-election, popular support for Jawara began to decline. He was the longest-serving head of state in Africa at the time, and he started to face growing internal criticism and calls for change, especially for failing to curb corruption and provide basic services. Despite the PPP's electoral dominance, The Gambia was home to a functional political opposition, and was in fact the longest-lasting multiparty democracy in Africa at the time. Jawara took about 59% in the 1992 elections, but an increasing number of civil society groups, university students and working Gambians were taking to the streets in the early 1990s to express their discontent.

On 22 July 1994 there was an angry protest by soldiers. This was mostly about their salaries, which were being paid several months late, but also about their poor treatment by Nigerian officers during peacekeeping duties in Liberia and Sierra Leone. Surprisingly this protest turned into yet another coup d'état. This time, however, the coup did not fail and Jawara was ousted from power, though he managed to escape to a US warship that happened to be in Banjul Harbour. He was later granted asylum in Senegal. The leader of the successful coup was a young lieutenant in the Gambian army named Yahya Jammeh. A new military government, the Armed Forces Provisional Ruling Council (AFPRC), took power, consisting of several senior military officers as well as civilian ministers from the previous government.

The coup had immediate and serious repercussions for The Gambia. On the advice of the British Foreign and Commonwealth Office (FCO), many thousands of British tourists cancelled reservations and several of the major tour companies halted all flights to The Gambia, forcing many tourism-related businesses to close. The annual number of visitors dropped by over 65% to fewer than 40,000. The USA cut all aid to The Gambia, and there was an exodus of non-government organisations and charities from the country. The FCO withdrew its travel warning in spring 1995, and tourism slowly began to stabilise.

Yahya Jammeh won 56% of the vote in 1996, and Jammeh's renamed Alliance for Patriotic Reorientation and Construction (APRC) won 33 of the 45 parliamentary seats in 1997. Despite the encouraging release of several opposition members who had been imprisoned immediately after the coup, Amnesty International described the situation in the country as one of 'democratic reforms without human rights'.

From the mid 1990s, The Gambia enjoyed a degree of political stability and economic growth, but in an increasingly repressive climate. Several coup attempts, of varying degrees of seriousness, provided a pretext for a continual ratcheting up of repression. Protest was criminalised and those speaking out against the government were subject to arbitrary arrest, enforced disappearance and torture.

The country remained nominally a democracy, with at least three parties contesting each of the 2001, 2006 and 2011 presidential elections, which returned Jammeh to power with 53%, 67% and 71.5% of the vote respectively. But opposition activists were routinely hounded and abused, and subject to severe limitations on campaigning; the Economic Community of West African States (ECOWAS) described the pre-electoral landscape in 2011 as being characterised by 'an unacceptable level of control of the electronic media by the party in power, and an opposition and electorate cowed by repression and intimidation'. In the same year, activist Amadou Scattred Janneh was sentenced to life in prison for the crime of distributing anti-dictatorship T-shirts.

The climate of repression and fear that characterised The Gambia in the 2000s was not limited to opposition politicians alone. Journalists were another target, and operated at significant, even fatal risk to themselves. The respected editor of *The Point* newspaper, Deyda Hydara, was assassinated in 2004, as was outspoken journalist Ebrima Manneh following his arrest by security police in 2006. Newspapers were shut down, bought out or intimidated into self-censorship. An ignominious string of alleged human rights abuses include the police killing of a dozen protesters during a student demonstration in 2000, the murder of 59 West African migrants in 2005 and the abduction and detention of more than 1,000 suspected witches at the instigation of government-sponsored 'witch-doctors' in 2009. Freedom House's 'Freedom in the World' ranking (based on political rights and civil liberties) gave The Gambia an abysmal aggregate score of 18 out of 100, categorising the country as 'not free' in 2016. United Democratic Party secretary and opposition activist Solo Sandeng was beaten to death in custody in the same year.

Abroad, The Gambia was perhaps best known for Jammeh's shocking flights of dictatorial fancy and bombastic rhetoric. In 2007, Jammeh announced that he had discovered a herbal HIV/AIDS cure, which he forced some 9,000 infected people to take instead of anti-retroviral drugs, even performing 'treatments' in State House himself. An unknown number died from this dangerous quackery, but a refusal to participate could result in a prison sentence. In 2008, Jammeh launched a crusade against homosexuality with the announcement that the APRC intended to execute all gay and lesbian people by implementing laws 'stricter than those in Iran'. In 2010, he described atheists as being 'even below a pig', and a year later he suggested to the BBC that he would 'rule this country for one billion years...if Allah says so'. But it was not to be. It was in this bizarre and severely repressive climate that the 2016 elections took place, returning a shock result that would change The Gambia forever.

GAMBIA HAS DECIDED The 2016 elections saw a seven-party unity coalition take on Jammeh. Despite the fact he was chosen as the unity ticket's candidate at the last minute (several better-known opposition activists like Ousainou Darboe had been imprisoned to prevent them from contesting the elections), property developer and political newcomer Adama Barrow emerged as the shock victor, besting Jammeh by 43.3% to 39.6%. Equally surprisingly, Jammeh conceded defeat almost immediately. The country was electrified, and the streets filled with revellers celebrating this almost unimaginable turn of events.

But the mood darkened in an instant: in a typically mercurial return to form, Jammeh made a dramatic U-turn a week later, going on TV to reject the results outright and call for new elections. The Gambia was now in the throes of a full-fledged crisis. Troops occupied the electoral committee HQ. Barrow fled to Senegal. ECOWAS heads of state visited Banjul, attempting to persuade Jammeh to leave off. And ordinary Gambians stood for the election results, rallying behind the slogan #GambiaHasDecided, which overnight appeared on walls and T-shirts all over the country.

As the official handover date approached, ECOWAS and the African Union declared that they would no longer recognise Jammeh's presidency at the expiration of his mandate on 19 January, and ECOWAS convened a military force to ensure the transition in the face of Jammeh's increasingly intransigent posture. Barrow was inaugurated as the third president of The Gambia on schedule – but at the

1

Gambian embassy in Dakar – and subsequently requested that the ECOWAS troops positioned along the border enter The Gambia. The troops faced little resistance, but it took another two days to force Jammeh out, and he finally departed to exile in Equatorial Guinea – along with his fleet of luxury cars – on 21 January. Barrow arrived back in The Gambia to jubilant scenes later that week, and the Jammeh era officially came to a close.

ADAMA BARROW AND THE 'NEW GAMBIA' To say Barrow's in-tray was full upon taking up the mantle of the presidency would be an understatement. In his first month in office, he freed hundreds of political prisoners and returned The Gambia to its previous status as a secular, rather than Islamic, republic. In 2018 alone, The Gambia rejoined the Commonwealth (Jammeh had withdrawn in 2013, calling it a 'neo-colonial institution'), launched the Truth, Reconciliation and Reparations Commission (TRRC) to investigate wrongdoing under the previous government, and convened a constitutional convention, tasked with touring the country and seeking public opinion as they drafted a new law of the land. The independent press has also blossomed since the transition, and there are now more than 30 radio stations and half a dozen TV stations and newspapers broadcasting with minimal government interference. Since the Barrow administration took power, The Gambia has improved every year in Freedom House's Freedom in the World ranking; as of 2023 it was considered 'partly free', scoring a 48 out of 100.

But despite these commendable efforts to right the ship of state, it hasn't been all smooth sailing under the Barrow administration either. Many of the reforms initiated in the early days of the administration have wound up bogged down or abandoned in favour of political ambition or expediency. The first major controversy arrived in 2020, when, despite an agreement with the 2016 unity coalition that he would serve in a transitional capacity and leave office after three years to make way for a new election conducted on a truly level playing field, Barrow refused. Instead, he declared he would serve to the end of his legally mandated five-year term and suppressed the growing 'Three Years Jotna (enough)' protest movement in the lead-up to this anniversary.

Thanks to this refusal to relinquish power, Barrow's relationship soured with his coalition partners and his former party, the United Democratic Party (UDP). He therefore formed a new party to contest the 2021 elections, the National People's Party (NPP) – and promptly further shocked his former partners and the Gambian public at large by inking an alliance with the APRC, the party of former dictator Jammeh. This new NPP–APRC alliance also torpedoed the final draft of the new constitution in September 2020, leading to speculation that concern over a retroactive clause on term limits led them to sink the bill, potentially allowing Barrow another crack at the top office.

And Barrow did ultimately win the 2021 elections against the UDP and his former vice president Ousainou Darboe, securing another five-year term with 53% of the vote. After hundreds of interviews and thousands of hours of research, the TRRC submitted its findings in December 2021, recommending numerous prosecutions of Jammeh-era officials – including the former president – but no action had been taken on these recommendations as of mid 2023. Barrow again promised to launch a new constitutional process in December 2021, but it remains to be seen where it will go – and how and why it might succeed where the previous attempt failed. Until then, the Jammeh-era constitution promulgated in 1997, and amended some 50-odd times at the dictator's whim, remains the highest law of the land.

Barrow's alliance also won the most recent parliamentary elections in 2022, but the increasingly close result (the NPP and APRC took 29% and 3% respectively, while the opposition UDP took 28%) indicates the Gambian public may be cooling on what many have considered an alliance of naked political ambition. Regardless, most Gambians are still glad to see the back of the past administration, but complaints of increasing crime, corruption and public disorder under the new administration indicate a growing disillusionment with what the new authorities have managed to deliver.

Thus, the high hopes of 2017 have returned a decidedly more mixed outcome. There have been many commendable gains, and Gambians today are generally free to speak, write and assemble as they see fit. However, many of these developments remain unconsolidated, at risk of erosion from political machinations and selfish interests. So as for who and what will be on the ballot at the next set of elections in 2026 and 2027, just ask – any Gambian will be happy to give you an earful. Because while progress may inevitably come in fits and starts, Gambians have definitively found their voice.

ECONOMY

There are no significant mineral or similar natural resources to be found in The Gambia. Subsistence agriculture has traditionally been the backbone of the economy, though its role has been shrinking for some years and the service sector is now The Gambia's primary earner by a significant margin. But in rural areas, nearly 75% of the population is employed in agriculture, and farming contributes around 18% of the country's gross domestic product (GDP). Production is for two main markets, the first of which is local. Rice, millet, maize, sorghum, findo (a small-grained millet also known as fonio), fruits and vegetables are all grown for home consumption. Despite the fact that Gambians are some of the world's biggest consumers of rice, eating about 117kg per person annually (in the UK this is closer to 7kg per person), most of it is imported. Food is not in short supply in The Gambia, but agricultural products tend to come in gluts during their growing periods and capacity for secondary processing remains low. For example, vast amounts of mangoes are sold (as well as rot) everywhere during the rainy season, while at the start of the dry season you see huge piles of watermelons for sale on most street corners.

Groundnuts, cotton and sesame are the principal cash crops. Groundnuts have been the chief cash crop since the British introduced them in 1829 and still represent the country's largest export crop. Annual groundnut production is erratic and depends significantly on rainfall, which has become less predictable in recent years, thus significantly affecting the annual crop. The annual yield for most of the 1960s and 1970s was above 100,000 tonnes, but this reached a nadir of around 45,000 tonnes in 1996. Production today remains somewhat inconsistent, ranging between 80,000 and 120,000 tonnes annually in recent years.

Livestock farming is also an important contributor to GDP. Everywhere you go in The Gambia you will see herds of *ndama* cattle, sheep and goats, most of which are trypanotolerant (tolerant against sleeping sickness). Many of these animals are grazed in the bush during the day, where herdsmen stop them from wandering on to farm crops (most of the time), and they are staked out at night. Draught animals such as bullocks, donkeys and horses are also important to rural communities and carts drawn by these animals are still a common form of transport in such areas.

The Gambia lies within one of the richest fishing zones in the world and the natural productivity of the country's waters is further enhanced by the flow of nutrients from the River Gambia, so it comes as no surprise that fishing is an important industry here, or that fish is the primary source of protein for most Gambians. It is estimated that around 65,000 tonnes of fish are caught each year, with the majority (65%) of this being taken by fishermen using locally constructed fishing canoes, or *pirogues*, powered by outboard motors. Most of the catch is destined for home consumption as either fresh or locally smoked fish.

About 15–20% of the annual catch is done by industrial trawler, in large part by Chinese companies who also run a handful of fishmeal processing plants along the coast. These have been a source of great controversy with local fishermen and residents for their deleterious effects on fish hauls and the local environment, but Gambian fishmeal is a growing export and the government nets significant fees from these factories and trawlers. The final 15% of Gambian fishing takes place on the river and other inland waterways.

Forests are also an important resource in The Gambia, providing fuel, food, medicine and materials for the construction industry. However, Gambian forests are chronically overexploited and have declined markedly in both quantity and quality over the last several decades. Many people within the country now understand how important forests are, especially in the protection of soil against desiccation and erosion (a problem that is affecting much of the land in The Gambia), as well as for wildlife and recreation, but the degradation remains significant.

Industry plays a small but growing role in the Gambian economy, accounting for just under 20% of GDP in 2021 (up from 12% in 2012) but still employs only a small fraction of the national labour force. The sector can be split into small-, medium- and large-scale industries. Small-scale industries include poultry production, metalworking and welding, repair workshops, and various crafts such as pottery, carving, jewellery making and tie-dye and batiks. Most of The Gambia's medium- and large-scale industries are involved in fish processing and exportation. Mining for sand and gravel occurs throughout the country, for the most part supplying the local construction industry. Clay is also mined in some areas for use in pottery.

Generating more than 20% of the national GDP, tourism is the largest single industry in The Gambia and dates back to 1964 when Scandinavian tour operators first launched charter flights to the country. Since then the number of tourists has steadily risen, despite a few dips caused by a combination of local and global phenomena like (obviously) Covid-19, the 2019 collapse of Thomas Cook, the 2013–16 Ebola crisis (which did not actually reach The Gambia, not that that mattered for tourist numbers), and the 1994 coup. The majority of the tourists are British, but Dutch, Swedish, German, French and Danish visitors are also well represented. Some 42,000 people are directly employed by the industry (and a further 65,000 indirectly), accounting for about 18% of the workforce, although it has to be said that many of these jobs are insecure, poorly paid and limited to the tourist season. Many tourists visit The Gambia just for the sun, sea and sand of the Atlantic coast, and are happy to sit on beaches or around hotel swimming pools. However, lots do go on at least one organised trip away from the hotels during their stay. To facilitate this, the Ministry of Tourism and Culture has encouraged the creation of more grassroots ecotourism ventures, which generally allow local communities more direct benefits than more conventional tourist models.

PEOPLE

The majority of The Gambia's inhabitants belong to one of eight different ethnic groups. These are the Mandinka, Wolof, Fula, Jola, Sarahule, Serer, Aku and Manjango.

Many recent immigrants from surrounding countries live in The Gambia, including people from Senegal, Ghana, Guinea, Guinea-Bissau and Liberia. And The Gambia has a particularly close relationship with Sierra Leone, thanks to a shared experience of British colonialism (The Gambia was even administered from Freetown for many years) and the common historical origin of The Gambia's Aku people and Sierra Leone's Krios. Thousands of Sierra Leoneans also fled to The Gambia during their homeland's civil war in the 1990s, and many chose to put down roots and remain.

Mauritanians (also called Narr in The Gambia), easily spotted in their billowing blue robes, also live throughout The Gambia, often running village shops and small businesses. Traders from Ghana run The Gambia's biggest fishery complex at Ghana Town. And as in many West African countries, there is also a long-settled Lebanese population, who have been engaged here as traders and professionals for generations; a number of significant businesses in The Gambia (and throughout West Africa) are Lebanese–Gambian owned. Many Europeans have also chosen to make The Gambia their home, either as retirees or having married a Gambian spouse.

Each ethnic group has its own traditions, language and background. Conversely, the small size of the country, generations of intermarriage and the unifying force of Islam have all contributed to a great sharing of cultural heritage among the peoples of The Gambia.

Mandinka trace their origins to the Mandé peoples of the Manding (Mali) Empire who spread across West Africa with the expansion of the empire starting around 1300. There are dozens of groups throughout the region whose origins can be traced to these migrations, including the Mandinka, Bambara, Soninké, Djallonké and others, but in The Gambia the Mandinkas (also known as Malinké) predominate, representing 42% of the population. There are more than 11 million Mandinka people throughout West Africa, but nowhere do they make up a larger share of the population than in The Gambia. Traditionally they were subsistence farmers and today they remain engaged in business and farming, especially the production of groundnuts throughout the country. The *griot* bard traditions (page 24) found across West Africa and the prevalence of the *kora* harp have origins with the Mandé and their presence throughout the region.

The **Fula** (also known as Fulani, Fulɓe or Peul) are The Gambia's second-largest group, representing some 22% of the population and typically living upriver. They form part of an enormous ethno-linguistic group numbering more than 40 million people living in nearly two dozen countries stretching from Senegal and The Gambia in the west to Sudan, the DRC and the western fringes of Ethiopia in the east. Likely originating in the area north of the Senegal River, the Fula are traditionally nomadic pastoralists, herding cattle with the seasons, but a large and growing number are now settled, working as farmers, artisans and traders. With the AD1030 conversion of the king of the ancient state of Takrur, the Fula living in the Senegal River valley were the first group anywhere in Senegambia to adopt Islam.

The **Wolof** are Gambia's third-largest ethnic group (13%), and by far the largest in neighbouring Senegal. They are thought to have originated in southern Mauritania, from where droughts and raids forced them south into western Senegal, where they formed a cluster of autonomous kingdoms from the 1200s onwards. During the religious wars of the 19th century, the Wolof established themselves in Banjul and on the North Bank of the Gambia River as traders and shipbuilders. The Wolof heartland is also largely concurrent with the area known as the peanut basin, where the aforementioned nut has been the main cash crop since the 1840s. The Gambia sits along the southern fringes of this area, and most Gambian Wolof live on the North Bank where they still farm and sell groundnuts, as well as in Banjul, where they are influential in business, commerce and the civil service. Most Wolof people follow Sufi Islam, and many belong to the Mouride and Tijaniyyah Islamic brotherhoods.

The earliest settlers in the area south of the River Gambia were the **Jola** (13% of the population), who are thought to have been practising wet rice farming in the region for up to a millennium. Long resistant to outside incursions, fiercely refusing to cede power to either their Mandinka neighbours or the European colonialists alike, the Jola farming and fishing communities in southwestern Gambia and Senegal's Casamance region have generally retained their traditional practices and beliefs in ways that have been lost elsewhere. Though most Gambian Jola converted to Islam during the Soninke–Marabout wars of the 19th century, there are many Animist and Christian Jola as well.

The **Serahuli** (also known as Soninké or Sarakole; 7% of the population) were, along with the Fula, among the first groups in Senegambia to adopt Islam in 1076. Their roots go all the way back to the first millennium as rulers and merchants in the Ghana Empire (from which the modern state gets its name). The heartland of the empire was situated in what is now western Mali and southeastern Mauritania, and the first Serahuli arrived in The Gambia after the empire's collapse, with a second wave during the 19th century as refugees from religious conflict in Senegal. Nowadays many are farmers living along the eastern Gambian border, but they remain famous for their gold- and silver-trading activities throughout West and Central Africa.

The **Serer** (3%) are among the oldest ethnic groups in the Senegambia region, with ancestral lands just over The Gambia's northern border around the Sine-Saloum Delta and Petite Côte in Senegal. Long resistant to Islamisation from the surrounding Wolof, Fula and Mandinka communities, the Serer were among the last Senegambian groups to adopt Islam. Though Serers today are largely Muslim, they – much like the famously independent-minded Jola – retain a stronger presence of Christianity and traditional Animist beliefs (known in Serer as *a fat Roog* or 'the way of the divine') than in most parts of the country. Today they are found mainly along the river mouth, with fishing as their main trade.

The **Manjango** (or Manjack) come from what is now northern Guinea-Bissau, and began to arrive in Senegambia as migrant workers in the 19th century, seeking better wages and conditions than could be found in Portuguese Guinea at the time. They share a staunchly egalitarian philosophy and history of resistance with their Jola neighbours, along with a long tradition of wet rice cultivation and palm wine production. Today they are mostly Christian, and many still have identifiably Portuguese names.

And last but very much not least, the **Aku** (1%) are the descendants of local women and colonialists, as well as liberated people who resettled in Gambia after the abolition of enslavement. They are closely related by blood and culture to the Krio people of Sierra Leone. The Aku played an especially influential role in Gambian economic and governmental life during the colonial period, and despite their small population, continue to figure prominently in Gambian commerce and the civil service. Today most Aku are Christian and have identifiably Anglo-European names.

SOCIAL STRUCTURES A historical caste system can be found among several of The Gambia's ethnic groups, including the Mandinka, Fula, Serahuli and Wolof, who traditionally organised their societies along hierarchical lines with status determined by birth. Marriage between the various classes was uncommon.

Broadly speaking, these class structures consisted of three broad groups – the freeborn, the artisans and the slaves. At the top were the freeborn who consisted of nobles and commoners. The former were the royal lineages and great warrior families; the latter included farmers, traders and marabouts. Lower down the scale were the artisans who consisted of specialised workers such as blacksmiths, leather workers, woodcarvers and weavers. Although not enslaved, the artisan families were attached to the freeborn families in a patron–client relationship. Musicians were also a lower caste but highly respected. A particular type of court musician called a *griot* or *jeli* (page 24) performed song and poetry, containing stories of a family, village or clan as a form of oral history.

These traditional hierarchies still inform many social relationships within The Gambia today, though increasing urbanisation and levels of formal education continue to erode the practice. But discrimination between the descendants of 'noble' and 'slave' castes continues in some parts of the country to this day – there have been several outbreaks of community unrest sparked by caste discrimination in Koina, Upper River Region, as recently as 2019.

FESTIVALS AND CEREMONIES During your stay in The Gambia, you are very likely to hear, before you see, a Gambian ceremonial occasion taking place. Festivities such as weddings, naming ceremonies, initiation ceremonies and other special Muslim and Christian festivals are celebrated by lavish feasting, drumming, music and dancing. A village will also celebrate the arrival of a special guest, the event being marked by the dancing of the *kanali* – a group of women dancers.

Festivals and ceremonies are loud and colourful events, with participants having new clothes made and dressing elegantly. Of course they are also costly affairs and so traditionally contributions are made to the host family in the form of money or food. If you are invited to a celebration, you will be expected to bring something. You should also expect to give a present or some money to the *griots* (musicians and oral historians) that come to these events.

Festivals and ceremonies are very important and much of West African life is centred on such events, which help to reinforce social cohesion and harmonious community life.

Marriage
Traditionally, marriages in The Gambia are arranged. However, this practice is less common now in the urban areas. The marriage ceremony itself is the finale of a week's activities, involving the exchange of gifts and visits to relatives. The official ceremony takes place at the mayor's office and is followed by eating and dancing at someone's compound. The procession of cars from the office to the home is marked by much blowing of car horns and shouting, and by the decoration of the bride and groom's car, so much so that it's hard to miss this one!

Initiation ceremonies and Female Genital Mutilation
Traditionally, circumcision in many African countries is an event that marks the transition from childhood to adulthood. Boys and girls are circumcised separately in groups, usually between the ages of eight and 12, although it can occur at an earlier age. After the operation, the groups are taken into the bush and taught about their adult responsibilities and rules of behaviour while they are healing. When the children return to their villages there is much feasting and socialising, and the initiated individuals are given new clothes and decorations by their parents. Special dancing with masquerades, such as the *kankurang* (a man dressed from head to foot in a costume made of tree bark – there is a life-size model outside the National Museum in Banjul, page 100) also marks the return of the initiate.

As part of these initiation rites, Female Genital Mutilation (FGM) remains widespread in The Gambia. The practice, which involves partial or total removal of the external female genitalia, is widely considered to be an integral aspect of Islamic teaching in The Gambia, though it causes extreme pain and distress to the individual concerned, and may result in healing problems, long-term health issues, or even death caused by infection. The practice was officially banned in The Gambia in 2015, but to date there have been no convictions and the overall prevalence remains extraordinarily high: around 75% of Gambian women have been cut.

A number of individuals and organizations in The Gambia have been working with local communities to develop culturally grounded alternatives to FGM and to bring this harmful practice to an end, but it remains an uphill struggle. The Gambia Committee on Traditional Practices Affecting the Health of Women and Children (GAMCOTRAP; w gamcotrap.gm) has been advocating against FGM and for improved access to sexual and reproductive health services since 1984, and Tostan (see above) has been administering their rights-based Community Empowerment Program in dozens of communities here since 2007.

More recently, Gambian activist Jaha Dukureh (f JahaMarieDukureh) has been recognized globally for her work towards ending FGM, alongside her organization, Safe Hands For Girls (w safehandsforgirls.com). She is the UN Women Goodwill Ambassador for Africa, was named one of *Time Magazine*'s 100 Most Influential People in 2016, and was the subject of a biopic film, *Jaha's Promise*, in 2017 – which can be viewed here: w youtu.be/rJ0KJwbo6tY. Though progress can seem agonisingly slow, these collective efforts have begun to bear some fruit: today's FGM prevalence for girls under 14 has dropped to 50%.

Naming ceremonies One week after a baby is born, an important ceremony takes place when the infant is named. An elder, who either shaves the baby's hair or cuts a lock and says a silent prayer, performs this ceremony in the morning (around 10.00). The elder whispers into the infant's ear the name the parents have chosen, which is proclaimed aloud by a griot. While the name is being whispered, a chicken, goat or sheep is slaughtered. A 'charity' of kola nuts, cakes or other special foods is distributed to the guests, and the baby's tuft of hair is buried. Guests bring small gifts for the infant and the griots as well. Later in the day, a meal is prepared followed by drumming and dancing. If you are informed of a naming ceremony, even in casual conversation, this is an invitation to attend. It is an informal invitation, and you will be most welcome.

Muslim and Christian holidays As a predominantly Muslim country, the people of The Gambia celebrate many religious holidays. Observance of these holidays usually involves special prayers and the offering of charity followed by feasting and dancing. They are also occasions for Gambians to dress up and visit friends and relatives. On Tobaski (Eid al-Adha), all heads of families who can afford it slaughter a sheep, goat or cow and divide the meat among friends, relatives and the poor as charity. Christian ceremonies are also observed in The Gambia, particularly in cities where a large proportion of the population is non-Muslim, such as Banjul.

LANGUAGE

English is the official language. The main local languages are Mandinka, Fula, Wolof, Serakhulle and Jola, among others. In practical terms, you will have no problem locating English-speaking people in the western areas and being able to communicate with them. Head further upriver and English-speakers can become harder to find (though you will usually manage without too much trouble). Gambians seem to have a gift for picking up different languages, probably because they live in a highly multilingual society. As a result, there are also a few guides, based mostly at the hotels, who can speak passable German, Dutch or French.

RELIGION

Around 95% of the population follows Islam. The remaining 5% are mostly Christian, and there's also a small minority of people (less than 1%) who follow age-old forms of animistic religion like traditional Jola and Serer belief – though this rather underrepresents the prevalence of traditional worship in the country, as beliefs here tend to be fairly syncretic and many people continue to partake in older traditions while identifying as Muslims and Christians.

Indeed, much behaviour is still governed by animist beliefs that endow natural objects and phenomena, idols, fetishes and individuals with supernatural forces or the power to protect or to use such forces. Many Gambians, from tiny babies to senior citizens, wear amulets, commonly called *jujus* or *gris-gris*, on their body around the waist, neck, arms or legs. The jujus are often leather packets, or cowrie shells, which contain writings from the Koran as a spell, or charm, which is said to protect the wearer. The juju will have been provided at birth, naming or initiation ceremonies by the local griot, or animist priest. Alternatively, the spell or charm may have been prescribed by a marabout. Gambians consult marabouts for a variety of reasons, but the following are the most common: to protect against evil spirits; to improve one's status; or to remedy an undesired situation.

As with most things Gambian, there is a distinct lack of inter-religious animosity within the country. Everyone is free to worship how and who they want, without prejudice, and there is nothing but a healthy curiosity about others' modes of worship and beliefs.

EDUCATION

Education in The Gambia appears to be the best it has been since independence but there are still big problems to overcome. Most areas of the country now have schools

There are many taboos in Gambian culture. It is widely held, for instance, that if a person dreams of seeing raw fish or a snake, it is a sure sign of pregnancy, or that seeing a shooting star is a portent that a prominent person will die. Another common belief is that anything done on a Saturday will be repeated in the future, for which reason many people avoid visiting the sick and making condolences on this day. It is taboo to buy or sell items like soap, needles or charcoal at night, and it is also forbidden to whistle after dark, since all these things will lead to bad luck. It is also taboo for a widow to go out of her home during her mourning period.

Many animals are believed to have magical or special powers. In rural areas, most people will not kill or eat certain animals because they believe they have some ancestral connection with them. Despite this, many traditional beliefs impact negatively on wildlife. An example is the widespread fear of owls – thought to be transformed wizards and witches whose haunting call announces an impending death – that often results in its subject being killed. By contrast, geckoes and chameleons live charmed lives, in the sense that they are also very widely feared and usually left alone, although this updater's Jola wife once made an offering of her breast to a chameleon in order to protect her newborn baby.

Dragons or *ninki nanka* are the most feared of all animals in The Gambia. They live in remote areas and are usually hostile beasts who are able to kill by merely looking at someone. Fortunately, however, there also exist professional dragon slayers who are immune to such effects, and who for vast sums of money will go and slay these nefarious dragons. Since no-one else can look at a dragon without dying, clients must rely on the word of the dragon slayer that the deed has been done.

Gambians are also great believers in the sanctity and holy power of certain places. The sacred crocodile pools provide examples, as do the many special sites scattered throughout the country. These sacred sites range from crocodile pools, groves, trees and stone altars through to tombs, burial sites and places where esteemed holy men have prayed. The sanctity of such places is a blessing in disguise as it is prohibited to cut down the trees or otherwise disturb the sites – and so a small part of The Gambia remains untouched.

although many teachers are unqualified and poorly paid. Many schools also have a lack of teachers, which means that they have to be run on a shift basis, with one set of pupils being taught in the morning and another set in the afternoon. Even so, many classrooms are very crowded, with high pupil-to-teacher ratios, and have poor resources. The school system is state-run but there are also a number of Islamic schools that are operated in conjunction with the state system by local mosques. Most children in the country get an education up to primary level but then the number falls dramatically for various reasons. Many pupils do not pass their exams and therefore cannot go on to secondary level. Additionally, many families are so poor that they cannot afford secondary-school fees, school uniforms and books. Many children, especially girls, are also kept out of school to work in the fields or gardens. The literacy rate stands at slightly more than 50%, representing roughly 40% of women and 60% of men.

CULTURE

ART Artwork is all around you in The Gambia. Not only in the market stalls, or *bengula* (meeting place), near the hotels or craft markets in Banjul, but also in the metalworkers' yards, and the woodworkers' and tailors' shops along every road.

At the markets you can buy all kinds of woodcarvings, straw and wicker work, leather work, pottery, jewellery, textile work (including weaving) and metalwork. Many of the woodcarvings are finished by the stall owners who sell them, but beware as their colour is a result of staining with shoe polish and will fade with time without constant attention. Having said this, the carvings of African masks, bowls, male and female figures and animals make good purchases and gifts.

The woven cloth you see in the markets represents the most important material in The Gambia in the form of cotton. Cloth is made by *maabo*, a caste of weavers who traditionally come to The Gambia in the rainy season and produce it on demand for clients. Traditionally these clothes were used for special occasions such as marriage ceremonies, circumcisions and burials. The dyes used for colours in the weaving are made traditionally from natural sources; for example the ironwood tree (*Prosopis africana*) gives a red colour while the mango tree produces black.

Tie-dye and colourful batiks also abound. You will also see clothes that have been crafted in the traditional Gambian style – loose with embroidery – or made on more Western lines. You may want to bring pictures of clothes that you would like made up while staying here. Many of the tailors are able to turn a photograph into a made-to-measure designer dress or suit before your very eyes (or in a week at the most).

Away from the markets, other creative forces are at work. You only have to glance at the metalworkers' yards to see intricate gate designs and the handiwork made from recycled material. Goods range from spoons and ladles through to saucepans, brightly painted metal boxes and candleholders.

MUSIC Much like its neighbours, Senegal and Mali, The Gambia is renowned for its hereditary *griot* praise-singers and storytellers (page 24). These griots, also known as *jali* (Mandinka), *gewel* (Wolof) or *gawlo* (Fula), act as historians in many West African societies – particularly in places once part of the Manding (Mali) Empire – recounting ancient leaders, traditional ceremonies, famous deeds, clan lineages and more. It's a centuries-old tradition that often goes hand in hand with the indigenous West African harp known as the *kora*, and the country has produced numerous masters of the beloved and otherworldly-sounding instrument.

These Gambian kora luminaries include some of the first to take the sound beyond West Africa: **Alhaji Bai Konte** was the first kora soloist to tour in North America in the 1970s, and **Foday Musa Suso** collaborated with Herbie Hancock and Philip Glass in the 1980s and 90s. Alhaji's son **Dembo Konte** also took up the mantle and became a world-renowned player in his own right, followed by a series of musical grandchildren – the family tradition continues at their compound in Brikama (page 184). But the most famous Gambian kora practitioner today is also perhaps one of the most unlikely: in a tradition long reserved exclusively for men, female kora virtuoso **Sona Jobarteh** has become one of the most recognisable voices in Gambian music, touring extensively and penning the anthemic 2015 tune 'Gambia'.

In addition to the kora, the griot tradition is closely associated with several other instruments, including the *balafon* wooden xylophone (listen to Guinean master El

Hadj Djeli Sory Kouyate) and the smaller *ngoni* harp (listen to Grammy-nominated Bassekou Kouyaté from Mali). Gambian traditional music also frequently involves a combination of *sabar* and *tama* (talking) drums. The *sabar* (referring to both the drum and related dance tradition) is connected with Wolof and Serer people, and

THE GRIOT

When one talks about music in West Africa, one often hears talk of *griots* (pronunciation 'gree-oh'), but the term, derived from the Portuguese for 'troubadour', doesn't even begin to adequately describe the meaning. Not simply musicians, griots are the oral historians and praise singers of societies, descending through families since the times of ancient West African empires. The Mandinka word for griot is 'jeli', which means blood, and you could describe the griot as the lifeblood of a culture. In fact, it is said that when a griot dies, it is as if a library has burned to the ground. In the times before writing, the griot was the only way in which histories of early mankind could be passed along from the elders to younger generations.

My first contact with a griot, at my local mechanic's in Brikama, was less than romantic. While sitting under the mango tree, one of the lads pointed out a house nearby and told me that it belonged to Pa Bobo Jobarteh, one of The Gambia's top *kora* players and a big star. Before long, he came out and started playing the kora, before beckoning me to join him. You could say it's the Gambian equivalent of popping over for tea with Bruce Springsteen, who plays for you while you wait for your car to be serviced. After he'd played a few beautiful songs as his brothers brewed *attaya*, we started chatting.

'I was born into a griot family in Brikama, and I started playing kora at the age of six. When I was 11, I played at WOMAD festival in England, then aged 22, I toured Europe, Asia, Australia and USA. I am good friends with Peter Gabriel and as a boy I played for the Queen, in Buckingham Palace.'

Given the humble surroundings it seems hard to believe, but it's true – I've seen the pictures. As we spoke, Pa Bobo showed me an older CD of his where he's pictured with members of Fairport Convention, recording in an English stately home.

'Historically we griots were the oral historians and custodians of the empire of western Sudan, playing traditional instruments such as the kora, balafon, drums and many more. But our future – the future of the griot – depends on our work being protected and promoted. We have to earn a living to carry on.'

In January 2017, during the height of the troubles after the election, Pa Bobo was forced into exile in Senegal having released a pro-democracy song that went viral on YouTube. With a €10,000 price on his head, he wasn't taking any chances, but thanks to the power of social media, the griot still managed to sing to thousands and was an influential part of the #GambiaHasDecided movement that eventually propelled President Jammeh out of power and into exile.

Pa Bobo's work is available on Spotify, Apple Music or Bandcamp (w pabobojobarteh.bandcamp.com). If you'd like to stay with Pa Bobo, you can contact him on m 617 7550, via WhatsApp on m 390 5045/209 9668, or on Facebook (f pabobo.jobarteh).

Extract adapted and edited from Chasing Hornbills *by Simon Fenton.*

can be heard on the compilation *Wolof Music of Senegal and The Gambia*, or in the music of **Yandé Codou Sène** and **Doudou N'Diaye Rose** (both from Senegal).

Senegambia is also considered to be the spiritual home of the banjo, whose origins can be traced convincingly to the *akonting*, a three-string lute traditionally played among the Jola. It can be heard on the 2023 compilation *Ears of the People: Ekonting Songs from Senegal and The Gambia*. Daniel Laemou-Ahuma Jatta, who features on the album, arranges lessons at the Akonting Center (m 959 9393) in Mandinari (page 181). The Tanje Village Museum (page 163) also displays many traditional instruments.

If it wasn't already clear, it bears emphasising that there are significant musical and cultural commonalities to be found between The Gambia, Guinea, Mali and Senegal – all countries of the former Manding Empire – and just as with the two countries' geography, there is also no meaningful separation between the music of Senegal and The Gambia. The two countries share common musical roots, and they've also embraced a similar range of more contemporary sounds, encompassing everything from Cuban rumba to reggae and hip-hop.

But perhaps nothing unites The Gambia and Senegal more than the homegrown dancefloor rocket fuel of *mbalax*. The off-kilter, frenetic, stuttering drums of this local pop genre dominate airwaves and dancefloors on either side of the border, with Senegalese legend Youssou N'Dour known for bringing this uniquely Senegambian sound to the world. And though the rhythms have sacred origins in the Serer *njuup* initiation ceremonies, today they're the thrumming backbeat to any party worthy of the name – and inspiration for some decidedly secular dance moves as well. Many of the traditional instruments named above can also be heard on *mbalax* recordings, particularly the sabar and tama drums.

While The Gambia's recorded output is decidedly smaller than that of its powerhouse neighbours, there are still a few bona fide Gambian bands emphatically worth chasing down, most of which are now easily found on various streaming platforms.

Starting in the late 1960s, the **Super Eagles** are still legendary among African music aficionados for their vintage soul and Congo rumba-inspired sounds. About a decade later, **Guelewar** showed up on the scene, playing a fiery mix of psychedelic rock and traditional Gambian melodies. In the 1980s and 90s, **Ifang Bondi**, which included several former members of the Super Eagles, recorded a number of albums of wide, spacey Senegambian grooves with some jazz and Latin vibes thrown in. And **Laba Sosseh** played Cuban-inspired 'salsa Africana' for decades, starting in the late 1960s.

In recent decades, Cuban influence has largely given way to another Caribbean island. **Reggae** and dancehall sounds have a huge following in The Gambia today, with artists like Benjahmin ('Sweet Gambia'), Rebellion the Recaller and Royal Messenjah producing Jamaican-inspired tunes with a Gambian twist. **Hip-hop** is also massive – listen out for a growing roster of acts like ST Da Gambian Dream ('the lyrical Musa Molloh'), Dogfather, M Kay, and Attack. For something a bit lighter, dig into some danceable pop and Nigerian-inspired **Afrobeats** from Nobles, Miss Jobizz, Oboy & Gambian Child, and Jizzle.

While the above attempts to spotlight Gambia-specific acts, widely known Senegalese and Malian artists such as Orchestre Baobab, Youssou N'Dour, Ali Farka Toure, Amadou and Mariam, Rokia Traore, Oumou Sangare, Nahawa Doumbia and Fatoumata Diawara are also widely known and listened to in the country.

DANCE Traditional West African dances come in a wide variety of styles and form an integral part of most traditions and ceremonies in The Gambia. Dance may be used to illustrate stories at a wedding or naming ceremony, or to represent traditional beliefs where inanimate objects come to life or spiritual powers enter a human or animal. Or it may depict something altogether more mundane, including everyday scenarios like hunting, fishing and working in the fields. Music and dance inform all aspects of life in The Gambia, and there are few more characteristic sounds than the beating of drums, which can be heard on most nights of the week, almost anywhere in the country.

Of these many traditions, *sabar* is perhaps the most popular and important drum and dance form in Senegambia today. With its origins in the Serer traditions that also gave birth to *mbalax*, sabar refers to not only the dance, but the style of music accompanying it, the drums it's played on, and the events where the drumming and dancing take place. Played with one hand and one stick, the taut goatskins crackle in a flurry of syncopation, spurring the meticulously coiffed female dancers on to a showstopping routine of extraordinarily wild leaps and unabashedly sensual manoeuvres. It's from here in the traditional sabar that mbalax gets its high-flying leaps. (Though it is less common for men to dance sabar than mbalax.) These risqué moves have also put the tradition at odds with some of the region's more conservative elements, and sabar was even banned at one point in neighbouring Senegal.

The sabar parties are massively loud spectacles that can be heard from blocks around and carry on until the wee hours, so the best way to check one out for yourself is simply to keep your ears open and follow the drums. Alternatively, many of the larger coastal resorts will hire dancers and musicians to perform sabar and other traditional dances to entertain guests.

If you don't manage to track down a sabar yourself, take a moment to stream Doudou N'Diaye Rose's 1992 album *Djabote*. Recorded in the open air on Gorée Island in Senegal, with an ensemble of more than 50 drummers and 80 singers, it's the booming, thrumming, unbelievably precise work of a master and his musicians and an enormously compelling document of the tradition.

TRADITIONAL DRESS Much of Gambian dress in urban areas is wonderfully varied and colourful. Traditionally most men prefer to wear a two-piece combination consisting of a *turkia*, a three-quarter-length long-sleeved loose shirt, together with a pair of loose-fitting Arabic-style trousers called *sirwals*. The suit can be made in all types of material, from plain white through to many different batik designs and lacy embroidered fabric in a full range of bold colours.

Many Gambian men wear woolly hats with a striking zig-zag pattern – these are in fact Czech *zmijovka* hats, locally known as *laafa Banjul* or more commonly 'Cabral' after the Bissau-Guinean revolutionary who popularised the look, allegedly after picking up the style on a trip to political ally Czechoslovakia in the early 1960s. Fula men can often be spotted wearing the *tengade*, a conical straw hat trimmed in leather and perfect for blocking out the sun.

The most characteristic dress of Gambian women is the *granbuba*. This is a full-length dress which sometimes has a highly embroidered neck. It has simple seams down the sides below large sleeve holes. The dress is worn over a full-length skirt or wrap, either in the same material or a contrasting colour. Women will also wear a matching headdress.

Friday is a great day for fashion-spotting as people put on their 'Friday best' to attend communal afternoon prayers (and to look sharp for the weekend). Public and religious holidays are also a time for Gambians to dress up. If you are out and about on such a day, every street feels like a runway show.

SPORTS AND GAMES

WRESTLING Commonly known as *boreh* or *laamb*, this is the oldest sporting activity in the Senegambian region, dating from before the 13th century and probably originating in Mali. Successful wrestlers were – and still are – seen as extremely important and able men with great innate spiritual and physical powers. Traditionally, the wrestling match is between contestants from two different villages. Each team is called a *kato*. The event is usually marked by a sense of progression with the youngest and least-skilled wrestlers starting first. The entire match builds up towards a climax in which the final bout is between the champions of each team.

As with all Gambian ceremonial occasions, the events are colourful and noisy affairs and music is inseparable from traditional Gambian wrestling. The basic instrument is the drum, with each ethnic group having its own traditional wrestling tunes. Unlike Western wrestling there are no long-drawn-out holds and techniques like head, leg or arm locks; simply the first to be knocked down loses.

> After a particularly well-fought fight, friends and well-wishers, especially women, will rush into the arena to press coins into the hands of a favourite contestant and rush out again. Successful wrestlers are believed to possess a superior endowment of spiritual strength, which the Mandinka call *nyamo*.
>
> Extract from *Wrestling in the Gambia* by B K Sidibe and W Galloway

Large numbers of amulets are worn on every part of their body and magic potions are taken to increase their power. Wrestling was once the Gambian national sport. Today it is still popular but has to a large extent been replaced by football. Wrestling is no longer included on the school curriculum so there are fewer people able to take part in the sport. If you wish to watch a wrestling match, they still occur regularly in Serekunda and a few other places throughout the country. The best way to see a contest is to organise a visit through an official guide or a Gambian friend, or check in with the Gambian Wrestling Association (m 370 3003; f gamwrestlers) to see what's on.

FOOTBALL Youngsters can be seen on any open patch of ground or on beaches playing football barefoot, and a few of them have gone on to be international stars in foreign teams. In the evenings you can often see crowds gathered around TV sets by the roads or in bars to watch national and international matches. And while foreign teams typically draw the most attention, the GFA League First Division (w gambiaff.org) has 16 teams that play in Banjul, Serekunda and at the

Independence Stadium in Bakau, where games against neighbouring countries also take place and draw large crowds.

In 2005, The Gambia hosted the African Under-17 Football Championships, a qualifying competition for the Under-17 World Cup. To the sheer delight of Gambian fans, their team qualified for the finals in Peru, culminating in a true David-and-Goliath match where The Gambia took on Brazil – and won! Delirious fans spilled out of houses, bars and hotels to celebrate the shock 3–1 victory. Although The Gambia's team did not win the tournament, the young athletes came home to a heroes' welcome. The adult national team has yet to qualify for the FIFA World Cup, however. The men's and women's teams shared a similar, if somewhat dispiriting respective FIFA ranking of 120th and 122nd in 2023.

But The Gambia was blessed with perhaps its most thrilling year of football ever in 2021, when the men's national team earned their first-ever qualification for the Africa Cup of Nations. The Scorpions arrived as the tournament's lowest-ranking team and quickly set about shocking everyone – Gambians included – by defeating Tunisia in the group stages, one of the continent's best-ranked teams. They went on to reach the quarter-finals before being knocked out by hosts Cameroon. Senegal's Lions of Teranga ultimately took home the trophy, and most Gambians, already fizzing with the home team's unexpectedly stellar performance, were more than happy to keep the buzz going to cheer on their neighbours.

DRAUGHTS AND *WARRI* You may often see small groups of men sitting under trees or in cosy areas around a large board. They will either be playing draughts or the national board game known as *warri*. A typical place to see this is the courtyard of the Serekunda post office. Warri boards can be purchased at many of the craft markets and stalls in the coastal resorts and the stallholder will be only too glad to show you the rules of the game – though they are not simple.

2

Natural History

The Gambia is justifiably proud of its rich natural heritage. This pride is manifested in many different ways, including the Banjul Declaration of 1977, the far-reaching and forward-thinking wildlife law, and the provision of eight protected sites totalling nearly 4.9% of the land area. The Gambia is also meeting its international obligations in preserving the world's biodiversity by being a signatory to many international conventions, including the Convention on Biodiversity.

One of the tools used to prevent overexploitation of wildlife is the Wildlife Act of 1977. In essence the law is fairly simple: in order to safeguard the country's wildlife and natural history, *all* wildlife is protected by law, and anyone who is found hunting, selling, importing or exporting, or keeping wild animals as pets is breaking the law and may be prosecuted, fined and imprisoned. The only exception to this rule is the hunting of a number of species that are considered to be pests. These include warthog, giant pouched rat and francolin. Such hunting is licensed and organised by the Department of Parks and Wildlife Management.

The Gambia is also a signatory to the Convention on International Trade in Endangered Species of Flora and Fauna (CITES). Please remember this if you are offered any live or indeed any part of a *dead* wild animal to buy (eg: a skin, horns or turtle shell). It is illegal to export any of these items from The Gambia, or even to have them in your possession while in the country. If you see an infringement of this law during your visit to The Gambia, *please* inform

THE BANJUL DECLARATION

It is a sobering reflection that in a relatively short period of our history, most of our larger wildlife species have disappeared together with much of our original forest cover. The survival of the wildlife still remaining with us and the setting aside of protected natural habitats for them are concerns for all of us.

It would be tragic if this priceless natural heritage, the product of millions of years of evolution, should be further endangered or lost for want of proper concern. This concern is a duty that we owe to ourselves, to our great African heritage and to the world.

Thus I solemnly declare that my government pledges its untiring efforts to conserve for now and posterity as wide a spectrum as possible of our remaining fauna and flora.

His Excellency the President of the Republic of The Gambia,
Sir Dawda Kairaba Jawara, 18 February 1977

the Department of Parks and Wildlife Management (✆ 437 6973; m 981 7559/391 7559; e info@thegambiawildlife.com; w thegambiawildlife.com). All information received is treated as strictly confidential. You can help to safeguard the wildlife of The Gambia.

GEOLOGY AND GEOGRAPHY

The Gambia is a flat country with its highest point only 53m above sea level. It lies on a vast plateau of sedimentary sandstone that stretches from Mauritania in the north to Guinea Conakry in the south, and is tilted slightly towards the Atlantic. The main feature of the country is the River Gambia, which enters The Gambia about 680km from its source in the Fouta Djallon Highlands in Guinea. The river flows in a general east–west direction until it empties into the Atlantic Ocean, and cuts a winding, shallow valley for itself through the surrounding sandstones and claystone. The river has also laid down a series of alluvial deposits such as clay and sand which have partly filled this valley. Some of these deposits have been fairly recent in geological time. The river flats are normally separated from the surrounding plateau by a series of low sandstone hills, especially in the east of the country. In some places, though, extensions of the plateau have formed impressive cliffs that overlook the river.

HABITATS

THE COAST For about 40km from the coastline the offshore seas are shallow and lie on the continental shelf, before dropping sharply down into the depths of the ocean. These shallow waters are an important source of fish, not only for people but also for the numerous birds that feed here. Although the seabed is mainly composed of sand, there are large outcrops of rocks and extensive beds of sea grass that form huge sun-warmed meadows. The sea-grass meadows are grazed by green turtles (*Chelonia mydas*) while dolphins, minke whales (*Balaenoptera acutorostrata*) and Mediterranean monk seals (*Monachus monachus*) hunt the abundant shoals of fish. The coastline of The Gambia consists of a long, recently deposited (in the geological timescale anyway) sandy beach, interrupted in only a few places by low cliffs and associated rockfalls. The top of this beach is clothed with creeping, sand-binding and salt-tolerant plants. Behind the beach is a series of ancient raised beaches. They are generally covered with coastal scrub, a rich habitat of small shrubs and grassland interspersed with taller trees such as baobab (*Adansonia digitata*) and rhun palm (*Borassus aethiopum*). Beyond the scrub most of the coast was once lined with moist coastal forest dominated by tall, thick stands of rhun palms and other salt-tolerant trees. This has now largely disappeared from many parts of the country.

MANGROVES AND *BANTO FAROS* Mangrove swamp, or forest, covers much of the transitional zone between aquatic and terrestrial habitats around the mouth of the River Gambia. It also extends inland along the edges of the river and many of the *bolongs* (creeks), as far as 200km from the sea. There are two main types of mangrove tree. White mangroves colonise dry land edges that are rarely inundated by the tides and are therefore less saline. Red mangroves grow right down into the edge of the sea and are very salt-tolerant. The two types are easy to tell apart as white mangroves poke up aerial roots from below the mud, while red mangroves prop themselves up on curving stilt-like roots. Coastal mangrove forests are fairly low in height, but further upriver they can tower to 20m. Mangroves grow only in tropical and sub-tropical waters and are an endangered habitat throughout the world. One reason for this is that they are often thought of as 'wasteland', and therefore cleared for development. This sometimes has drastic consequences because mangroves form a natural barrier between the sea and low-lying coastal land susceptible to erosion. In fact mangroves actually create dry land by binding mud and sand together. As the mangroves grow they periodically shed their leaves, which gradually builds up the fertility and depth of the soil in which they grow. This continues over hundreds and thousands of years until eventually the swamp becomes dry land. New mangroves grow further out on the edges of the swamp all the time and the process continues. Mangroves are also of enormous benefit in many other ways; for example many of the fish that are caught as adults in offshore waters actually spawn among the roots of mangroves. The swamps also act as a very important nursery for young fish before they head out to the open sea. In addition mangrove swamps are the only source of mangrove oysters (*Grassostrea tulipa*), which are collected and sold by many Gambian women, as well as being a source of timber for firewood and building.

Behind the mangrove swamps you will find the *banto faros*. These are large flat areas of land reclaimed from the sea by the mangroves and then abandoned. Often these flats can be barren, coated in a crystalline layer of salt crusts. In the less saline parts they are covered in thick mats of low-growing succulent plants.

WETLANDS There are many different types of wetland habitats within The Gambia. These range from coastal salt pans, lagoons and marshes, through mangrove swamps, mud flats, saltwater rivers and bolongs, flooded sand mines, animal watering holes, rice fields and permanent freshwater pools lined with reed beds, to vast seasonally flooded marshes. Most of these habitats are extremely rich in crustaceans, annelid worms and molluscs which are harvested by vast numbers of wading birds, especially during the dry season when resident species are supplemented by thousands of migrants from Europe and other areas in the north.

FARMLAND Much of The Gambia is now covered in land managed for agriculture. In the past this was under a rotational regime, where land was traditionally worked every 20 years or so. During the intervening years it was left fallow and covered in regenerating scrub and woodland. Recent rapid population growth means more pressure is being applied to increase crop production to feed people, and some of the agricultural land is now managed on a much shorter rotation, being left fallow for only two or three years in places. Much of this agricultural land is used to grow crops such as sorghum, millet, and especially groundnuts. When the land is cleared for crops, useful trees such as baobab, figs (*Ficus* species), winterthorn (*Faidherbia albida;* previously in the *acacia* genus) and African locust bean (*Parkia biglobosa*) are left intact. After the harvest, the remains of the crops and other vegetables are grazed by herds of cattle and flocks of sheep and goats. During the growing season and into the dry season these animals also range throughout the savannah and woodlands.

SAVANNAH AND THE SAHEL Two types of savannah are found in The Gambia: Guinea savannah (also known as Guinean forest–savannah mosaic) and Sudan (or Sudanian) savannah. In the West Coast Region (in areas of higher rainfall up to the Bintang Bolong), the type of savannah that is commonly found is called southern Guinea savannah. This type of savannah is made up of a rich mixture of over 50 tree species, which are dense and grow fairly tall. East of the Bintang Bolong, and covering the whole of the North Bank of the River Gambia, Guinea savannah is gradually replaced by Sudan savannah. This type of habitat consists of dry, open woodland with well-spaced trees of moderate height and tall grasses. It occurs frequently on lowland soils and the slopes of low laterite (red clay) hills and ridges, and is characterised by tall red termite mounds that have been formed on the lateritic (approaching the composition of laterite) soils. This woodland is also interspersed with a few taller trees, such as baobab and red-flowered silk-cotton trees (*Bombax costatum*) which are a haven for birds that feed on their nectar-rich, large waxy flowers. In some areas of the Sudan savannah, deeper soils support taller thicker woodland composed of dry-zone mahogany (*Khaya senegalensis*) and African rosewood (*Pterocarpus erinaceus*).

All savannah is subject to bush fires that can occur almost annually in some areas. Some of these are natural fires caused by lightning strikes, etc, but people start many of them, either deliberately or accidentally. These fires change the composition of the savannahs, favouring fire-resistant trees, eliminating species that cannot cope with fires and severely reducing the natural regeneration of the vegetation.

The southward spread of Sahelian savannah, a dry habitat characterised by sparse short grass and scattered shrubs, is expanding through Senegal to The Gambia owing to decreased rainfall and massive deforestation by a timber-hungry population. Already parts of the country north of the River Gambia are showing signs of drying out. It has been noted by a few ornithologists that some birds of the dry Sahel are spreading south into The Gambia too. Only a massive injection of time and effort can possibly hope to stop the Sahel from pushing even further into The Gambia.

GALLERY FOREST To the untrained eye, gallery forest looks much like the rainforest found in other parts of West and Central Africa. However, the two differ in one main respect. Rainforest is fed from rain, while gallery forest is fed from ground water. It doesn't sound an important distinction, and certainly both types of forest are very moist, especially in the rainy season. In fact, it is quite an important variance, as a different range of trees and plants prefer the environmental conditions of gallery rather than rainforest, and vice versa, though there is also a considerable overlap in the plant species that are found in both of these habitats. It is a less important distinction to animals, which tend to be more mobile, and therefore the same, or similar, species are generally found in both. Gallery forests are a natural component of the savannah woodlands and are considered to be the vestiges of the closed, moister forests occurring in southern West Africa. Gallery forest is now a very rare habitat in The Gambia and can be found in only a few places such as Abuko Nature Reserve, Pirang Forest Park and some of the fringes of the freshwater stretches of the River Gambia.

URBAN HABITATS Urban habitats are widespread, though most of the larger urban centres are found in the West Coast Region. Urban habitats range from the smallest of country villages to the vast sprawl of Serekunda, including everything in between. In some areas these habitats are covered in concrete and tarmac and are devoid of life, except for the usual pest species that can be found anywhere in the world, such as some insects and larger animals, for example rats and mice. Other areas contain large open green areas and many trees, especially mango (*Mangifera indica*). These areas are richer in wildlife, with frogs, toads, lizards, snakes (even large ones like the African rock python, *Python sebae*) and birds making their homes there.

Many people think of West Africa as being relatively poor in wildlife, especially when compared with the great national parks of East Africa. And it is true that the region is now relatively impoverished in terms of glamorous large mammals. All the same, there is wildlife everywhere in The Gambia, whether it be sparkling dragonflies or colourful butterflies, noisy frogs, scampering lizards or sleepy crocodiles. And there are still some large mammals, too, including hippos, warthogs, dolphins and a range of monkeys. Furthermore, The Gambia is a well-known hotspot for birdwatchers. Even a simple walk around the grounds of a hotel will reveal numerous firefinches and cordon-bleus, sunbirds and gonoleks, while a week's steady searching could well see you amass over 200 species, depending on how serious you are and how much effort you put in.

TIPS FOR WATCHING WILDLIFE Successful wildlife watching can be quite an art. Its nearest equivalent is probably stalking and hunting food to eat – only taking your shot through a lens rather than a barrel! If you're an outdoor type then most of the following tips will already be well known to you. For people that are less used to the outdoors and to the rigours of watching wildlife, they may seem a little obvious and archaic. But they are well worth following if you don't want to waste your time in fruitless searches for wildlife. The main point is that if you walk slowly and pause often, your chances of spotting something good will be multiplied.

The one thing that you cannot guarantee, however, is luck. Wild animals are unpredictable. You can be in the right place at the right time, with the right clothes and equipment, and follow all the rules for good wildlife stalking, but still not see anything. Conversely you can walk down a busy main street in a town and see something quite unexpected. Luck is the one thing that we cannot help you with. However, you can help yourself by reading and following the advice below.

The right equipment No special equipment is necessary for watching wildlife although a good set of binoculars can be extremely useful, as getting really close to wild birds and animals is often difficult. A pair in the 7–10 magnification range and 30–56 lens range, with a ratio of 1:4 (eg: 8x32) or 1:5 (eg: 8x42) will usually stand you in good stead.

The right clothes It is important to try and blend into your surroundings as much as possible but also to keep cool at the same time. A set of khaki safari-type clothes is a good compromise. Remember it is sensible to wear long trousers in the bush, not only because of the small danger of snakes (trousers will prevent most of them from biting into your leg) but also because of the myriad tiny biting insects such as ants that just love bare flesh. Tuck your trousers into a good pair of light, stout boots and you are almost snake-proof and can walk around without worrying about stepping on something nasty. It will also stop insects from crawling up your legs. A sunhat with a wide brim is a good idea too, not only to protect you from the sun but also to help break up the outline of your head and shoulders (page 34).

The right place This is fairly obvious. You cannot expect to see dolphins if you walk through a forest, or warthogs from a boat at sea. Animals all have particular habitats that they adhere to, though there are some species, notably birds, which are far more mobile and can be encountered anywhere. It is not always necessary to go for miles into the bush to spot wildlife. Well-known sites such as Abuko Nature

Reserve (page 178) can be excellent for watching animals at close quarters, simply because so many people visit. The animals have become accustomed to visitors and do not run off at the first sight or sound of a human.

The right time This is very important in The Gambia. It gets so hot during the middle of the day that many animals do the sensible thing and have a siesta, normally away from prying eyes. The best times for wildlife watching are from first light to around 11.00, and again from 16.00 to dusk. Of course there are always exceptions. Many butterflies are best seen around midday, and some of the larger animals, especially predators, are best looked for during the first and last few hours of darkness. Take a drive upcountry in the dark and you stand a fair chance of spotting animals dashing across the road that you would not normally see during the daylight. Ask permission at any of the protected areas and they will generally allow you to walk through in the dark and have a torch-lit safari. It is wise, though, and potentially required, to take a local guide with you.

Staying inconspicuous Try and disguise the **shape** of your body, which is a dead giveaway to cautious wildlife, even at a distance. The shape that really gives us away as human is our square shoulders with our head perched on top. Wear a floppy hat or scarf and this will go a long way to breaking up your outline.

It is much harder to see things when they are in deep shadow, so try it yourself and use **shade** to your own advantage. For example, walk along a line of trees within their shade while you scan adjacent fields, or sit in shade when you rest. It will give you a much better chance of seeing things before they see you. There is also the added benefit that it is much cooler in shade.

Like shape, the human **silhouette** is instantly recognisable to wild animals, so try to avoid standing on skylines where you stand out like a sore thumb. Remember, too, that you can be silhouetted against other plain objects – for example, ploughed fields or bodies of water.

Wearing clothes or carrying equipment that has a shiny reflective surface is a serious no-no for wildlife watching. The **shine** of such objects can give you away very easily, so go for matt surfaces – and watch those sunglasses.

When searching out mammals, try to walk into the wind so that your **scent** is carried away behind you. This will prevent animals having an advance warning and disappearing before you can see them. Some wildlife, especially mammals, are more reliant on their powerful sense of smell to pick up danger than they are on their other senses. As humans, with our poor sense of smell, we often forget this simple rule.

Fast, sudden **movements** betray your presence, so try to move slowly and deliberately. This also helps by allowing you more time to scan the ground around you for those well-camouflaged and difficult-to-see species, before they burst away in a cloud of noise and dust. One point that is easily overlooked is that moving vegetation is a dead giveaway too, so proceed carefully through tall grass or bushes so that you don't scare everything away. This is perhaps the most important of our tips for watching wildlife.

WILDLIFE PHOTOGRAPHY It is difficult to obtain decent wildlife photographs in The Gambia without a good specialist lens, eg: 200mm or 300mm. Having said this, many birds and animals are highly approachable, especially in hotel gardens and around water bodies towards the end of the dry season. The hides at Abuko Nature Reserve (page 178) and the sewage ponds at Kotu (page 132) provide excellent conditions for close-up views of many bird species.

In addition, The Gambia is home to a great variety of plants and insects. Throughout the year both the native flowers and those of the introduced varieties in the hotel grounds can be quite spectacular. In particular, the first rains result in an explosion of new flowers (eg: the scarlet fireball lilies (*Scadodox multifloris*), which can be seen lining the road leading to the airport terminal), and bright colourful insects, including many butterflies and moths.

Lighting is a critical factor in every type of photography and it is especially true of nature photography. The quality and quantity of light vary enormously during the day in The Gambia. Lighting is at its best in the hours just after dawn and before sunset. At this time it is not too harsh and allows details to be recorded. The light also comes from a lower angle in the sky and helps provide depth to images from the shadows that are created.

If you find yourself taking pictures in the middle of the day, you will see that the natural light becomes very intense, making it impossible to record the detail and contrast of subjects. One way to approach this problem is to use a polarising filter, especially if you are taking pictures of water. The filter removes the unwanted glare from the surface of the water and has the effect of increasing the contrast between any subject and the background.

An overcast cloudy sky will always produce a softer and even lighting, regardless of the time of day. The diffuse light in this situation causes shadows to become indistinct or non-existent, with the result that fine details are revealed.

One more tip is that wildlife photography often requires patience and quite a few hours of sitting or crouching in hot, sticky and cramped conditions. Don't forget to take your insect repellent, sunscreen, hat and plenty of water! And for advice on equipment, see page 65.

THE WILDLIFE

PRIMATES At present, five primate species are widespread and relatively common in The Gambia: western red colobus, patas monkey, green (or callithrix) monkey, Guinea baboon and Senegal bushbaby. The first four are fairly easy to see diurnally in the right habitat. The country also supports an introduced population of common chimpanzee, confined to three islands in the River Gambia National Park (page 240), and possibly a relict population of Campbell's monkey.

Temminck's western red colobus (*Procolobus badius temminckii*) This is a large slender leaf-eating monkey with hind legs longer than the arms. The head is small and round, with a short muzzle and flat, broad nose. The upper parts are generally dark grey while the lower limbs and underparts range from rich red to light orange. The face is bluish to black, and the long, tuftless tail is dark, sometimes with an orange tint. As with other colobus monkeys, its thumbs are reduced to mere stumps. It lives in troops of typically around 15–30 individuals, and inhabits various forest and woodland habitats. Despite being found throughout a large area of West Africa, it is disappearing rapidly and listed as endangered, mainly from habitat loss through logging and clearing of forests. Nevertheless, significant populations are present in protected areas such as in Kiang West and the River Gambia National Park, Bijilo Forest Park and Abuko Nature Reserve.

Guinea baboon (*Papio papio*) The largest and most ferocious looking of Gambian monkeys is the Guinea baboon, a West African endemic listed as Near Threatened by the International Union for Conservation of Nature (IUCN) owing to habitat loss within its small range. Grizzled reddish-brown in colour, it has a large dog-like muzzle, and adult males also possess a sharply defined mane and weigh up to 19kg. Baboons are predominantly terrestrial but do visit trees and are quite capable of climbing even smooth palm trunks. They are adaptable feeders, eating most edible plants found in their range, supplemented with small animals ranging from grasshoppers to birds and even young antelopes. Baboons obtain all the water they need to survive from their food and dew, but also like to drink regularly. The Guinea baboon is fairly common upcountry but increasingly scarce along the coast, although it can still be seen in protected areas such as Makasutu Cultural Forest.

Patas monkey (*Erythrocebus patas*) This slender monkey is sandy grey in colour with a russet-red tail, crown and hindquarters, pale facial skin and a dark nose. Males weigh up to 25kg, but females reach a maximum of 14kg. Sometimes dubbed the 'greyhound' of monkeys, it is mainly terrestrial and has long limbs that allow it to travel at up to 50km/h. Though considered Near Threatened by the IUCN, it remains fairly common throughout The Gambia, inhabiting several vegetation types, from open grassland to dry woodland, and is sometimes seen crossing roads upcountry.

Green monkey (*Chlorocebus sabaeus*) A long-legged species associated with forest margins and savannah, the green monkey is grizzled golden-green with off-white underparts, pale grey hands and feet, and a red-tipped tail. The male has a very pale blue scrotum, and can weigh up to 7.5kg. It is adapted to practically all wooded habitats outside of rainforests, but being smaller than a baboon and slower than a patas, it cannot afford to venture as far from the safety of the trees, and is also more dependent on trees for food. Once regarded as a subspecies of the widespread vervet monkey, the green monkey is now considered to be a full species resident only in West Africa. It is the most numerous monkey in The Gambia and can be found throughout the country.

Campbell's mona monkey (*Cercopithecus campbelli*) The Gambian status of this dark, long-tailed, arboreal monkey is uncertain. It once inhabited heavily wooded parts of the country and may still have a very limited presence in the southwest.

Senegal bushbaby (*Galago senegalensis*) Distantly related to the lemurs of Madagascar, bushbabies or galagos are small primates that emit a scream so loud you'd think it was coming from a chimpanzee or gorilla. The Senegal bushbaby is the only one of around a dozen species that occurs in The Gambia. Nocturnal and quite difficult to find, it can sometimes be picked out by tracing the cry to a tree and shining a torch or spotlight in its general direction to look for the reflection of its large eyes.

CARNIVORES
Spotted hyena (*Crocuta crocuta*) Probably the most common large predator in The Gambia, the spotted hyena has a bulky build, sloping back, brown-spotted coat, powerful jaws and dog-like expression. Contrary to popular myth, it is not exclusively a scavenger, nor is it hermaphroditic (an ancient belief that stems from the false scrotum and penis covering the female's vagina). Sociable animals, and fascinating to observe, hyenas live in loosely structured clans of about ten, led by females who are stronger and larger than males. It is normally nocturnal and is

seldom seen, though its loud, repetitive and reverberating hoot 'whoo-up' carries for up to 5km.

Leopard (*Panthera pardus*) This medium to large spotted cat (the largest males grow up to 2m in length and weigh up to 90kg) is solitary and secretive but very habitat-tolerant, typically favouring areas with plenty of cover, such as riverine woodland and rocky slopes. It is adept at remaining concealed in dense vegetation, aided by its beautiful colouring, which also provides a very practical camouflage. As recently as 50 years ago, leopards were so common that they could be watched quite regularly on the outskirts of Banjul. These days they are all but extinct in the country, and the last reliable sightings were in the early 2000s. They may still cross in from Senegal periodically, but this would be to very remote areas like Kiang West National Park or Jinack Island, if at all.

Smaller carnivores Small carnivores are common in the Gambian countryside, but you have to be lucky to see any, as they are elusive and mostly nocturnal. The species recorded so far include **side-striped jackal** (*Canis adustus*), which is widespread, and the **sand fox** (*Vulpes pallida*), which appears to be restricted to the North Bank of the River Gambia. The **African clawless otter** (*Aonyx capensis*) inhabits many wetlands, especially the mangrove creeks, and this is the largest species of otter found in Africa. The black-and-white-striped **zorilla** (*Ictonyx striatus*) is a skunk-like animal that has been rarely recorded in The Gambia, as has the **honey badger** (*Mellivora capensis*), otherwise known as the **ratel**. The ratel is a small but ferocious carnivore that is well known because of its habit of raiding bee nests for their honey. The shaggy, dog-like **African civet** (*Civettictis civetta*), with its ornate pattern of blotches, spots and stripes and a boldly marked face, is said to be common. There are three species of **genet** (looking almost like a cross between a spotted cat and a mongoose) which are very good climbers and feed on fruit, insects, snakes, birds and rodents. The **two-spotted palm civet** (*Nandinia binotata*) is a similar-looking animal that in The Gambia has only ever been recorded in Abuko Nature Reserve and Pirang Forest Park. Five species of mongoose are found in The Gambia. These range from the pack-living **banded mongoose** (*Mungos mungo*), which may be seen hunting in the daylight in and around Kiang West National Park, to the nocturnal and very common **marsh mongoose** (*Atilax paludinosus*), which lives a mostly solitary existence. This animal has extremely nimble fingers and survives by capturing crabs at the water's edge. The **African wild cat** (*Felis silvestris lybica*) looks very like a domestic tabby and may be the commonest of the cats in The Gambia. Other species include the rare lynx-like **caracal** (*Caracal caracal*) with a reddish-fawn coat, and the long-legged and beautifully spotted **serval** (*Leptailurus serval*), which are both widespread but uncommon. Identifying any of these species can be difficult.

UNGULATES
Hippopotamus (*Hippopotamus amphibius*) The country's largest ungulate can weigh in at up to a staggering 3,200kg, and have a body length of up to 3.5m. Dependent on fresh water, hippos are resident along the River Gambia upstream of Elephant Island, but sometimes come closer to the coast. The IUCN's 2016 estimate put The Gambia's entire national population at only about 40 hippos, but you can spot them at least somewhat consistently near River Gambia National Park. Hippos spend the day submerged in deep water, emerging from the river just before darkness falls to graze on nearby grassland for 4–5 hours before returning to the

water to digest the food. There are many existing and potential conflicts between people and hippos, not least of which is that hippos cause considerable damage to agricultural crops on the riverbanks, especially rice fields.

Common warthog (*Phacochoerus africanus*) Often, but erroneously, referred to as a bushpig, the warthog is a large animal, with males weighing up to 150kg, though females are normally a lot smaller with a maximum weight of 75kg. It is relatively long-legged with prominent curved tusks, and a crest of lank dark hair extending from the crown to the nape of the neck and hanging over the shoulders. The 'warts' are three pairs of thickened pads of skin that protect the jaws, eyes and muzzle. It is widespread and common in wooded, bush and savannah habitats upriver, largely because the majority of the population is Muslim, and therefore does not eat pork. This does not mean to say that warthogs live in perfect harmony with people. They can be quite a pest to crop farmers, and are also hunted to provide meat for tourist-oriented restaurants.

Bushbuck (*Tragelaphus scriptus*) This handsome medium-sized antelope has a reddish coat (though mature males become progressively darker with age), with vertical and horizontal white stripes, numerous spots on the haunches, and white markings on the face and ears, above the hooves and under the broad woolly tail. Though common and widespread, it is rather shy and tends to stick to deep cover, where it can remain virtually invisible, announcing its presence only when it bounds off in a blaze of noise and movement, often accompanied by a loud warning bark. The large bushbuck population in Abuko Nature Reserve is relatively accustomed to people and easy to see.

Maxwell's duiker (*Cephalophus maxwelli*) This tiny antelope is often very hard to spot as it makes its way through the grass and trees. Most sightings are made as it crosses open paths. Again it is very common at Abuko and this is one of the best places to see it. Just over 30cm in height, with a maximum weight of 5.4kg, it is a forest species that lives mainly on fruit but will also eat leaves and shoots, and even ants and other insects. It can often be found following troops of monkeys, waiting for them to drop some half-eaten fruit on the ground.

Sitatunga (*Tragelaphus spekei*) This large but secretive antelope is still present in fair numbers along the banks of the River Gambia. Associated with marshes and other wetland areas rather than forest, it is the world's only aquatic antelope, with widely splayed hoofs and a thick oily coat that repels water. Probably the country's best site for observing sitatunga as they emerge from cover to feed is along the southern bank of the River Gambia in Kiang West National Park.

Roan antelope (*Hippotragus equinus*) This is one of the largest antelopes in Africa and is a very impressive and powerful-looking creature. A male might weigh up to 300kg, with a head and body length of up to 2.4m, and massive arched horns up to 1m long. A herd of these magnificent antelopes frequently wanders into Kiang West National Park from southern Senegal during the wet season.

AARDVARK The aardvark, or ant bear (*Orycteropus afer*), is a strange-looking nocturnal creature that is said to be widespread. It is a large animal with a very long nose, squared-off head and long rabbit-like ears. It spends the day living underground in warrens and even when foraging above ground at night it is very shy, so is seldom spotted. It feeds by digging out colonies of ants and termites and sweeping up the insects into its small mouth with its long, sticky tongue.

BATS Like other mammals, bats (or *tonso* in Mandinka) can regulate their body temperature, and give birth to live young and suckle them on milk. Unlike other mammals, however, they are able to fly, a unique ability that has led to their colonising of almost every ecosystem on earth. Indeed, bats account for almost a quarter of the world's 5,000-odd mammal species, and at least 30 species occur in The Gambia, though they have been little studied as yet.

Bats come in two main types: large fruit bats, with wingspans of up to 75cm, and much smaller insect-eating bats. Fruit bats are the more commonly seen, since they roost communally in trees, often in urban areas. They have large eyes and are quite able to see in the dark as they fly from tree to tree, though their sense of smell is also acute and they often use this to locate their food. Fruit bats eat fruit of course, but also pollen and nectar from flowers. The commonest species in The Gambia is probably the **Gambian epauletted fruit bat** (*Epomophorus gambianus*) which can be found just about everywhere.

The insect-eating bats are amazing creatures. Their eyesight is relatively poor but they compensate by using a form of sonar, hearing rather than seeing their surroundings. Depending upon the species in question, they emit short sharp sounds from either their mouths or specially adapted noses. These sounds are sent out in waves around them as they fly, and when these sounds hit an object such as a branch or perhaps a flying insect they bounce back and are picked up by the bats' ears (or their noses in specially adapted species). The sounds are then processed in the bats' brain to produce a 'sound picture' of their environment. These animals are so well adapted that they can detect the location of insects as small as 1mm long, and work out the direction and speed that they are flying. This is even more amazing when you think that they do all of this while they themselves are twisting and turning in very fast flight in complete darkness. These bats are very beneficial to man. They eat vast quantities of insects that are pests to farmers and even the smallest species of bat can eat up to 3,000 mosquitoes per night, helping to keep the numbers of these malaria-carrying insects at manageable levels. Some species have been known to live as long as 30 years.

INSECTIVORES This is a group of small insect-eating mammals that to date have been little studied in The Gambia. The **African four-toed hedgehog** (*Atelerix albiventris*) has been recorded at scattered locations around the country, including in Abuko Nature Reserve. Other species include the **giant shrew** (*Crocidura olivieri*) and the **savannah shrews** (*C. nanilla* and *C. lamottei*).

HARES The **African savannah hare** (*Lepusmicrotis senegalensis*) is a widespread and common species throughout The Gambia, locally often referred to as a rabbit. It is generally solitary and nocturnal, living in any area where there is tall grass or scrub.

RODENTS Rodents are a large group of poorly studied animals within The Gambia and contain a variety of species from the very large porcupines to the tiny **pygmy mouse** (*Mus musculoides*), which weighs 2–3g. One thing that they all have in common is that they eat vegetable matter such as grass, fruits and seeds, and they all have teeth that are constantly growing and therefore need to be kept worn down by gnawing. The **crested porcupine** (*Hystrix cristata*) is widespread but nocturnal and difficult to see, though probably common. Its relative, the **brush-tailed porcupine**

(*Atherus africanus*) has only been recorded by the coast at places like Bijilo Forest Park and Abuko Nature Reserve.

On a walk or drive through the countryside you are much more likely to see **squirrels**. Two species, the **striped ground squirrel** (*Xerus erythropus*) and the **Gambian sun squirrel** (*Heliosciurus gambianus*), are particularly common. The former is almost always seen on the ground and can be identified by the white stripe along its flank. The latter is found mainly in trees and has a black-and-white-ringed tail. The **red-legged sun squirrel** (*Heliosciurus rufobrachium*) can also be seen at Abuko Nature Reserve, where it is an uncommon resident of the gallery forest. It is slightly larger than the Gambian sun squirrel and can be identified by its red legs. There are also numerous species of rats, mice and gerbils, including the very common (and edible) **giant pouched rat** (*Cricetomys gambianus*), a completely harmless animal that can weigh up to 1.4kg. This species is grey in colour with a long, naked tail that is white for the last half of its length. This is not really a 'rat', in spite of its English name, but belongs to a very old family of rodents found only in Africa. It has large cheek pouches that it stuffs with food, which it then carries to an underground den to be stored so that it can be eaten at leisure and in relative safety.

DOLPHINS At least two species of dolphin are regularly sighted off the coast – the **Atlantic hump-backed dolphin** (*Sousa teuszii*) and the **bottlenose dolphin** (*Tursiops truncatus*). The bottlenose dolphin is also known to swim upriver about as far as the Senegambia Bridge, and is frequently sighted east of the Tanbi Wetland Reserve (south of Banjul) and across the river by Dog Island. It has also been known to enter bolongs in both Niumi and Kiang West national parks.

The bottlenose dolphin can grow up to 3.9m long and weigh anything from 150kg to 650kg. It is a uniform grey colour with an off-white, light grey or pinkish underside. Its main distinguishing features are the prominent dark dorsal fin, and an inquisitive and active nature. It is usually found in groups of up to ten animals but as many as 500 have been seen together offshore. It is highly active at the surface, frequently riding the bow and wake of boats, and sometimes leaping several metres high out of the water. It is a powerful swimmer but dives seldom last longer than 3–4 minutes.

The Atlantic hump-backed dolphin is the smaller of the two species with an adult length of 2–2.5m and a weight of 100–150kg. It is distinguished from the bottlenose by the conspicuous elongated hump in the middle of its back and relatively small dorsal fin on top. The colour is slate-grey on the back and sides, with the underside usually paler. The body may be speckled. It usually swims in groups of three to seven animals, but schools of up to 40 have been sighted off the coast. It appears to prefer shallow coastal and estuarine water less than 20m deep, especially around mangrove swamps. It is often quite difficult to approach and tends to avoid boats by diving and reappearing some distance away in a different location. It surfaces every 40–60 seconds but can stay underwater for several minutes. It seldom rides the bow-waves of boats but is known for co-operating with fishermen by driving fish towards their nets.

Watching dolphins in the wild is one of the ultimate wildlife experiences. Several tour operators and hotels offer dolphin-watching trips on the River Gambia, and they can also sometimes be seen from the deck of the Banjul–Barra ferry.

MANATEES The West African manatee (*Trichechus senegalensis*) is large and cylindrical in shape, reaching a length of up to 3.6m and weighing in at 350–450kg.

It has a dark grey wrinkled skin, which is lighter underneath and is almost entirely hairless except for whiskers on its upper lip. Often manatees can look green as the 5cm-thick skin on the back is sometimes covered with a growth of algae. The thick, fleshy upper lip is quite mobile and the head is rounded with very small eyes, no external ears and small round nostrils on the top of the large muzzle. The body tapers into a tail that ends in a rounded fin. The front limbs have evolved into short flippers, each with three rudimentary nails. The hind limbs are no longer outwardly present.

Manatees are entirely aquatic and cannot come out on to land at all. They are superbly adapted to an aquatic existence with nostrils and eyes placed on top of the head so that they can remain almost entirely submerged but still able to breathe and see above the surface. They can dive for up to 15 minutes in an emergency though an ordinary dive lasts between only 1 and 2 minutes. To help them dive their nostrils close with the aid of a valve and oily tear ducts allow them to see under the water. Their normal speed is around 10km/h but when frightened they can swim at considerably faster speeds.

Manatees live mostly in estuaries, coastal lagoons and large rivers and are sometimes encountered in the sea in shallow coastal waters. They are wholly vegetarian, eating a variety of water plants and the leaves of mangroves and other vegetation overhanging the water. They live (but are not easily seen) far up the River Gambia, from the mouth to at least as far as Baboon Island. The West African manatee is now considered vulnerable throughout its range.

REPTILES
Crocodiles Crocodiles have changed very little in the last 65 million years and are perfectly adapted to living in water. Their eyes and nostrils are located on top of the head and they have webbed hind feet. Their nostrils also have watertight valves and there is a flap at the back of the throat, which allows them to feed underwater. Three species are present in The Gambia. Most common is the **West African crocodile** (*Crocodylus suchus*), which was split from the similar-looking but quite distantly related **Nile crocodile** (*C. niloticus*) of eastern and southern Africa in 2011. It can live for up to 100 years in the wild and can attain a length of 6m, with a weight exceeding 1,000kg. The **African slender-snouted crocodile** (*C. cataphractus*) has been recorded occasionally in the vicinity of Georgetown and the River Gambia National Park. The **dwarf crocodile** (*Osteolaemus tetraspis*) is thought to be extinct in The Gambia.

The future of the West African crocodile in The Gambia is almost assured thanks to human intervention. A small population of this species is fully protected in Abuko Nature Reserve. Early in the wet season the crocodiles breed close to the Darwin Field Station in the reserve. Even more significant than the group at Abuko are the populations present at the three sacred crocodile pools. There is one such pool on the North Bank of the River Gambia, at Berending, one in the southern part of the country at Kartong, and the most famous of them all at Kachikally, in Bakau. This last pool, although small, has a large crocodile population. Not only do these pools protect wild populations of this species but they also act as breeding and dispersal centres where excess animals can bolster the wider crocodile population.

Marine turtles These massive shelled reptiles are represented by perhaps five species in Gambian coastal waters. Though they live in the sea, all turtles are tied to land for reproduction and must face many dangers as they haul themselves onto the shore to lay their eggs. In the sea they are powerful and elegant swimmers that cover vast distances during their lifetimes. On shore they are heavy, clumsy creatures that must drag their huge weight through soft sand using only the massive strength of their flippers. Four turtle species have been confirmed as nesting on The Gambia's beaches. Most numerous is the **green turtle** (*Chelonia mydas*), a very large species, up to 1.4m long and 300kg in weight, with a hard smooth shell, a compact and relatively small head, and a tail in both sexes.

Three other species, the **hawksbill** (*Eretmochelys imbricata*), **olive ridley** (*Lepidochelys olivacea*) and giant **leatherback turtle** (*Dermochelys coriacea*) have also been observed nesting in The Gambia, but in considerably smaller numbers than the green turtle.

The leatherback, which can reach a length of 1.8m and an incredible weight of 646kg, is probably the scarcest species inhabiting Gambian waters. Easy to identify as it lacks a horny shell, being covered instead with thick, smooth skin that resembles vulcanised rubber, it is a common target for poachers. One other species, the **loggerhead** (*Caretta caretta*), is also thought to live along the coast, but it is unknown whether they use Gambian beaches to breed.

Lizards These are the most common and familiar reptiles in The Gambia; indeed, there can hardly be a house or compound in the country that does not have a resident gecko or agama. The country's most striking smallish lizard is the **agama**, or **rainbow lizard** (*Agama agama*) which is found almost everywhere in all types of habitat. During the dry season they are generally dull brown in colour, but a month or so before the rains begin the females develop a bright-orange patch along their flank and the males become very gaudy in colour with yellow heads and bright-blue bodies. You can often see the males displaying to one another, with their front feet planted firmly on the ground and their heads bobbing up and down. The agama is active during the day and feeds almost exclusively on termites and ants.

The largest group of lizards in The Gambia is the **geckoes**, and five species have been found here. These common lizards have amazingly adapted feet and eyes. Gecko feet have toe-tips with groups of scales covered in masses of minute hairs that allow them to 'stick' to seemingly smooth surfaces, even glass. The eyes have transparent eyelids that are fused permanently and thus cover the eye with a 'spectacle' that protects it. Geckoes are found in many habitats, but are best known as living in houses where they happily feed on a diet of insects such as cockroaches, mosquitoes, flies and crickets. Geckoes are mainly nocturnal and adapted to living in cooler temperatures than many other lizards. One of the most common species is **Brook's house gecko** (*Hemidactylus brooki angulatus*).

Skinks are another large group of lizards. Four species are found in The Gambia. They look much more like typical lizards than geckoes, are mainly ground-dwelling and are active during the day. They feed almost exclusively on small insects, which they seize in their jaws after a short rush from cover. The **orange-flanked skink** (*Mabuya perrotetii*) and the **brown-flanked skink** (*M. affinis*) both appear to be extremely common and widespread in many different habitats, even in and around urban areas, though the former is normally active only during the wet season. The other two species of skink are much rarer. The **snake-eyed skink** (*Leptosiaphus nimbaense*) has been found only twice in The Gambia. **Armitage's cylindrical skink** (*Chalcides armitagei*) is an uncommon coastal species (page 110).

Chameleons are unmistakable lizards and are famous for their ability to change the colour of their skin to match their background and mood. There are two species of chameleon in The Gambia: *Chamaeleo gracilis* and *C. senegalensis*, which look fairly similar. Chameleons have toes that are bound together and oppose so that they can effectively grip branches. Their tails are prehensile and unlike those of geckoes, agamas and skinks they cannot be shed or regenerated. The eyes of chameleons appear to be placed in turrets and move independently of one another as they search for food. Insects form the main prey of these creatures. These are caught with a telescopic tongue (sometimes longer than the chameleon's body) which can be shot out and has a sticky pad at its tip.

Last but no means least are the **monitor lizards**. There are two species in The Gambia: the **savannah monitor** (*Varanus exanthematicus*) and the **Nile monitor** (*V. niloticus*). The latter is the commonest and also the largest of all the monitor lizards in Africa, reaching a maximum length of 2m. They are powerful-looking animals with well-developed limbs and strong claws. They have a long tail and a long, flexible neck. These lizards are real predators and will eat almost anything from insects to birds and mice. They will also dig up and eat the eggs of turtles and crocodiles and even catch and eat young crocodiles that have just hatched. The Nile monitor is a great swimmer and is therefore usually found in or near water, while the savannah monitor is found in more arid areas, mostly during the wet season.

Snakes At least 37 species of snake have been identified in The Gambia, though most of these are rarely seen or are confined to certain restricted habitats such as gallery forest. However, some species are widespread and can be found in the bush, woodlands, gardens and wasteland. The snakes that you are most likely to see are the beauty snakes, pythons and cobras. Although feared by people, snakes are not the most dangerous animals in the country. Far more people die from malaria, which is carried by the humble mosquito.

Only nine Gambian snakes are regarded as being seriously venomous and dangerous to humans. Snakes do not strike at people because they wish to kill them or eat them; they strike because they are stood on by accident or because they are cornered and cannot escape, because they are frightened or because they are protecting their young just as a human parent would protect their children. The ordinary town dweller or visitor is unlikely ever to see a snake, never mind be struck by one. However, if you do see a snake, then do not go near it or attempt to catch it. Back away and leave it in peace and it will do the same to you. Often a snake will see you before you see it and will rapidly slide away in fear.

AMPHIBIANS At least 33 species of amphibian are found in The Gambia, ranging from toads through bullfrogs to reed and tree frogs. The square-marked toad, or **common African toad** (*Bufo regularis*), is probably the most common and regularly encountered. It is a typical large and compact toad with a warty skin. It is dark olive-brown in colour and the skin between the tiny warts on its sides often appears almost black. It is covered by dark patches that are often arranged more or less symmetrically on the back, looking like pairs of dark squares running along either side of the spine – hence one of its English names. In addition, younger animals have a light stripe which runs along the backbone, sometimes yellow in colour, though this often fades in older animals.

This toad is encountered in most types of habitats, including coastal scrub and woodland, forest, farmland, swamps and even in urban areas, especially in the irrigated grounds of hotels and gardens. However, its main natural habitat appears to be Guinea savannah. Toads must keep their skin moist in order to survive. They do this by becoming nocturnal, hiding by day beneath rocks and fallen logs or in holes, and emerging at night to hunt. Their favourite prey appears to be ants but

2

other insects are also eaten, with termites making up a larger proportion of their diet in damper weather. Adult toads make up the diet of a lot of other creatures, including Nile monitors, crocodiles, herons and egrets.

FISH Fish not only play a large role in the ecology of Gambian waters but they are also the mainstay of a thriving local industry. Saltwater fish are common in the shallow seas off the coast. Walk along any beach and you will see dozens of dead fish washed up on the tideline, including stingrays and triggerfish. If you are really interested, a visit to one of the many fishing villages, such as at Tanji, especially when the catches are being brought in, will satisfy even the most ardent of fishwatchers. Commonly caught fish include **bonga** (*Ethmalosa fimbriata*) and **African red snapper** (*Lutjanus agennes*), but even larger species such as sharks are sometimes landed. Along the River Gambia and its bolongs there is a small-scale fishing industry that provides much of the protein needs of the Gambian population. The Gambia is also well known throughout the world for its sportfishing, and indeed some of the largest specimens of freshwater fish ever caught in the world have been hooked here by keen foreign anglers.

Tilapia and **mullets** are perhaps the most common fish in the country. The juveniles of these can be found in vast quantities among the mangroves, which act as a natural nursery. These fish in turn provide food for huge numbers of birds such as herons, egrets, ospreys and fish eagles.

Perhaps the strangest fish of all, and one which you are bound to see wherever there are mangroves, is the **Atlantic mudskipper** (*Periophthalmus papillo*). When the tide is out and the mud is exposed, mudskippers can be seen creeping about using their strong pectoral fins like miniature legs. They are sometimes mistaken for amphibians but they are true fish and have developed their walking ability so well that they can even climb up on to the exposed lower roots of the mangroves.

CRABS The most abundant species of crab in The Gambia is the **West African fiddler crab** (*Uca tangeri*). This species can be seen in huge numbers on the mud alongside mangrove swamps. The males have one small claw and one large claw that they wave around to warn off other males and to attract females. A walk on the beach at night with a torch is the best way to see **African ghost crabs** (*Ocypoda africana*). They inhabit the shoreline and have distinctive eyes on long stalks. They will often scuttle off into the surf and all you can then see is the tops of their eyes looking at you from above the water like miniature periscopes.

INSECTS Of all the creatures inhabiting our world, insects are by far the most numerous. Science has recognised over 1 million species so far and there are many, many more that as yet remain undiscovered and undocumented. For this reason it is obviously not possible to write about all of the insects in The Gambia in a short section, so we will give a general account that will hopefully give you an overview of this diverse and fascinating group of animals. We have selected some species which are common and therefore more likely to be seen, and those that are particularly interesting or important to people.

Dragonflies and damselflies These are brightly coloured insects, some quite large, with long transparent wings. They are remarkable fliers, being able to hover with ease and even fly backwards. They live most of their lives as nymphs beneath the surface of ponds, streams and rivers. Dragonflies are voracious predators, both as nymphs and, later, as they emerge, as flying adults. They are very beneficial insects, eating millions of smaller insects such as mosquitoes each year. Very common species include the **scarlet dragonfly** (*Crocothemis erythraea*), which is bright red, and the **globe skimmer** (*Pantala flavescens*), a dull brown species that can be found almost everywhere in the tropics. An uncommon species in The Gambia is the **emperor dragonfly** (*Anax imperator*). This is a large, blue-bodied dragonfly that can also be found in many parts of Europe. Altogether there are over 70 species of dragonfly and damselfly in The Gambia.

Stick insects These lengthy and slender insects have long and very thin legs and antennae. They are coloured brown or green and spend long periods remaining absolutely still, making them very difficult to find as they look just like twigs or sticks. Some species can grow as large as 10–12cm. They are all vegetarian but do not usually occur in large enough numbers to cause damage. They can usually be found hiding among grass stems.

Cockroaches Well known to many of us, cockroaches originate from the tropics, but are now found almost everywhere around the world. Although some species are considered pests because they damage books and clothes and contaminate foodstuffs, many are found only in forests and the bush and cause no harm to humans whatsoever.

Mantids These attractive insects always give the impression of being alert and intelligent animals because their long neck allows them to twist their head and follow movement with their eyes, but really they are no more intelligent than other insects. They are beneficial because they prey on many species that are pests. They have well-developed wings and fly mostly at night when they are attracted to lights. Beware: the larger specimens have powerful jaws and can inflict a painful bite. The front legs of mantids are wonderful adaptations for seizing other insects with lightning force before being drawn to the mouth and eaten.

Ants, wasps and bees These are mostly highly social insects, though some species live solitary existences. There are hundreds if not thousands of species in West Africa but some of the most interesting, and in many ways most frightening, are the **army ants**, or **driver ants**. This ant travels in dense columns that may be hundreds of metres long. The workers are all female and blind, with large powerful jaws. The queen is seldom seen but is three or four times the size of the workers and is also blind. There is also a soldier caste with very large-toothed jaws. They all have a powerful bite and once their jaws are locked into position it is very difficult to make them let go. They were once used to suture open wounds by getting them to bite both edges of the wound together, then twisting off their bodies and leaving the head and jaws in place. Their nest is formed in the ground and colonies can contain hundreds of thousands of individuals. Periodically the nests will move, and this is when the ants form a column. Eggs, larvae, pupa and food are carried by the workers who are flanked and protected by the soldiers. If you happen to step on to a column by mistake you will be instantly subjected to numerous painful bites! When a nest has moved the ants then spread out and forage over a wide area. They are mainly carnivorous and have been known to kill and devour animals as large as pythons. Chickens and guineafowl have been stripped to the bone by these ants in hen houses where they cannot escape, and there are stories of tethered horses being eaten in the same way. In contrast, the males are large winged insects that are entirely harmless. They are known as 'sausage ants' and are often attracted to lights in the evening. A good place to see army ants is at Abuko Nature Reserve, where columns are seen frequently crossing the footpaths.

A common feature of the countryside is **termite mounds**. These massive castle-like structures have smooth ventilation shafts that keep the inside of the nest at a constant temperature. They are often used as hiding places by snakes, bats and other animals, so never stick your hand down one! Termites are seldom seen during the day and are mostly small and inoffensive, although they can cause considerable damage to wooden buildings. They are highly social insects with a queen, kings, workers and soldiers. The soldier caste guard the nests and have ferocious bites.

Butterflies The rainy season is undoubtedly the best time to see a huge variety of differently coloured butterflies, of which there are over 170 species in The Gambia, but there are also many that fly during the dry season. Below we have selected two species that can be commonly seen during the whole year and are fairly easy to identify.

The first of these is the extremely common **citrus swallowtail** (*Papilio demodocus*). This species is large, with a wingspan of 7–11cm. It is mainly blackish but also heavily marked and dusted with yellow. There is a yellow band across the hindwing and a similar but broken yellow band on the forewing. On each hindwing there are two large blue, black and orange-marked eyespots. The edges of the hindwings are also scalloped. The citrus swallowtail occurs in open country, cultivated areas, gardens and forest margins. Very commonly found on cultivated and wild citrus trees such as orange, lime, grapefruit and lemon, its caterpillar devours enormous quantities of leaves and is sometimes considered a pest.

The **African tiger** (*Danaus chrysippus*) is another very common butterfly. It is slightly smaller than the citrus swallowtail with a wingspan of around 7–8.5cm. It is an orange-brown butterfly with black borders to the wings and a large triangular black patch on top of the forewings which encloses several white spots. The form of the African tiger found in West Africa also has a large white patch on the hindwings. Both sexes are almost identical but the male has four black spots on the hindwing while the female has only three. This butterfly has a foul taste and is mimicked by the females of other butterflies, which apparently taste better, so that they can escape the hungry attentions of birds and lizards. The African tiger butterfly can be seen flying in many different habitats, including open and bush country, gardens, woodlands and the margins of forests. Its flight is very slow and sailing, giving the impression of being very relaxed. Sometimes you may come across small groups of them in the evening as they prepare to roost together for the night. The caterpillars are very distinctive: smooth and ringed with yellow and black bands.

BIRDS Birds are a major and vital part of every habitat in The Gambia and can be seen just about everywhere. Unlike many of the 'little brown jobs' that can be found in Europe and North America, Gambian birds tend to be more colourful and confiding, therefore making a birdwatching trip to the country a visit to remember. It can also be a great introduction to many species that can be found elsewhere in Africa. Although thousands of birdwatchers visit The Gambia each year, many of them concentrate on the best-known and most easily accessible sites. This means that for the more adventurous there is still a real chance of adding a new species to the country list, as we ourselves have done on several occasions. Almost 600 bird species have been recorded in The Gambia, a phenomenal number considering the small size of the country. Yet there are many reasons why this is so, including the vast array of different habitats, ranging from the coast, through saltwater and freshwater wetlands, Guinea and Sudan savannah, woodlands and forests, to agricultural land, towns and villages. The Gambia is also visited by hundreds of thousands of European birds during the northern winter, as well as by smaller numbers of African birds that migrate from the north and south during the summer.

A visit to each habitat will reveal its own specialised birds. Starting at the coast, there are miles of open, gently sloping sandy beaches where the most common birds are the shoreline waders such as **ruddy turnstone** (*Arenaria interpres*), **sanderling** (*Calidris alba*) and **whimbrel** (*Numenius phaeopus*). These are joined by numbers of **western reef heron** (*Egretta gularis*), **grey heron** (*Ardea cinerea*), **osprey** (*Pandion haliaetus*) and **pied kingfisher** (*Ceryle rudis*). Offshore, and around the scattered fishing centres, **grey-headed gulls** (*Larus cirrocephalus*) are numerous, as are various **terns**. You may be lucky and spot a few **skuas** chasing the other birds and forcing them to drop their hard-earned food, especially around the port at Banjul. Two rarities that are well worth looking out for include the **kelp gull** (*Larus dominicanus*), which has been found breeding in The Gambia, and **Audouin's gull** (*Larus audouinii*), a bird of global conservation concern which winters in moderate numbers along the coast.

The next major habitat on the coastline is the mangrove forest, which stretches far inland along the course of the River Gambia. A canoe trip along a mangrove-lined bolong is a relaxing and satisfying way to see some serious birds, including **pelicans, spoonbills, yellow-billed stork** (*Mycteria ibis*) and **goliath heron** (*Ardea goliath*), plus lots of waders, especially at the beginning of the dry season. Others to look out for include **blue-cheeked bee-eater** (*Merops persicus*) and **mouse-brown sunbird** (*Anthreptes gabonicus*). The river itself and its many tributaries are good places to spot the magnificent **African fish eagle** (*Hieraaetus spilogaster*) perched on an overhanging tree. Other wetland habitats are sure to provide you with a good list of spectacular species such as **African darter** (*Anhinga rufa*), **white-faced whistling duck** (*Dendocygna viduata*), **sacred ibis** (*Threskiornis aethiopicus*), **palm-nut vulture** (*Gypohierax angolensis*), **crakes, greater painted-snipe** (*Rostratula benghalensis*) and **African jacana** (*Actophilornis africanus*) – the famous lily-trotter – to name just a few of the commonest species.

Inland from the coast are the coastal forests, a prime example of which is Bijilo Forest Park, and a few small patches of gallery forest like Abuko Nature Reserve, Pirang Forest Park and the River Gambia National Park. These forests hold small populations of secretive birds such as **grey-headed bristlebill** (*Bleda canicapilla*), **yellowbill** (*Ceuthmochares aereus*), **ahanta francolin** (*Francolinus ahantensis*), **white-spotted flufftail** (*Sarothrura pulchra*), **western bluebill** (*Spermophaga haematina*) and the beautiful **green turaco** (*Tauraco persa*). Walking around the shady footpaths of these forests is like stepping back into primeval times. There are huge buttress-rooted trees and thick tangles of vines and creepers on all sides and the forests echo to the weird calls of birds.

Next we come to the Guinea savannah, which ranges from open areas of grassland through to thickly wooded patches. This is the habitat that once covered huge chunks of the countryside but has gradually been whittled away. Even here, though, you will find spectacular birds such as **bee-eaters, green wood-hoopoe** (*Phoeniculus purpureus*), **blue-bellied roller** (*Coaracias cyanogaster*), **barbets, African golden oriole** (*Oriolus auratus*) and the dinosaur-like **Abyssinian ground hornbill** (*Bucorvus abyssinicus*) – a huge black bird that stalks through the grass, seldom taking to the air.

Further inland, and also on much of the North Bank of the River Gambia, you will see a gradual transition to Sudan savannah, which is much drier and dominated by massive red termite mounds. Look out for a wide range of birds of prey, especially the large and impressive **martial eagle** (*Polemaetus bellicosus*), plus buntings, coursers and sparrow-weavers. In the north and east of the country you can find dry and sparsely vegetated Sahelian landscapes, which are encroaching slowly southwards. Look out here for **northern anteater chats** (*Myrmecocichla aethiops*), which at a distance seem very dark until they open their wings in a short flight and reveal large white wing patches.

Agricultural land ranges from vegetable gardens and dry fields of groundnuts to vast rice fields whose roots and lower stems are perched in shallow water. These are the special domain of the **weavers, finches, doves** and **glossy starlings**, among others. Where cattle graze you are also bound to find flocks of **cattle egret** (*Bubulcus ibis*) and **black magpie** (*Ptilostomus afer*), stalking around the feet of the cows and darting after insects that have been disturbed. You should also keep a sharp lookout for the **yellow-billed oxpecker** (*Buphagus africanus*) perched on the back of cattle. Here, they provide a good service in picking off ticks and other bothersome parasites.

Surprisingly, one of the best habitats for birds comes from a totally unexpected source. These are the grounds of the many resort hotels along the coast. A combination of year-round watering and the planting of exotic flowers in hotel gardens attract many birds to these miniature green oases. These include the **long-tailed glossy starling** (*Lamprotornis caudatus*), **yellow-crowned gonolek** (*Laniarius barbarus*) and many different types of brilliantly coloured **sunbird**. These are considered by some as the most beautiful of all the birds of The Gambia.

3

Practical Information

WHEN TO VISIT

The peak tourist season, and the most pleasant time to visit in climatic terms, broadly coincides with the northern-hemisphere winter, ie: late October to April. During these dry months, a high quota of cloudless skies and blazing sunshine is practically guaranteed to those seeking to escape colder and more northerly climes. Other advantages of travel between October and April are that it tends to be cooler and more comfortable at night, there are fewer mosquitoes and other biting insects about, and dirt roads upriver are less likely to be impassable. In addition, plenty of scheduled flights run to The Gambia from the UK (and the rest of Europe) between October and April, so it is often possible to pick up cheap last-minute package deals inclusive of flights and accommodation.

Out of season, May and June are also good for independent travel, with the advantage that the coastal resorts will be much quieter. Over July to September, the average monthly rainfall is above 200mm, and even though much of the rain falls overnight (and the storms can be pretty spectacular), these months are probably best avoided. The rainy season also carries a higher risk of contracting malaria, as mosquitoes tend to be abundant, while the hot and humid conditions can be very uncomfortable at night, particularly upriver where air conditioning is a rare luxury.

For birders, the early dry season, from late October to December, is the optimum time to visit. Following the rains, most wetland habitats will be at their best, attracting huge numbers of passage migrants from Europe, while weavers, bishops and other resident species displaying marked seasonal plumage variations tend to be in full breeding colours. Birding remains rewarding throughout the dry season, as a significant proportion of migrants overwinter in The Gambia, but from February onwards seasonal wetlands tend to have dried up, and there is generally less wildlife around, particularly over May into early June. The beginning of the rainy season is the time when life starts to show itself again: butterflies and dragonflies fill the air, lizards and birds take on their breeding colours, and mango trees attract large numbers of straw-coloured fruit bats. Overall, though, watching the birds and other wildlife in the rainy season becomes difficult because the vegetation is so thick.

HIGHLIGHTS

JINACK ISLAND AND NIUMI NATIONAL PARK It's hard to believe this wild isle sits barely 10km from the bustling capital city. Here, the only traffic jam you'll encounter involves cows passing each other on the beach.

RIVER GAMBIA NATIONAL PARK This lush, lazy bend in the Gambia River is home to a cluster of islands where a rescued and resettled chimp population has lived since the 1970s. Take a boat safari and peer into the undergrowth where more than 140 chimpanzees now run the show.

WASSU AND KERR BATCH STONE CIRCLES Wonder aloud at these massive megaliths left behind by civilizations past. Thought to be burial sites, they're a glimpse into an ancient Gambia that has largely been lost to time.

LAMIN LODGE This terrifically teetering multi-level wooden construction overlooks the mangroves between Banjul and Brikama, and makes a superb setting for a lazy lunch – take the scenic route and get here by boat.

BINTANG BOLONG Far enough upriver to feel like an excursion, but really just a short drive away, this tranquil riverside town is home to some of the finest accommodation anywhere away from the coast.

KARTONG Go all out in The Gambia's southernmost town, where you can feast on a fresh-caught lobster while watching the boats putter back and forth across the delightfully scenic Allahein River to Senegal.

JANJANBUREH Head upriver to this timeworn port town, without which The Gambia may have long ago disappeared from the map. Hop in a kayak or go for a guided hike to see traditional life along the river as it's been practised for generations.

MAKASUTU CULTURAL FOREST Take a day trip to this celebrated forest, where conservation and culture go hand in hand. Visitors are taken on a birding and nature walk before being treated to a vibrant and educational display of traditional Gambian music and dance.

SOUTH COAST BEACHES Unwind along The Gambia's prettiest stretch of coast, refreshingly free of the major development found to the north. Here, farmers and fishers tend to their respective trades, palm-wine tappers scale to dizzying heights to collect their toddy, and rootsy eco-lodges tempt with swinging hammocks.

ALBREDA AND KUNTA KINTEH ISLAND Take in one of the darkest chapters in modern history at this UNESCO World Heritage Site encompassing a former slaving fort-island and surrounding villages, made globally famous in the TV series *Roots*.

RIVER CRUISES Shake off the road dust and set sail on The Gambia's most defining asset. Though it's woefully underutilised these days, there are a few possibilities for getting out on these waters for a few hours or a few days at a time. And you can even spot dolphins.

BASSE SANTA SU Forget what anyone's told you about The Gambia being 'Africa-lite' in this quintessential regional market town, where crowds of traders and artisans from all over West Africa make their livings sewing, scraping, herding and hawking.

SUGGESTED ITINERARIES

ONE WEEK With a week in-country, you can get a good taste of what The Gambia has to offer, taking in some of the well-trodden tourist sites along with a few lesser-visited corners of this oblong land. Flying into Banjul, start off with a couple of nights in the main tourist district, picking a favourite between Bakau, Fajara, Kotu and Kololi based on your tolerance (or lack thereof) for package-holiday paradise.

Beyond just taking the opportunity to chill on the beach, many of The Gambia's most visited sites are within easy reach from here: scope out the scales at Kachikally Crocodile Pool, meet the monkeys at Bijilo Forest Park and ogle with the ornithologists at the birding hotspot of Kotu Bridge. Alternatively, take in a varied slice of urban Gambia with a visit to the country's uniquely sleepy island capital, followed by a shock wake-up at the irrepressibly energetic Serekunda Market.

Afterwards, head down the coast and leave the city behind. Drop into Tanji en route for a walk through the coastal bird sanctuary, then carry on south to stake out a spot at one of the tranquil eco-lodges found around Sanyang, Gunjur and Kartong. Here you can breathe easy on the rural-feeling south coast, taking in traditional villages and the patchwork farm fields that surround them, or check out the crush of canoes at Gunjur's artisanal fishing harbour.

Next, head upcountry! It's a straight shot west to Bintang Bolong, where a couple of very appealing lodges overlook the mangrove-lined shores of a Gambia River tributary. Take a day trip across the river to UNESCO-recognised Albreda and Juffureh villages and Kunta Kinteh Island, made famous in the TV series *Roots*. The ruins of the infrastructure supporting the inglorious trade in human beings makes for a sobering sight, and an important memorial to the region's difficult history.

From here, you'll need to start heading back towards Banjul. If you've got an extra night or two (and a bit of extra cash), there would be no better cherry on top than a stop at the Makasutu Cultural Forest, where you'll find a celebrated combination of conservation and culture, and the fabulous Mandina Lodges, home to some of the country's most innovative luxury accommodation.

TWO WEEKS With two weeks, you've got time to do all of the above and continue east from Bintang for an upcountry adventure. Make your first stop at the riverfront village of Tendaba, where you can take a boat trip through the myriad creeks of the Bao Bolong Wetland Reserve or stay landside and look for wildlife at the little-visited Kiang West National Park.

From here, keep on until the historic town of Janjanbureh, where several admirable ecotourism initiatives are working to capitalise on their town's historic and natural assets. Visit a weekly *lumo* (market) in the area, where traders from around the region hawk a dizzying variety of wares, or hop in a kayak and get to know life in the villages along the river – both are as genuine a slice of rural Africa as you'll get anywhere on the continent.

From Janjanbureh, turn back west and make a stop at River Gambia National Park to spot the rescued chimps that call several river islands here home. The park houses an excellent tented lodge, or you can stay on the other side of the river in Kuntaur – which is also the jumping-off point for the mysterious megalithic stone circles at Wassu, which are also recognised by UNESCO (and printed on the D50 note).

Continuing back west along the North Bank, it's possible to arrange a memorable homestay in Njau with the admirable Women's Initiative Gambia, led by The Gambia's 'Queen of Recycling', or birders might consider stopping off for a couple of nights at Morgan Kunda Lodge, which overlooks the landward side of the Bao Bolong Wetland Reserve. Those less keen on birding might prefer to keep on towards the coast, aiming for the delightfully wild Jinack Island for a couple of nights spent soaking up the silence in this forgotten-feeling corner of the country, before boarding the Banjul ferry back to the big smoke – just 10km, but a whole world away.

Once back on the Banjul side of the water, celebrate your successful journey with an ice-cold beverage (frilly umbrella optional) and a couple of creature comforts on the Senegambia Strip – you've earned it!

TOURIST INFORMATION AND TOUR OPERATORS

The **Gambia Tourism Board (GTB)** (✆ 446 2496; e info@gtboard.gm; w visitthegambia.gm; f gogambia) has their head office on Bertil Harding Highway, halfway between Kotu and Palma Rima Junctions, and a smaller office on Senegambia Junction in Kololi, plus branch offices in each region of the country. Its website includes several downloadable brochures and other helpful links, as well as a form for submitting queries.

The operators listed below specialise mostly in all-inclusive fly-in packages from the UK or elsewhere. Companies offering domestic excursions from the coast are listed in the introduction to the *Greater Banjul* chapter (page 87).

UK
Birdfinders ✆ +44 (0)1258 839066; e info@ birdfinders.co.uk; w birdfinders.co.uk. Fixed-departure tours to The Gambia with a focus on birding.

Explore Worldwide ✆ +44 (0)1252 391140; w explore.co.uk. Offers an adventurous 2-week programme combining Senegal & The Gambia for small groups.

The Gambia Experience ✆ +44 (0)1489 866939; w gambia.co.uk. This supremely knowledgeable outfit, boasting more than 35 years' specialist experience in the country, offers a wide choice of flights & accommodation, including package trips. Though a good port of call for generic beach holidays, it is also the sole or primary booking agent for several top eco-lodges & boutique hotels, & it offers a range of bespoke & fixed-departure birding tours, the latter usually led by Chris Packham or his recommended local guide Malick Suso. It also operates the only year-round scheduled flight from the UK. Check the website for last-minute special offers.

Heatherlea ✆ +44 (0)1479 821248; e info@ heatherlea.co.uk; w heatherlea.co.uk. Fixed-departure ornithological tours to The Gambia.

Naturetrek ✆ +44 (0)1962 733051; w naturetrek.co.uk. Fixed-departure guided group tours to The Gambia with an emphasis on birding.

Overlanding West Africa ✆ +44 (0)1728 862247; e info@overlandingwestafrica.com; w overlandingwestafrica.com. Independent operator whose overland trip from Dakar to Freetown passes through The Gambia.

US
Birding Ecotours ✆ +1 937 238 0254; e info@ birdingecotours.com; w birdingecotours.com. Specialists in birding with a 10-day tour in The Gambia.

Palace Travel ✆ +1 800 683 7731; e info@ palacetravel.com; w palacetravel.com. Offers a range of tours from 7 to 10 days. Can also be coupled with Senegal.

Spector Travel of Boston ✆ +1 617 351 0111; e tryafrica@spectortravel.com; w spectortravel.com. Offers a 9-day tour through Senegal & The Gambia that showcases their cultural heritage.

WEST AFRICA
African Adventure Tours ✆ +220 449 7313; e info@adventuregambia.com; w adventuregambia.com. Based in Fajara, this operator offers a variety of tours including river cruises & 4x4 excursions as well as trips to Senegal.

Bushwhacker Tours m +220 991 2891/706 2502; e info@bushwhackertours.com; w bushwhackertours.com. Run by expert guide Alieu Bayo, this Banjul-based venture offers fishing trips, 4x4 excursions & combined tours with Senegal.

FairPlay Gambia m +220 233 4176; e dave@ fairplaygambia.com; w fairplaygambia.com. Based out of Janjanbureh, this commendable

The Gambia is a very popular destination with birdwatchers; so much so that it has developed a significant guiding subculture based solely on avitourism. There must be hundreds of self-professed bird guides who hang around the main ornithological hotspots in Greater Banjul, ranging from bumsters-with-binoculars who would barely know a sparrow from an eagle, to a core of very skilled and dedicated guides who possess great expertise when it comes both to identifying difficult species and locating rarities. The best local birding guides also have a phenomenal talent when it comes to calling up birds, with whistles that mimic the calls of many species. If you want a great example of this, try getting a birding guide to call a pearl-spotted owlet on Fajara Golf Course.

Many hotels now have official birding guides who will take guests out and about. Otherwise, the best place to look for a reliable guide is the Gambia Bird Guides Association next to Kotu Bridge (page 130). The guides here can take you around locally and they also arrange trips upcountry in search of special birds, at reasonable but negotiable prices. However, before making any such arrangement, you are strongly advised to spend an hour or two with your guide birding in the vicinity of Kotu Bridge, which is one of the finest ornithological sites along the coast.

If you would like to make advance arrangements with a particular guide, the following is a short selection of recommended guides:

Burama Keita m +220 329 6385; e keitaguide@yahoo.com; w birdsofgambia.net; f burama.keita
Hassan Gindeh m +220 704 0618; e hassan.gindeh@gmail.com; w hassanbirding.com; f Hassan Birding - in The Gambia and Senegal
Kebba Sosseh m +220 394 1839; e ksosseh@gmail.com;

w birdseekerstours.com; f Bird Seekers Tours – Kebba Sosseh
Mass Sanyang m +220 992 4761/310 2161; e masssanyang55@hotmail.com; f mass.sanyang
Musa Jatta m +220 270 0858/988 2167; e info@turacobirding.org; w turacobirding.org; f Turaco Birding and Expedition

social enterprise specialises in extended river trips between the coast & MacCarthy Island on their liveaboard pirogue, as well as hiking & kayaking trips upcountry.
Gambia Tours +220 446 2601/2; e info@gambiatours.gm; w gambiatours.gm. Family-run outfit based in Banjul offering a range of tailor-made tours & excursions, as well as car hire & airport transfers.
Scoot West Africa m +223 7032 0344, +221 77 387 80 46; e info@scootwestafrica.com;

w scootwestafrica.com. Independent operator running unique small group trips taking in Senegal, The Gambia & Guinea-Bissau (among others) atop 110cc moto-scooters, with a focus on slow travel & taking the road less travelled.
Senegambia Birding m +220 701 8174; e contact@senegambiabirding.com; w senegambiabirding.com. Based at Mandinari River Lodge (page 181), this Gambian–Dutch outfit runs private & group birding & photography tours in The Gambia & Senegal.

RED TAPE

A valid passport is required, and the expiry date should fall after your scheduled date of return to your home country. Arriving by plane at Banjul International Airport, holders of UK, EU, Commonwealth and African passports do not require a visa and will be given a 28-day entry stamp on arrival, free of charge. US citizens do require a visa and will be issued a five-year multiple-entry visa on arrival for D7,000 (increased from D3,000 in early 2023). A separate airport security fee of US$/€/£20 or D1,000 – payable in cash – is levied on arrival and departure. (You save on the exchange rate by paying in Dalasi as of mid 2023.)

At land borders, things get a bit fuzzier, and Gambian immigration is known for making up a variety of different fees and requirements that often have no basis in law – your experience can vary wildly from border to border, officer to officer and day to day. Generally speaking, if you are entitled to visa-free entry at the airport, you should be here as well, but you may receive a 15-day entry stamp instead of 28. However you arrive, your period of stay is renewable for two more 28-day periods (D2,000/renewal) at the Gambia Immigration Department (GID) in Banjul or at police/GID stations in Senegambia, after which you are expected to apply for a residence permit.

Gambian embassies abroad also issue visas, but fees can vary considerably between them (charging the equivalent of £160 in Washington or £50 in Dakar, for example). You may also wish to consult the tourism board for further information, and perhaps even save or print a copy of the Ministry of Foreign Affairs' communiqué on visas (found at the link below) to have on hand in case of difficulties at the border, though note that their page on the topic contained partially contradictory information at press time: w visitthegambia.gm/visas-and-passports.

All Covid-related entry and movement restrictions were lifted in December 2022. If you are travelling from a country where yellow fever is endemic (most other African countries including Senegal), you may be asked to show a valid yellow fever vaccination certificate, and might theoretically be refused entry if you can't.

A driving licence from any country, so long as one of the languages used is English, is valid for up to three months. For longer stays, an international driver's licence is required.

For security reasons, it's advisable to write up all your important information in a document and email copies to yourself and a few trusted friends or relatives, together with a scan of your passport (which will facilitate getting a quick replacement if it is lost or stolen). Other information you might want to include in this document are your flight details, travel insurance policy details and 24-hour emergency contact number, details of relatives or friends to be contacted in an emergency, bank and credit-card details, camera and lens serial numbers, etc.

EMBASSIES AND CONSULATES

A comprehensive list of embassies and consulates found in The Gambia is available at w embassypages.com/gambia. Greater Banjul is home to a good selection of West African diplomatic missions and can be a useful place to get visas if travelling around the region. Côte d'Ivoire, Ghana, Guinea, Guinea-Bissau, Liberia, Mali, Mauritania, Nigeria, Senegal and Sierra Leone are all represented.

GETTING THERE AND AWAY

BY AIR Most UK-based tourists visit The Gambia on a package, including flights and accommodation. The Gambia Experience (w gambia.co.uk) runs their own scheduled flights from the UK several times weekly, which are the only direct connection from the UK. Coming from the UK or elsewhere in Europe, other charter companies worth checking out in season (October–April) are Corendon Dutch Airlines (**w** corendon.com) and TUI Airways (**w** tui.co.uk). Options are more limited between May and September, but include Air France (**w** airfrance.com), Binter Canarias (**w** bintercanarias.com), Brussels Airlines (**w** brusselsairlines.com), Royal Air Maroc (**w** royalairmaroc.com), TAP Air Portugal (**w** flytap.com) and Vueling (**w** vueling.com).

Coming from North America, Royal Air Maroc serves Montreal, New York, Washington and Miami, allowing for a one-stop connection in Casablanca. You can do the same with Air Senegal (**w** flyairsenegal.com) from New York or Baltimore via Dakar. Delta (**w** delta.com) also serves Dakar from New York. And of course there are many possibilities for routing through Europe.

OVERLAND FROM EUROPE To travel overland from Europe, via Morocco/Western Sahara, Mauritania and Senegal, is fairly straightforward, and can now be done entirely on tarmac roads following the Atlantic Coast. Anybody planning an expedition of this sort is pointed to Siân Pritchard-Jones and Bob Gibbons's dedicated guidebook *Africa Overland*, also published by Bradt (see **w** bradtguides.com/shop for more details).

HEALTH   *with Dr Daniel Campion*

The Gambia, like most parts of Africa, is home to several tropical diseases unfamiliar to people living in more temperate climates. However, with reasonable precautions – ie: malaria prophylaxis – your chances of a serious incident are minute. In fact, as in much of Africa, it is road travel that presents the greatest risk to life and limb you're likely to face.

Within The Gambia, a range of adequate (but well short of world-class) clinics, hospitals and pharmacies can be found around Banjul, Serekunda and the main resort areas. Most of the larger beach hotels also have their own clinic or a doctor on call. Facilities are far more limited and basic upriver. Wherever you go, however, doctors and pharmacists will generally speak fluent English, and consultation and laboratory fees (in particular malaria tests) are inexpensive by international standards – so if in doubt, seek medical help.

PREPARATIONS Sensible preparation will go a long way to ensuring your trip goes smoothly. Particularly for first-time visitors to Africa, this includes a visit to a travel clinic to discuss matters such as vaccinations and malaria prevention. A list of current travel clinic websites worldwide is available on **w** istm.org. For other journey preparation information, consult **w** travelhealthpro.org.uk (UK) or **w** cdc.gov/travel (USA). All advice found online should be used in conjunction with expert advice received prior to or during travel. The following summary points are worth emphasising:

- Don't travel without comprehensive medical **travel insurance** that will fly you home in an emergency.
- Make sure all your **immunisations** are up to date. A yellow fever vaccination is advised to protect you against disease and you may need to show proof of immunisation upon entry if you are entering The Gambia from another yellow fever endemic area. A yellow fever vaccination certificate will then be required on entry. Since July 2016, any yellow fever certificate is considered to last for life if you are over two years of age and/or you are not immunosuppressed

3

at the time of having the vaccine. If either of those criteria applied then revaccination is recommended at ten years. If the vaccine is not suitable for you then you would be wise not to travel, as West Africa has the highest prevalence of yellow fever and there is up to a 50% mortality rate. It's also unwise to travel in the tropics without being up to date on tetanus, polio and diphtheria (available as a three-in-one vaccine), hepatitis A and typhoid. Immunisation against rabies, meningitis, hepatitis B and possibly tuberculosis (TB) may also be recommended.

- The biggest health threat is **malaria**. Despite encouraging research and trials in recent years, there is no vaccine against this mosquito-borne disease available to travellers, but a variety of preventative drugs is available, including mefloquine, atovaquone/proguanil (Malarone) and the antibiotic doxycycline. Malarone and doxycycline need only be started two days before entering The Gambia, but mefloquine should be started two to three weeks before. Doxycycline and mefloquine need to be taken for four weeks after the trip and Malarone for seven days. It is as important to complete the course as it is to take it before and during the trip. The most suitable choice of drug varies depending on the individual and the country they are visiting, so visit your GP or a specialist travel clinic for medical advice. If you will be spending a long time in Africa, and expect to visit remote areas, be aware that no preventative drug is 100% effective, so consider carrying a course of treatment too (Artemether and lumefantrine combination therapy (Coartem) is often used). It is also worth noting that no homeopathic prophylaxis for malaria exists, nor can any traveller acquire effective "natural" immunity to malaria after infection. Those who don't make use of preventative drugs risk their life in a manner that is both foolish and unnecessary.

- Though advised for most travellers, a **pre-exposure course of rabies vaccination**, involving three doses taken over a minimum of 21 days, is particularly important if you intend to have contact with animals, or are likely to be 24 hours away from medical help. If you have not had this then you will almost certainly need to evacuate for medical treatment, as it is very unlikely that The Gambia will have the necessary treatment.

- Anybody travelling away from major centres should carry a **personal first-aid kit**. Contents might include an antiseptic, Band-Aids, suncream, insect repellent, aspirin or paracetamol, antifungal cream (eg: clotimazole or Canesten), loperamide (Imodium) for diarrhoea, antibiotic eye drops, tweezers, condoms or femidoms, a digital thermometer and a needle-and-syringe kit with accompanying letter from a health-care professional. Antibiotics for severe diarrhoea (usually azithromycin) may be recommended for certain high-risk travellers.

- Bring any **drugs or devices relating to known medical conditions** with you. That applies both to those who are on medication prior to departure, and those who are, for instance, allergic to bee stings, or are prone to attacks of asthma. Always check with the country website to identify any restricted medications. Carry a copy of your prescription and a letter from your GP explaining why you need the medication. This is particularly important in The Gambia, thanks to the unpredictable application of its drug laws (page 62).

COMMON MEDICAL PROBLEMS
Malaria This potentially fatal disease is widespread in low-lying tropical parts of Africa, a category that includes all of The Gambia, and while the risk of transmission

is highest in the rainy season, it is present throughout the year. Since no malaria prophylaxis is 100% effective, one should take all reasonable precautions against being bitten by the nocturnal *Anopheles* mosquitoes that transmit the disease (page 60). Malaria usually manifests within two weeks of transmission, but it can be as little as seven days and anything up to a year. Any fever occurring after seven days should be considered as malaria until proven otherwise. Symptoms typically include a rapid rise in temperature (over 38°C), and any combination of a headache, flu-like aches and pains, a general sense of disorientation, and possibly even nausea and diarrhoea. The earlier malaria is detected, the better it usually responds to treatment. So if you display possible symptoms, *get to a doctor or clinic immediately* (in the UK, go to the local emergency department (A&E) and say that you have been to Africa). A simple test, available at even the most rural clinic in Africa, is usually adequate to determine whether you have malaria. You need three negative tests to be sure it is not the disease. And while experts differ on the question of self-diagnosis and self-treatment, the reality is that if you think you have malaria and are not within reach of a medical facility, it would be wisest to start treatment. Malaria treatment kits can be obtained before travel at many travel clinics, but a course of artemether and lumefantrine (Coartem) can also be purchased in most Gambian pharmacies. Any medicines purchased locally should be sourced from the major, reputable pharmacies in Greater Banjul whenever possible. If you use a self-treatment kit, you should still seek medical assistance as soon as possible, for definitive diagnosis and treatment.

Traveller's diarrhoea Many visitors to unfamiliar destinations suffer a dose of travellers' diarrhoea, usually as result of imbibing contaminated food or water. Rule one in avoiding diarrhoea and other sanitation-related diseases is to wash your hands regularly, particularly before snacks and meals. As for what food you can safely eat, a useful maxim is: "peel it, boil it, cook it or forget it". This means that fruit you have washed and peeled yourself should be safe, as should hot cooked foods. However, raw foods, cold cooked foods, salads, fruit salads prepared by others, ice cream and ice are all risky. It is rarer to get sick from drinking contaminated water but it happens. Bottled water is safe and widely available, but to reduce plastic waste you may wish to consider a re-useable filter bottle such as Aquapure.

If you suffer a bout of diarrhoea, it is dehydration that makes you feel awful, so drink lots of water and other clear fluids. These can be infused with sachets of oral rehydration salts. If diarrhoea persists beyond a couple of days, it is possible it is a symptom of a more serious illness (typhoid, cholera, hepatitis, dysentery, worms, etc), so you should see a doctor. If the diarrhoea is greasy and bulky, and is accompanied by sulphurous (eggy) burps, one likely cause is *Giardia*. This gut parasite can cause persistent symptoms but is treatable. Again, seek medical advice if you suspect this.

Bilharzia Also known as schistosomiasis, bilharzia is an unpleasant parasitic disease transmitted by freshwater snails most often associated with reedy shores where there is lots of water weed. It cannot be caught in hotel swimming pools or the ocean, but should be assumed to be present in any freshwater river pond, lake or similar habitat, even those advertised as 'bilharzia free'. The most risky shores will be within 200m of villages or other places where infected people use water and wash clothes. Ideally, however, you should avoid swimming in any fresh water other than an artificial pool. If you do swim, you'll reduce the risk by applying DEET insect repellent first and staying in the water for under 10 minutes. Drying off vigorously with a towel after an accidental brief water exposure may help to prevent the *Schistosoma* parasite from penetrating the skin, but should not be relied upon. Bilharzia is often asymptomatic in its early stages, but some people experience an intense immune reaction, including fever, cough, abdominal pain and an itching rash, around four to six weeks after infection. Later symptoms vary but often include a general feeling of tiredness and lethargy. Bilharzia can be tested for at specialist travel and tropical medicine clinics, ideally at least six weeks after exposure. Fortunately, it is easy to treat at present, typically with one or two doses of Praziquantel (Biltricide).

Meningitis The Gambia lies within Africa's "meningitis belt" where periodic outbreaks can occur, especially in the dry season. Transmitted by close contact and respiratory droplets, this bacterial infection can kill within hours of the appearance of initial symptoms, typically a combination of a blinding headache (light sensitivity), blotchy rash and high fever. Outbreaks tend to be localised and are usually reported in local media. Fortunately, immunisation with a conjugate meningococcal ACWY vaccine protects against the most serious bacterial form of meningitis and lasts for five years. Nevertheless, other less serious forms exist which are usually viral, but any severe headache and fever – possibly also symptomatic of typhoid or malaria – should be sufficient cause to seek medical advice immediately.

Rabies This deadly disease can be carried by any mammal and is usually transmitted to humans via a bite or a scratch that breaks the skin. In particular, beware of village dogs and monkeys habituated to people, but assume that *any* mammal that bites or scratches you (or even licks on intact skin) might be rabid even if it looks healthy. First, scrub the wound with soap under a running tap for a good 10–15 minutes, or while pouring water from a jug, then pour on a strong iodine or alcohol solution, which will guard against other infections and might reduce the risk of the rabies virus entering the body.

Whether or not you underwent pre-exposure vaccination, it is vital to obtain post-exposure prophylaxis as soon as possible after the incident. Post-exposure vaccine is readily available in most locations. Those who have not been immunised will need a full course of four or five injections as well as rabies immunoglobulin (RIG), but this product is expensive and may be hard to come by – another reason why pre-exposure vaccination should be encouraged. If you have had the full three doses of pre-exposure vaccine, then you will not need the RIG, but just two further doses of vaccine three days apart. It is important to tell the doctor if you have had pre-exposure vaccine – carry your vaccine record with you. Treatment should include RIG (regardless of previous vaccination) if your immune system is significantly weakened, eg: if you take immunosuppressant medication. Death from rabies is probably one of the worst ways to go, and once you show symptoms it is too late to do anything – the mortality rate is almost 100%.

Tetanus Tetanus is caught through deep dirty wounds, including animal bites, so ensure that such wounds are thoroughly cleaned. Immunisation protects for ten years, provided you don't have an overwhelming number of tetanus bacteria on board. If you haven't had a tetanus shot in ten years, or you are unsure, get a booster.

HIV/AIDS With around a 2% prevalence, rates of HIV/AIDS infection in The Gambia are in line with regional trends in West Africa, but this is still ten times the prevalence rate found in the UK. The infection rate is many times higher among sex workers, and other sexually transmitted diseases are rife. Condoms (or femidoms) greatly reduce the risk of transmission.

Tick bites Ticks in Africa are not the major disease vectors that they are in the Americas, but they may spread African tick bite fever (ATBF) along with a few other dangerous rarities.

Ticks should ideally be removed complete, and as soon as possible, to reduce the chance of infection. You can use special tick tweezers, which can be bought in good travel shops; or failing this, with your fingernails, grasp the tick as close to your body as possible, and pull it away steadily and firmly at right angles to your skin without jerking or twisting. Applying irritants (eg: Olbas oil) or lit cigarettes is to be discouraged as a means of removal since they can cause the ticks to regurgitate and therefore increase the risk of disease. Once the tick is removed, if possible douse the wound with alcohol (any spirit will do), soap and water, or iodine. If you are travelling with small children, remember to check their heads, and particularly behind the ears, for ticks. Spreading redness around the bite and/or fever and/or aching joints after a tick bite imply that you have an infection that requires antibiotic treatment. In this case seek medical advice.

Skin infections Any mosquito bite or small nick is an opportunity for a skin infection in warm humid climates, so clean and cover the slightest wound in a good drying antiseptic such as dilute iodine, potassium permanganate or crystal (or gentian) violet. Prickly heat is a fine pimply rash that can be alleviated by cool showers, dabbing (not rubbing) dry and talc, and sleeping naked under a fan or in an air-conditioned room. Fungal infections also get a hold easily in hot moist climates so wear 100%-cotton socks and underwear and shower frequently.

Eye problems Bacterial conjunctivitis (pink eye) is a common infection in Africa, particularly for contact-lens wearers. Symptoms are sore, gritty eyelids that often stick closed in the morning. They will need treatment with antibiotic drops or ointment. Lesser eye irritation should settle with bathing in salt water and keeping the eyes shaded. If an insect flies into your eye, extract it with great care, ensuring you do not crush or damage it, otherwise you may get a nastily inflamed eye from secreted toxins.

Sunstroke and dehydration Overexposure to the sun can lead to short-term sunburn or sunstroke, and increases the long-term risk of skin cancer. Wear a T-shirt and waterproof sunscreen when swimming. On safari or walking in the direct sun, cover up with long, loose clothes, wear a hat, and use sunscreen. The glare and the dust can be hard on the eyes, so bring UV-protecting sunglasses. A less direct effect of the tropical heat is dehydration, so drink more fluids than you would at home.

Other insect-borne diseases Although malaria is the insect-borne disease that rightly attracts the most attention in Africa, there are others, most too uncommon to be a significant concern to short-stay travellers. These include dengue fever and other arboviruses (spread by day-biting mosquitoes), sleeping sickness (tsetse flies), and river blindness (blackflies). Bearing this in mind, however, it is clearly sensible, and makes for a more pleasant trip, to avoid insect bites as far as possible (page 60). Two nasty (though ultimately relatively harmless) flesh-eating insects associated with tropical Africa are tumbu or putsi flies (*Cordylobia anthropophaga*),

The *Anopheles* mosquitoes that spread malaria are active at dusk and after dark. Most bites can thus be avoided by covering up at night. This means donning a long-sleeved shirt, trousers and socks from around 30 minutes before dusk until you retire to bed, and applying a DEET-based insect repellent to any exposed flesh. It is best to sleep under a net, or in an air-conditioned room, though burning a mosquito coil and/or sleeping under a fan will also reduce (though not entirely eliminate) bites. Travel clinics usually sell a good range of nets and repellents, as well as Permethrin treatment kits, which will render even the tattiest net a lot more protective, and help prevent mosquitoes from biting through a net when you roll against it. These measures will also do much to reduce exposure to other nocturnal biters. Bear in mind, too, that most flying insects are attracted to light: leaving a lamp standing near a tent opening or a light on in a poorly screened hotel room will greatly increase the insect presence in your sleeping quarters.

It is also advisable to think about avoiding bites when walking in the countryside by day, especially in wetland habitats, which often teem with diurnal mosquitoes. Wear a long loose shirt and trousers, preferably 100% cotton, as well as proper walking or hiking shoes with heavy socks (the ankle is particularly vulnerable to bites), and apply a DEET-based insect repellent to any exposed skin.

known as mango worms in The Gambia, which lay eggs, often on drying laundry, that hatch and bury themselves under the skin when they come into contact with humans, and jiggers, which latch on to bare feet and set up home, usually at the side of a toenail, where they cause a painful boil-like swelling. Drying laundry indoors and wearing shoes are the best way to deter this pair of flesh-eaters.

OTHER SAFETY CONCERNS

Wild animals Don't confuse habituation with domestication. Most wildlife in Africa is genuinely wild, and widespread species such as hippo or hyena might attack a person given the right set of circumstances. Such attacks are rare, however, and they almost always stem from a combination of poor judgement and poorer luck. A few rules of thumb: never approach potentially dangerous wildlife on foot except in the company of a trustworthy guide; never swim in lakes or rivers without first seeking local advice about the presence of crocodiles or hippos; never get between a hippo and water; and never leave food (particularly meat or fruit) in the tent where you'll sleep.

Snake and other bites Snakes are very secretive and bites are a genuine rarity, but certain spiders and scorpions can also deliver nasty bites. In all cases, the risk is minimised by wearing closed shoes and trousers when walking in the bush, and watching where you put your hands and feet, especially in rocky areas or when gathering firewood. Only a small fraction of snakebites deliver enough venom to be life-threatening, but it is important to keep the victim calm and inactive, and to seek urgent medical attention.

Car accidents Dangerous driving is probably the biggest threat to life and limb in The Gambia. On a self-drive visit, drive defensively, being especially wary of stray livestock, gaping pot-holes and foolhardy or bullying overtaking manoeuvres. Many vehicles lack headlights and most local drivers are reluctant headlight-users, so avoid driving at night and pull over in heavy storms. On a chauffeured tour, don't be afraid to tell the driver to slow or calm down if you think they are too fast or reckless.

SAFETY AND HASSLES

The Gambia is generally a very safe travel destination, certainly in terms of crime and associated issues. Indeed, the biggest concerns for most travellers should be malaria (page 56) and road accidents associated with public transport. It should be pointed out that, as is the case almost anywhere in the world, breaking the law, in particular the usage of illegal drugs (which includes marijuana), could land you in trouble.

CRIME Theft is not a major concern for tourists, but it is worth following a few common-sense rules, as detailed below:
- Most casual thieves operate in busy markets, particularly those in Serekunda and Banjul, as well as in bus stations and the crowded ferry crossings. Keep a close watch on your pockets and possessions in such places, and avoid having valuables or large amounts of money loose in your daypack or pockets.
- Keep all your valuables and the bulk of your money in a hidden money-belt. Never show this money-belt in public. Keep any spare cash you need elsewhere on your person.
- Where the choice exists between carrying valuables on your person or leaving them in a locked room, we would tend to favour the latter option, particularly after dark, but obviously you should use your judgement and be sure the room is absolutely secure. If you do decide to carry large sums of money, or other valuables, with you after dark, then use taxis; don't walk around.
- Leave any jewellery of financial or sentimental value at home.
- Avoid quiet or deserted places, such as unlit alleys by night, or deserted beaches by daylight, particularly if they lie close to or within a major urban area. When in doubt, take a guide, though preferably one who has been recommended to you by your hotel or by other travellers. Known places where muggers occasionally prey on tourists are the beach going south from Bijilo, the beach going north from Calypso Restaurant at Cape Point, and the beach going towards Banjul from Denton Bridge.
- Car break-ins are an occasional problem in built-up areas. A favourite trick is to slash the rubbers holding the windows in place and to remove the glass to get access. Never leave money or valuables in a car unless someone you trust is guarding it.
- If you are carrying expensive gear such as cameras, binoculars or telescopes, then keep them out of sight in a rucksack unless you are actually using them. Be extra careful when using them in out-of-the-way and lonely places.
- When swimming, be very careful about leaving your valuables on the beach, as people often get their things stolen while they are splashing about, having fun in the sea. Leave them in a prominent place and keep a sharp eye on them while you are in the water, or better still leave at least one person with them at all times.

If all of this talk of crime is putting you off, bear in mind that violent crime is very rare indeed. You have far more chance of being mugged in New York,

3

London, Berlin, Johannesburg or Sydney than you ever have in Banjul or Bakau. And you are also extremely unlikely to be threatened with a gun of any sort in The Gambia.

If, by some unlucky happenstance, you are robbed in The Gambia, please report it to the police. If you don't report a crime, how are the police to know about it and to do something to stop it happening again? Remember, too, that if you want to claim off your insurance you will need a police report number. It may take a little time to write a statement, etc, but it's worth the effort.

BRIBERY AND BUREAUCRACY Bribery and corruption are a fact of life in The Gambia. In interactions with tourists, this most often takes the form of officials simply 'giving it a shot' on the off chance they might get something, and so long as you keep a good attitude, it doesn't usually go further than that. And while these chancer officials can be enormously tiring, they are rarely malicious – The Gambia is certainly the only country where a border guard stamping me in asked me not about my background or plans in The Gambia, but if I would take him to *my* country instead!

MEDICINE MUDDLE

Gambian authorities, in particular agents of the Drug Law Enforcement Agency, The Gambia (DLEAG), will occasionally mount an unusually thorough search of travellers' baggage. This typically takes place on arrival at land borders, but occasionally also at the airport or at a road checkpoint. It is generally done to find your first-aid/medical kit and see what's in it.

This is because, as in most countries, many drugs are prescription-controlled in The Gambia. Having found your medicines, DLEAG agents may accuse you of having 'illegal' prescription drugs if you cannot show a written prescription alongside the medicines in question. Many of these prescription-controlled drugs can be purchased without paperwork at Gambian pharmacies, however, so they rely on your inability to produce documentation in order to accuse you of a crime and therefore solicit a bribe.

While you may not be able to fully avoid this selective law enforcement, your experience of being extorted can vary wildly based on your attitude. You can firstly inoculate yourself against this scheme and reduce your hassle significantly by keeping your medicines in their original packaging and bringing the written prescription wherever possible. (This is best practice regardless!) DLEAG agents may confiscate certain medicines (codeine or diazepam are known to be problematic, even with a prescription), but they may also attempt to manufacture further non-existent issues with your paperwork that can only be solved through payment. Depending on what you have been accused of, it may be difficult to avoid making some kind of payment, but as with any interaction with the authorities, remain cool, calm, and collected – and especially patient. A friendly, unhurried, respectful demeanour is your best defence against any accusation, so don't be afraid to take your time and see if you can talk it through over a fresh pot of *attaya*.

You can see a list of controlled drugs in The Gambia at w visitthegambia. gm/health-medication, and it should go without saying that in light of the above, carrying illicit drugs in The Gambia – such as the produce of Jinack Island (page 203) – is a fool's errand and should be strictly avoided.

So at borders and police, military and other roadblocks, you may be subject to either direct requests for cash, or more likely presented with some sort of fabricated issue with your paperwork which is subject to a fine. That being said, this advice rests on the assumption that your paperwork is in fact fully in order, so note that in The Gambia it's required to have a valid licence, car insurance, fire extinguisher (in date!) and warning triangles if you are driving. If you don't have these, or commit another type of driving infraction, you may find yourself on the hook for a small payment.

And do try to keep a bit of perspective on the matter. It's eminently unfair, and unfortunately quite common, for foreigners to gripe about corrupt officials while being legitimately in breach of the laws themselves! So assuming your documents are in order, most of these attempts are just a bit of opportunism and can be defused with a bit of chat, a bit of patience and a smile.

When it comes to other official interactions, the tendency to portray African bureaucrats as difficult and inefficient in their dealings with tourists is also often overstated. Indeed you come across the odd unhelpful official, but then such is the nature of the beast everywhere in the world. It is worth noting that the treatment you receive from officialdom will be determined partly by your own attitude. Try to be friendly and patient, and accept that the person to whom you are talking may not speak English as fluently as you, or may struggle to follow your accent.

And finally, you should also be cautious of flashing a camera around in the vicinity of official buildings, bridges, military camps and the like (for example in Kanilai), as the security police might take exception to it, in which case you could well find yourself in for a long and tedious conversation, or worse.

SWIMMING In the wrong conditions, an element of risk is associated with swimming on any beach, even those generally regarded as relatively safe. Swimmers risk being dragged away from shore by riptides, strong undertows and whirlpools, particularly in stormy or windy weather, though it is not always easy to determine the presence of a strong undertow until you are actually in the water. Some tourist beaches in The Gambia display flags indicating whether swimming conditions are safe. Most don't, in which case you should ask local advice before you swim, particularly on quiet beaches where there are no other swimmers about. Weak swimmers should also avoid water deeper than their waist unless they are using some sort of flotation device. If you are caught in a riptide or whirlpool, it is generally advisable not to fight the current by trying to swim directly to shore, but rather to save your strength by floating on your back or swimming parallel to shore until the tide weakens, and only then to try to get back to land.

WOMEN TRAVELLERS *Juliana Peluso*

Whether they want them or not, women travelling alone in The Gambia will certainly not find themselves lacking for new friendship opportunities. Foreigners are the centre of attention wherever they go, and lone women only more so; it is considered unusual for a woman to travel without the company of her husband, so when the assumption of singlehood is combined with stereotypes about the relative sexual liberation of Western women (and/or certain assumptions being made about why she has chosen to take her holiday in The Gambia), unwanted advances can at times be overwhelming.

While the attention is rarely dangerous or threatening in nature, it can be ubiquitous (particularly on the coast), so it's wise to have a plan to brush off romantic solicitations simply and quickly in order to streamline what will be a frequent shut-down process. Whether speaking with women or men, it is inadvisable to admit to being unmarried, and some female travellers will go so far as to wear a fake wedding ring in order to bolster their claims to being 'taken', which are usually respected (though not without requisite, good-natured teasing as to the superiority of Gambian men over their Western counterparts). Even the most patient women will find it tempting to give in to their frustration at times, but this usually only ends with relentless taunting and bad blood; it's better to respond icily to particularly aggressive suitors, which should eventually garner disinterest.

DRESS Expectations of modesty in dress vary dramatically by region, and women are advised to err on the side of the discreet in order to avoid even further harassment. Generally speaking, regions upriver are known to be particularly conservative, and are also therefore the strictest when it comes to limiting exposed skin; while outfits are as tight as anywhere else, shoulders and calves are rarely exposed in public. In contrast, the skimpiness exhibited in greater Banjul's nightlife scene rivals that of any Western city, and daytime apparel can reasonably accommodate shorts, mid-thigh-length skirts and vest tops. The best practice is usually to observe the clothing of local women your age in order to discern what's acceptable in the city, town or village in question.

TRANSPORTATION Women travelling long distances, especially in gelly-gellys, would do well to choose a car with other female travellers whenever possible; bathroom breaks are begrudgingly allotted by the driver, who may not be feeling particularly generous on a given day, and having backup when vying for a petrol station or locale with enough tree cover to provide for dignity will help your case. Following other common-sense rules of thumb, such as avoiding travelling after dark whenever possible and only taking 'official' means of transport (as official as purchasing a ticket from a garage can be, that is), should go a long way in terms of self-preservation.

SANITARY PRODUCTS Finally, also note that getting hold of tampons or sanitary towels upcountry can be impossible, though it is easy to buy them from any supermarket in the coastal resorts. So take a supply if you are travelling upcountry and remember that when travelling in the tropics it is common for women to have heavier and more irregular periods than they might normally have at home.

LGBTQIA+ TRAVELLERS

Any act of consensual same-sex sexual activity is criminal in The Gambia, and so-called 'serial offenders' currently risk a life sentence in prison for 'aggravated homosexuality' – an amendment passed under the notoriously homophobic Jammeh government in 2014. The Barrow government confirmed in 2020 that no review of these laws was on the cards, citing 'the norms of [The Gambia's] people'. And, indeed, LGBTQIA+ individuals are highly stigmatised in Gambian society. Of course none of this means that homosexuality doesn't exist here; only that of necessity it is clandestine. Setting aside the rights and wrongs of the matter, and at risk of stating the blindingly obvious, this clearly isn't a destination suited to travellers in search of anything approximating a gay scene, and same-sex couples who visit should exercise maximum discretion.

The UK's **gov.uk** website (w gov.uk/government/publications/disabled-travellers/disability-and-travel-abroad) has a downloadable guide giving general advice and practical information for travellers with a disability (and their companions) preparing for overseas travel. The **Society for Accessible Travel and Hospitality** (w sath.org) also provides some general information.

WHAT TO TAKE

Almost anything you are likely to need can be bought from one of the many markets and supermarkets dotted around Greater Banjul, and even though specialist imported items might be pricier than they are at home, there is no need to arrive laden down with a hoard of inexpensive inessentials. Indeed, for the many visitors who base themselves in a resort hotel and spend most of their time on the beach or by the swimming pool, there's probably no need to pack any more elaborately than one might for a beach holiday in Greece or France. A little more thought and care might be advisable for anybody heading upriver for a few days, but even so, unless you plan on travelling more extensively in West Africa or will be working in a remote part of the country, there's no reason to go overboard on luggage.

CARRYING LUGGAGE For most package tourists, it will matter little whether you bring your luggage in a suitcase, duffel bag or rucksack. If you'll be travelling around a lot, especially on public transport, some type of backpack is strongly advised. Either way, a small daypack will also be useful for carrying water, lunch, field guides, binoculars, etc, on day trips.

CLOTHES Light cotton wear is ideal for the tropical Gambian climate. Depending on how long you'll stay in the country and how static or itinerant you are, that might include two pairs of long trousers and shorts for men or three to four skirts or shorts for women, two swimming costumes, plus as many shirts, socks and underwear as you reckon you will need. A wide-brimmed hat provides good protection against the sun, but even a baseball cap is better than no headgear.

Nights are warm, so one sweater should suffice, supplemented by a light waterproof windbreaker if you travel during the rainy season. Again, depending on your mode of travel and whether you'll be sunning on the beach or birding in the bush, bring at least one solid pair of shoes or boots for walking, and one pair of sandals or other light shoes for casual use. And if your bag starts to become uncomfortably heavy or bulky, bear in mind that any item of clothing that breaks or tears can easily be replaced in Greater Banjul.

It's also important to bear in mind that The Gambia is overwhelmingly Islamic and, while it's quite laid-back as these things go, it's worth taking note of a few considerations when planning your outfits. Women generally shouldn't wear skirts or shorts above the knee, and tops that cover your shoulders would be a good idea as well. For men, knee-length shorts are acceptable but tend to be looked upon as an outfit for schoolboys, not grown men. As a rule, the most conservative areas of the country are upriver, while attitudes are considerably more relaxed along the coast, and Western dress predominates in Greater Banjul – though this varies greatly by the neighbourhood that you happen to be in. (Attitudes in Banjul proper or Serekunda, for instance, are more in line with their country cousins upriver than with the Senegambia Strip, only a few miles away.) So while you may see travellers doing it in a few of the main tourism hotspots, wearing your skimpy swimwear outside of the immediate beach area (where it's no problem) is not appropriate anywhere else.

OTHER USEFUL ITEMS The content of this list will depend on what you intend to do on your holiday. A must for most people, **suncream** and **insect repellent** are very useful (and can easily be bought after you arrive), and a small **medical kit** may also come in handy (page 56). A water bottle can be nice to have, but conversely may be of limited utility unless you have access to filtered water.

If you're a birdwatcher or otherwise interested in wildlife and natural history, then don't forget the **binoculars**, whatever you do. Serious birders will of course need to bring their **telescope** and **tripod**. Another vital piece of equipment if you intend to wander about in the bush unguided is a **GPS device** or **phone** (with supplementary **power bank**) or, for the old school, a **compass**.

A good **torch** is a must in case of blackouts. **Loo paper** cannot always be found when you most need it so carry a roll in your bag. Other sundry items include **tampons** or **sanitary pads**, as they are not always easy to get hold of upcountry.

ELECTRICAL DEVICES Electricity is 220–240V. If you intend to operate delicate electrical equipment then you should make sure you use a stabiliser or voltage regulator, as the voltage does tend to fluctuate quite a lot. Adapters are needed for appliances using 110V. A few three-/two-pin adapters could be useful.

MONEY

The unit of currency since 1971 – The Gambia decimalised the same year as the UK – is the dalasi (denoted as 'D'), a Wolof word that probably derives from the English word dollar or French *dala* (a type of five-franc coin). It is subdivided into 100 bututs. The dalasi has devalued steadily over time, though never in a particularly dramatic way. The rate of exchange in October 2023 stood at US$1 = D66, £1 = D80 and €1 = D69. The highest banknote is D200, which has a value of around £2.60. Other banknotes in circulation are D100, D50, D25, D20, D10 and D5. Coins come in denominations of D1, 50 bututs and 25 bututs – though bututs have largely disappeared with inflation. Several series of banknotes (the newest introduced in 2019) are in circulation and accepted, so don't be surprised if you receive a quite varied collection of notes.

ORGANISING YOUR FINANCES Arriving in The Gambia, you ideally need to carry an international Visa card supplemented by a stash of hard currency cash. Unlike in the majority of African countries, the most widely recognised hard currency in The Gambia is the British pound sterling. The US dollar and euro are also accepted at all foreign-exchange outlets, but more obscure currencies will be difficult to change. The best place to change money is usually private bureaux de change (known locally as forex bureaux), which tend to be more efficient than banks, keep longer hours and offer a slightly more favourable rate. There are forex bureaux dotted all over Banjul and in major resort areas such as Bakau, Kotu and Kololi. Alternatively, small Mauritanian-run shops are often willing to change money with little fuss and at a fair rate – and these are often your only option upriver. Many hotels also have foreign-exchange desks, but the rates tend to be poor. Avoid changing money on the street, as it is illegal, and also carries a higher risk of being cheated or robbed.

With the exception of some upmarket hotels and car-rental companies, pretty much every price in The Gambia is quoted in the local currency, dalasi, and can be paid for that way. Indeed, in many situations, attempting to pay in anything other than dalasi would create complete confusion. In an ideal world, we would follow suit in this book, by quoting all prices in dalasi. However, because of the currency's ongoing devaluation and comparatively high local inflation rate, we feel that aside from basic costs such as entry fees and public transport, converting dalasi prices to a hard currency equivalent is more likely to provide a reliable medium-term indicator of current prices. As it is clearly the most widely used hard currency in The Gambia, we have opted to use British pound sterling for this purpose and converted October 2023 prices at an approximate exchange rate of D80 to the pound.

If you carry a card, make sure it has the Visa or MasterCard insignia, as other brands, including Diners and American Express, are borderline useless in The Gambia. Be aware too that the cards are of use primarily for withdrawing local currency from ATMs. GT Bank, Standard Chartered and EcoBank accept both Visa and MasterCard. When it comes to direct payments, most larger hotels will accept credit cards, as will a few tourist-oriented shops and restaurants in Greater Banjul and Kololi, but they are not accepted at smaller outlets and will be practically useless upcountry.

Travellers heading outside of the Greater Banjul area should be aware that ATM distribution around The Gambia is very uneven, and so you may need to plan accordingly. There are a handful of suitable ATMs at Banjul International Airport, and dozens more are scattered around the capital and resort area as far south as Brusubi Turntable and inland to Brikama. By contrast, there is only one operational ATM along the South Bank between Brikama and Basse (in Soma, plus three in Basse itself), while the only ones on the North Bank are in Barra and Farafenni, and the most southerly one on the coast is just south of the Brusubi Turntable. Most ATMs impose a withdrawal limit of D4,000 (about £50), but EcoBank's limit was double this in mid-2023. You can usually do several transactions per banking day, depending on the limit set by your own bank, but this can become expensive if you are charged fees.

A few precautions for those relying primarily on a credit card for funds: the first is to let your bank know where and when you will be travelling, so they don't become suspicious at a few withdrawals in The Gambia and put a hold on your account. The second is that even a valid card might be stolen, swallowed by an ATM or otherwise rendered useless, so it's best to carry a second card as a backup, keeping it separate from the rest of your funds. Finally, though credit-/debit-card scams are not commonplace, they have been reported and most usually involve somebody copying a card number and using it to make a fraudulent payment. This sort of thing can largely be avoided by keeping the card out of sight at all times, and by using your card to make a bulk cash withdrawal from an ATM rather than to pay lots of small bills directly.

Carry your hard currency and cards (plus passport and other important documentation) in a money-belt, ideally one that can be hidden beneath your clothing. The money-belt should be made of cotton or another natural fabric, and everything inside it should be wrapped in plastic to protect it against sweat.

Once in The Gambia, try to keep a fair selection of different-sized notes and coins in your pockets, as no-one, anywhere, ever seems to have change for larger notes.

COSTS AND BUDGETING Although The Gambia is not a cheap destination, it remains quite inexpensive and very good value in an African context.

So far as travel basics go, accommodation for one or two people will probably average out at around £20 per day (and slightly cheaper upcountry) if you always go for the cheapest option. You're looking at more like £25–50 per day for a moderate room with air conditioning, and £50–200 or upwards for upmarket comfort.

For food, expect to spend around £5 per head per day if you stick to street food and very cheap restaurants, £10 if you eat once daily in a restaurant, and maybe £20 per day to eat pretty much what you like (excluding really upmarket places). For advice on tipping, see page 80.

Depending on how often and how far you travel, public transport shouldn't average out at more than a few pounds per person per day, while a charter taxi ride in most towns costs no more than £3.

The main thing you need to add to the above on a daily basis is liquid. Unless you restrict yourself to tap water (not advisable) or the slightly chemical-tasting but perfectly acceptable water in sachets, you'll spend a fair bit of money just keeping your thirst quenched in this hot climate – say £4 per head daily if you stick to bottled water and soft drinks bought in shops, perhaps £10 daily if you add on a couple of beers.

Put this together, and you're looking at a rock-bottom budget of £25/35 daily (again, perhaps a touch less upcountry) for one/two people using the cheapest accommodation and avoiding proper restaurants and bars. To travel thriftily but with a bit more freedom and comfort, a budget of around £50/75 for one/two people would be feasible. If you want air-conditioned rooms, two solid meals, and the rest, budget on upwards of £75/115 for one/two people.

The above reckoning excludes one-off expenses such as excursions and guiding fees, factors that tend to create the occasional expensive day, markedly so for those on a tight budget.

GETTING AROUND

MAPS As with anything, travellers are increasingly relying on online, rather than paper maps. For that purpose, Google Maps is fairly reliable in The Gambia, but you may also wish to refer to/compare against Open Street Maps (w openstreetmaps. org) and the Maps.me (w maps.me) offline mapping app, which often captures details and changes that Google may miss. Otherwise, the most recent paper map is Reise Know-How's *1:550,000 Senegal & The Gambia* from 2016. There is also an *Official Map of Historic and Cultural Sites* produced by the National Centre for Arts & Culture, with inset detail of Banjul. A fine collection of historical maps can be found at w maps.lib.utexas.edu/maps/gambia.html.

AROUND GREATER BANJUL Getting around the Greater Banjul area, and the rest of the southern coastal belt, is very straightforward. Indeed, if you are staying at one of the resort hotels in Bakau, Kotu or Kololi, almost everything you're likely to need on a day-to-day basis – beach, restaurants, supermarkets, bars, and banks – will be within easy walking distance of your hotel. And for day excursions further afield, you have the choice of hiring a taxi, renting a bike, using public transport, or joining an organised excursion set up by a local tour operator or registered guide.

Tourist taxis Two main types of charter taxi operate in Greater Banjul, both on a similar basis to taxi cabs in many Western cities, except that they are unmetered so it is conventional to agree the fare before the journey starts. The more expensive are the specially licensed tourist taxis (usually green with a white diamond on the side) that can be found outside any of the tourist hotels. These are regulated by the Gambia Tourist Authority and should be fully insured. They will run you to any destination, and usually ask a fixed price for a return trip, inclusive of a period of waiting, so may be negotiable for one-way trips or where no waiting is required. The current list of fixed fares is detailed on boards outside most hotels, as well as in the main taxi ranks in the tourist zones.

Shared taxis The preferred option of budget-conscious travellers is shared taxis, which are usually painted bright yellow with green stripes, and tend to be far cheaper than tourist taxis. These unregulated and often uninsured taxis normally ply a set route and pick up passengers along the way for a set fare of usually D15. But they are also quite willing – indeed, usually very eager – to be chartered on a 'town trip', which is where one person hires the whole taxi to wherever they want to go for a negotiable price – typically around £2.50 per 5km, half of what a tourist taxi would ask. These taxis move freely all around Greater Banjul but are not allowed into the Senegambia Strip or Kotu without special permission, so if you are staying in these areas it is best to walk to the junction with Bertil Harding Highway and pick one up there.

Ride-hailing services Finally, while none of the major international ridesharing companies are active in The Gambia, there is now a homegrown version known as **1Bena** (w 1bena.com). Launched in 2021, the increasingly popular app is available on both Android and iOS, and has the distinct advantage of telling you the price of your journey in advance. Even if you don't use it to get a ride, it can be a useful way to get a sense for the approximate price of a given trip.

Bicycles A rented bicycle is a good way of getting around the hinterland immediately outside Banjul and the resorts, with the great advantage of letting you see the towns and countryside at your own pace. Do be careful when out riding though, as Gambian drivers often pass dangerously close to bicycles or cut them up. Furthermore, many roads are full of pot-holes or have their edges worn unevenly, which can force cyclists into the flow of traffic. There are bicycle-hire outlets outside the African Village and Cape Point hotels in Bakau, Kombo Beach Hotel in Kotu, and the Kairaba Hotel in Kololi. Rates are about £2 per hour for short usage or £5–10 per day for longer periods.

Organised day excursions If you're booked into a package hotel for the duration of your stay, an organised day excursion is the easiest way to see something more of the Gambian countryside, especially if time is tighter than money, or independent travel isn't your thing. A very popular day trip is the full-day Roots Excursion, which runs by boat to the North Bank villages of Albreda and Juffureh, as well as Kunta Kinteh Island, UNESCO World Heritage Sites covered in greater detail from page 198. For birders and wildlife enthusiasts, other worthwhile goals for day excursions include Abuko Nature Reserve (page 178) and Makasutu Cultural Forest (page 186), while beach lovers seeking to fulfil a Robinson Crusoe fantasy are pointed to Jinack Island – often marketed as Treasure or Coconut Island (page 203). Urban adventurers will enjoy a day tour of Banjul city centre and Albert Market, whereas those seeking something a little more active could join a south-coast excursion embracing a kayak trip on the Tanji River and a visit to Tanji fishing beach and village museum. For a list of operators in the Greater Banjul area, see page 87.

FURTHER AFIELD Although most visitors to The Gambia never stray far outside the Greater Banjul area, there is a whole country out there to be explored, whether on public transport or on a self-drive basis. Note that there is no rail system in The Gambia, nor any domestic flight network, nor any river transportation (save for a few pokey ferries that connect the South and North banks), which means that public transport is all but restricted to the roads.

Transport infrastructure
There is an increasingly good network of roads. Since 2021, the entirety of the North Bank and South Bank roads are surfaced all the way east until their meeting point at Fatoto. Most trunk roads west of Brikama are also surfaced, as is the coastal road from Banjul to Kartong on the southern border with Senegal (Casamance). An increasing number of feeder roads have also been surfaced in the past several years, notably including the road to Albreda/Juffureh.

Many rural villages, however, can still only be reached along sandy dirt tracks. These are fine during the dry season but some of them become impassable during the heavy downpours of the rainy season, such as the road from Kanuma through Niumi National Park towards Jinack Kajata. It is unlikely that many of these roads will be paved in the near future.

As the roads' importance has grown, that of the river has waned, and the River Gambia – navigable all the way from the coast to the eastern border with Senegal – is today almost entirely unutilised as a transport corridor. Four steamers used to ply the river, calling at 28 ports during the week-long trip to Basse (and 33 if they were going all the way to Fatoto): the *Prince of Wales* (1922–53), the *Lady Denham* (1929–46, sunk in a collision near Kuntaur), the *Lady Wright* (1949–77) and the *Lady Chilel Jawara*, which was the last passenger ship to serve on the river, from 1978 until it capsized just downriver of Farafenni in 1984, causing four deaths. Despite this somewhat chequered navigational history, the river is such an outstanding resource – not to mention arguably the country's defining feature – that it is really a shame there are so few options to travel this way. FairPlay Gambia's *Fula Princess* cruising pirogue (page 252) is a noteworthy exception, with regular departures in season, while the Gambia Experience (page 52) also runs occasional river cruises on the 44-passenger *Harmony G* yacht.

Public transport
Road transport is very cheap (a fiver gets you from one side of the country to the other), but most vehicles are quite rundown, slow, sweaty, crowded and poorly driven. Further details of individual routings are included in the regional chapters of this guide, but generally the best option, at least for the time being, is the privatised Gambia Transport Service Company (GTSC). Based in Kanifing (Serekunda), the GTSC operates several scheduled departures daily along the South Bank Road to Soma, Janjanbureh and Basse, as well as the North Bank Road between Barra, Lamin Koto and Foday Kunda/Passamas, all in Ashok-Leyland buses, some of which have air conditioning.

The distinctly inferior but much more flexible alternative to the GTSC buses is the private passenger vehicles known as *gelly-gellys* (minivan size or larger) or shared/bush taxis (saloon cars or station wagons) that cover pretty much every conceivable route in the country, offering variable degrees of unreliability and discomfort. The focal point of the passenger vehicle network in the far west is Serekunda, where

I usually turn up sometime before the sun rises for a long trip as it's cooler and I have more chance of bagging the front passenger seat which has some leg room. Otherwise, I'd be stuck in the third row – what would normally be a car boot – where they put a seat for three more people. Once I have my place, it's a waiting game. Prices are set by the government and profit margins are non-existent, so drivers are forced to cram in as many people and as much luggage as possible to ensure they make a few pennies.

I'll usually grab myself a couple of *café toubas*. I'm still not entirely sure what gives this local coffee its distinctive liquorice-like taste, but it's good, if a little too sweet. There's invariably a stall on wheels, where a boy will scoop coffee from a cauldron and then pour it back and forth between two cups, building up a cappuccino froth of impressive heights.

Then there are the urchins: little ragged boys called the *talibe*, often barefoot, faces covered in dust and snot, normally wearing a T-shirt branded with Unicef, Barack Obama 'Time for Change', or these days more commonly #GambiaHasDecided. Groups of them, carrying old tomato purée tins, walk around chanting for spare change. Tragically, they are controlled by gang leaders who will beat them if they don't reach their quota. One modern-day Fagin was charged recently in neighbouring Senegal for beating a boy to death. Years of working with homeless people has led me to believe it's best to give money to an organisation rather than to an individual, but in this case it's hard to resist.

Market stalls sell just about everything, as long as it's cheap and Chinese. Women sell *wanjo*, a Ribena-like drink made from hibiscus, and mangoes from large enamel bowls carried in on their heads. A more modern phenomenon is men selling mobile-phone top-up cards. Small stalls with dubious hygiene standards make omelettes and stick them in rolls with brown lumpy mayonnaise stored in unrefrigerated buckets. Often there's a choice of a spaghetti roll or a macaroni roll, so it's lucky I'm not on the Atkins diet.

Elsewhere, Baye Fall boys with their large turbans, masses of beads and long robes, collect for charity. Goats wander round hoovering up the discarded mango skins and other rubbish. There's a motley collection of bush taxis, buses, trucks and abandoned vehicles that are in a really bad way. On top of all of this are the mad men, the hucksters, the Liberian refugees looking for an English speaker, the baggage handlers and the mass of people seemingly moving all of their worldly possessions.

An edited excerpt from Squirting Milk at Chameleons *by Simon Fenton.*

the two main stations are Westfield Junction (for elsewhere in Greater Banjul and Brikama) and Dippa Kunda (for the south coast). For passenger vehicles from the coast to most places further upriver, the main South Bank terminus is Brikama while the sole terminus on the North Bank is Barra.

Car rental Perhaps the most satisfying way to explore The Gambia, though far more costly than using public transport, is in a rented 4x4. Brits should be aware, however, that although The Gambia is a former British colony, it follows the European and American model and drives on the right-hand side of the road.

Practical Information GETTING AROUND

3

And while the North Bank and South Bank roads are great, with smooth surfaces (and plenty of speed bumps) that tend to encourage a relatively orderly approach to road usage, all aspirant drivers should be prepared for a somewhat more anarchic environment than the one they are used to.

Driving in The Gambia presents a number of unfamiliar hazards. On older pot-holed roads and dirt roads, vehicles swerve unpredictably to avoid obstacles, and use whichever side of the road they fancy. Especially in the rural areas, dogs and livestock frequently wander into the road, as do children, and even adults, often without looking to see what's coming their way. Then there are the slow-moving donkey-, horse- and bullock-drawn carts, and the bush taxis that swerve madly to avoid colliding with them. Fortunately, outside of Greater Banjul, traffic volumes are low, so driving is not too stressful, especially if you take it slow and easy, and give yourself those vital extra milliseconds to react to the unexpected. Driving at night is best avoided (there are no street lights and many vehicles lack headlights), as is driving in heavy rain.

Another repeat nuisance is the ubiquitous police, immigration, customs and military roadblocks that force drivers to slow down every few kilometres. Usually you'll be waved on, no problem, but sometimes you'll be stopped and asked to produce your driver's licence and vehicle insurance, and more occasionally your reflector triangle and fire extinguisher. More often than not, this sort of interrogation is quite good natured, and feels more like a pretext for a chat than anything else, but if your papers are not in order, you could be in for a rough ride.

Two reputable car-rental companies are the budget-oriented **AB Rent a Car** (Palm Rima Junction, Kotu; ℡446 0926; m 764 9743/932 0776; e info@ab.gm; w ab. gm; f Ab rent a car gambia), who offer vehicles from £30 per day, and the newer and more upmarket **Afriq Cars** (The Village, Kololi; m 770 0900, 207 7900; e info@ afriqcars.com; w afriqcars.com; f afriqcars.motors).

An alternative to conventional car rental is to strike up a deal for transportation with a taxi driver, ideally one you have used for a few local rides, and with whom you feel comfortable. This will generally work out more cheaply than renting a car, and it shifts the responsibility for driving or dealing with any breakdown or other hassles to somebody experienced in local conditions. A major disadvantage of going this route is that costs (and tensions) can quickly mount if the exact terms are not agreed upfront – for instance, whether the rate includes or excludes the driver's accommodation, food, and other expenses, as well as fuel and any fines imposed at roadblocks.

Ferries After the recent opening of the bridges at Farafenni, Basse and Fatoto, there are now five places countrywide where vehicle ferries continue to operate between the South and North banks. From west to east, these are Banjul–Barra, Kau-ur–Jakoto, Barajali–Wali Kunda, Janjanbureh–Lamin Koto and Bansang–Bush Town. Note well, however, that breakdowns are not uncommon and ferries can sometimes be out of commission for weeks at a time. It's also possible for foot passengers to cross the river via pirogue at several other locations, ie: Kuntaur or Jarreng.

Organised upriver excursions As is the case with local day trips, most tourists who venture upriver do so as part of an organised overnight excursion, which can be booked through upmarket hotels or any of the operators listed on page 52. The most popular excursions are one-night trips to Tendaba Camp or Bintang Bolong, which usually incorporate at least one boat trip into the mangroves and creeks that line the main river, or further upriver to Janjanbureh, ideally for at least two nights. It's also possible to set sail from Bintang Bolong for a few days all the way upriver to Janjanbureh. For wildlife enthusiasts, arguably the most rewarding

ACCOMMODATION PRICE CODES

Prices are based on a standard double room.

$$$$$	Over £150
$$$$	£100–150
$$$	£50–100
$$	£20–50
$	Under £20

trip out of Greater Banjul, doable as a one-night excursion though two nights is better, is to the wonderful camp run by the Chimp Rehabilitation Project in the River Gambia National Park. Few trips head further upriver than Janjanbureh unless they are continuing into eastern Senegal.

ACCOMMODATION

The coastal resorts of Greater Banjul are dense with accommodation that caters mainly to tourists but ranges in quality from world-class package or boutique hotels, such as Ngala Lodge, to scruffy small lodges aimed mainly at backpackers, volunteers and others on a tight budget. Accommodation on the coast north of the River Gambia or south of Tanji tends to consist of modest but pleasant eco-lodges and more basic beach camps catering to those on a low to medium budget, while accommodation upriver is mostly quite basic, but with an encouraging few exceptions like the Chimp Rehabilitation Project Camp in the River Gambia National Park.

Detailed accommodation listings for all towns, resorts and other places of interest can be found in the regional chapters of this guide. Entries are categorised under five main headings: exclusive/luxury, upmarket, mid-range, budget and shoestring. Broadly speaking, the **exclusive or luxury** bracket comprises package and boutique hotels that would approach four- or five-star status anywhere in the world. Places listed as **upmarket** would typically be comparable to a three-star hotel in international terms. **Mid-range** hotels are one- or two-star lodgings that don't quite meet international standards, but would still be comfortable enough for most tourists, offering a range of good facilities such as air conditioning, satellite television, en-suite hot showers and toilet. **Budget** accommodation consists mostly of ungraded hotels that definitely don't approach international standards, but are still reasonably comfortable and in many cases have air conditioning and en-suite facilities. **Shoestring** accommodation consists of the cheapest rooms available, and ranges from nice backpacker-type set-ups to genuine dives. This categorisation is not rigid, since it is based on the feel of any given hotel as much as the price, and there are many borderline cases, but it should nevertheless help readers isolate the option best tailored to their budget and taste. Within each category, we have, where appropriate, highlighted any genuine standouts (often but not exclusively owner-managed places with a strong individual character) as an author's pick ✳.

EATING AND DRINKING

Greater Banjul must host at least 100 restaurants catering mainly to tourists, and numerous international cuisines are represented in resort areas such as Kololi, Kotu and Bakau. Standards are high and prices relatively low. The options upriver are generally limited to hotel restaurants and a few local eateries serving a limited and fairly predictable selection of local dishes. Everywhere in the country, except perhaps the main tourist resorts, a varied selection of street food is sold at kiosks, usually close to the market.

In the morning, breakfast sandwiches are king. They're served up on either a rather uninspired machine-baked baguette or the also-baguette-shaped, slightly denser and much more interesting handmade *tapalapa*; just scan the roadsides for a woman sitting behind a pile of stainless steel bowls arranged around her like a drum set. Inside these lurks a variety of savoury sauces, including green peas, black-eyed peas (*niebe*) and caramelised onions, or chocolate spread if you prefer. They'll often have some coals or a gas cooker on which to fry up omelettes as well. The whole affair comes wrapped in an old Arabic newspaper and won't run you more than about £1.

Evenings, on the other hand, are for *afra* – essentially a streetside barbecue, often run by Hausa immigrants from Nigeria or Niger. With a variety of meats grilled up or slow-cooked over a wood fire and wrapped in ersatz butcher paper – usually a repurposed cement bag – afra is about as no-frills as it gets, and the theatrics of the grillmaster chopping up your meal with a hatchet or a machete are worth the price of admission alone. Served with some grilled onions, mustard, salt, a few dashes of Maggi sauce and no silverware anywhere in sight, it's a guaranteed greasy good time.

Throughout the day you can happily graze on an enviable selection of seasonal fresh fruit, fire-roasted peanuts and cashews, fried dough balls (known as *panket*), Madeira cake and coconuts – in both water and fruit form.

Many restaurants have Gambian dishes on their menus, although some may require notice for their preparation. This usually comprises rice or millet served with a spicy fish, meat or chicken stew, which comes in a few main types: *domoda* (groundnut sauce), *yassa* (stewed or marinated in onion and lemon), and *plassas* (a sauce of stewed greens thickened with peanut butter). Another popular choice, known elsewhere in West Africa as jollof rice, *benachin* (literally 'one pot') is a spicy risotto-like Wolof dish made with fish, chicken or beef. Also popular is *superkanja*, a tasty okra soup whose name derives from the Portuguese *sopa* (soup) and Mandinka *kanja* (okra). Worth trying too are shrimps fried with garlic in the Gambian style, and Lebanese-style *shawarmas*, comprising thin slices of lamb (or other meats) with salad and hummus in pitta bread.

Vegetarians and vegans may struggle somewhat, but there are usually a few options to lean on, in addition to the obvious fruit and nut snacks mentioned above. In the tourist areas, choices are unsurprisingly much wider, including Indian, Lebanese and Jamaican restaurants with vegetarian options available, as well as numerous places serving pizzas, pastas, etc. Otherwise, the sauces in the breakfast sandwiches mentioned above are typically meatless, and traditional dishes like *domoda* can be made without meat, but only on request – those served as a dish of the day will almost always have been cooked with meat inside. Dairy is

RESTAURANT PRICE CODES

Prices are based on a full meal for one.

$$$$$	Over £15
$$$$	£10–15
$$$	£6–10
$$	£3–6
$	Under £3

SENEGAMBIAN GLOSSARY

There are a number of dishes, drinks and products common in both Senegal and The Gambia, but commonly known by different names depending on which side of the border you're on. These names derive from a combination of Mandinka, Wolof, English, French and beyond. Here are a few translations of some terms that differ on either side of the border.

English	Gambian	Senegalese
barbecue	afra	dibiterie
jollof rice	benachin	thieboudienne
peanut sauce/stew	domoda	mafé
puff-puff/fried dough	panket	beignet
shea butter	bambô-tulô	karité
hibiscus	wanjo	bissap
baobab	sito	bouyé
Saba senegalensis fruit	kabba	madd
velvet tamarind	kosito	solom

more easily avoided, and not found in most Gambian dishes. If you eat fish, you'll have an easier time, as it's the most common protein in *benachin*, which is perhaps The Gambia's most common dish.

The usual range of international soft drinks is sold cheaply all over The Gambia. Unfortunately Banjul Breweries, producers of the award-winning local lager JulBrew, folded in 2020, and JulBrew (whose label reads 'The Gambia's Best Beer') is now produced in Senegal, which has left it more expensive and harder to find than European imports like Cristal and Cody's. Most restaurants and bars on the coast also serve a selection of imported wines and spirits, though this is less common upriver.

Despite The Gambia being predominantly Islamic, the vast majority of restaurants serve alcohol, but this is progressively less common as you continue up the river. Wanjo is a sweet but refreshing drink made from hibiscus flowers, and ginger and baobab juices are also common. All around the country, people drink a strong green tea called *attaya,* popular across much of West Africa. Served in clear shot glasses with copious amounts of sugar, the tea is brewed several times in a tiny enamel teapot, becoming less bitter and more sweet as you go along. The preparation of *attaya* takes about an hour and is as much for drinking as it is for socialising, as everyone sits around and chats while the pot is brewing.

PUBLIC HOLIDAYS

In addition to the fixed holidays below, the following variable religious holidays are recognised: Koriteh (Eid al-Fitr), Tamharit (Ashura), Laylat al-Qadr (ten days before the end of Ramadan), Mawlid (Milad an-Nabi), Tobaski (Eid al-Adha), Good Friday and Easter Monday. Aside from the closure of banks and offices, these holidays have a limited effect on tourists. During the fasting month of Ramadan, however, it is customary to refrain from smoking, eating or drinking in the presence of Muslims between dawn and dusk. All of the large hotels and restaurants remain open during Ramadan, some smaller businesses may open late and close early, and others might not open at all.

Initiated by former President Jammeh in 2004, Set Settal (meaning 'clean and be clean' in Wolof), also called Operation Clean The Nation, is a public programme designed to keep streets and other public areas free of unsightly non-biodegradable litter and organic waste that helps foster disease-carrying bacteria. It was discontinued after the 2017 change in government, but Environment Minister Rohey John Manjang announced its return in January 2023.

It is usually enacted on the last Saturday of every month, though it may sometimes be cancelled, or held over to another Saturday, where this date clashes with a public holiday or another important event. It runs from 09.00 to 13.00, with the idea being that everybody chips in to clean up their private compound and/or neighbourhood, though for many it was simply a pretext to take a morning off work or to sleep in.

Under Jammeh, all private and public transport, including taxis, was halted for the morning, and most shops, restaurants and other businesses were also closed. This does not seem to be the case for the recently revived Set Settal, which was declared to be purely voluntary. Just what that means for participation and effectiveness, on the other hand, remains to be seen!

1 January	New Year's Day
18 February	Independence Day
1 May	Labour Day
25 May	Africa Day
15 August	Assumption of Mary
25 December	Christmas Day

ROTATING HOLIDAYS Note that Islamic holidays are based on the lunar Hijri calendar, and the dates below marked with a * are predictions. Islamic holidays usually shift by about 11 days annually when compared with the Gregorian calendar, but this can move around by a day or two depending on when the moon officially kicking off the holiday is sighted.

	2024	2025	2026	2027
Mawlid*	15 Sep	4 Sep	25 Aug	14 Aug
Easter Monday	1 Apr	21 Apr	6 Apr	29 Mar
Koriteh (Eid al-Fitr)*	9 Apr	30 Mar	19 Mar	9 Mar
Tobaski (Eid al-Adha)*	16 Jun	7 Jun	27 May	17 May
Tamharit (Ashura)*	16 Jul	5 Jul	25 Jun	14 Jun

MEDIA AND COMMUNICATIONS

NEWSPAPERS Since the installation of the new government in 2017, the Gambian press has operated largely free from governmental interference. The Gambia ranked number 50 in the 2022 Reporters Without Borders Press Freedom Index, outranking nine EU countries and coming in at number eight in Africa. This is a radical break from the past – The Gambia was ranked 152nd in 2013, a tie with Myanmar.

A number of legal changes have supported this freer and more transparent climate. Defamation was declared unconstitutional in 2018, and President Barrow signed the Access to Information Act in 2021. The law ensures that individuals can access records from public institutions and authorities. Half a dozen English-language newspapers are produced and sold inexpensively in Banjul, the best of which include *The Standard* (w standard.gm) and *The Point* (w thepoint.gm).

RADIO AND TELEVISION The national television and radio company is the state-run Gambian Radio and Television Service (w grts.gm), which broadcasts throughout the country. They lost their monopoly with the change of government in 2017, and The Gambia now boasts 32 private radio stations and five private TV networks. Many hotels and restaurants supplement these services with a bouquet of international satellite channels provided by the South African company DSTV (w dstv.com).

POST International post is inexpensive and usually gets to its destination reasonably quickly during the dry season (when there are more flights) but more tardily during the rains. Post coming into the country is often delayed, sometimes for months, and unverified stories of registered post being stolen by postal workers abound.

TELEPHONE As in much of the world, landline phones (where they existed) are disappearing, and mobile network access and uptake is expanding. The international country code is +220; there are no area codes, and all numbers (land or mobile) have seven digits. If you bring an unlocked mobile with you, a local SIM card is very cheap, as is airtime and/or a data bundle. The main providers are Africell (w africell. gm), Qcell (w qcell.gm), Gamcel (w gamcel.gm), and Comium (w comium.gm), all of which have service centres dotted all over Greater Banjul. The first numeral in any seven-digit number will tell you the identity of the provider, as per the table below:

2, 7	Africell
3, 5	Qcell
4, 56, 57	landline
6	Comium
8, 9	Gamcel

WHATSAPP

This messaging app is enormously popular in The Gambia, and is strongly recommended if you will be moving around the country independently and making your own arrangements with hotels, service providers, guides, etc. It allows you to call, text and send multimedia messages to others who have the app installed, using the data connection on your mobile. Many businesses now rely on it heavily for bookings. It is also the easiest way to reach The Gambia from abroad, and practically free.

To see if a number has WhatsApp, simply save it to your contacts list **with the country code**, in this case +220. Then open the app and start a new chat – if your would-be interlocutor is on the app, you will see their name in the contacts list and can send them a message immediately. If they are not, you will be given an option to 'invite' them by SMS, but in practice you will be better off checking another number. Many Gambians have several numbers (one for each service provider), but usually only one of these will be linked to WhatsApp.

INTERNET Greater Banjul has reasonable internet connections. Most hotels have Wi-Fi, even if the connection can sometimes be erratic, and getting online using mobile data is typically reliable enough. If you expect to spend a lot of time online, it will pay to get a local SIM card and data bundle with one of the mobile providers mentioned on page 77. There are also now a handful of co-working spaces in greater Banjul, notably AFB Workspace (w afbworkspace.com; f afbworkspace; day use from £5) with locations in Kotu, on Kairaba Avenue, and near Brusubi Turntable.

Upriver, most hotels do not necessarily offer Wi-Fi – or do so in a primarily theoretical capacity – so you'll want to come armed with a mobile data connection if you need to get online. Connection upriver is still much patchier than on the coast, but this has improved significantly in recent years, and most communities over a certain size now have a mobile mast.

ELECTRICITY SUPPLY The power grid is administered by the National Water & Electric Company (NAWEC), and since 2018 has been propped up by the Karadeniz Powership Koray Bey, a 36MW floating power plant docked in Banjul that provides 60% of the national supply. As such, power delivery has improved significantly, but most tourist hotels on the coast operate a standby generator just in case. A number of lodges on the coast south of Tanji operate on solar power, and the erratic power supply upriver is by all accounts much improved in recent years – though who knows what might happen if the powership sets sail again.

CULTURAL ETIQUETTE

The Gambia is an amiable and peaceful country full of convivial people whose approach to life tends to be very laid back – sometimes frustratingly so for Western visitors used to a faster pace of life. Gambians themselves joke about GMT, an acronym not for Greenwich Mean Time but Gambia Maybe Time, and provided you are on holiday, not trying to push through deadlines, this relaxed attitude is part of the country's charm. Unfortunately, however, the innate friendliness of Gambian society is undermined somewhat by a small subset of so-called 'bumsters' who hang around the resort areas of Greater Banjul and habitually hassle any passing tourist, whether it be on the beach, on the street, or in a market. More about bumsters can be found on page 79, but it should be clarified upfront that while they can be extremely annoying, they are not representative of Gambians as a whole, and the whole phenomenon is more or less confined to a few specific resort areas. South of Tanji and upriver of Brikama, first-time visitors to Africa, or at least those with a pale complexion, may be surprised at the amount of attention they draw by virtue of their conspicuous foreignness – symptoms of which range from having every passing taxi blare its horn at you to being greeted by mobs of exuberant children chanting '*toubab*' (white person) as you walk past. At times, this can be exhausting, but it is essentially just an expression of curiosity and friendliness, and seldom underscored by malice.

ETIQUETTE The Gambia, like any country, has its rules of etiquette, and while allowances will normally be made for tourists, there is some value in ensuring they don't have to be made too frequently.

Greetings are very important in Gambian society. If you need to ask directions, or anything else for that matter, it is considered very rude to blunder straight into interrogative mode without first exchanging greetings – even when shopping. If there is one phrase you should learn, it is the greeting '*As-Salaam-Alaikum*' ('Peace be upon you'), the response being '*Wa-Alaikum-Salaam*' ('And upon you, too') – a universal Arabic exchange used widely among Gambians. Otherwise, just saying 'Hello' (and where appropriate shaking hands) will do the job.

Because The Gambia is predominantly Islamic, the left hand is traditionally reserved for ablutions. It is thus considered highly insulting (and unhygienic) to use your left hand to pass or receive something, or when shaking hands. If you eat with your fingers, it is customary to use the right hand only. Topless bathing is not acceptable on the beaches or at hotel swimming pools, and elsewhere visitors should be cognisant of conservative Islamic dress codes. Walking around half-dressed, as some tourists insist on doing, is totally inappropriate. Women should ideally wear a loose-fitting summer dress or slacks that that go below the knees, and a top that covers their cleavage and shoulders. Men can get away with wearing shorts but should not walk around topless. Gambians are generally quite tolerant, and they accept that visitors have different customs, but still it is impolite to go too far in flaunting local dress codes.

When visiting upcountry villages, there are some additional forms of etiquette that you should adhere to. One of these is that you should seek out the village *alkalo* and spend a few minutes greeting him before doing whatever it is you came for. It is also a good idea to bring him a small gift, either kola nuts, or a D25 or D50 note will do. This is not only polite but may also be very useful, as the alkalo will know everything that is going on in his village, and may be able to provide guides or translators if you require them. If you are introduced to the Muslim *imam* (holy man) of the village, and asked to enter his home, remember to remove your shoes and hat first, just as you would if entering a mosque.

BUMSTERS The one thing most likely to spoil your holiday in The Gambia is bumsters, the local nickname for a rather parasitic type of young man who habitually latches on to tourists hoping to get something – anything – from the exchange. In the resort areas of Greater Banjul, you'll have only to leave your hotel for a walk and you'll meet at least one bumster. There are a number of classic ways that bumsters approach tourists. Generally they will ask you your name or where you come from, or what hotel you're staying at. More cunningly, some might say something like 'Hey, remember me? I work at your hotel', hoping to embarrass tourists into conversation. And whatever the approach, the conversation usually ends up with an offer of guide services, or sex, or drugs, or failing that just a straight request for money. If that doesn't work, most bumsters will shrug it off, but a small minority might become rude and intimidating, accusing their victim of being a racist, in the hope it will shame them into giving him something.

If this is your first trip to The Gambia, don't let bumsters put you off visiting. The Gambia is a wonderful country, full of wonderful people, but it's better to be forewarned and forearmed when it comes to dealing with the one major exception. Most of the time, the best approach to bumsters is to acknowledge their greeting with a cool but friendly 'Hello', without slowing down your pace, or looking like you have any intention of stopping or allowing yourself to be drawn into a conversation. If they persist beyond this, telling them you are busy and/or saying 'maybe later' usually works. But do keep it friendly: it's important to remember that most of these guys are facing a chronically difficult economic situation and may see this as the best of a bad set of options available to them. That doesn't mean you ought to pay them, of course, but you can afford to be respectful and firm – and losing your temper will only escalate the interaction. If you are a non-confrontational sort of

3

person, another tack would be to hire an official tour guide, who will not only keep bumsters away, but can also help you find out more about The Gambia. Better still, travel upcountry for a few days, away from the tourist areas, to experience The Gambia at its bumster-free best.

SEX WORKERS Sex work is low-profile but relatively common in some tourist areas, specifically in a few particular nightclubs and bars in Greater Banjul where single men are likely to be approached quite immediately (sometimes even if their partner has just nipped out to the loo). It is also conspicuous in the form of frequent proposals aimed at unaccompanied women – The Gambia's reputation for 'holiday romances' between young bumster types and much older Western women means that these types of propositions are considerably more common than in other countries in the region. (See *Women Travellers*, page 63.) Throughout the sex trade, sexually transmitted diseases are prevalent.

BEGGING Wherever you go in The Gambia, the chances are that someone will ask you for money. This could be a kid walking down the street who will ask for ten dalasi, or his mother who will ask for D50. It could be your taxi driver who needs money for repairs to his taxi, or a hotel worker who needs money to fund his education. You will have to decide the merit of each case, but remember that ripping off *toubabs* is a way of life for some Gambians, who are under the impression that everybody living in Europe or North America possesses unlimited wealth. However, we must strongly discourage tourists from handing over money, pens, sweets or other goodies to random children or opportunist beggars. For one, it helps foster a culture of dependency on handouts. It also often entices children living in villages regularly visited by tourists to bunk or abandon their schooling in favour of begging. And more selfishly, it creates a very unpleasant basis for interaction between visitors and locals. If you want to help people in The Gambia, then a far better option is to give money, books, computers or medical supplies to an existing charity or directly to an institution like a village school or clinic (see opposite).

What might be termed 'real beggars' is a completely different case. Go to any supermarket or restaurant and you are likely to find someone sitting outside and begging for money. Many of these people are mentally or physically disabled, and genuinely in need of help as they cannot find work or fall back on social security as they might in the West. Just take a moment to watch what Gambians do when they are asked for money. Nine times out of ten they will reach into their pockets and give him or her a dalasi or two. There's no harm in you doing the same.

TIPPING Among locals, tipping in restaurants is not near-obligatory as it is in the USA or some parts of Europe. However, a tip will usually be expected at more touristic restaurants, and it will always be appreciated at local eateries too. If you've enjoyed your meal and the service was good then give a good tip; 10% would be a fair guideline, though with change so often being an issue in The Gambia, just rounding up the bill to an amount that doesn't require change is also often a sensible approach.

The semi-official guides available at most nature reserves and museums generally provide a free service that's included in the entrance fee. A tip is therefore expected, and should be given, assuming that you are happy with the service. It is difficult to give a guideline, as it depends so much on the age, attitude, experience and skill of the guide, but around D100–200 per party per hour or D800–1,000 for a full day's guiding would feel about right. Skilled birding guides should be paid a little more, as often they have years of experience or training behind them. That said, while it is appropriate to tip genuine guides who have been of real value to you, it is not advisable to tip bumsters or other hangers-on who simply latch on to tourists and try to act like a guide or to make you feel sorry for them.

BARGAINING AND OVERCHARGING Prices in hotels, restaurants, shops and public transport are generally fixed, and overcharging is too unusual for it to be worth challenging a price unless it is blatantly ridiculous (though many hotels will be open to negotiating a discounted rate, particularly for longer stays). However, tourists must be prepared to bargain over prices in certain circumstances, for instance when chartering private taxis, organising guides or shopping in markets.

The main instance where bargaining is customary, bordering on essential, is when buying handicrafts. Stall owners will generally quote a price knowing full well they are likely to be bargained down, so it is not necessary to respond aggressively or accusatorially. It is impossible to say by how much you should bargain the initial price down. Some people say that you should offer half the asking price and be

---

GETTING INVOLVED IN THE GAMBIA

These are just three of the many worthwhile educational charities operating in The Gambia. For a more comprehensive list, see the 'Charity Directory' on The Gambia Experience's website (w gambia.co.uk/charity).

AFRIKAYA (e afrikayathecharity@gmail.com; w afrikaya.co.uk; f Afrikaya) This UK-based charity was formed in 2007 with the aim to build a nursery school for children who struggled to access education in The Gambia. The charity has succeeded in its goal, and the nursery school in New Yundum near Brikama currently serves 135 children between the ages of three and seven. The school is built around a Kebba tree, which in The Gambia is a symbol of strength, growth and life. They organise various fundraising events in the Wiltshire area, or you can sponsor a child to cover basic costs such as school uniform, reading materials and a healthy lunchtime meal.

FRIENDS OF THE GAMBIA (w fotga.org.uk; f fotga.official) This UK-registered charity is run by volunteers and works to support improved educational and health outcomes in The Gambia. It operates a very successful 'sponsor a child' scheme (and is always in need of new sponsors to give disadvantaged children the chance of education), provides educational and medical equipment for schools, clinics and hospitals and funds sustainable projects in schools and villages throughout the country.

GOAL FOR THE GAMBIA (e goalforthegambia@hotmail.co.uk; w goalforthegambia.co.uk; f goalforthegambia) A UK-registered charity, GOAL for The Gambia supports education and training opportunities for young people in The Gambia. Currently they sponsor over 400 children from nursery to university in three schools and two nurseries. Sponsorship costs from £7 a month and covers fees, uniforms and books. Additionally, they support school-building projects such as toilets, classroom blocks and new roofs. School visits can be arranged.

prepared to settle at around two-thirds, but many stall owners are more whimsical than such advice allows for. A sensible approach is to ask the price of similar items at a few different stalls before you actually contemplate buying anything.

In fruit and vegetable markets and stalls, bargaining is often the norm, even between locals, and the healthiest approach is to view it as an enjoyable part of the Gambian experience. There will normally be an accepted price band for any particular commodity. To find out what it is, listen to what other people pay and try a few stalls. A ludicrously inflated price will always drop the moment you walk away. When buying fruit and vegetables, a good way to get a feel for the situation is to ask for a bulk discount or a few extra items thrown in. And bear in mind that when somebody is reluctant to bargain, it may be because they asked a fair price in the first place. No matter how tight your budget, most Gambians are much poorer, so don't lose your sense of proportion.

Part Two

GREATER BANJUL AND KOLOLI

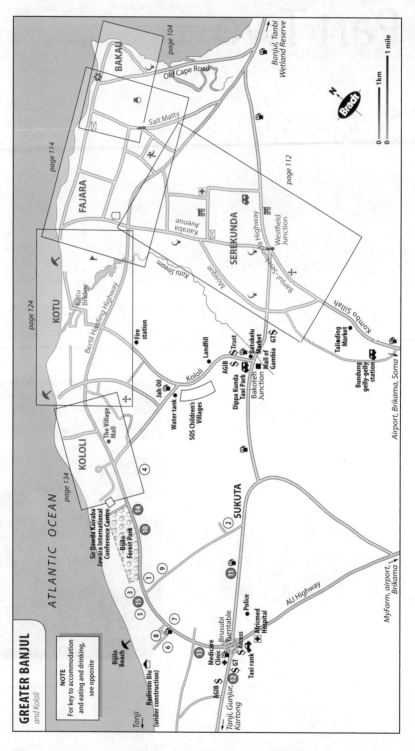

GREATER BANJUL
and Kololi

NOTE
For key to accommodation and eating and drinking, see opposite.

ATLANTIC OCEAN

page 124

page 134

page 114

page 104

KOTU

KOLOLI

FAJARA

BAKAU

Old Cape Road

Sait Matty

Bertil Harding Highway

Kotu Bridge

Kotu Stream

Sir Dawda Kairaba Jawara International Conference Centre

Bijilo Forest Park

The Village Mall

Radisson Blu (under construction)

Bijilo Beach

Tanji →

Fire station

Jah Oil

Water tank

SOS Children's Villages

Landfill

Kololi

Mosque

Kairaba Avenue

Banjul–Serekunda Highway

SEREKUNDA

Westfield Junction

Kombo Sillah

AGIB

Trust

Batokolu Market

Mall of Gambia

GT

Dippa Kunda Taxi Park

Bakoteh Junction

Talinding Market

Bundung gelly-gelly station

Banjul, Tanbi Wetland Reserve

page 112

SUKUTA

Brusubi Turntable

Medicare Clinic

Recess

Taxi rank

Africmed Hospital

Police

AU Highway

AGIB

GT

Tanji, Gunjur, Kartong ↓

MyFarm, airport, Brikama →

Airport, Brikama, Soma →

Brach

0 ___ 1km
0 ___ 1 mile

N

Greater Banjul and Kololi: An Overview

The Gambia's main population centre, as well as the focal point of its tourist industry, is the administrative region of Greater Banjul and neighbouring suburbs of Kololi, Bijilo and Sukuta. Despite extending over a mere 100km² (less than 1% of the country's surface area), this compact urban conglomeration supports around one-third of the national population, and probably hosts something like 90% of its hotels, restaurants, banks, supermarkets and such – a figure all the more remarkable when you consider that about half the region comprises the more-or-less uninhabitable mangroves and marshes of Tanbi Wetland Reserve.

Administratively, Greater Banjul is divided into two units: the Banjul Local Government Area (LGA) covering the island-bound city centre, and the tenfold-larger Kanifing LGA, accounting for Serekunda and all the beach resorts north of Kololi Point. Officially, Kololi, Bijilo and Sukuta actually lie in the West Coast Region, but in practice they feel like an extension of Greater Banjul the city rather than separate urban entities.

On the ground, Greater Banjul and Kololi are more neatly divided into three broad areas, each with its own distinct character. On the east side of the Tanbi Wetlands, the neat but tiny national capital Banjul, established on the confines of Saint Mary Island in 1816, is the country's administrative centre and a popular goal for day trips with tourists, but seldom used as an overnight base. West of the Tanbi Wetlands, an amorphous, chaotic and rather charmless sprawl of inland suburbs centred on Serekunda has overtaken the capital as the country's main centre of business and commerce. Further west still, following the Atlantic coastline south of the Gambia River mouth for around 12km, lies resortland: the string of well-developed beachfront suburbs – Cape Point and Bakau, Fajara and Koto, Kololi and Bijilo – that form the heart of The Gambia's package-tourism industry.

In terms of facilities, the coastal strip of Greater Banjul and Kololi, with its plethora of hotels, guesthouses, restaurants, casinos, nightclubs, bars, supermarkets and other shops, can come across much like a European resort annex grafted on to the west coast of Africa. Equally, a definite West African flavour is pervasive everywhere you go: whether it is the hot sun, sandy beaches and palm trees, the bright

GREATER BANJUL and Kololi
For listings, see from page 143, unless otherwise stated

🛏 **Where to stay**
1   Baobab Holiday Resort
2   Camping Sukuta
3   Coco Ocean Resort & Spa
4   Devon Lodge *p139*
5   Kasumai Beach Guest House
6   Lemon Creek Resort
7   Sardinka House
8   Seafront Residences
9   Shelley's

✖ **Where to eat and drink**
10   2 Rays
11   The Blue Kitchen
12   Chosaan
     Kasumai Beach Bar & Restaurant (see 5)
13   Mosiah's Jamaican Bar & Restaurant
14   Sea Shells
15   Sunbird Beach Bar & Restaurant

85

clothes of the locals, or the plentiful gorgeous birdlife flitting around hotel gardens. And you needn't go far inland to find yourself immersed in an unambiguously African landscape – just take a stroll through the backstreets of Bakau to Kachikally Crocodile Pool, or a shared taxi to the hectic Serekunda market, or a day tour to central Banjul.

One important point to note is that while the coastal resorts of Greater Banjul are a thriving hub of tourist activity during the holiday season (late October to April), they have a definite 'lights off' feel for the remainder of the year. Most hotels and restaurants cut down their services during the off-season, laying off a significant proportion of their staff for the duration, while others close entirely, particularly those owned or managed by expats or foreigners, who may go back to their home countries for a week, or a month, or longer to avoid the rainy season. It's impossible to let you know which places will be closed, or even when, because in many cases this varies year by year, but even at the lowest ebb of tourism, in July and August, there is enough going on that you'll have no problem finding a room, or a meal, or a well-stocked supermarket.

HIGHLIGHTS

Note that most of the sites covered here or in *Part Three* are easily visited as day trips from the resorts in Greater Banjul – this is a selection of some highlights.

NATIONAL MUSEUM OF THE GAMBIA Housed in the former Bathurst Club, this oft-overlooked, enjoyable museum in central Banjul is strong both on local history and on traditional cultures (page 100).

ALBERT MARKET Handicraft enthusiasts shouldn't miss out on Banjul's historic central market, which is a good place to buy woodcarvings, tie-dyed batik clothing and much else besides (page 101).

KACHIKALLY CROCODILE POOL Crocodiles so tame you can stroke their backs are the main attraction at this sacred pool in Bakau, though it also hosts a worthwhile museum (page 109).

BAKAU BOTANICAL GARDEN Almost a century old, this small, low-key and attractively laid-out garden makes for a peaceful retreat from bustling Bakau or Fajara (page 111).

FAJARA AND KOTU BEACHES Our favourite among several attractive beaches that line the Atlantic coastline of Greater Banjul is the long stretch of white sand connecting Kotu and Fajara (page 119).

FAJARA CLUB The par-69 18-hole course at the Fajara Club is a must for golfers, and the institution also offers several other sports facilities to day members (page 119).

SEREKUNDA MARKET The country's largest market, set in the heart of Serekunda, might not be for the faint of heart, but it does offer an uncompromising glimpse into the many faces of modern-day Africa (page 122).

KOTU STREAM A near-mandatory first stop for birders, Kotu Stream regularly yields 50-plus species in an hour or two, and the bridge across it is a good place to hook up with local bird guides (page 131).

SENEGAMBIA STRIP Love or hate this action-packed street in Kololi, there's no arguing with the abundant choice and overall quality of the dozens of restaurants that line it (page 137).

BIJILO FOREST PARK Red colobus monkeys, giant monitor lizards and plentiful forest birds are among the attractions of this small pedestrian-friendly reserve only 10 minutes' walk from the Senegambia Strip (page 145).

GETTING AROUND

Greater Banjul is the most compact part of The Gambia, and the easiest for getting around. There are plenty of tourist taxis available outside all the larger hotels, and a plethora of shared taxis ply all of the main roads and charge a fare of a few dalasi. If in doubt, head for Westfield Junction, which is the main public transport hub in Serekunda, and an easy place to pick up transport to central Banjul, Bakau, Fajara, Kotu and Kololi (as well as to most sites along the Brikama Road). It's now also possible to book a taxi, both immediately and in advance, through the 1bena app (w 1bena.com), the Gambian answer to Uber.

Day excursions to most sites treated as highlights in this or *Part Three* can be arranged at short notice through a number of **local operators**, of which African Adventure Tours (w adventuregambia.com), Arch Tours (w arch-tours.com), Bushwhacker Tours (w bushwhackertours.com), The Gambia Experience

---

MEDICAL FACILITIES

Most Gambian medical facilities of any quality lie within the area covered in this part of the guide. In case of a problem, however, probably your first course of action should be to visit the clinic in your hotel (assuming it has one), or to ask about the most suitable facility at reception.

Failing that, recommended options include the **Africmed Clinic and Laboratory** (↘441 0686; m 733 2101; e info@africmed-gm.com; w africmed-gm.com) about 200m southeast of Brusubi Turntable, as well as the **Bijilo Medical Centre and Hospital** (m 666 5555/998 0371; e drmusa@bijilomedical.org; w bijilomedical.org).

For dental problems, head to the **Smile Dental Clinic** (m 399 2409) in The Village on Kololi (or their two other locations on Kairaba Av & in Banjul). The **Medicare Clinic** pharmacy (m 953 3344) at Brusubi Turntable is open 24/7, while in Serekunda, the **Malak Pharmacy** (Kairaba Av; ↘ 437 6087; m 770 0719) has the next-longest hours, until midnight daily (and 22.00 on Sun).

(w gambia.co.uk) and West African Tours (w westafricantoursinfo.com) are recommended. Excursions are also bookable through the activity desks of most of the better hotels, or they can be arranged privately through the National Tour Guide Association kiosks at Senegambia Junction, Palma Rima Junction or Koru Market, or (if birds are your main interest) through any member of the Gambia Bird Guides Association, which is based at Kotu Bridge (page 130).

OTHER PRACTICALITIES

The region covered in this part of the guide breaks up into a number of hotel clusters, each of which is serviced by a selection of restaurants, bars, banks, ATMs, forex bureaux and supermarkets, as well as at least one craft market and taxi park. You are unlikely to need to walk much more than 10 minutes from your hotel to locate any of the above facilities. One shop worth singling out is Timbooktoo, in Fajara (page 119), which is the only quality vendor of books anywhere in the country.

EMBASSIES, HIGH COMMISSIONS AND CONSULATES IN THE GAMBIA The vast majority of consular services are in the more fashionable areas of Fajara and Bakau, rather than in Banjul proper – see w embassypages.com/gambia for a full list.

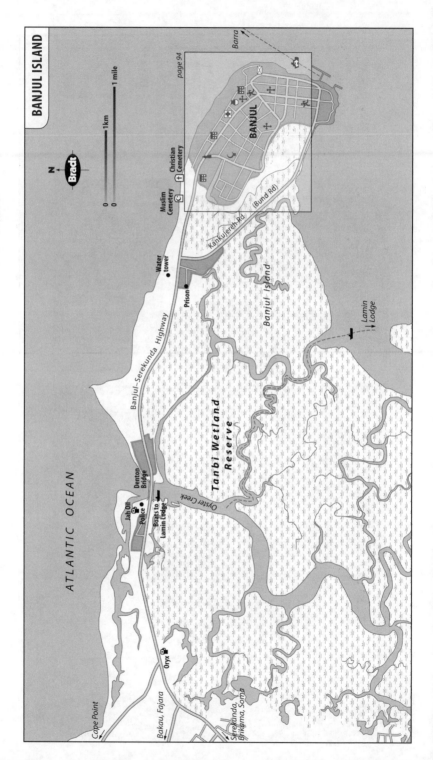

BANJUL ISLAND

page 94

BANJUL

Barra

Kankujereh Rd   (Bund Rd)

Banjul Island

Christian
Cemetery

Muslim
Cemetery

Lamin
Lodge

Water
tower

Prison

Banjul–Serekunda Highway

ATLANTIC OCEAN

Tanbi Wetland
Reserve

Cape Point

Jah Oil
Police

Denton
Bridge

Boats to
Lamin Lodge

Oyster Creek

Oryx

Bakau, Fajara

Serekunda,
Brikama, Soma

N

Bradt

0   1km
0   1 mile

90

4

Central Banjul

Banjul is the least populous capital city on the African mainland, and probably the most compact, with some 35,000 inhabitants confined to an area of around 3km². Occupying the easternmost quarter of a small island that protrudes hook-like into the southern mouth of the River Gambia, Banjul is lapped by open salt water on three sides, while its southwestern shore is dislocated from the mainland by the maze of mangrove-lined creeks that comprise the Tanbi Wetland Reserve. A solitary road, the Banjul–Serekunda Highway, links the capital to the rest of the country, crossing from the island to the mainland at Denton Bridge some 5km west of the city centre.

Despite being the capital, island-bound Banjul has long since surrendered much of its significance to the nearby mainland, where towns such as Serekunda, Bakau and Brikama now support significantly larger populations. (Between 1993 and 2013, Banjul lost 10,000 residents, while next-door Serekunda and surrounds gained 150,000.) In touristic terms, too, the capital city feels like something of an annex to the coastal resorts that blossom only 10km to its west: a sleepy urban anachronism often visited as a day trip by curious holidaymakers, but seldom viewed as an overnight destination in its own right. And yet Banjul still has many of the trappings of a capital. Most government departments have their headquarters in the city, which is also the site of State House, the administrative centre for the country, and the primary residence of President Barrow.

In its favour, the low-key Gambian capital possesses considerable character. Architecturally, Banjul is a real hodgepodge of old colonial properties, shantytowns and modern office buildings, none more than a few storeys high. And while the overall atmosphere is quite subdued and laid-back, certain areas can be very hectic, particularly the stretch of Liberation Avenue that follows the eastern waterfront from Albert Market south to the terminus for the Barra Ferry.

Culturally, Banjul is a West African melting pot. As you walk the streets, you'll see henna-painted Fulani women in golden hoop earrings and high heels, rubbing elbows with tall, blue-robed Mauritanian shopkeepers and Serahuli from upcountry in their traditionally dyed indigo gowns. Carry on and you'll find a kaleidoscope of impeccable outfits tailored from wild, colourful wax prints, and a parade of billowing boubous made from impossibly shiny *bazin* fabric, beloved by Gambians and Senegalese alike as their 'Sunday best', and regularly worn to Friday prayers. Throw in a clutch of Rastafarians in red, gold and green woven caps, Lebanese businesspeople in dark sunglasses, and a small army of suited-or-skirted office workers keeping the country's wheels turning, and you've got a small taste of what makes this small city tick. It's urban Gambia without the tourism, and a visit here can make for a fascinating peek at workaday West Africa beyond the beachfront bubble. And with a couple of interesting monuments and museums to boot, it's easy to spend an edifying afternoon in one of Africa's quirkiest capitals.

Little is known about the early history of Banjul. It seems that the earliest Portuguese explorers knew the island as Banjulo, a corruption of the Mandinka name for bamboo, which once grew profusely there. The British navigators who followed the Portuguese into the area called the island Combo or Kombo, after an important kingdom that occupied much of the mainland south of the river mouth. In 1651, the Duke of Courland (present-day Latvia) leased Banjul Island from the King of Kombo and James Island from the King of Barra. But while the Courlanders constructed the first fort on James Island, they appear never to have occupied Banjul, ownership of which eventually defaulted back to the King of Kombo. (And while the kingdom may be gone, Gambians today still refer to the entire Greater Banjul area from Brikama to the coast as Kombo or Kombos.)

Two external events conspired to bring Banjul back into the spotlight in the early 19th century. The first was the formal recognition of the River Gambia as a British possession under the Treaty of Versailles of 1783. The second, in 1807, was the passing of the British Abolition Act, which rendered the British slave trade out of Africa wholly unlawful and resulted in the official closure of the River Gambia to any further trade in captive humans. Unfortunately, however, this embargo was ignored by ships from anti-abolitionist France and Portugal, and also by the Americans, who had legislated against importing slaves in 1807, but allowed ships to transport them under the Spanish flag.

Initial British naval attempts to prevent slave ships entering the River Gambia enjoyed limited success. So it was that the Governor of Sierra Leone, Sir Charles MacCarthy, sent Captain Alexander Grant to Banjul Island in early 1816 to examine the possibility of setting up an anti-slaving garrison there. Impressed by the island's potential, Grant easily persuaded the King of Kombo, who had shortly before lost several family members to Spanish slavers, to cede the island in return for British protection, along with an annual payment of 103 iron bars. In April 1816, Banjul was formally handed over and renamed St Mary's Island. Three months later, MacCarthy and Grant's plan received written approval from the Earl of Bathurst, after whom the nascent settlement was named.

Captain Grant started work as soon as the treaty had been signed. Acclaimed for his personal energy and vigilance, he was well liked both by the local people and by his own men, who mostly despised the slave trade as much as he did. Construction began with a barracks to house 80 men and the erection of a battery of six 24-pounder guns and two field pieces (still present today in the grounds of State House, but out of bounds to tourists). A defensive trench was dug around the whole site, to help repel potential attacks from certain local chiefs who had profited so much from the slave trade that they violently opposed its abolition. Sir Charles MacCarthy strengthened the garrison by sending more troops from the Royal African Corps. He also stationed a sergeant's guard on James Island to prevent foreign ships from sailing further upriver. Within a few months, the garrison at Bathurst had captured five slave ships as they attempted to sail upriver, a hard and dangerous task given the high stakes involved (anybody found guilty of slave trading was automatically hanged).

Bathurst's growth was encouraged by offering free plots to legitimate merchants, providing that they built substantial brick or stone houses within a stipulated period. By 1818, the island's population stood at around 600, thanks to the relocation of many British merchants formerly operating out of Gorée Island (in present-day Senegal). By 1826, boosted by an influx of Wolof traders from Senegal and freed slaves from Sierra Leone, the non-military population of Bathurst had grown to around 30 Europeans and more than 1,800 Africans.

From here on, the population continued to grow at a phenomenal rate, and people settled in several distinct communities. Portuguese Town is where the wealthier traders – many of them mixed-race people who came here from Gorée and Saint-Louis – worked and erected their houses. Melville (later Jolof) Town is where the merchants' dependants and servants were housed, along with members of the artisanal class. Soldier Town is where the army was based. The poorest quarter, originally known as Mocam Town, later became Half Die, a graphic reminder that nearly half of its inhabitants died during an outbreak of cholera. These villages were separated originally by strips of cultivated land that eventually disappeared beneath buildings as the population grew, until they all joined up to form one cohesive town covering the entire habitable part of St Mary's Island.

The island may have been the perfect location for an anti-slaving garrison, but in hindsight it had little going for it as a future capital city. Hot, humid, low-lying and surrounded by standing water, it forms a natural breeding ground for tropical diseases such as cholera and malaria, and is prone to flooding – a growing concern in the age of climate change. Furthermore, the geographical constraints imposed by its small size have limited its physical and economic growth to such an extent that it must surely be the only African capital to have experienced a population decline over recent decades (the current population is more than 20% lower than the mid 1980s high of 45,000). Nevertheless, Bathurst continued to serve as the Gambian capital after independence in 1965, though both the island and the city officially reverted to their former name of Banjul in 1973.

GETTING THERE AND AWAY

Being small and island-bound, the town of Banjul is not itself a hub of domestic or international transport. All international flights land at Banjul International Airport, which despite its name actually borders the mainland village of Yundum, halfway between Serekunda and Brikama, and is closer by road to the coastal resorts between Cape Point and Tanji than to Banjul. Likewise, the various termini for buses and other public transport running upriver along the South Bank Road are clustered around Serekunda or Brikama, while all transport heading inland along the North Bank Road leaves from Barra, on the opposite side of the river mouth to Banjul. For further details of these connections, see the *Getting there and away* sections in the following chapters.

BY ROAD The only road connection to the capital is the Banjul–Serekunda Highway, which crosses Oyster Creek (the waterway that separates the mainland from the island) at Denton Bridge, which was built in 1986 to replace an older namesake. Many hotels and most tour operators based around the coastal resorts offer half-day trips to Banjul City. If you prefer to do your own thing, tourist taxis will readily take you from any resort hotel to anywhere in Banjul, and will wait for you while you do whatever it is you have come for. More affordably, a steady stream of bush taxis connects central Banjul to most other towns and resort areas on the mainland inland of Brikama, and fares are D20 from Serekunda. The bush taxi station for Bakau and Fajara lies on the south side of Independence Drive opposite the National Museum [95 F3], while the one for Kololi (Senegambia Junction), Serekunda (Westfield Junction) and Brikama is opposite the traffic circle at Gamtel House [95 F5] (the junction of Rene Blain Street and Freedom Lane).

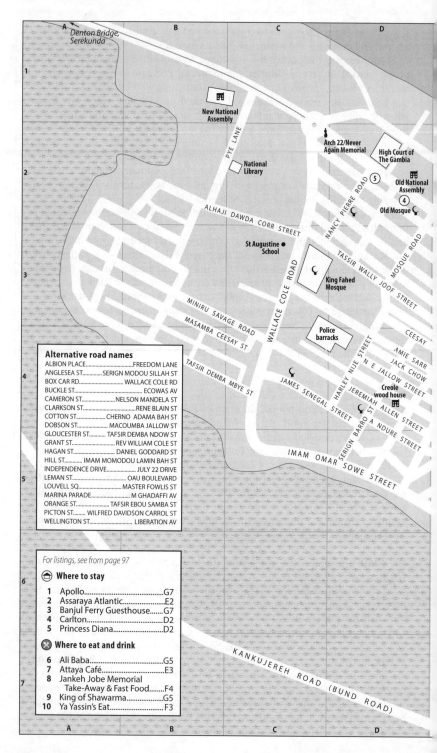

New National
Assembly

National
Library

PYE LANE

Arch 22/Never
Again Memorial

High Court of
The Gambia

Old National
Assembly
⑤

Old Mosque ☾
④

NANCY PIERRE ROAD

MOSQUE ROAD

ALHAJI DAWDA CORR STREET

St Augustine ●
School

WALLACE COLE ROAD

TASSIR WALLY JOOF STREET

CEESAY

King Fahed
Mosque

MINIRU SAVAGE ROAD

MASAMBA CEESAY ST

Police
barracks

AMIE SARR

JACK CHOW

HARLEY NJIE STREET

N E JALLOW STREET

Creole
wood house

TAFSIR DEMBA MBYE ST

JAMES SENEGAL STREET

JEREMIAH ALLEN STREET

JACK CHOW STREET

SERIGN BARRO ST

A NDURE STREET

IMAM OMAR SOWE STREET

KANKUJEREH ROAD (BUND ROAD)

Alternative road names

ALBION PLACE.............................FREEDOM LANE
ANGLESEA ST........ SERIGN MODOU SILLAH ST
BOX CAR RD............................ WALLACE COLE RD
BUCKLE ST...................................... ECOWAS AV
CAMERON ST.................NELSON MANDELA ST
CLARKSON ST..............................RENE BLAIN ST
COTTON ST............ CHERNO ADAMA BAH ST
DOBSON ST.................... MACOUMBA JALLOW ST
GLOUCESTER ST........... TAFSIR DEMBA NDOW ST
GRANT ST............................REV WILLIAM COLE ST
HAGAN ST....................... DANIEL GODDARD ST
HILL ST........... IMAM MOMODOU LAMIN BAH ST
INDEPENDENCE DRIVE.................... JULY 22 DRIVE
LEMAN ST....................................... OAU BOULEVARD
LOUVELL SQ.................. MASTER FOWLIS ST
MARINA PARADE........................... M GHADAFFI AV
ORANGE ST...................... TAFSIR EBOU SAMBA ST
PICTON ST......... WILFRED DAVIDSON CARROL ST
WELLINGTON ST........................... LIBERATION AV

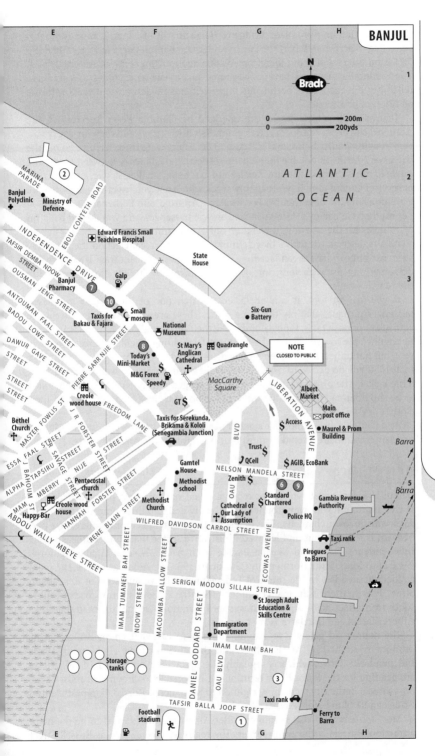

BANJUL

N

Bradt

0 ——————— 200m
0 ——————— 200yds

ATLANTIC

OCEAN

MARINA PARADE
(2)

Banjul Polyclinic
+

Ministry of Defence

INDEPENDENCE DRIVE

EBOU CONTETH ROAD

TAFSIR DEMBA NDOW STREET

OUSMAN JENG STREET

ANTOUMAN FAAL STREET

BADOU LOWE STREET

DAWUR GAVE STREET

STREET

STREET

STREET

Edward Francis Small
+ Teaching Hospital

State House

Galp
(7) Banjul Pharmacy

(10) Taxis for Bakau & Fajara

Small mosque

National Museum

PIERRE SARR NJIE STREET

(8) Today's Mini-Market

M&G Forex
Speedy $

GT $

Creole wood house

FREEDOM LANE

Taxis for Serekunda, Brikama & Kololi (Senegambia Junction)

St Mary's Anglican Cathedral †

Quadrangle

MacCarthy Square

Six-Gun
• Battery

NOTE
CLOSED TO PUBLIC

LIBERATION AVENUE

Albert Market

Main
✉ post office

• Maurel & Prom Building

Barra

Barra

MASTER FOWLIS ST

J R FORSTER STREET

Bethel Church +

ESSA FAAL STREET

TAPSIRU STREET

SAVAGE STREET

MBERRY

NJIE STREET

J BAHOUM ST

ALPHA

Pentecostal church +

Creole wood house

MAM ST

Happy Bar

ABDOU WALLY MBEYE STREET

HANNAH FORSTER STREET

RENE BLAIN STREET

Gamtel House

Methodist school

Methodist Church +

WILFRED DAVIDSON CARROL STREET

Trust $
♪ QCell

Zenith $

Cathedral of Our Lady of Assumption †

NELSON MANDELA STREET

BLVD

OAU

$ AGIB, EcoBank

$ Access

(6) (9)

Standard
$ Chartered

• Police HQ

Gambia Revenue Authority

ECOWAS AVENUE

IMAM TUMANEH BAH STREET

NDOW STREET

MACOUMBA JALLOW STREET

DANIEL GODDARD STREET

SERIGN MODOU SILLAH STREET

OAU BLVD

St Joseph Adult Education & Skills Centre

Immigration Department

IMAM LAMIN BAH

Taxi rank

Pirogues to Barra

(3)

Storage tanks

Football stadium

TAFSIR BALLA JOOF STREET

Taxi rank

(1)

Ferry to Barra

E   F   G   H

95

BY RIVER The long-promised bridge to Barra is still just that (a promise), so if you'd like to arrive or depart the city by water, the Banjul–Barra ferry terminal [95 G7] is on the east side of Liberation Avenue about 500m south of Albert Market. The Banjul–Barra ferries have a chequered history when it comes to safety and reliability, but there have been some improvements made in recent years with the addition of new ferries.

That said, all vehicle ferries are operated by **Gambia Ferry Services** (✆ 422 3729/9932/4107; m 783 3083; w ferries.gm; f GPAFerries), and they run every day, very roughly hourly between 07.00 and 23.00. There were three ferries making the trip as of 2023, with notable differences in speed and efficiency between them. The *Kunta Kinteh* is the best, with the *Kanilai* and *Johe* being smaller, slower, and often out of service. Encouragingly, you can now track which one you're getting and when it's arriving using the new Gambia Ferries App (Android only). The fare is D170/800 per motorcycle/car, or D35/60 per foot/bicycle passenger, and you should bank on 35 minutes for the crossing (travel time only!) at minimum.

As a pedestrian (or with a bicycle/moto), you can typically get on the first ferry to arrive, but car drivers can face long queues and a significant wait. If you'd rather do something else with your time, a 'priority ticket' for D1,500 allows you to skip the vehicle queue.

If you are on foot, it can be faster to catch one of the regular motorised passenger pirogues that ply the same route. These are effectively the waterborne equivalent of bush taxis, though, and – like their terrestrial counterparts – are often uncomfortable, overloaded and even a bit frightening. Incidents are fortunately rare, but not unheard of – seven people drowned when their pirogue capsized here in 2013. If you do decide to risk it, try to avoid stormy or windy weather and ask for a life jacket. The pirogue fare is D50 per passenger, plus about D10 on either side to be shoulder-carried from the shore to the boat (as most locals do, to keep their clothes dry!).

And if all this just sounds like a major headache, Roots tours to Juffureh, Albreda and James Island are offered by most tour operators at the coastal resorts.

ORIENTATION

Banjul is a compact town whose roads are laid out in a grid pattern, making it fairly easy to find your way around. It can be divided into three quite distinct areas, each with its own character. The oldest and most architecturally interesting part of town is the spacious and leafy administrative sector that runs southeast along Independence Drive and Marina Parade from Arch 22/Never Again Memorial [94 C2] to MacCarthy (former July 22) Square [95 G4]. Adjacent to this, the main residential area lies to the south of Independence Drive and west of Rene Blain Street. Finally, there is the main commercial centre, a grid of narrow roads running south from MacCarthy Square and west of Liberation Avenue (the road that links Albert Market and the Barra Ferry terminus).

The main road gateway to Banjul, about 5km east of Denton Bridge, is the prominent Arch 22. This is where the Banjul–Serekunda Highway becomes Independence Drive, which is arguably the main road on Banjul Island. If you are heading for the Barra Ferry terminus, it is possible to circumvent most of the busy streets in the city by turning right on to Kankujereh Road 3.5km past Denton Bridge and 1.5km before Arch 22.

Most tourists who visit Banjul consider Albert Market [95 G4] to be the main attraction, especially the craft market. The roads near here, such as Russell Street and Liberation Avenue, are also jam-packed with shops and market stalls, as are the pavements around MacCarthy Square. Apart from these and the main tourist attractions of the National Museum and Arch 22, though, there's really not a lot more to see. Note that the official road name changes implemented in the 1990s have not been widely adopted by locals, so most roads effectively have two interchangeable names.

SECURITY

Banjul is a reasonably safe city, even at night, though it would be foolhardy to walk around wearing flash jewellery or carrying more cash than you need. There are a lot of bumsters around, particularly in the vicinity of Albert Market, Arch 22/Never Again Memorial and the Assaraya Atlantic Hotel. Usually their motive is no more sinister than trying to insinuate themselves into your holiday as a guide or friend, but still it is best to shake them off firmly and politely rather than allowing them to draw you into conversation.

Around Albert Market, there are a few bumsters who work tourists in tag teams. One might, for instance, approach you with some sort of offer or a conversational gambit ('I work at your hotel?' or 'Do you remember me?'), keeping on persistently until the moment you show any sign of irritation or offishness, at which point he'll fling about angry accusations of racism, etc. The second guy then appears, perhaps claiming to be a security guard or a professional guide, and intervenes on your behalf by chasing off the first with a few angry words, hoping that will generate enough trust for you to take him on as a guide or to help negotiate with sellers on your behalf.

GETTING AROUND

If you're on foot, you can walk between pretty much anywhere you want in under 30 minutes, especially if you are just visiting the tourist attractions. Alternatively, shared taxis are commonplace and it shouldn't cost you more than D200 for a 'town trip' (chartered taxi) from one side of the city to the other.

WHERE TO STAY

Banjul itself offers a limited selection of accommodation compared with the resorts that line the coast to its west. Budget travellers are decently catered for, with a few acceptable choices that generally feel a lot more down to earth (or down at heel, depending on your perspective) than their counterparts in the nearby resort area. Unfortunately, the semi-legendary Radio Syd Guesthouse, formerly the best budget option near Banjul, burned down in 2020. The Swedish proprietors, who originally came to The Gambia in the 1970s as pirate radio operators, survived the fire, but the building was a total loss – it's now a petrol station.

MID-RANGE

Assaraya Atlantic Hotel [95 E2] (204 rooms) Marina Parade; m 290 9090, 291 9191; e reservations@assarayaatlantichotel.com; w assarayaatlantichotel.com. This has long been the best address in Banjul, though it's worth noting that there's not a lot of competition in that department & the best rooms in Banjul would be pretty tired by most other measures. Guests tend to be here on business, but there's a large swimming pool & shaded resto-bar attached, & the beachfront location is hard to argue with. *£30/46 sgl/dbl garden view, £34/52 sgl/dbl sea view, all rates B&B.* **$$**

BUDGET

Apollo Hotel [95 G7] (30 rooms) 33 Buckle St; m 784 3105. This long-serving multi-storey address has benefitted from some recent renovations & is definitely the nicest option near the ferry, but otherwise it's pretty basic & the options on Independence Dr are preferable. *£11/13 sgl/dbl with fan, £13/20 sgl/dbl with AC.* **$**

Carlton Hotel [94 D2] (40 rooms) Independence Dr; ✆ 422 8670, 422 5549; m 724 9761. This stalwart multi-storey hotel a few doors down from the Princess Diana, though comparable in quality to its neighbour, is probably a bit wonkier on the whole. But it does get points for the tree-shaded terrace sitting area, absent from the competition. *£9/12 sgl/dbl with fan, £13/18 sgl/dbl with AC.* **$**

Princess Diana Hotel [94 D2] (12 rooms) Independence Dr; ✆ 422 8715; m 518 6586. Probably the pick of the central cheapies, this obtusely named hotel close to Arch 22/Never Again Memorial seems to have undergone recent renovations, & the clean, tiled en-suite rooms with fan or AC seem pretty good value. *£11/13 sgl/dbl, £16 dbl with AC.* **$**

SHOESTRING

Banjul Ferry Guesthouse [95 G7] (16 rooms) Liberation Av; m 718 9366. A drop in standard from the above, but not so much in price, this rundown but potentially useful fallback has large en-suite rooms in a convenient location near the ferry terminal & that's about it. *£10 dbl with fan.* **$**

✕ WHERE TO EAT AND DRINK

Restaurant options in Banjul are limited, and many places have closed down in the past several years. The poolside restaurant and bar at the Assaraya Atlantic Hotel (page 97) is technically the nicest option in town, and at least one of the few places you can get a beer. Otherwise, you have a few choices, none of which serves alcohol:

Ali Baba Restaurant [95 G5] Nelson Mandela St; ✆ 422 4055; ◷ 08.00–19.00 Mon–Sat, 10.00–17.00 Sun. Something of a Banjul institution, this popular fast-food restaurant near the ferry terminal serves typical Lebanese dishes such as shawarmas & falafel sandwiches, along with a selection of burgers & Gambian & pasta mains. *Full meals cost around £4 & snacks around £1.50.* **$$**

King of Shawarma Restaurant [95 G5] Nelson Mandela St; ✆ 422 9714; m 773 3307; ◷ 09.00–19.00 Mon–Sat. Situated next to Ali Baba's, this is another good Lebanese restaurant serving similar dishes. The seafood & juices are recommended. *Around £4 mains or £1.50 snacks.* **$$**

Attaya Café [95 E3] Independence Dr; m 733 3344; ▮; ◷ 08.30–22.00 daily. Opposite the hospital, this little café serves a range of (proper!) coffees, juices, cakes & sandwiches. There's free Wi-Fi & a book corner with an eclectic selection of Gambian & international novels. *Daily dish/sandwiches around £2.* **$**

Jankeh Jobe Memorial Take-Away & Fast Food [95 F4] Independence Dr; m 219 2878; ◷ 07.00–22.00 Mon–Fri. This eatery opposite the National Museum does excellent & budget-friendly daily plates in a clean & casual setting. *Around £2 for the meal of the day or a sandwich.* **$**

Ya Yassin's Eat [95 F3] Independence Dr; m 391 8127, 344 4144. Not far down the road from Jankeh Jobe, this does a similar range of dishes – stop into both & see which plate of the day sounds better to you. *Around £2 for the plate of the day.* **$**

OTHER PRACTICALITIES

BANKING AND FOREIGN EXCHANGE Most **banks** are clustered around the junction of Ecowas Avenue and Nelson Mandela Street [95 G4–5], including EcoBank, GT Bank, AGIB, Standard Chartered, Access Bank and Trust Bank, all of which have ATMs. There are also a few private forex bureaux dotted around, including **M&G Forex** [95 F4] on Independence Drive and several in the vicinity of Albert Market.

Private moneychangers sometimes loiter outside Banjul post office, but they have a reputation for trickery, so are best avoided.

HOSPITAL The country's largest and oldest medical facility, established in 1853, is the **Edward Francis Small (formerly Royal Victoria) Teaching Hospital** [95 E3] (🎧 422 8224–7) on Independence Drive a block west of the National Museum. It has a casualty department, but for immediate attention it's probably wiser to visit one of the clinics in the Kololi area. The closest thing to a 24-hour pharmacy is the **Banjul Pharmacy** [95 E3] (🕘 09.00–21.00 Mon–Sat) on Independence Drive opposite the hospital.

INTERNET None of the hotels listed offers Wi-Fi except for Assaraya Atlantic Hotel (page 97), so if you don't have mobile data, head for the restaurant there or Attaya Café (see opposite).

POST The **main post office** [95 H4] on Liberation Avenue is a convenient place to post home goods bought at the adjacent Albert Market. If you are doing this, it's best to visit the parcel desk so staff can look at the contents and stick on a customs declaration before you finish wrapping it. This way you avoid your parcel being opened later and more roughly by customs officials. For stamp collectors, a special desk sells sets of Gambian stamps.

SHOPPING The **Albert Market** [95 G4] sells everything from vegetables and fruit to beauty products, clothing, shells, beads, fabrics and prints. Situated within the main market, the **Banjul Craft Market** is without a doubt the best place in Banjul to buy local crafts such as musical instruments, batiks, antiques and the usual colourful bracelets and necklaces. The **Kerewan Record Store** next to the entrance can load up a USB stick of Gambian and other West African music for you. Perhaps the best supermarket in town is **Today's Mini-Market** [95 F4] (🎧 420 1778; 🕘 09.00–21.00 daily) on Independence Drive, which stocks a fair selection of wines, spirits and other imported and packaged goods.

WHAT TO SEE AND DO

4

Banjul is rather short on 'must-see' attractions, the one arguable exception being the worthwhile and well-organised National Museum. However, you could easily dedicate a couple of hours to exploring the town centre, ideally starting in the far west at the distinctive Arch 22/Never Again Memorial, then following Independence Drive southeast down to the National Museum, possibly diverting north to the waterfront where Clean Earth Gambia (🛐) and Future Proof Banjul (🛐 futureproofbjl) have initiated a reforestation project, or south into the old residential area, then continuing further southeast via MacCarthy Square to Albert Market and the bustling stalls and shops that line Liberation Avenue as it runs south to the Barra Ferry terminus.

ARCH 22/NEVER AGAIN MEMORIAL [94 C2] (Independence Dr; 🕘 08.00–18.00 daily; entrance D100) Difficult to miss, towering as it does above the only road into the city, the imposing but otherwise unimpressive Arch 22 monument was unveiled in 1997, designed by the Senegalese architect Pierre Goudiaby to commemorate the 22 July 1994 military coup d'état that brought former president Yahya Jammeh to power. Since he was finally deposed in 2017, the question of what to do with a monument so inextricably linked with the former regime's dictatorial megalomania has somewhat bedevilled Banjulians and Gambian authorities alike. They started out by honking, cheering and joyfully driving back and forth under the arch when Jammeh fled the country – a privilege only enjoyed by the former president during his rule – and since then have been largely just letting it fall to pieces.

So the rather forlorn triumphal arch, comprising two rows of four pillars beneath a triangular roof, still stands a full 35m high, though the peeling paint and general disrepair makes its lofty Neoclassical pretensions seem more contrived than ever. A handful of exhibits on the three upper floors – reached by a giddying spiral staircase – are now mostly gone, so the only reason to come here is to take in the spectacular views. Stretching in all directions, across the city rooftops to the river mouth and sea, they're worth the price of admission alone.

In mid 2022, the Barrow government, in keeping with the findings and recommendations of the Truth, Reconciliation and Reparations Commission (TRRC), announced that Arch 22 would be reimagined as the Never Again Memorial Arch, and that it would be renovated to serve as a memorial to the victims of Jammeh's rule. At the time of writing, works had yet to begin, so while the shape of the future memorial remains unknown, it will continue to memorialise the former regime – just not in the way its creators may have imagined.

NATIONAL MUSEUM OF THE GAMBIA [95 F3] (Independence Dr; ☏422 6244; m 769 2772; e musmon@qanet.gm; w ncac.gm; ⊕ 08.00–18.00 Mon–Thu, 08.00–13.30 Fri, 08.00–14.00 Sat; entrance D100) Situated on the north side of Independence Drive, this is the country's premier museum, officially opened by President Jawara in 1985, and housed in an airy wooden-floored building that formerly served as the (whites-only) Bathurst Club. Many of the exhibits are a bit tired looking, but overall it is a very interesting place to spend an hour or two. Among the more absorbing collections is a varied set of monochrome photographs of Banjul taken in the early 20th century, some fabulous traditional masked dancing kits, displays about the Senegambia Stone Circle sites of Wassu and Ker Batch, Iron-Age societies in the Senegal River region, and the spread of Islam and the marabout tradition. In the pleasant gardens of tamarisk and palm trees, you'll find public toilets, the city's last functional well, a batik stall and a quality silversmith. Still photography is permitted, but not video.

INDEPENDENCE DRIVE AND MARINA PARADE Among the oldest roads in Banjul, these two parallel thoroughfares are lined with several of the city's most interesting 19th-century buildings. These include the **High Court** [94 D2], the former **National Assembly** [94 D2] (a new modernist-looking National Assembly building was inaugurated at the west end of town in 2014), the **Edward Francis Small (formerly Royal Victoria) Teaching Hospital** [95 E3] and various government offices. Also on Marina Parade but sadly off-limits to tourists is **State House** [95 F/G3], a majestic building whose grounds house the Six-Gun Battery raised by Captain Grant in 1816 to prevent slave ships entering the River Gambia (now part of the 'Kunta Kinteh Island and Related Sites' UNESCO World Heritage Site). Back on Independence Drive, two landmark sites of worship are the **Old Mosque** [94 D2], built in the first half of the 19th century by Bombeh Gaye, and the small but pretty **St Mary's Anglican Cathedral** [95 F4], which was constructed under the name King's Church in 1933. The church courtyard contains a small memorial to five police constables killed in the line of duty in Sankandi in 1900.

SOUTH OF INDEPENDENCE DRIVE One of the oldest parts of Banjul is the residential quarter that runs south from Independence Drive towards the mangroves that form the city's southern boundary. At the west end of this district, on Wallace Cole Road a few hundred metres south of Arch 22, the modernistic **King Fahed Mosque** [94 C3], built in 1988, is the city's largest and most prominent place of worship, graced by two tall octagonal minarets and with capacity for more than 6,000 male and female worshippers. At the other end of the district, on the junction of Macoumba Jallow and Rene Blain streets, a few hundred metres south of MacCarthy Square, is the oldest surviving place of worship in Banjul: the modest **Methodist (originally Wesleyan) Church** [95 F5] built in 1834. Between the two, the backstreets of this district are dotted with some of the city's finest examples of **mid-19th-century wooden Creole architecture**. Good examples can be seen next to the Happy Bar on Rev William Cole Street [95 E5], on Pierre Sarr Njie Street [95 E4] and on Sagarr Jobe Street [94 D4].

MACCARTHY SQUARE AND SURROUNDS Until recently known as July 22 Square in commemoration of the 1994 coup d'état that brought former president Yahya Jammeh to power, this green space at the heart of Banjul has since reverted to its old name, commemorating 19th-century anti-slavery campaigner Sir Charles MacCarthy (for whom the island on which Janjanbureh sits is also named). The park itself is a small quadrangle at the eastern end of Independence Drive, on the pivot that divides the western administrative region from the southern commercial district. The site of a World War I memorial and a commemorative fountain constructed for the coronation of King George VI in 1937, it is now often used for important ceremonial events, including presidential speeches, and the annual independence day festivities on 18 February.

On the square's western side is the **Quadrangle** [95 G4], or Government Building, the oldest building in Banjul, and now the home of the National Archives. Extended from the original barracks constructed by Captain Grant some 200 years ago, the Quadrangle is topped by a handsome clock tower donated by the Bavreres Company in 1892.

ALBERT MARKET [95 G4] Running south from MacCarthy Square to the Barra Ferry terminus on Liberation Avenue (formerly Russell and Wellington streets) is the vibrant commercial focal point of Banjul. Its centrepiece is Albert Market, which started life in the mid 19th century and is still going strong today, albeit behind a relatively modern façade constructed after it was razed by a fire in 1988. For curio-hunters, it is the site of the excellent **Banjul Craft Market**, an excellent place to buy everything from sculptures and traditional musical instruments to tie-dyed batik clothing and locally made jewellery. But even if you are not interested in buying, it is a fascinating place to stroll around, with different sections devoted to clothing, fish, meat, fresh produce, fetish stalls and hardware, all of them catering mainly to local buyers rather than tourists.

LIBERATION AVENUE AND HALF DIE South of Albert Market, Liberation Avenue is lined with Lebanese and Mauritanian cloth stores, and the workplaces of many local tailors who will convert the raw material to finished clothing for very reasonable prices. Also on this road are several old colonial-era warehouses, most notably the **Maurel and Prom Building** [95 H4], with its arched double-storey façade. Two blocks inland, on the corner of Daniel Goddard and Wilfred Davidson Carroll streets, the **Cathedral of Our Lady of Assumption** [95 G5], which celebrated its centenary in 2011, is an unusual Catholic building with an adobe exterior supported by heavy buttresses. Nearby at 20 Ecowas Avenue, the **St Joseph Adult Education & Skills Centre** [95 G6] (✆ 422 8836) is known for the high-quality handcrafted clothes and other artefacts produced by its female students. Further south, around the Barra Ferry terminus, the old and rundown suburb of Half Die (originally known as Mocam Town but renamed in memory of the many victims of a cholera outbreak in 1869) is the site of some of the city's last remaining Creole-style wood-and-bamboo-weave houses.

TANBI WETLAND RESERVE Established in 2001, this 45km² reserve protects the extensive maze of mangroves, open channels, mud banks and other saline wetland habitats that separate Banjul Island from the mainland, running south almost all the way to the small town of Lamin on the Serekunda–Brikama Road. Long known as a birding hotspot, the main road runs adjacent to a large expanse of tidal mud that is exposed at low tide, often giving excellent views of herons, egrets, African spoonbill, pelicans and various waders including pied avocet. It is one of the best sites in The Gambia for rarities, which have in the past included great 'ticks' like saddle-billed stork, European spoonbill and lesser yellowlegs.

A popular access point to the northern wetlands is Kankujereh Road (formerly Bund Road), which skirts the southern fringe of Banjul for about 3km (and sees a lot of heavy truck traffic). It's also possible to access the wetlands by boat, which can be hired from the small marina on the south side of the Banjul–Serekunda Highway immediately west of Denton Bridge. Boats can go as far south as Lamin Lodge if you wish, and also offer fishing trips through the mangroves, birding trips or dolphin-spotting excursions in the open sea. Expect to pay around £15–25 per hour, depending on the size and type of boat. Recommended operators include **Angling Tours Gambia** with skipper Alhagie (m 779 9104, 379 9104; e ag_sarr@ yahoo.com; ⨍) and **Jane's Boats** (m 776 8074; e jane@janesboats.gm; w janesboats. gm), who operate the lazy day cruise through the mangrove creeks that has been popular for 20 years. Book online or via the major tour operators (£40 pp for cruise, £30 pp for fishing; half price for children, inc some drinks, lunch & hotel transfer).

5

Bakau and Cape Point

The third-largest town in The Gambia, with a population of 75,000, bustling Bakau is perched atop low red cliffs running southwest from Cape Point, the north-facing promontory at the juncture of the Gambia River mouth and Atlantic Ocean coastline. One of the first parts of The Gambia to be developed as a resort area, Cape Point also separates two beaches that could hardly be more different in character. The strip of Atlantic coastline southwest of Cape Point, below the cliffs of Bakau, is essentially a fishing beach, lined with dozens of colourful pirogues, and the site of a chaotic market where the day's catch is gutted and sold. By contrast, the flat sweep of golden sand running southeast of Cape Point ranks among the most attractive swimming beaches in the country, offering distant views to the North Bank on a clear day, and with a relatively quiet and uncrowded feel compared with most other resort areas.

Although a lot of Bakau's seafront has been turned over to residential use, there are also plenty of hotels dotted around, and beach tourism remains arguably the main economic activity today. That said, Bakau is also very much a working town: Atlantic Boulevard, the main thoroughfare, is flanked by the whiffy fishing beach and a large produce market, while the narrow dusty roads running inland through the old town retain a surprisingly organic and lived-in character. As a result, tourist facilities in Bakau seem to exist in less of an industry bubble (and to be rather less heavily bumstered; page 79) than their counterparts in, say, Kololi or Kotu.

HISTORY

Unsurprisingly, the existence of Cape Point was documented by the earliest Portuguese explorers, who christened it Cabo de Santa Maria (a name that later became associated with Banjul Island, known as St Mary's Island in British colonial times). The oldest part of Bakau, Kachikally was most likely founded by the Bojang clan, which has since produced several local Mandinka chiefs (and more recently MPs and other politicians), and which still claims traditional ownership of the sacred crocodile pool in the heart of the old town. Bakau is first name-checked by Lemos Coelho, a Portuguese explorer who landed there in 1669 and noted that it housed a European slave-trading post. Over the subsequent three years, Coelho used the 'very attractive port' as a base for exploring further upriver, and later wrote that if he 'were to return upriver today, he would live nowhere else'. In 1816, Captain Grant, the founder of Banjul, established a sanatorium at Cape Point, close to what is now the British High Commission, and also arranged for a lantern to be hung there at night as a navigational aid. In 1823, Bakau became the site of a primary school founded by the Quaker missionary Hannah Kilhan and two male colleagues. Integrated into the British colony of Gambia in 1888, Bakau was

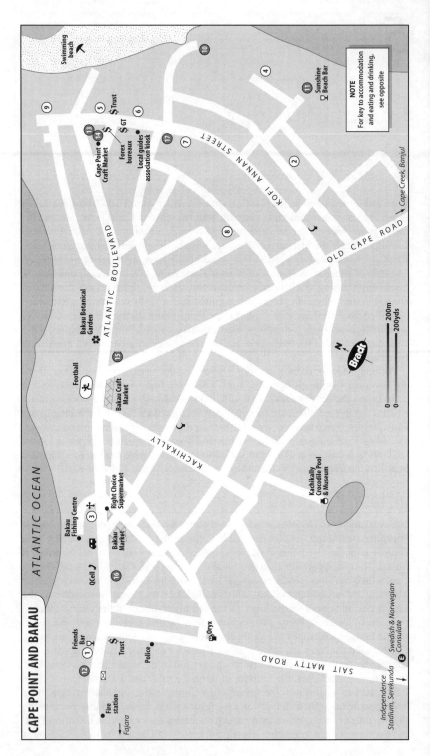

CAPE POINT AND BAKAU

ATLANTIC OCEAN

Swimming beach

Trust

GT

Cape Point Craft Market

Forex bureaux

Local guides association kiosk

KOFI ANNAN STREET

Sunshine Beach Bar

OLD CAPE ROAD

Cape Creek, Banjul

NOTE
For key to accommodation and eating and drinking, see opposite

ATLANTIC BOULEVARD

Bakau Botanical Garden

Football

Bakau Craft Market

KACHIKALLY

Kachikally Crocodile Pool & Museum

N

Bradt

0   200m
0   200yds

Bakau Fishing Centre

Right Choice Supermarket

QCell

Bakau Market

Friends Bar

Trust

Police

Oryx

SAIT MATTY ROAD

Independence Stadium, Serekunda

Swedish & Norwegian Consulate

Fire station

Fajara

partially destroyed by flooding in 1906. Several old colonial buildings still stand, however, among them the quaint St Peter's Church opposite the market, and several grand clifftop residences.

GETTING THERE AND AWAY

For new arrivals heading to Bakau from Banjul International Airport, it's a drive of around 20km via Serekunda or 25km via the Bertil Harding Highway; taxis to any hotel in the area cost around £20.

Bakau lies about 11km west of Banjul via the Banjul–Serekunda Highway and the Old Cape Road, a route covered by regular bush taxis, which leave Banjul from the station on Independence Drive opposite the National Museum, and cost around D20. There are also regular shared taxis to Serekunda and Kololi.

Coming to or from Fajara, a steady flow of shared taxis runs along Atlantic Boulevard, the 4km road between the north end of Kairaba Avenue and Cape Point, and they will pick up passengers anywhere en route.

The main taxi and public transport rank in Bakau is on Atlantic Boulevard opposite the Bakau market, but there are also taxi ranks close to the junctions with the Old Cape Road and Sait Matty Road.

WHERE TO STAY *Map, page 104*

The only truly upmarket hotels in Bakau are Ocean Bay and Sunbeach. There are several good cheaper options, including the new Bojang River Lodge and the characterful One World Village Guesthouse or Ann's Guesthouse. Bakau is also home to two long-serving and busy but otherwise rather indifferent package set-ups in the form of the Cape Point and African Village hotels.

EXCLUSIVE

❋ **Sunbeach Hotel & Resort** (111 rooms)
Kofi Annan St; ☏ 449 7190; m 278 1338; e info@
sunbeachhotel.gm. Among the most appealing
large resort hotels in The Gambia, this sleek
address has a modern North African feel & the
smart sgl-storey blocks offer modern rooms with
flatscreen TVs, safe, AC, hot shower & verandas
offering mostly sea views. The open & spacious
grounds host 2 restaurants & 2 swimming pools,
& various activities such as beach volleyball, yoga,
badminton & games are on offer. Other services
include valet, laundry, babysitting & tours. *Contact
The Gambia Experience (page 52) for bookings &
rates.* **$$$**

Ocean Bay Hotel & Resort (195 rooms)
Kofi Annan St; ☏ 449 4265, 449 5787; e info@
oceanbayhotel.com; w oceanbayhotel.com. This
wheelchair-friendly complex lies in spacious
& well-maintained palm-shaded gardens that
lead out to a semi-private swimming beach
perhaps 300m south of Cape Point. Set in
Mediterranean-style dbl-storey pastel blocks
with terracotta tiled floors & roofs, the spacious,
if somewhat dated, rooms come with king-size
or twin bed, dark wood furniture, fan, AC, sat
TV, private balcony & en-suite hot shower. Other
facilities include a large rectangular swimming

CAPE POINT AND BAKAU
For listings, see from page 105

◉ **Where to stay**
1 African Village
2 Ann's Guesthouse
3 Atlanticoast Residence
4 Bojang River Lodge
5 Cape Point Hotel & Restaurant
6 Ocean Bay Hotel & Resort
7 One World Village Guesthouse
8 Roc Heights Lodge
9 Sunbeach Hotel & Resort

✖ **Where to eat and drink**
10 Calypso
11 Gibbi's on the Beach
12 Kunta's Bar & Grill
13 Mr Bass Bendula Garden
14 Rising Sun Bar & Restaurant
15 Saffie J Bar & Restaurant
16 Solomelo
17 Zaika Restaurant & Bar

pool, a choice of 5 indoor & poolside restaurants & bars, 24hr laundry & valet service, tennis courts, watersports, tours, babysitting, foreign exchange & a library. *From £75/85 standard sgl/dbl B&B.* **$$$**

MID-RANGE

* **Roc Heights Lodge** (22 rooms) Samba Breku Rd; 449 5428; m 709 1543; e enquiries@ rocheightslodge.com; w rocheightslodge.com. Compromised only by its suburban location 5–10mins' walk from the beach, this classy boutique-style lodge is set in luxuriant tropical gardens centred on a swimming pool. Notable for its attentive service & tasteful African décor, it offers accommodation in a variety of en-suite dbl or twin rooms with TV, balcony, fan, AC & sitting area. Self-catering apts & penthouse suites (with distant sea views) are also available. There is a stylish restaurant with indoor & garden seating. *£42/58 sgl/dbl room, £44/61 sgl/dbl penthouse suite, £56/74 sgl/dbl apt.* **$$$**

Bojang River Lodge (13 rooms) Off Kofi Annan St; m 202 2988; e bookings@bojangriverlodge. com; w bojangriverlodge.com; f. This new lodge opened in 2021 & features comfortable & brightly coloured 2-storey roundhouses with AC overlooking a heart-shaped swimming pool (with bar) & Cape Point Beach beyond. The restaurant does grills & Gambian favourites for around £5. Good value. *£34/41 standard/superior dbl, B&B.* **$$**

Cape Point Hotel & Restaurant (75 rooms) Kofi Annan St; 449 5005; m 267 2553; e info@ capepointhotel.net; w capepointhotel.net. This family-run hotel lies a few paces' walk from the beach immediately south of Cape Point, & it has good facilities including a swimming pool, children's pool, bar & restaurant. The grounds are small & crowded, making it feel very packaged, & the décor is a little frayed at the edges. The en-suite rooms are reasonably sizeable & come with TV, fridge, bathroom with tub/shower & AC. *£48 dbl B&B.* **$$**

BUDGET

* **One World Village Guesthouse** (7 rooms) Kofi Annan St; m 735 8241, 308 0441, 683 4569; e aita@oneworldvillage.eu; f. Owned & managed by a Gambian–Swedish couple, this refreshingly down-to-earth & funky little

guesthouse is set in attractive leafy gardens centred on a circular swimming pool about 500m south of Cape Point & the beach. The standard rooms using shared bath are on the functional side, but very neat & clean, & they come with a fan & netting. There is also 1 larger en-suite room, & 1 mini suite with optional AC. There is no restaurant, but b/fast can be provided at £2.50 per head, while for other meals you can either use the communal self-catering kitchen or head to any of a dozen good eateries within easy walking distance. *£16 dbl with shared bathroom, from £21 en-suite dbl.* **$$**

African Village Hotel (73 rooms) Atlantic Bd; 449 5034; m 307 9645, 717 6255; e africanvillagehotel@yahoo.com; w africanvillagehotel.gm. One of the oldest & most packagey hotels on the Gambian coast, the lively & friendly African Village is a little rough around the edges, but it remains a popular & good-value choice, not least thanks to its superb location, on a low cliff overlooking the fishing beach, in the heart of Bakau. Facilities include a compact swimming pool area, a restaurant with a clifftop wooden deck, & a rather eroded private beach that offers good swimming tidally. Accommodation is in simply decorated en-suite rooms & thatched roundhouses. *£17/25 standard sgl/dbl with fan, £32/39 sgl/dbl with AC & sea view.* **$$**

Ann's Guesthouse (6 rooms) Off Kofi Annan St; m 227 3617, 777 3332; e annlindholm@ yahoo.com; f. This small, Swedish–Gambian guesthouse is a calm & comfortable address with tidy AC rooms opening onto a green garden & swimming pool area. It's quite good value & popular with long-stay visitors for that reason. *£22/25 dbl with shared/en-suite bath, B&B.* **$$**

SHOESTRING

Atlanticoast Residence (29 rooms) Atlantic Bd; m 368 5773, 283 3276; e atlanticoastresidence@gmail.com. Formerly known as the Bakau Guesthouse, this long-serving 4-storey hotel opposite Bakau Market is notable above all for the superb views over the fishing beach & harbour from the sea-facing rooms. These are basic & rather timeworn but spacious & serviceable enough for the price, & it's hard to argue with the private sea-facing balconies. *£13/25 dbl with street/sea view.* **$**

When it comes to eating out, you could spend a week in Bakau without repeating a venue. There are restaurants in most of the hotels, but generally the better option is standalone eateries, in particular the cosmopolitan cluster around the Ocean Bay Hotel, which includes Calypso, Zaika and Mr Bass.

UPMARKET

✻ **Calypso Restaurant** Off Kofi Annan St; m 692 0201; ⏰ 09.00–23.00 daily (the bar stays open later at w/ends). Established in 1988, this Bakau institution has an idyllic location on the edge of a large reed-lined pond that supports plentiful crocodiles & waterbirds, & Cape Point Beach extending away to the north. There is the choice of eating in the open-sided thatched main restaurant, in one of the summer houses next to the crocodile pool or beach, or in a wooden treehouse-like construction behind them. It is a popular meeting point for expats on Fri & Sat nights, when there is also often live music. An excellent menu dominated by seafood, steak & pasta dishes is complemented by more affordable snacks & sandwiches. It also has a full bar & tapas menu. Come between 16.00 & 17.00 to see the crocodiles being treated to a fish supper. Overall, a very agreeable lunch spot & great night out, though not the cheapest. *Mains around £10, snacks around £5–6.* $$$$

MID-RANGE

Gibbi's on the Beach Off Kofi Annan St; m 755 9192; w gibbis.eu. This new address has a huge 1st-floor dining room overlooking the beach, & serves excellent seafood, including lobster, shrimp & butterfish, alongside pizzas & other grills. There's live music on busy nights. *Mains around £8.* $$$

Solomelo Atlantic Bd; 🏢 solomelosgambia. Half music venue, half restaurant, this is a fine choice for lunch, & an even better choice for dinner, drinks & live music at w/ends. The music is Gambian, but the menu leans international with coconut prawns, Thai fish cakes & more. Check their Facebook for upcoming events. *Mains around £6.* $$$

Zaika Restaurant & Bar Kofi Annan St; m 707 9220, 788 1955; ⏰ 16.00–late daily (high season). This is one of the best Indian restaurants anywhere on the coast, with indoor & outdoor seating & a massive menu of dishes including a great vegetarian selection & some Chinese &

European favourites, as well as a well-stocked bar. Rather low on character but exceptional food. *Expect to pay £5–8 per main, inc rice or naan.* $$$

✻ **Mr Bass Bendula Garden** Atlantic Bd; 📞 449 8223; ⏰ 08.00–02.00 daily. A well-known landmark situated opposite the Cape Point Hotel, this vibey rendezvous has the ambience of a street café, with shaded seating spilling out onto the pavement. A varied international menu includes Asian, Mexican & continental dishes, but the main specialities are pizzas, seafood & excellent Gambian staples such as fish with benachin rice. It is particularly popular over w/ends, when you can watch live Premier League football accompanied by chilled draught beers. There is also live music on Mon, Wed, Fri & Sat, usually starting at around 21.00. A great place to settle into for a lively evening. *Mains in the £4–6 range.* $$

Kunta's Bar & Grill Atlantic Bd; m 770 1499; ⏰ 08.00–late daily. Probably the pick of several moderate pavement eateries clustered around the entrance of the African Village Hotel, this place has a pleasant outdoor ambience, cheap beers, & a varied menu concentrating on Chinese, Gambian & seafood dishes. *Mains £4–6.* $$

BUDGET

Rising Sun Bar & Restaurant Off Atlantic Bd; m 755 9192; ⏰ Nov–Apr 07.00–23.30 daily. This low-key local eatery next to Cape Point Craft Market focuses on fresh seafood & also has a good vegetarian selection. *Vegetarian dishes around £3, other mains around £5.* $$

Saffie J Bar & Restaurant Old Cape Rd; m 739 5656; ⏰ 10.00–late daily. This relaxed & friendly open-air pavement restaurant opposite Bakau Craft Market might look like little more than a local drinking hole, but it has a long & surprisingly varied menu offering everything from meatballs or beef stroganoff with boiled potatoes to grilled prawns or fish & chips. Down to earth & great value. *Most mains around £4.* $$

ENTERTAINMENT AND NIGHTLIFE

Most of the restaurants listed on page 107 double as bars. Several also host live music at weekends and more occasionally on weekday nights. We recommend Calypso Restaurant for a sedate beachfront drink, while Mr Bass Bendula Garden is a good place to enjoy live Premier League football or (later in the evening) live music at weekends. **Sunshine Beach Bar** (m 744 9260) is popular with locals and a great place to sit under the beachside bantaba and soak up the bass-heavy reggae vibes – grills and bar snacks are available too.

OTHER PRACTICALITIES

BANKS AND FOREIGN EXCHANGE There are several private **forex bureaux** clustered around the north end of Kofi Annan Street opposite the Cape Point Hotel, along with two ATMs, from **Trust Bank** and **GT Bank**. Further west, there's another ATM at **Trust Bank** on the junction of Sait Matty Road and Atlantic Boulevard. Package hotels such as Ocean Bay and Cape Point also have foreign-exchange facilities.

GUIDES If you want an official guide to show you around Bakau or to arrange excursions elsewhere, the local guides association has a kiosk on Kofi Annan Street opposite the Ocean Bay Hotel.

SHOPPING For self-caterers, **Bakau Market** has a superb selection of fresh fruits and veggies, while the surrounding stalls and small shops stock bread and other locally produced perishables. For imported goods, frozen meat, wines and spirits, your best bet is the **Right Choice Supermarket** (✆ 449 7156; ⏰ 09.00–21.00 daily) next to the market. The **Bakau Craft Market** at the junction of Old Cape Road and Atlantic Boulevard and the **Cape Point Craft Market** behind Mr Bass Bendula Garden both have dozens of stalls selling woodcarvings, batik clothes and tablecloths, jewellery and other locally crafted items.

WHAT TO SEE AND DO

The main tourist focal point is the **swimming beach** immediately southeast of Cape Point. If your hotel doesn't offer direct access to this, it can easily be reached along a sandy eastern extension of Atlantic Boulevard north of the Cape Point Hotel. By contrast, the working beach southwest of Cape Point has suffered badly from erosion, and attempts to reverse its decline have met with limited success. While swimming here is still possible tidally at certain spots, notably below the African Village Hotel, it is wise to ask local advice before you take the plunge. (Cape Point itself sits behind a 500m rock barrier erosion defence similar to, but much older than, that found at Kololi.)

Away from the developed area, a lovely undisturbed beach lined with palms, mangroves and salt marsh runs southeast of the Ocean Bay Hotel and on towards Banjul. Be warned, however, that muggings have been reported from the beach southeast of the Calypso Restaurant, so best not to carry any valuables there, and/or to walk in a group.

Bakau is a lively, agreeable and often fascinating place to explore on foot, the sporadic attentions of bumsters offering to 'show you the crocodiles' notwithstanding. Well worth a look is the colourful fresh produce **market**, which lies on the landward side of Atlantic Boulevard, and is aimed mainly at locals rather than tourists. On the opposite side of the road, easily found by following the fishy smell, a short track curves downhill to the fascinating **Bakau Fishing Centre**, a fishing beach and market that is busiest in the late afternoon but bustles with colourful pirogues and mercantile activity throughout the day. About 1km inland of Atlantic Boulevard, **Independence Stadium**, built with Chinese assistance in 1983, is the country's premier stage for sporting events and political celebrations, with a capacity of around 30,000.

KACHIKALLY CROCODILE POOL AND MUSEUM (⊕ 13.4768 -16.6726;
🄵 Katchikally; 📷 sarjo_kachikally; ⏲ 07.00–19.00 daily; a D100 fee covers entrance to both the pool & the museum, but you pay extra for an optional guide) The most popular tourist attraction in Bakau is an ancient freshwater pool situated in the heart of the labyrinthine residential suburb of Kachikally (sometimes spelt Kachikali) about 700m south of Atlantic Boulevard. The pool is under the custody of a chiefly clan called Bojang, whose ancestors reputedly settled in the area around 500 years ago. According to oral tradition, shortly after the Bojang arrived in the area, they were visited by the fertility spirit Kachikally in the form of an apparently distraught elderly woman who pretended that her daughter was drowning in the pool. The family did everything they could to assist Kachikally, who rewarded them by entrusting the pool into their care and asking them to populate it with wildlife. A few weeks later, the family captured and released into the pool a pair of crocodiles which are ancestral to the 80 or so individuals that inhabit it today, and act as intermediaries with the spirit Kachikally. During the rainy season, many of the pool's residents disperse into the surrounding town and countryside, and you hear occasional tales of people waking up to find a young crocodile next to their bed!

Although it is a bit of a tourist trap, the pool is still a popular pilgrimage site for women experiencing difficulties conceiving, who come from far and wide to douse themselves in its curative water (any child born after a ritual bathing of this sort is invariably named Kachikally). On a good day you might see more than half-a-dozen crocodiles sunning on the bank, including at least one albino and several 2m-long individuals that are totally habituated to human visitors and even allow themselves to be touched on the back or tail (cue enthusiastic photo-taking all around). The largest of these reptilian giants, a 75-year-old 3m-long male named

5

SACRED CROCODILE POOLS   *By Craig Emms and Linda Barnett*

Three sacred crocodile pools can be found along the Gambian coast. The best-known and most accessible of these is Kachikally in Bakau, but there are also similar pools at Kartong, close to the southern border with Senegal, and at the North Bank village of Berending. People come to these pools from all over The Gambia, even from elsewhere in West Africa, bringing kola nuts for the guardians who will in turn offer up their blessings or prayers. Usually, an elder custodian will bring water from the pool and bless it before the visitors wash in it. The ceremony ends with drumming and dancing, and then the visitor is asked to abstain from unbecoming behaviour. The pools are most often visited by infertile women for curative purposes, but they also attract men wanting to reverse their bad fortune in business or other matters, parents hoping to protect their children during circumcision ceremonies and wrestlers seeking victory in a competition.

Charlie (reputedly after the first tourist who had the nerve to touch him), seldom makes an appearance these days, though the guides insist he still lives there. The pool itself is often covered in water cabbage, a floating plant that provides shelter for numerous groove-crowned bullfrogs, which form the staple diet of the crocodiles. Be careful close to the water's edge, as crocodiles that seem docile on terra firma might well attack somebody who falls into their watery home.

At the entrance to Kachikally, an informative little museum includes some interesting displays about the history of Bakau and Gambian involvement in World War II. The museum also displays a good collection of African musical instruments, including the harp-like *kora*, a 1.5m-long wooden xylophone and several tall ceremonial drums, plus a selection of traditional masquerade costumes and masks. The leafy pool grounds also host a surprisingly varied birdlife, with the likes of blue-breasted kingfisher, black-headed paradise flycatcher and yellow-throated leaflove likely to be seen flitting about.

Kachikally Crocodile Pool is poorly signposted, but easily reached from Atlantic Boulevard by following the surfaced Kachikally Road inland from the west side of Bakau Craft Market. Turn left on to a dirt road after about 500m (where Kachikally Road forks sharply to the right) then to the right after another 100m, and you will see the painted entrance in front of you. Anyone will point you in the right direction, but be warned that any bumster who gets involved in guiding you there will expect a fee.

CREATIVE ARTS TUNGEENA (m 707 9310; e kanimoury7@gmail.com; f) For the artistically inclined, a morning or afternoon spent with artist Karamo Saidykhan is a real treat. Specialising in batik fabrics, he leads workshops at his atelier near the Kachikally Crocodile Pool. Here, he will walk you through all stages of local batik production, from initial design and application of wax to cloth dyeing. Classes cost £13 per person for groups of up to three and £10 per person for groups of four to eight. You can try your hand at any kind of design you like, applied on T-shirts, tablecloths, wall tapestries and more.

BAKAU BOTANICAL GARDEN (Atlantic Bd; ⏱ 09.00–17.00 Mon–Sat; entrance D50) Established in 1924, this small botanical garden, on the seaward side of Atlantic Boulevard alongside the British High Commissioner's residence, is packed with a wide variety of indigenous and exotic plants, many of which are labelled. A series of winding footpaths, interspersed with benches in shady places, make it a very pleasant place for a morning or afternoon stroll. Considering its small size and urban location, the garden hosts quite a rich birdlife including nesting pairs of hamerkop and a variety of colourful finches and other small passerines.

CAPE CREEK Bisected by the Old Cape Road about 500m south of Bakau, Cape Creek (⊕ 13.4746, -16.6621) is an extensive saline wetland comprising patches of marsh, mangroves and open water, as well as exposed mud flats at low tide. The area is very good for birds, with exciting views of pied kingfishers hunting from nearby power lines over the creek. At low tide, scan the mud flats for waders such as black-winged stilt, Eurasian oystercatcher and common greenshank. It is also worth searching the mud and shrubby vegetation for smaller and more elusive species such as red-billed quelea and various migrant warblers. During the rainy season, you have a good chance of spotting a yellow-crowned bishop performing its strange bumblebee-like display flight in the reed beds running towards the junction known as Sting (or sometimes Camaloo) Corner, where the Bertil Harding Highway and the Banjul–Serekunda Highway meet.

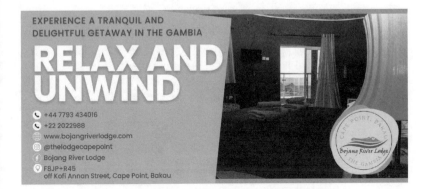

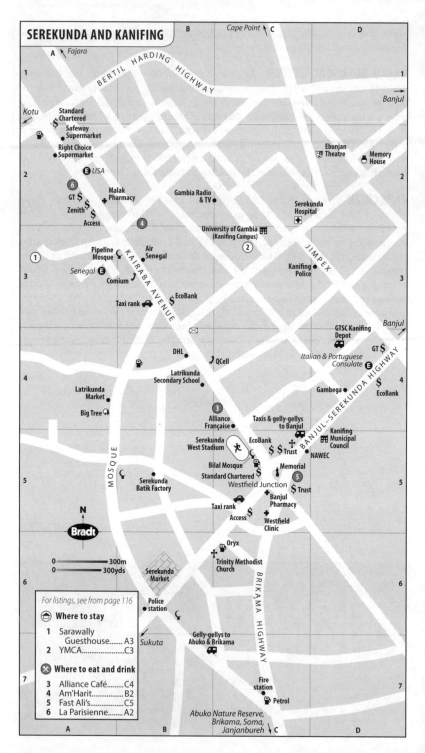

SEREKUNDA AND KANIFING

Fajara
Cape Point
Kotu
Banjul

BERTIL HARDING HIGHWAY

Standard Chartered
Safeway Supermarket
Right Choice Supermarket
USA
GT
Zenith
Access
Malak Pharmacy
Pipeline Mosque
Senegal
Comium
Air Senegal
Taxi rank
EcoBank

Gambia Radio & TV
University of Gambia (Kanifing Campus)

Ebunjan Theatre
Memory House
Serekunda Hospital

Kanifing Police

JIMPEX

Banjul

GTSC Kanifing Depot
Italian & Portuguese Consulate
GT
EcoBank
Gambega

DHL
QCell

Latrikunda Secondary School

Latrikunda Market
Big Tree

MOSQUE

Alliance Française

Serekunda West Stadium
Taxis & gelly-gellys to Banjul
EcoBank
Kanifing Municipal Council
NAWEC
Trust

Bilal Mosque
Standard Chartered
Westfield Junction
Memorial
Trust

Serekunda Batik Factory

Taxi rank
Access
Banjul Pharmacy
Westfield Clinic

BRIKAMA HIGHWAY

N

Bradt

0   300m
0   300yds

Oryx
Trinity Methodist Church

Serekunda Market
Police station
Sukuta

Gelly-gellys to Abuko & Brikama

Fire station
Petrol

Abuko Nature Reserve, Brikama, Soma, Janjanbureh

For listings, see from page 116

🏠 **Where to stay**
1 Sarawally Guesthouse....... A3
2 YMCA....................... C3

✖ **Where to eat and drink**
3 Alliance Café.......... C4
4 Am'Harit................ B2
5 Fast Ali's.............. C5
6 La Parisienne.......... A2

6

Serekunda, Fajara and Kairaba Avenue

Probably the busiest thoroughfare anywhere on the Gambian coast, the 4km-long Kairaba Avenue connects the inland Westfield Junction (a well-known landmark and transport hub) to the intersection with Atlantic Boulevard 200m from Fajara Beach. Formerly known as Pipeline Road, and still often referred to by that name, Kairaba Avenue was until the early 1970s a rough dirt track flanked for much of its length by working fields and scattered homesteads. Today, it is a wide, straight, built-up and heavily trafficked asphalt road that bisects two substantial but somewhat contrasting settlements: the bustling and chaotic town of Serekunda to the south of the intersection with Bertil Harding Highway (universally known as 'Traffic Light', as it was home to The Gambia's first one ever, installed here in 2000), and the leafy coastal residential suburb of Fajara to the north.

Sprawling inland of the coastal resorts, Serekunda is in fact the country's largest and most economically vibrant town, with a population estimated at 350,000, as well as being the most important route crossroads and public transport hub south of the River Gambia. Despite this, it is an oddly amorphous and ill-defined entity. Physically, Serekunda seems to lack clear boundaries, merging almost imperceptibly into the coastal resorts to its northwest and the smaller town of Sukuta to the southwest. Serekunda also lacks a clear political status, often being treated as all-but-synonymous with the Kanifing Municipal Council (a Local Government Area encompassing the entire Greater Banjul Region aside from Banjul Island).

One thing that Serekunda doesn't lack is vitality. Indeed, coming from sedate and orderly Banjul, or from the inherent artificiality of the coastal resorts, Serekunda feels like urban Africa at its most unapologetically raw and energetic. The streets, a seething mass of human enterprise and dodgem traffic, are lined with a hodgepodge of medium-rise office blocks, bright new supermarkets, colonial-era façades and jerry-built tin-roofed homesteads, all crowded together with the absence of design one might expect of a town that has grown enormously, and seemingly without restriction for decades. Everywhere there is noise and colour and movement and crowds of people. And an amazing variety of businesses and shops line the roads: bakeries, metalworkers, welders, car-repair yards, timber merchants, hair salons, spare-part shops...name it and you can probably find it somewhere in Serekunda.

At the northern end of Kairaba Avenue, past the US Embassy and intersection with Bertil Harding Highway, Serekunda gives way to Fajara, a relatively affluent suburb that runs west from Sait Matty Road to Kotu Stream, along a coastline dominated by low cliffs that slope towards an expansive sandy beach in the west. Fajara, like Serekunda, is not particularly well developed for tourism, boasting only

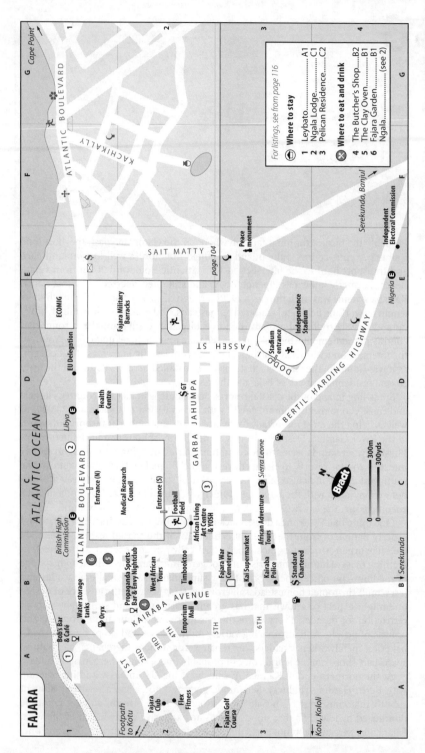

FAJARA

Cape Point

ATLANTIC OCEAN

ATLANTIC BOULEVARD

KACHIKALLY

Footpath to Kotu

Kotu, Kololi

Bob's Bar & Café

Water storage tanks

Oryx

Fajara Club

Flex Fitness

Fajara Golf Course

British High Commission

6

5

Propaganda Sports Bar & Envy Nightclub

West African Tours

Timbooktoo

Emporium Mall

KAIRABA AVENUE

1ST
2ND
3RD
4TH
5TH
6TH

4

Fajara War Cemetery

Kai Supermarket

Kairaba Police

African Living Art Centre & YOSH

Football field

Entrance (N)

Entrance (S)

Medical Research Council

3

African Adventure Tours

Sierra Leone

Standard Chartered

Libya

ECOMIG

EU Delegation

Health Centre

GARBA JAHUMPA

GT

Fajara Military Barracks

2

SAIT MATTY
page 104

Peace monument

JASSEH ST

DODO

Stadium entrance

Independence Stadium

BERTIL HARDING HIGHWAY

Nigeria

Independent Electoral Commission

Serekunda, Banjul

Serekunda

B

N

Bradt

0   300m
0   300yds

For listings, see from page 116

Where to stay
1	Leybato........................	A1
2	Ngala Lodge..................	C1
3	Pelican Residence.........	C2

Where to eat and drink
4	The Butcher's Shop......	B2
5	The Clay Oven.............	B1
6	Fajara Garden.............	B1
	Ngala...........................	(see 2)

a handful of hotels, but it does house some of the country's finest restaurants, most of them within a block of Kairaba Avenue. Well-known landmarks include the Fajara Military Barracks, the British High Commission and the Gambian headquarters of the Medical Research Council (a British-funded institution with a high profile in the field of malaria research). The most westerly part of the suburb, bordering Kotu Stream, is given over to the Fajara Club and the 18-hole Fajara Golf Course.

HISTORY

Also spelt Serrekunda, Serekunda is named after Sayerr (or Serre) Jobe, a Wolof marabout who, together with an entourage of relatives and slaves, migrated from the Sine-Saloum region of Senegal to the present-day Gambia in the mid 19th century. Local tradition has it that Sayerr Jobe first settled in the vicinity of Jinack Island, then in Banjul, before relocating to the southern mainland close to the existing village of Sukuta, where he established Serekunda. A successful merchant as well as a respected holy man, Sayerr Jobe is said to have fathered seven sons prior to his death in 1896, when he was buried at Serekunda Cemetery, near what is now the primary school. By the early 1960s, Serekunda had grown to be a small town, but it was only in the post-independence era that it outstripped Banjul as a population and commercial centre, eventually expanding along Kairaba Avenue to merge with Fajara – a posh residential suburb since colonial times – during the economic boom of the 1980s.

ORIENTATION

The four-way intersection at the south end of Kairaba Avenue [112 C5], known as Westfield Junction after a clinic founded there in 1972, is not only the focal point of activity in Serekunda, but also the most important road hub in the whole country. The Banjul–Serekunda Highway runs northeast from Westfield Junction to Banjul. Southeast of Westfield Junction, the Brikama Highway runs past Banjul International Airport and Abuko Nature Reserve to the important junction town of Brikama and the start of the main South Bank Road east to Soma, Janjanbureh and Basse. Southwest of Westfield Junction, Sayerr Jobe Road runs right past the covered Serekunda Market, then bisects the inland suburbs of Sukuta and Brusubi, before continuing along the south coast to Brufut, Tanji, Gunjur and Kartong. Then finally there is Kairaba Avenue itself, which runs northwest from Westfield Junction to Fajara, and is flanked by several supermarkets, banks and restaurants, as well as the US Embassy.

GETTING THERE AND AWAY

FAJARA For new arrivals heading to Fajara from Banjul International Airport, it's a drive of around 22km via Serekunda, costing around £20 in a taxi. Coming to or from Bakau, a steady flow of shared taxis runs along Atlantic Boulevard between the north end of Kairaba Avenue and Cape Point, and they will pick up passengers anywhere en route. A number of shared taxis also run along Kairaba Avenue between Fajara and Serekunda's Westfield Junction (the best place to pick up transport to Banjul), and also along the Bertil Harding Highway to Kotu or Kololi (Senegambia Junction) for just D15 per leg.

SEREKUNDA Serekunda is the most important transport hub anywhere on the South Bank, and also the main focal point for public transport around Greater Banjul and along the coast further south.

AROUND GREATER BANJUL Shared taxis and *gelly-gellys* (private minibuses) to and from Banjul terminate at the southwest end of the Banjul–Serekunda Highway, at a taxi station on the north side of the road close to Westfield Junction (on the Banjul side, they terminate at the station on Rene Blain Street opposite Gamtel House). Public transport to and from the other resorts in Greater Banjul (Fajara, Bakau, Kotu and Kololi) can also be picked up around Westfield Junction, or anywhere along Kairaba Avenue.

However, if the prospect of public transport is daunting, or you want to head straight to one of the coastal hotels, it may be easiest just to charter a taxi – they are not expensive and can be found easily at several stands along Kairaba Avenue or in the vicinity of the market. Perhaps even easier still, there is always the increasingly popular 1bena app (w 1bena.com), the Gambian answer to Uber, where you can request a taxi, either immediately or in advance, on your phone.

SOUTH COAST AND BRIKAMA Transport inland to Abuko or Brikama leaves from a small station along Mosque Road [112 B7] about 500m southeast of the junction with Sayerr Jobe Road (✪ 13.4355, -16.6793). Transport heading to the south-coast towns of Brufut, Tanji, Sanyang, Gunjur and Kartong leaves from Dippa Kunda Taxi Park [map, page 84] (✪ 13.4341, -16.6913), which lies on the north side of Sayerr Jobe Road at Bakoteh Junction (the intersection with Kololi Road) about 1km west of the junction with Mosque Road.

FURTHER AFIELD Situated off Jimpex Road, about 600m northeast of Kairaba Avenue, the GTSC's Kanifing Depot [112 D4] (✪ 13.4527, -16.6701; m 794 1106, 438 0152, 201 2222, 713 0939; w gtsc.gm; f gambiatransport) is the primary departure point for the daily GTSC buses that run east along the South Bank Road to Basse via Soma and Janjanbureh. A small handful of these affordable buses leave between 06.00 and noon daily. If you're willing to get up for it, the daily express bus is considerably faster and only slightly more expensive – but it leaves at 06.30. Unfortunately there is still no formal system for booking seats in advance, but the GTSC may be prepared to accommodate tourists who want to reserve a seat for the next morning – call or pop by the office to see what can be done. (And as the schedules are often subject to change anyway, it's clever to reconfirm the departure schedule in advance.)

If you miss out on the GTSC buses, or opt not to use them, your best bet for gelly-gellys and other transport along the South Bank Road is the hectic main bus station in the town of Brikama, which lies about 23km south of Westfield Junction. Coming from Banjul or Serekunda, you'll find that plenty of shared taxis run back and forth to Brikama all day, leaving Banjul from Rene Blain Road and Serekunda from the south end of Mosque Road. The other place to pick up gelly-gellys and shared taxis upriver is Bundung Taxi Park (✪ 13.4187, -16.6764), also known as Buffer Zone, which lies opposite Bundung Police Station 500m northwest of the Brikama Road and 4km south of Westfield Junction. However, while Bundung is significantly closer to Serekunda, it is less convenient to get to than Brikama, and departures inland are less regular.

WHERE TO STAY

Accommodation options in Fajara and Serekunda are surprisingly limited, but do include what is arguably the country's premier beachfront boutique hotel in the form of Ngala Lodge. There are also a couple of well-established and justifiably popular cheaper options close to Kairaba Avenue, notably the YMCA, which is well positioned for catching public transport upriver from the GTSC bus station.

EXCLUSIVE/LUXURY

☀ Ngala Lodge [114 C1] (24 suites) 64 Atlantic Bd, Fajara; ☎ 449 4045; m 247 1072; e info@ngalalodge.com; w ngalalodge.com. One of the country's most prestigious & luxurious hotels, Ngala Lodge is a sedate, child-free, all-suite retreat set in a converted 1940s ambassadorial residence perched on a low cliff overlooking the beach close to the British High Commission. Each of the suites & semi-suites are individually decorated, but they all share a strong sense of style & fun in the choice of vintage & contemporary artworks from Africa (& further afield), very comfortable furnishings including a king-size bed with walk-in mosquito net, & excellent facilities including AC, fan, minibar & in most cases a private balcony or garden. A separate Manor House comprises 4 suites, a private garden & a sitting area with TV. The 6 Macondo sea-view suites are newer, each unique & spacious featuring touches such as private libraries, & 3 have private plunge pools making them among the best rooms in The Gambia. Rooms in the main hotel are centred on the small infinity pool, which leads down to the (exceptional) terrace restaurant, then through lush & shady tropical gardens to the cliff & a short footpath down to a semi-private swimming beach. Other facilities include live music on most nights, an excellent library & easily arranged excursions to most sites of interest. The whole experience is enhanced by the dynamic, responsive management & attentive staff. *Book through The Gambia Experience (page 52): from £162/204/256 lodge/manor/Macondo suites B&B.* **$$$$$**

MID-RANGE

Pelican Residence [114 C2] (10 rooms) Garba Jahumpa Rd; ☎ 449 5360; m 388 5085; e reservation@pelicanresidence.com; w pelicanresidence.com. Lying 500m east of Kairaba Av & not far from Timbooktoo bookshop, this is a clean & quiet option with comfortable & modern en-suite rooms set in a trim green garden. Good value. *£23/26/53 basic/standard/suite.* **$$**

BUDGET

☀ Leybato Hotel [114 A1] (19 rooms) Off Atlantic Bd, Fajara; ☎ 449 7186; m 990 2408, 311 4147; e leybato47@hotmail.com. One of the oldest & best-known establishments in this part of The Gambia, this sprawling lodge is set among a little oasis of tropical trees & plants at the base of a fairly steep cliff on the eastern verge of Fajara Beach. A popular hangout for expats & volunteers, it has the chilled feel of a superior backpacker hostel, epitomised by the thatched summer huts & hammocks scattered through the shady grounds. The en-suite African-style huts are a bit gloomy inside & certainly showing their age, but clean & acceptable enough considering the price & location, & they come with queen-size bed, net & fan. A restaurant/bar serves inexpensive meals & drinks. It's reached 250m along a winding dirt road that extends northward from the junction of Kairaba Av & Atlantic Bd. Good value. *£20/26 dbl with fan/AC.* **$$**

Sarawally Guesthouse [112 A3] (5 rooms) off Kairaba Av; m 343 5682; e marionaffbb22@gmail.com; 📷. Hidden away about 400m west of Kairaba Av, this homey address is ideal if you don't need to be right on the water. Rooms are scrupulously clean & come with canopy beds & fans. *£16/19 sgl/dbl with shared bath, £19/23 sgl/dbl en-suite.* **$$**

SHOESTRING

YMCA [112 C3] (34 rooms) MDI Rd, Kanifing; ☎ 439 2647; m 245 5413, 760 9081, 316 0592; e reservation@ymca.gm; w ymca.gm. Situated around the corner from Serekunda Hospital & about 10mins' walk north of the GTSC bus station, this clean & well-managed 3-storey hostel is one of the best shoestring–budget options in Greater Banjul. A variety of rooms & small apts are on offer, all with fan, & substantial discounts are available for longer stays. A restaurant serves meals in the £2–3 range from 09.00 to midnight except Sun. *£7/8/12 room with shared bath/en-suite/AC.* **$**

✗ WHERE TO EAT AND DRINK

UPMARKET

☀ Ngala Restaurant [114 C1] 64 Atlantic Bd; m 728 6647, 247 1107; w ngalalodge.com; ⏰ 07.30–10.30 & 12.30–22.00 daily; booking recommended in high season. The small restaurant at Ngala Lodge is one of the most exclusive places to eat in The Gambia, offering the option of sitting in the open-sided interior or on a wide terrace perched on a clifftop overlooking the sea. The emphasis is on seafood, but not exclusively so, & the imaginative fusion menu, prepared by a European chef, is supplemented by several daily specials, depending on the availability of fresh ingredients. Lunch includes a selection of light pasta dishes, while the dinner menu has a strong selection of Thai dishes. The wine list is exceptional too, largely exclusive to only Ngala, & there is live music most nights. Unlike the majority of other restaurants, there is usually only 1 evening sitting so you can make a whole night of it. *Mains in the £9–12 range (lunch), or £15–25 (dinner).* $$$$$

The Butcher's Shop [114 B2] Kairaba Av; \ 449 5069; f TheButchersShopGambia; ⊕ 09.00–23.00. Another perennially popular veteran of the Fajara dining-out scene, this stylish bistro & delicatessen, which opened in 1993, has a varied continental-style menu, with the main emphasis on meat, though vegetarians & pescetarians will also find plenty to choose from among the salads & pastas. Seating is on a lovely tree-shaded wooden terrace, & it has an excellent wine & dessert menu. *Mains mostly in the £7–10 range.* $$$

MID-RANGE

✳ **Fajara Garden** [114 B1] Off Atlantic Bd; m 371 7777, 383 7056; ◙ thefajaragarden. Opened in early 2023 under the same management as the Alliance Café, it's hard to say no to the garden party vibes & Afro-international cuisine (try the profiteroles with baobab crème) at this classy new address. B/fast, lunch & dinner daily; drop by in the evenings for kora, jazz or salsa. *Mains £6–8.* $$$

The Clay Oven [114 B1] 1 block south of Atlantic Bd; \ 449 6600, 449 6978; m 797 3737; e vimal@ theclayoven.gm; w theclayoven.gm; ⊕ noon–23.30 daily. Widely regarded to be the country's best Indian restaurant, The Clay Oven has been under the same hands-on owner-management team since it first opened its doors at Cape Point in 1991. Now situated on a back road in Fajara, it offers garden or AC indoor seating & an extensive menu of oven-baked tandoor dishes & curries, as well as a varied Chinese selection. Vegetarians are well catered for, the bar is well stocked, & there's Wi-Fi. *Mains £6–10 inc rice or naan.* $$$

BUDGET

✳ **Alliance Café** [112 C4] m 371 7777; w alliancecafegm.com. Drop in to this charming garden café at the Alliance Française for waffles, pastries, brunch, Gambian plates & probably the best coffee in town. Wi-Fi. *Meals £3–5.* $$

Fast Ali's [112 C5] Westfield Junction; m 991 1229; ⊕ 10.00–23.00 Mon–Sat. This Lebanese fast-food institution at Westfield Junction serves up quick & easy shawarmas alongside heaping plates of *ful*, hummus, stuffed grape leaves & other Levantine delights for bargain prices. No alcohol. *Meals £2–5.* $$

La Parisienne [112 A2] Kairaba Av; m 766 0676; f laparisiennegambia; ⊕ 08.00–01.00 daily. Established in 1996 in a prime spot opposite the US Embassy, this excellent café has the choice of indoor seating with blasting AC or outdoor seating on a wide veranda. A good spot for b/fast & good coffee or pastries, croissants, sandwiches, homemade ice cream & light meals anytime. Wi-Fi. *Meals £3–5.* $$

Am'Harit [112 B2] m 789 6181; f amharit.gm. This friendly local hangout just off Kairaba Av does a good & very affordable array of Gambian plates (including a daily dish) &, apropos of nothing, also has a virtual reality gaming setup! *Mains £2–5.* $–$$

ENTERTAINMENT AND NIGHTLIFE

✳ **Bob's Bar & Cafe** [114 A1] Off Atlantic Bd; m 904 5291. This locally run bar is on the sandy track leading over a ridge towards the Leybato Hotel & is a fantastic spot to enjoy the local Rasta vibes. Enjoy a cold beer in the brightly painted roundhouse or the small garden courtyard while listening to reggae. Bob can rustle up meals on demand & can also organise drumming lessons. Not only that, but he's a skilled hat maker, & displays his wares around the bar.

Propaganda Sports Bar [114 B2] Kairaba Av; m 750 7356. About 300m & an entire world away from the rootsy atmosphere at Bob's, this shiny new bar complex is fully on-trend, with a cool modernist vibe, shisha, billiards & plenty of footy on the TVs. If you'd rather dance, Envy Nightclub (m 348 8891) is in the same building & equally glitzy.

Bakau's most popular tourist attraction, Kachikally Crocodile Pool, is home to over 50 crocs PAGE 109

right
(AVZ)

Diminutive red-flanked duikers can be spotted in Bolong Fenyo Community Wildlife Reserve PAGE 169

below left
(mG/S)

Listen out for the spotted hyena's eerie nocturnal hooting, which can be heard for up to 5km PAGE 36

below right
(DH/S)

Green monkeys are the most numerous monkey species in The Gambia PAGE 36

bottom left
(SP/S)

Gambia is home to two species of chameleon, which can be found throughout the country PAGE 42

bottom right
(IZ/S)

top left
(PP/S)
Hundreds of pelicans roost in the Tanji Bird Reserve every year, with numbers peaking over June to August PAGE 158

top right
(DJ/S)
Kotu is renowned for offering a great introduction to birdwatching in The Gambia, hosting gorgeous specimens like the blue-bellied roller PAGE 47

above left
(PP/S)
There is a well-known colony of red-throated bee-eaters at Bansang, towards The Gambia's eastern frontier PAGE 254

above right
(APA/S)
Rarities like western bluebill can be spotted without even leaving the city at Bijilo Forest Park PAGE 145

below
(PP/S)
Numerous pools, marshes and swamps throughout the country are reliable haunts for the elegant African jacana PAGE 47

African fish eagles keep a regular watch over the Gambia River and its many tributaries PAGE 47

above
(DJ/S)

Malachite kingfishers are often found near the Kau-ur Swamp PAGE 234

right
(TC/S)

Watch pied kingfishers hunt at Cape Creek, just outside of Bakau PAGE 111

below left
(DM/S)

Oriole warblers can be spotted at the Abuko Nature Reserve, as well as several of the coastal resorts PAGE 180

below right
(APA/S)

left
(JD/S)
Peanuts are a staple crop in The Gambia and can be bought freshly roasted throughout the country PAGE 74

below left
(AVZ)
Drumming is an essential part of African music and, particularly in rural areas, the beating of drums is a typical Gambian sound PAGE 23

below
(LM/S)
Locally grown gourds are used to shake out a rhythm in traditional Gambian music and dance PAGE 23

bottom
(CP/S)
Tanji is one of the country's busiest fishing ports, where hundreds of colourful pirogues haul their catch up on to the beach every day PAGE 162

The ruins of Fort James on tiny Kunta Kinteh Island form the most important relict of the slave trade in The Gambia PAGE 202

above
(PPL/S)

The twin villages of Albreda and Juffureh are an important pilgrimage site, particularly for members of the African diaspora PAGE 198

right
(s/S)

Zimba is one of many masquerade styles in The Gambia, which are displayed at the annual Janjanbureh Kankurang Festival PAGE 251

below
(AVZ)

above
(SS)

The cliffs that dominate the coastline around Fajara give way to open swathes of sand that make up the gorgeous Fajara Beach PAGE 119

left
(AVZ)

The central feature of the country is the River Gambia, bisecting the North and South banks PAGE 30

below
(CP/S)

Mangrove-lined *bolongs* (creeks) splay out in all directions from the mighty River Gambia PAGE 30

Within the Makasutu Cultural Forest and set alongside Mandina Creek, Mandina Lodges is home to both plentiful birdlife and a peaceful bush atmosphere PAGE 187

above (AVZ)

The Bijilo Forest Park is one of the best-preserved habitats of its type in the country, home to a dense population of red colobus and the more elusive patas monkey PAGE 145

right (AVZ)

The sandy beach, dotted with palm trees, is Kololi's main attraction PAGE 133

below (AVZ)

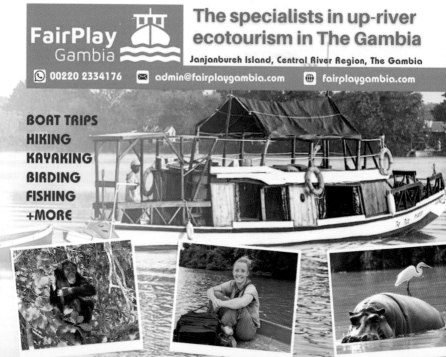

OTHER PRACTICALITIES

BANKING AND FOREIGN EXCHANGE Serekunda is serviced by the largest concentration of banks and ATMs in the country. These include branches of Standard Chartered Bank [112 A1], Access Bank [112 A2], GT Bank [112 A2] and EcoBank [112 B3] on Kairaba Avenue, as well as another EcoBank [112 D4] and GT Bank [112 D4] on opposite sides of the Banjul–Serekunda Highway near the turn-off to the GTSC station, as well as a GT Bank on Sayerrjobe Avenue near Serekunda Market. There is also a cluster of banks around Westfield Junction [112 C5].

If you are staying in **Fajara**, the closest banks with an ATM, depending on exactly where you are, would be the Standard Chartered Bank [114 B3] at the junction of Kairaba Avenue and Bertil Harding Highway, or the Trust Bank on Atlantic Boulevard in Bakau. For private foreign-exchange facilities, there are a few forex bureaux around Serekunda Market [112 B6], but this is quite a busy area so you're better off changing large sums elsewhere.

INTERNET All hotels in the area now offer Wi-Fi.

MEDICAL Though not exactly operating to Western standards, the **Westfield Clinic** [112 C5] (Westfield Junction; m 329 0065; w thewestfieldclinic.com; f wfcgambia) is one of the best-equipped clinics in the country. The well-regarded **Malak Pharmacy** [112 A2] (Kairaba Av; ☏ 437 6087; m 770 0719) near the US Embassy is open until midnight daily (22.00 Sun).

SHOPPING In addition to the chaotic but compelling **Serekunda Market** [112 B6], Serekunda is endowed with many good supermarkets, most of them concentrated along the north end of Kairaba Avenue near the US Embassy and Fajara. Perhaps the best stocked is the **Safeway Supermarket** [112 A2], which also keeps quite long opening hours (⊕ 09.00–20.00 Mon–Sat, 10.00–20.00 Sun). One shop that warrants a special mention is:

✳**Timbooktoo** [114 B2] Garba Jahumpa Rd; ☏ 449 4345/6; m 503 3448; f TimbooktooGambia; ⊕ 10.00–19.00 Mon–Fri (closed 13.00–15.00 on Fri), 10.00–20.00 Sat. Far & away the best bookshop in The Gambia, Timbooktoo spreads across 2 storeys & stocks an excellent range of reference books about the country (& West Africa in general), as well as current & classic English-language fiction, popular non-fiction, textbooks, guidebooks, field guides, maps, newspapers & local music CDs. It also has a selection of secondhand novels.

WHAT TO SEE AND DO

FAJARA BEACH Fajara feels more suburban than resort-like, and most of its coastline is hemmed in by low cliffs and cut off from public access by private properties. The main exception is in the far west, where the cliffs give way to the open swathes of sand that comprise the popular Fajara and Kotu beaches. This lovely beach can be accessed either by following the footpath to Kotu that runs along the northern boundary of the golf course and Fajara Waterfront housing complex, or else by taking the dirt road that runs from the north end of Kairaba Avenue to the Leybato Hotel.

FAJARA CLUB [114 A2] (⊕ 13.4668, -16.6974; m 705 3821; f TheFajaraClub; ⊕ 08.00–sunset daily) An offshoot of the colonial Bathurst Club, established in the

6

1930s and originally housed in what is now the National Museum, the Fajara Club was renamed and relocated to its present-day location between Kairaba Avenue and Kotu Stream at some point in the mid 1970s. Its main point of interest is the 18-hole par-69 golf course, which opened in 1973 to replace an older course at Denton Bridge near to Banjul. An unusual feature of the course, attributed to the sandy soil on which it stands and the seasonally dry climate, is that instead of the usual greens, it has 'browns' which need to be tidied up by brown-sweepers between games. Other facilities include a swimming pool, tennis and squash courts, a full-size billiards table, a reasonably priced restaurant serving decent pub grub, and a lively bar dominated by a large-screen TV that draws big crowds for major international sporting events.

The Fajara Golf Course [114 A3] is also renowned as a very good birding spot. There is a range of habitats from open areas to coastal scrub and a few tangled patches of woodland. The course also lies alongside part of Kotu Stream and holds lots of different birds, with black-headed plover and wattled plover on the open areas, Senegal coucal and African silverbill among the scrub, and pearl-spotted owlet in the taller trees. The black-shouldered kite is one of several birds of prey sometimes seen flying over the course.

The Fajara Club is a members-only institution, but visitors are welcome to take out temporary membership. For golfers, this works out at £26 per person per round, inclusive of green fee, club hire, balls, caddy, brown-sweeper and mat, with a discount if you have your own clubs. Note that quite a strict golfing dress code is maintained: no denim, and all shirts must have a collar and sleeves. For other facilities, you are looking at around £4 per person per day for use of any of the following: swimming pool, tennis or squash courts, or billiards table. Access to the bar and restaurant costs around £1.50, though it is included in all the above fees. The well-equipped **Flex Fitness** (m 299 9777; ◙ flexfitnessgambia) gym is also located here.

FAJARA WAR CEMETERY [114 B3] Maintained by the Commonwealth War Graves Commission (w cwgc.org), this military cemetery on the east side of Kairaba Avenue contains the graves of 203 soldiers, mostly Gambian and British in origin, who died in combat in World War II, when Banjul (then Bathurst) was an important Allied naval base. In keeping with the racist attitudes that informed European colonialism, the graves are segregated into clusters, some exclusively for soldiers of indigenous Gambian origin, others reserved for combatants of European descent. All but four of the combatants are identified by name, and there are ten non-war service burials and three war graves of non-Commonwealth nationalities. The cemetery also contains the Royal West African Frontier Forces (RWAFF) Memorial Tablet, which commemorates another 33 Gambians who died in service but whose last resting place is either unknown or cannot be maintained.

AFRICAN LIVING ART CENTRE [114 C2] (Garba Jahumpa Rd; m 706 6607, 744 9090; w gambiaweddingplanners.com; ◷ noon–18.00 daily; entrance free) Owned and managed by an extraordinary Gambian hairstylist and beautician who learned his craft in the fashion and beauty houses of New York, the African Living Art Centre is an eclectic and idiosyncratic set-up that operates primarily as an upmarket salon and 'beauty sanctuary' specialising in hairdressing, massage, chiropractic treatments, manicures, pedicures, facials, bodywork, makeovers, bridals and wedding planning. It also incorporates an art gallery, where textiles, masks, beads and statues can be bought, and exhibitions, vernissages and group events – like

PAPER RECYCLING SKILLS PROJECT   *By George Riegg, General Manager*

Established in 2001 as the first paper mill in The Gambia, the Paper Recycling Skills Project (PRSP) (m 770 7090, 774 8058; e icecool@qanet.gm; PaperRecyclingGambia) is a registered non-profit organisation based in Fajikunda, about 3km south of Westfield Junction off the Brikama Road. In its early days, the PRSP introduced the traditional craft of papermaking to The Gambia, allowing it to recycle used paper and other waste materials into handcrafted value-added products. All profits from the sale of the various products were invested into supporting education either by distributing free learning materials to needy students (over 45,000 exercise books plus pens, pencils and reading books) or by providing training and teaching assistance in environmental-awareness building through lectures, workshops and community outreach programmes.

After moving to the PRSP Craft Village compound in Fajikunda in 2007, the organisation developed new programmes to expand its positive impact on the environment and in the community. It developed a technique to turn freely available waste materials (such as paper, grasses, leaves, sawdust and other biomass) into fuel briquettes to be used for cooking instead of firewood or charcoal. It has also helped develop a cleaner-burning fuel-efficient domestic stove which can use the briquettes (as well as wood and charcoal), saving the user up to two-thirds of normal fuel expenditure. These initiatives are creating economic and health benefits for the community, while the reduced need for wood and charcoal saves many trees in a country with an ever-depleting forest cover. An 18-month project during 2011/12 firmly established PRSP as the country's foremost 'Biomass Recycling Research and Training Centre', and it now trains community groups to replicate the technology elsewhere in the country.

Since 2012, the PRSP compound has been turned into a 'walk-the-talk' showpiece for sustainable living and a balanced ecosystem, demonstrating that living in harmony with the environment brings many benefits. More than 80 trees representing 30-plus species have been planted alongside 60 other types of plants (flowers, shrubs, herbs and vegetables) to create a diverse mini ecosystem using permaculture techniques. Recycled tyres, old bricks and other waste materials have been used for the hard landscaping. Compost toilets provide nutrition for the plants and reduce waste. Grey water is used for the gardens, and a small solar installation provides electricity. A tree nursery has been established to provide seedlings of fruit-bearing trees free to the community.

The Craft Village is also home to the 'Greenie' movement, which links together environmental initiatives in schools and communities with various private, corporate and institutional partners. The 'Greenie' mascot is a little doll used to promote environmental activities understandably through media such as school books, posters, leaflets and training guides. Environmental awareness is a complex issue, and personalising it 'Greenie' helps to communicate positive messages to children and adults alike. True to the 'Greenie' motto 'together we CAN do it', the PRSP team warmly welcomes visitors interested in real sustainable community action.

painting and wine nights – are regularly held. See their social media for details. The centre's highly rated restaurant and bar, YOSH (m 712 2121; yosh_gambia;

mains £8–10; $$$), serves an impressively eclectic menu ranging from Africa all the way to Asia and the Caribbean – sometimes in the same dish!

SEREKUNDA MARKET [112 B6] If you want a taste of unadorned modern-day West Africa, try a visit to Serekunda Market, on the corner of Sayerr Jobe and Mosque roads. This is a hive of activity and you can buy anything from traditional African clothes to stiletto heels, alongside sticky tape, USB sticks, fine fabrics, traditional medicines, TVs and tools. It is crowded and noisy and sometimes smelly (especially near the stalls that sell spice), so it can be a real culture shock to those more used to pushing a shopping trolley along sanitised aisles in a spotlessly clean supermarket. This is a good safe place to meet ordinary Gambians and see what their world is really like, but do keep your valuables tucked away and a wary eye open for pickpockets. If you are at all nervous about visiting the market, take an official guide or a Gambian friend with you. They'll look out for you and show you around.

THE 'BIG TREE' AND SEREKUNDA BATIK FACTORY Situated close to each other along Mosque Road in the area known as Dippa Kunda, these two attractions are well worth combining with a visit to the nearby Serekunda Market. The more interesting for craft hunters is the batik factory [112 B5] (\ 439 2258), started by the late Mussu Kebba Drammeh, where you can see the tie-dye process in action, from the design, waxing and boiling to the finished product, and also buy batiks at source. To get there from the direction of the market, follow Mosque Road north for around 1km, then turn to the right, and you should see it on the right-hand side of the road behind a woodcarving factory. If in doubt, ask directions, as the place is well known locally, or call for directions as you get close. Far more easily located is the 'Big Tree' [112 A4], a massive silk cotton tree on the west side of Mosque Road about 500m past the batik factory next to Latrikunda Market.

ALLIANCE FRANÇAISE [112 C4] (Kairaba Av; \ 437 5418; e info@afbanjul.org; w afbanjul.org; �f AllianceFrancaiseBanjul) Serekunda's Alliance Française de Banjul is a French cultural centre whose primary purpose is to hold French classes and art and photography exhibitions, as well as cinema screenings and a variety of cultural performances. It's also home to the excellent Alliance Café (page 118). The centre's website is a good place to check out not only what is happening at the Alliance Française itself, but also what's happening culturally in the rest of the country.

MEMORY HOUSE [112 D2] (w aneked.org/memory-house; ⊕ 10.00–17.00 Tue–Sat) This powerful new museum-memorial chronicling abuses committed under former president Yahya Jammeh and the victims' ongoing quest for justice is a sombre counterpoint to The Gambia's freewheeling, 'smiling coast' package-tour reputation. After Jammeh's election loss and 2017 flight to exile in Equatorial Guinea, a government-mandated Truth, Reconciliation and Reparations Commission (TRRC) was formed to discover and catalogue the many human rights abuses committed during his 1994–2017 reign. Over this time, hundreds of people, from journalists and activists to people accused of witchcraft and unfortunate bystanders, were disappeared and murdered by government forces. Hundreds testified before the committee, which released its findings in December 2021, recommending dozens of prosecutions – which have yet to be carried out. The small museum, administered by the African Network against Extrajudicial Killings and Enforced Disappearances (ANEKED), displays portraits, testimonies and personal effects from some of the regime's many victims as part of its permanent exhibition, 'The Duty to Remember'. ANEKED also continues the work begun by the TRRC, employing agents to collect, preserve and share testimony from victims and their relatives around the country.

EBUNJAN THEATRE [112 D2] (m 998 1336, 351 8188; ⏹ EbunJan) Gambia's only theatre was founded in 2011 by indefatigable UK-trained dramaturge Janet Badjan-Young, better known as Auntie Janet. Performances here are emphatically not a spectacle for tourists: the troupe's animating philosophy is to share ideas and discuss social issues, utilising theatre arts as a medium and a tool for social development in The Gambia. As such, some of the performances have a pedagogical bent, discussing contemporary questions of clandestine migration or the traditional practice of female genital mutilation, while others reach deep into the African theatrical canon, like the run of Nigerian author Wole Soyinka's 1959 play *The Lion and the Jewel*. Performances are typically in English, and sometimes in Wolof or Mandinka. Check their Facebook page to see what's on; tickets are available at Timbooktoo bookshop (page 119).

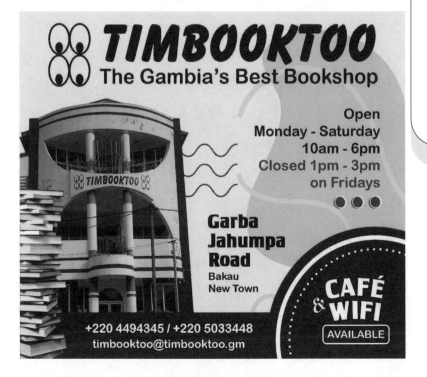

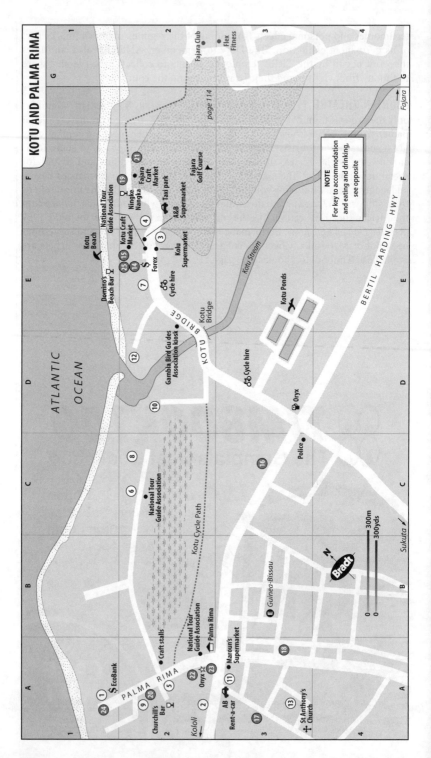

KOTU AND PALMA RIMA

ATLANTIC OCEAN

PALMA RIMA

Kotu Beach

Domino's Beach Bar

National Tour Guide Association

Kotu Craft Market

Forex

Cycle hire

National Tour Guide Association

Gambia Bird Gu des Association kiosk

KOTU BRIDGE

Kotu Bridge

Ningke Nangka

Fajara Craft Market

Taxi park

A&B Supermarket

Kolu Supermarket

page 114

Kotu Stream

Kotu Ponds

Fajara Golf Course

Fajara Club

Flex Fitness

BERTIL HARDING HWY

Fajara →

Kotu Cycle Path

Craft stalls

National Tour Guide Association

Palma Rima

Onyx ☆

Maroun's Supermarket

AB Rent-a-car

St Anthony's Church

Churchill's Bar

EcoBank

Cycle hire

Police

Oryx

E Guinea-Bissau

Kololi →

Sukuta →

NOTE
For key to accommodation and eating and drinking, see opposite

Bradt

N

0   300m
0   300yds

124

7

Kotu and Palma Rima

Ranking second only to nearby Kololi as the most developed resort area along the Gambian coast, Kotu lies on a wide sandy beach that runs southwest from Fajara for about 2km. The area is bisected by and named after Kotu Stream, a small mangrove-lined waterway which, despite its relatively small catchment area of around 60km², can lay claim to being the busiest birdwatching site in the country. Indeed, Kotu Bridge, which crosses the stream about 400m upriver of its mouth, and whose north bank houses the official Gambia Bird Guides Association kiosk, has become such a popular rendezvous for avitourists that on a busy day it can look a bit like a binocular salesperson's convention!

Although Kotu is a popular and recommended base for birdwatchers, the area is also well suited to more conventional beach tourism, being rather more hassle-free than its counterpart at Kololi, and endowed with several new upmarket package hotels, as well as dozens of restaurants, beach bars and other tourist facilities. The main cluster of development, generally referred to as Kotu, flanks a short strip of surfaced road that runs from the north bank of Kotu Stream to Kotu Beach. About 1.5km west of the stream lies a secondary cluster of developments generally known as Palma Rima (after the well-known resort hotel that lies at the junction with the Bertil Harding Highway). These two built-up areas are separated from each other by a largely uninhabited area of coastal marsh that runs west from Kotu Stream and can be explored from the pedestrian-friendly 1.2km Kotu Cycle Path. Palma Rima in particular has seen a cluster of new upmarket hotel developments open here in recent years, while several long-serving Kotu hotels have also undergone extensive renovations.

KOTU AND PALMA RIMA
For listings, see from page 126

Where to stay
1 African Princess Beach...................A1	8 Kunta Kinteh Beach Complex...............C2
2 Bakadaji...A2	9 Luigi's Apartments...................................A2
3 Bakotu...E2	10 Palm Beach...D2
4 Bungalow Beach.................................F2	11 Riyan Apartments.................................A3
5 Calabash Residence..........................A2	12 Sunset Beach..D2
6 Kalimba Beach Resort......................C2	13 Teranga Suites..A3
7 Kombo Beach.......................................E2	

Where to eat and drink
14 Ali Baba Pizza......................................E2	19 Paradise Beach Club.............................F2
15 Aroma Bar & Restaurant...................E2	20 Patta Patta Restaurant & Bar..............A2
16 Bamboo Garden Chinese.................C3	21 Sailor's Bar & Restaurant....................F2
17 Blagger's...A3	22 Samba's Kitchen...................................A2
18 Cafe Denmark....................................A3	23 Shiraz..A2
Kunta Kinteh Beach..................(see 8)	24 Solomon's Beach Bar & Restaurant......A1
Luigi's Pizza & Pasta House......(see 9)	25 Tandoor...E2

Coming directly from Banjul International Airport, it's a drive of around 22km to Kotu via Yundum and Sukuta, costing around £20 in a taxi.

Heading to Fajara or Bakau, the easiest option (at least from Kotu itself) is to walk along the footpath that runs uphill from the east of the beach through the new Fajara Waterfont housing development to the cul-de-sac at the west of Atlantic Boulevard, from where a steady flow of shared taxis runs past the north end of Kairaba Avenue to Cape Point.

The most direct connection between Kotu and Palma Rima is the Kotu Cycle Path, which can be walked in about 10–15 minutes. To travel between them by car, you need to head back south to the Bertil Harding Highway.

Kotu lies about 16km west of Banjul via the Banjul–Serekunda Highway and Bertil Harding Highway. Catch one of the regular bush taxis to Kololi (Senegambia) that leave Banjul from the station on Rene Blain Street opposite Gamtel House, ask to be dropped at Kotu Police Station (for Kotu) or Palma Rima, then walk or catch a taxi.

Taxis to pretty much anywhere you want can be picked up on the main strip through Kotu, where the main taxi stand is tucked away opposite the Bungalow Beach Hotel. However, since they are official tourist taxis, they tend to be quite expensive. A cheaper option is to walk up to the junction with Bertil Harding Highway and pick up a shared or private taxi there.

 ## WHERE TO STAY

UPMARKET/LUXURY

African Princess Beach Hotel [124 A1] (141 rooms) Palma Rima Rd; ✆ 446 2426; m 733 3354; e info@africanprincesshotel.com; w africanprincesshotel.com. On the beach at the end of the Palma Rima Rd, this large new resort boasts some seriously stylish Sahel-inspired architecture, 8 swimming pools, 2 restaurants, gym, beauty salon & a very convenient EcoBank ATM. Opened in 2018, the rooms are modern & handsomely appointed, & ground-floor rooms have swim-up terraces where you can relax on a chaise longue set ankle-deep in the water. *From £150 dbl B&B, with low season discounts.* **$$$$$**

Bakadaji Hotel [124 A2] (80 rooms) Bertil Harding Hwy; m 222 5556; w bakadajihotel.gm; ◻ bakadajihotelgambia. Completely rebuilt & reopened in 2023, this beautiful new option may have the same name, but is unrecognisably chic compared with its previous incarnation. Situated on the north side of Palma Rima Junction, the modern rooms here are set along a street-facing 1st-floor terrace, or clustered around the freeform swimming pool; all are finely equipped & done up in African décor. There's a spa & fitness centre, plus a restaurant serving buffets & BBQs at w/ends.

£80/100 standard sgl/dbl, £105/120 deluxe sgl/dbl, all rates B&B. **$$$$**

Kalimba Beach Resort [124 C2] (91 rooms) Off Palma Rima Rd; m 290 0364, 732 7777; e bookings@kalimbaresort.com; w kalimbaresort. com. Opened at the end of 2019, this new resort is one of The Gambia's most modern feeling, with whitewashed villas facing an angular swimming pool that snakes its way across the whole beachfront property. The large rooms are handsomely appointed with canopy beds & rainfall showers, & you can swim right up to the deluxe rooms. There's also a gym, spa & 2 restaurants. *From £108 dbl B&B, with low season discounts.* **$$$$**

Sunset Beach Hotel [124 D2] (97 rooms) Kotu Stream Rd; ✆ 446 3876, 446 6397; e info@ sunsetbeachhotel.gm; w sunsetbeachhotel.gm. This friendly, unpretentious & well-managed package hotel combines an attractive beachfront location on the east shore of the Kotu Stream mouth with good facilities including a pleasant swimming-pool area, free Wi-Fi, mini market, beauty salon & live music most nights. The spacious standard rooms come with twin/dbl bed & have tiled floor, bright modern décor, AC, sat

TV & en-suite hot shower. *From £100/130 sgl/dbl all-inclusive. Good low-season discounts available (B&B).* **$$$$**

Kombo Beach Hotel [124 E2] (258 rooms) Kotu Beach; 446 5466; m 712 6013; e info@ kombobeachhotel.gm; w kombobeachhotel.gm. The largest, busiest & smartest of the package hotels in Kotu, Kombo Beach can come across as a little impersonal, which is understandable given its size, but it has a great beachfront location, good service & a vast swimming pool, beach bar, clinic, gift shop, good spa & salon, & sports such as table tennis, tennis, volleyball, billiards, darts, archery & an outdoor gym. The entire complex was undergoing significant renovations as of mid-2023, so the resort ought to be looking especially sharp by the time you read this. *Rooms from £45/55 standard sgl/dbl, but rates are likely to change after renovations are complete.* **$$$**

MID-RANGE

✳ **Kunta Kinteh Beach Complex** [124 C2] (21 bungalows) 446 4875; m 515 3680, 900 3922; e kuntakintehcomplex@gmail.com; w kuntakinteh.com. Accessed via a 1km road running east from Palma Rima Rd opposite Luigi's, this complex next to the beach restaurant of the same name offers self-catering accommodation in 2-bedroom bungalows scattered along the beach immediately west of the Kotu Stream mouth. All apts come with dbl beds, well-equipped kitchens, sitting rooms with sat TV, clean bathrooms & private balcony. If you choose not to self-cater, you can eat at the neighbouring beach restaurant (page 129). There is a hair salon that also offers beauty treatments, a craft shop & a tailor that can knock up local attire. Several sports such as football, beach volleyball & fishing can be organised. Good value. *£52 standard dbl; £370/ week up to 2 people. Price inc airport transfers if required.* **$$$**

Bakotu Hotel [124 E2] (88 rooms) Kotu Stream Rd; 446 5555; e bookings@bakotuhotel.com; w bakotuhotel.com. This appealing medium-sized family-run hotel on the landward side of the main strip is perhaps the best of the cheaper package options in Kotu. It has also long been a popular choice with birdwatchers thanks to its leafy gardens & short nature walk leading to a well-positioned private viewing platform overlooking

Kotu Stream. It is only a couple of mins' walk from Kotu Beach, & has an agreeable swimming-pool area with sun terrace. The en-suite rooms are simply but tastefully furnished, & there is also an annex of apts with kitchenette, living area & private terrace overlooking the Kotu Stream. Other facilities include an on-site mini market, 2 good restaurants, a bar & evening entertainment. *From £60/65 sgl/dbl B&B.* **$$$**

Calabash Residence [124 A2] (15 rooms) Palma Rima Rd; 446 2293; m 777 6600; e info@ calabashresidence.gm; w calabashresidence. gm. Located a few doors up from Luigi's, this agreeable complex offers accommodation in modern spacious studios or 1- or 2-bedroom apts distinguished by their warm earth colours & above-average facilities. Each bedroom is en suite with combined tub/shower & queen-size or dbl bed, & the 1-bedroom apts also have a large open-plan sitting area with sat TV & well-equipped kitchen. The swimming pool is in a pretty tropical garden with attractive thatched umbrellas & palm trees to provide shade. *£53 dbl studio, £70/105 1-/2-bedroom apt.* **$$$**

Riyan Apartments [124 A3] (19 rooms) Bertil Harding Hwy; 446 3734; e riyanapartments@ gmail.com; w riyanapartments.com. Though it isn't very convenient for the beach, this apt complex on the junction of Palma Rima Rd seems like a pretty classy set-up, centred on a courtyard swimming pool shaded by palms with bar. The spacious & modern apts all come with a proper kitchen, a comfortable sitting area with sat TV, dark-wood furnishing, private balcony & 1 or 2 bedrooms with twin or dbl beds & nets. *€38/65 sgl/dbl, with attractive discounts for low season or longer stays.* **$$$**

BUDGET

✳ **Luigi's Apartments** [124 A2] (33 rooms) Palma Rima Rd; m 990 8218; e info@luigis. gm; w luigis.gm. Situated in Palma Rima 200m from the beach, this smart & reasonably priced owner-managed lodge is justifiably one of the most popular in The Gambia. A variety of spacious & immaculately clean en-suite rooms & apts is available, all with stylish modern furniture, funky décor, AC, free Wi-Fi, flatscreen TV, room safe & tea/coffee. Self-catering apts also have private balconies & a well-equipped kitchen. The courtyard swimming pool area has deckchairs (but is rather lacking in shade or character) & 24hr generator backup. A hidden garden around the back contains an attractive lily pond hosting geese & peacocks. There's also an excellent Italian restaurant (see below) on the ground floor, & plenty of other good eating options within easy walking distance. *From £30/40 standard sgl/dbl B&B, from £70 self-catering apts. Weekly rates are slightly cheaper.* **$$**

Bungalow Beach Hotel [124 F2] (110 rooms) Kotu Stream Rd; 446 5288, 446 5623; e info@ bbhotel.gm. Set in large gardens in the heart of Kotu, this long-serving package hotel has been feeling rather rundown for several years now, but it's still got a great beachfront location & decent facilities including a swimming pool, children's pool, playgrounds, beach bar & restaurant, so could be an OK option if you'd like to save a few pounds without leaving the beachfront. *£35/45 sgl/dbl B&B.* **$$**

Palm Beach Hotel [124 D2] (160 rooms) Off Kotu Stream Rd; m 278 7744, 221 1938; e palmbeachhotel@hotmail.com. About the cheapest package hotel on this part of the coast, the Palm Beach has in its favour a wonderful isolated beachfront location on the west bank of the Kotu Stream mouth, & the en-suite rooms with sat TV, wooden furnishings & AC are very reasonably priced. It is rather more difficult to enthuse about the tacky décor & rather rundown & cramped feel of the dbl-storey blocks, unless you are a fan of concrete dolphin statues. Facilities include a restaurant, swimming-pool area & beach seating. With realistic expectations, it seems pretty good value. *From £35/42 standard sgl/dbl B&B.* **$$**

SHOESTRING

Teranga Suites [124 A3] (18 rooms) m 705 8886; e terangasuites@gmail.com; w terangasuites.com. Set in the backroads south of Palma Rima Junction, about 1km from the beach, this owner-managed dbl-storey lodge offers accommodation in dated but clean en-suite rooms with fan & AC. There's a small swimming pool & bar, & plenty of restaurants within easy walking distance. Timbuktu Guesthouse across the street is similarly priced but more rundown. *£12/15/25 sgl/dbl/trpl rooms.* **$**

 # WHERE TO EAT AND DRINK

There are dozens of eateries dotted around Kotu and Palma Rima, and most of the hotels also have restaurants. The following is a selective mix of well-established favourites and some interesting new places.

UPMARKET

✳ **Luigi's Pizza & Pasta House** [124 A2] Palma Rima Rd; m 710 2102, 890 5055; w luigis.gm; ⏱ 08.00–16.00 & 18.00–23.30 daily. With its airy high-ceilinged interior & pleasant terrace, this genuine Italian restaurant is something of a Gambian institution, & widely regarded to serve the best pizzas around, along with various pasta & seafood dishes, & cheaper salads & baked potatoes with toppings. It has a fully stocked bar & also serves killer coffee. *Mains £5–8.* **$$$**

✳ **Shiraz Restaurant** [124 A2] Palma Rima Rd; m 767 0000, 770 0010; ⏱ 09.00–late daily in season, 19.00–23.00 out of season. Situated close to the junction with Bertil Harding Hwy, this widely adored restaurant is The Gambia's best Lebanese, with indoor & outdoor seating, & an excellent selection of Mediterranean-style grills, shawarmas & meze dishes, plus a full bar & good selection of wine. *Mains around £6–8.* **$$$**

Paradise Beach Club [124 F2] Kotu Beach; m 707 4444; paradisebeachclubgambia; ⏱ 11.00–22.00 Tue–Sun. Bright & breezy, this stylish new address is done up in whitewash, wood & linen, with a beachfront luxury vibe that takes its cues from Bali & the Balearics & offers a brunch-friendly seafood menu. *Prices start from £6.* **$$$**

Samba's Kitchen [124 A2] Palma Rima Rd; m 988 4620, 713 9744; sambaskitchenthegambia; ⏱ 09.00–23.45 daily. Under joint British–Gambian owner-management, this restaurant at the south end of Palma Rima Rd receives plenty of good feedback. It's a multi-faceted set-up with relaxed outdoor seating on the terrace or in the courtyard, a more formal indoor dining area, & a separate sports bar with large-screen TVs, pool tables & darts. The award-winning Gambian chef is something of a celebrity & the well-crafted menu includes a varied selection of attractively presented meat & seafood dishes, as well as salads, sandwiches & other light meals. It caters for vegetarians & vegans, & will also cook fishermen's catches by request. Live music on Fri nights & all-you-can-eat buffet roast Sun lunch. *Mains in the £8–10 range, Sun buffet £9.* $$$

MID-RANGE

✳ **Sailor's Bar & Restaurant** [124 F2] Kotu Beach; m 773 2388, 777 4064; ⊕ 08.00–23.00 or later daily. Situated at the far eastern end of the road along Kotu Beach, this long-serving restaurant is one of the most consistent in the area. The funky interior is adorned with African artworks, & there's also a breezy terrace sitting area & a thatched stilted wooden platform on the beach. The focus of the dinner menu is seafood, with specialities such as paella (for 2), grilled prawns & fish, but there are also plenty of meat & chicken dishes. Light meals & sandwiches are served during the day. *Mains £6–10.* $$$

✳ **Kunta Kinteh Beach Restaurant** [124 C2] m 990 1283, 990 7294; ⊕ 08.30–midnight daily. Boasting a great beachfront location in the shade of a grove of coconut trees along a dirt road running east from Palma Rima Rd, this popular place offers the option of sitting indoors or on an umbrella-shaded terrace. The à la carte menu is dominated by seafood, steak & chicken dishes in a variety of international styles, & it does a beach BBQ buffet on Sun. It also has free sun loungers, plus entertainment on Tue, including acrobats & fire eaters. *Mains £4–6.* $$

✳ **Solomon's Beach Bar & Restaurant** [124 A1] Palma Rima Rd; m 763 0007, 994 1031; f solomonsbeachbarresto; ⊕ 08.00–23.00 daily. One of the country's longest-serving beach bars, Solomon's is set in a large round building with thatched roof at the north end of Palma Rima Rd. It serves excellent fish, prawns & other seafood, with fish & chips in foil being the speciality, & also rents out sunbeds for a nominal daily fee. *Mains £5–7.* $$

✳ **Tandoor** [124 E2] Kotu Craft Market; m 220 4144; f Tandoor.Gambia; ⊕ Oct–Mar 16.00–23.00 daily. This superb outdoor Indian restaurant fills up early at the height of the season, & little wonder when it is so reasonably priced.

Tandoor dishes such as fish or chicken tikka are particularly recommended, but it also does a good line in curries, with vegetarians being well catered for. There's inexpensive house wine & draught beer too, & an excellent traditional kora player most nights. *Expect to pay around £6 per head for mains with rice or naan bread.* $$

Cafe Denmark [124 A3] Kololi Rd; m 998 3590, 707 5102; ⊕ 08.00–late. A popular haunt for expats, locals & tourists, with a large terraced area just off the road, this serves typical Gambian & European dishes as well as a few Danish specials. There is also occasional live music & Saturday discos. *Mains £5–8.* $$$

Ali Baba Pizza [124 E2] Kotu Craft Market; m 711 2618; ⊕ Oct–Mar 17.00–23.00 daily. Situated right next to the superior Tandoor, this relaxed outdoor eatery serves good pizzas & some Gambian dishes. *Mains £5–7.* $$

Bamboo Garden Chinese Restaurant [124 C3] Bertil Harding Hwy; m 314 9995; ⊕ 16.00–midnight daily. This well-established Chinese restaurant recently moved to a new location on Bertil Harding Hwy & serves the same good range of meat & vegetarian dishes at reasonable prices, as well as excellent king prawns. *Mains with rice around £4–7.* $$

Patta Patta Restaurant & Bar [124 A2] Palma Rima Rd; m 254 7435; ⊕ 08.00–late daily, Thu–Sat in low season. This relaxed & popular owner-managed restaurant has an outdoor setting next to Luigi's & a varied menu with plenty of seafood options, as well as Gambian dishes. There's a buffet on Thu, karaoke on Sun & live local music from 22.00 on Thu, Fri & Sat. There are also 10 small but clean rooms (£30 dbl) behind the bar. *Mains are mostly around £5–7.* $$

BUDGET

Aroma Bar & Restaurant [124 E2] Kotu Craft Market; m 770 0877. Good curries, grills & smaller snacks on a relaxed shaded terrace facing the craft market. There's a full bar & a friendly owner who aims to please, but don't be in a hurry. *From £4.* $$

Blagger's [124 A3] Off Bertil Harding Hwy; m 251 7979, 203 3675. Popular with expats, this serves traditional British pub favourites, including a regular Sun roast & daily specials during the week. There is a large outdoor terrace, or head inside to catch the footie on TV. Great value. *£4–5 for most mains.* $$

ENTERTAINMENT AND NIGHTLIFE

As is the case elsewhere on the Gambian coast, the line between bars and restaurants is often quite blurred. Several of the places listed from page 128, including any of the beach restaurants, are good for a few drinks, while the likes of Samba's Kitchen, Cafe Denmark and Patta Patta have live music several nights of the week. More dedicated nightspots include **Domino's Beach Bar** [124 E1] (Kotu Beach; m 368 8104, 709 0356; ⏲ 24hrs), which has something going most nights of the week, including campfires and drumming on Tuesdays and Saturdays, and Friday and Sunday reggae nights from 22.00 'until mama call'. If you're after something a bit more familiar, **Churchill's Bar** [124 A2] (m 740 1954; ⏲ 08.00–02.00 daily) has cheap beer and affordable pub-grub in an atmosphere strongly reminiscent of a British 'local'. The **Ningke Nangka** (m 791 5622) bar and restaurant complex on the beach was being refurbished in 2023, but will likely be back hosting parties during the lifespan of this edition. And for bottle service and bling, **Onyx Nightclub** (m 211 1311; ⏲ until 06.00 daily) is probably the glitziest address in the whole of The Gambia.

OTHER PRACTICALITIES

BANKS AND FOREIGN EXCHANGE The only ATM in Kotu/Palma Rima can be found at the African Princess Hotel [124 A1], where EcoBank has a machine. Several private **forex bureaux** can also be found within 100m or so of Kotu Craft Market [124 E2] at the east end of Kotu Stream Road.

BICYCLE HIRE Two cycle-rental stands can be found along Kotu Stream Road: one opposite the Kombo Beach Hotel [124 E2] and the other closer to the junction with Bertil Harding Highway [124 D3]. Rates are about £2 per hour for short usage or £5–10 per day for longer periods.

GUIDES The **Gambia Bird Guides Association** [124 E2] (m 753 5788, 529 6803; e infogambiabirds@gmail.com; w birdguidesassociationthegambia.com), which includes around 75 official bird guides, is based in a summer house on the west side of Kotu Stream Road immediately north of the bridge. Its members guide locally but can also arrange guided day trips to birding sites elsewhere on the coast, and longer trips upriver to Tendaba, Janjanbureh and even into Senegalese sites such as Niokolo-Koba and Djoudj national parks. You can book trips ahead of time, but you can also reliably find a handful of guides in attendance at any time between 07.00 and 19.00. The guides are all competent and many are very knowledgeable indeed. Expect to pay around £10 per person for a 2-hour guided bird walk or canoe trip around Kotu Stream and Ponds, which is also a good way to feel out whether you would like a guide for trips further afield.

The **National Tour Guide Association** (m 917 3332, 999 7711) has three offices in the area: one at the entrance to Kotu Craft Market, [124 E2] one at Palma Rima Junction next to the Palma Rima Hotel, [124 A2] and a new one in front of the Kalimba Beach Resort [124 C2]. This association was created in 1997 and all its guides have official status and are government trained. They can guide to most sites in and around the Gambian coast (though you are better taking a dedicated bird guide for ornithological sites) and also set up visits to wrestling competitions and other local activities. Guide fees are around £30 per party for a half-day tour and £50 for a full day.

HEALTH AND BEAUTY Several of the smarter hotels, such as Kombo Beach and Bakotu, have spas and beauty salons attached.

INTERNET All of the hotels here now offer Wi-Fi.

SHOPPING For handicrafts and other souvenirs, the largest and best stocked of three markets in the area is **Kotu Craft Market** [124 E2], which lies on the beach side of Kotu Stream Road opposite the Bakotu Hotel. It is rivalled in scope by **Fajara Craft Market** [124 F2], which lies about 5 minutes' walk further east just before Sailor's Bar and Restaurant, and a smaller cluster of stalls in Palma Rima along the road running east towards Kunta Kinteh Beach Complex. Most of the larger hotels also have gift shops selling a more limited selection of local handicrafts at fixed prices.

For grocery shopping, the best-stocked option is the superb **Maroun's Supermarket** [124 A3] (w marounssupermarket.com), which lies on the south side of Bertil Harding Highway opposite Bakadaji Hotel, and incorporates a good butchery, delicatessen and wines and spirits section. Several lesser but still quite well-stocked **mini markets** lie along the eastern end of Kotu Stream Road within 100m or so of Kotu Craft Market, while the fresh produce market next to Fajara Craft Market is recommended for fruit and veggies.

WHAT TO SEE AND DO

The main attraction at Kotu and Palma Rima is the beach, which, despite being bisected by the Kotu Stream mouth, is now probably the best along the developed part of the Gambian coast, being less affected by erosion than its counterparts at Kololi and Bakau. The main clusters of beach developments are in Kotu immediately east of Kotu Market, and at the north end of Palma Rima Road, and both sites are serviced by several beach bars and restaurants (many of which are listed individually earlier in this chapter) serving food and chilled drinks, and renting out sunbeds for a nominal fee.

KOTU STREAM [124 D2–G4] Kotu is renowned in ornithological circles for offering a great introduction to birdwatching in The Gambia, and a good deal of this is due to the presence of Kotu Stream, which is most easily accessed where it passes beneath the road at Kotu Bridge (⊕ 13.4616, -16.7048) before it empties into the sea. International birdwatchers have been visiting this site for decades now, and even though the surrounding areas have become more urbanised, it still retains a good number of birds. Indeed, accompanied by a knowledgeable guide (and several are available at the Bird Guides Association kiosk north of the bridge, see opposite), it should be possible for an Africa novice to clock up around 40–50 species in a 2–4-hour walk, while those more experienced in local conditions might be looking at closer to 70. Especially at low tide, the mangrove-lined mud flats host plenty of waders and herons, including greater painted-snipe, pied avocet, whimbrel, spur-winged plover and Senegal thick-knee, while half a dozen kingfisher species range from the very common pied to the more elusive giant kingfisher. The site is also good for osprey and for several species associated more with woodland and thicket, including the eagerly sought oriole warbler, African silverbill and various bee-eaters.

KOTU CYCLE PATH [124 A–D2] Another famous birding site that has an amazing array of birds along its length, and has provided many thousands of birders with

7

new species for their life lists, is the 1.2km cycle path (✿ 13.4586, -16.7065) that runs between Kotu Stream and Palma Rima roads. The selection of birds here depends quite a lot on season, and how marshy conditions are, but among the more common aquatic species likely to be seen are white-faced whistling duck, African jacana, African spoonbill, squacco heron and black egret (also called the umbrella bird, for its habit of fishing with its wings ballooned outwards to form a shaded canopy). The sedge and reed beds here can be good for warblers, finches, widow birds and the localised red-billed quelea, while a notable grassland species is the yellow-throated longclaw, which often performs conspicuous aerial displays in breeding season. At dusk, this can be a good place to see the spectacular standard-winged and long-tailed nightjars.

KOTU PONDS [124 D–E3] A third key birding site is the so-called Kotu Ponds (✿ 13.4582, -16.7044), which in fact comprise a trio of flooded sewage pits reached via a short dirt road opposite Badala Park Hotel. The pits are separated from the road by about 50m of open woodland that often hosts interesting species such as blue-bellied roller, yellow-crowned gonolek and various babblers. An amazing range of waterbirds can sometimes be seen in the ponds, and the best thing is that they allow you to get fairly close. Among the hundreds of waders that might congregate around the pool margins, look out for black-winged stilt, common greenshank, wood sandpiper and spur-winged plover. There is also often a large flock of white-faced whistling duck, plus grey-headed gull, white-winged black tern and various kingfishers. Rarities here have included red-necked phalarope and tufted duck. Be warned that the sewage ponds are a working environment and trucks come regularly to empty their loads of liquid waste, so you have to be a bit careful when walking around. You may be asked a nominal fee for entry, and though this is not official, paying it will encourage the workers to keep the place hospitable for birds.

8

Kololi and Environs

There's nowhere else in West Africa quite like Kololi. Situated on the Atlantic coastline 15km west of Banjul, this once unremarkable small Gambian village, having first been exposed to tourism in the 1970s, today forms the hub of the country's booming package resort industry. Here, within an area of about 2km², you'll find a couple of dozen hotels, including such venerable landmarks as the Kairaba and Senegambia, along with a cosmopolitan and seemingly inexhaustible selection of restaurants and bars, and other tourist facilities such as nightclubs, supermarkets, banks and craft markets. Kololi is also, you'll quickly notice, a major stomping ground for bumsters, whose attentions might be daunting on initial exposure, though mostly they're quite innocuous and quickly lose interest in familiar faces.

The main touristic focal point in Kololi is the tight cluster of hotels and restaurants that runs west from Senegambia Junction (on Bertil Harding Highway) to the Senegambia Hotel and Kololi Beach Club. This area is most often referred to simply as 'Senegambia', or 'The Strip', and almost every visitor to The Gambia ends up here at some point, for a meal, or a drink or a night out. Other important tourist centres are Seaview Boulevard, a few hundred metres north of Senegambia Junction, and a more dispersed group of hotels dotted around Bijilo to the south. The main attraction of this area is emphatically the beach, followed by the busy and wonderfully varied restaurant scene. However, it also boasts one genuinely worthwhile attraction for wildlife enthusiasts in the form of Bijilo Forest Park, a patch of bird- and monkey-rich coastal woodland running along the beach between Kololi and Bijilo.

NORTHERN KOLOLI

Although tourism in Kololi traditionally centres on the bunched cluster of restaurants and other facilities immediately west of Senegambia Junction, two important focal points sit a short distance further north. The first of these is a pair of shopping malls, The Village and the Tropic Shopping Centre (opened late 2021), situated on either side of Bertil Harding Highway about 600m north of Senegambia Junction, where you'll find supermarkets, several boutique shops and a handful of restaurants and cafés. The second is an 800m-long road, sometimes referred to as Seaview Boulevard (or the Duplex Strip or Djeliba Plaza, after former businesses), which runs west from Bertil Harding Highway to the beachfront Poco Loco bar. This road in particular has seen a huge turnover of restaurants and hotels in recent years, with many longstanding addresses closed pending redevelopment as of 2023.

GETTING THERE AND AWAY Coming from Senegambia Junction, it's less than 10 minutes' walk to the Tropic Shopping Centre and perhaps 20 minutes to Seaview Boulevard. From further afield, any shared taxi or other public transport heading

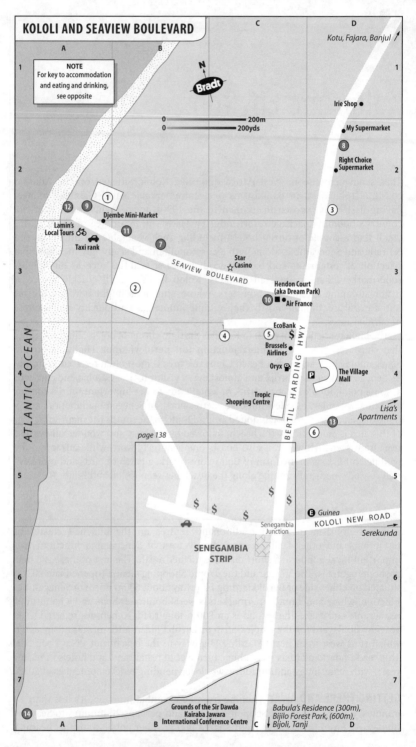

KOLOLI AND SEAVIEW BOULEVARD

NOTE
For key to accommodation
and eating and drinking,
see opposite

Bradt

0 ——— 200m
0 ——— 200yds

Kotu, Fajara, Banjul

Irie Shop ●

● My Supermarket

(8)

Right Choice
Supermarket ●

(3)

(1)

(12) (9)

Djembe Mini-Market

Lamin's
Local Tours
Taxi rank

(11)

(7)

SEAVIEW BOULEVARD

Star ☆
Casino

Hendon Court
(aka Dream Park)

(10) ● Air France

(2)

EcoBank

(4)   (5) $

Brussels
Airlines ●

Oryx

The Village
Mall

P

Tropic
Shopping Centre

*Lisa's
Apartments*

(13)

(6)

BERTIL HARDING HWY

ATLANTIC OCEAN

page 138

$ $

$ $ $ $

E *Guinea*

KOLOLI NEW ROAD

Senegambia
Junction

Serekunda

**SENEGAMBIA
STRIP**

(14)

Grounds of the Sir Dawda
Kairaba Jawara
International Conference Centre

*Babula's Residence (300m),
Bijilo Forest Park, (600m),
Bijoli, Tanji*

along Bertil Harding Highway can drop you along the way. Otherwise, catch a taxi, and pick up another when you are ready to leave (there's a vehicle rank at the end of the road near Poco Loco).

WHERE TO STAY Two of the largest hotels on Seaview Boulevard, Djembe and Djeliba, were defunct as of 2023, but given their locations, it's reasonably likely that they could reopen (most probably under new names and management) during the lifespan of this edition.

Upmarket

Balafon Beach Resort [134 A2] (70 rooms) Seaview Bd; m 209 7777; e bookings@ balafonresort.com; w balafonresort.com. Opened in 2016, this adults-only hotel is set in large, well-manicured grounds built around a small mangrove creek & freeform swimming pool, & faces directly on to the swimming beach at the end of Seaview Bd. Rooms are built in African-inspired 2-storey roundhouses, & while all are comfortably equipped with queen-size canopy beds, sat TV, fridge, AC & private balcony/terrace, there's something to be said for the deluxe rooms with access to a private pool directly from your terrace. There are plenty of restaurants within 200m of the hotel. *From £80/85 standard sgl/dbl, £100/105 deluxe sgl/dbl, all rates B&B.* **$$$**

Mid-range

Bamboo Village [134 B3] (25 rooms) Seaview Bd; \ 446 6543, 446 6542; m 729 5817; w bamboovillage.gm. About 250m from the beach, this new property on the south side of

Seaview Bd is centred around a large swimming pool that surrounds the central restaurant & swim-up bar. Rooms are in comfortable thatched rondavels done up in modern African décor. Good value. *From £45/52 standard sgl/dbl B&B, with significant low season discounts.* **$$**

Budget

Dandimayo Apartments [134 D2] (12 rooms) Bertil Harding Hwy; m 789 8321; e terrymaher1967@gmail.com. Set back just off the highway, these apt blocks surround a swimming pool just behind a large bar/restaurant area that serves English favourites including a Sun roast. The rooms are perfectly acceptable, if slightly garishly decorated, & come with AC, safe & fridge. *£35 for apt inc English b/fast.* **$$**

Paradise Suites Hotel [134 C4] (53 rooms) m 990 6857, 342 4942; e gmparadisehotel@ outlook.com. This rather rundown hotel next to the Seaview lies in uninspiring grounds with a very small swimming-pool area, but it's only 5mins' walk from the beach (through a gate at the back) & even closer to the restaurants & other amenities at Tropic Shopping Centre/The Village. The en-suite rooms are nothing to shout about, but they do have AC, queen-size bed, plenty of cupboard space, sat TV & sizeable bathroom with tub. With realistic expectations, it's fair value. *£37/45 sgl/dbl.* **$$**

Seaview Gardens Hotel [134 C4] (78 rooms) \ 446 6660; m 351 0071, 674 1012; e reservations@seaviewgardenshotel.gm; w seaviewgardenshotel.gm. Situated along a cul-de-sac running off Bertil Harding Hwy parallel to & about 150m south of Seaview Bd, this classy but disingenuously named hotel lies about 10mins' walk from the sea & has no garden worth talking about. The spacious & airy en-suite rooms are in dbl-storey Mediterranean-style blocks & come with sat TV, AC & free Wi-Fi. Good value. *From £21/26 standard/deluxe dbl B&B.* **$$**

KOLOLI AND SEAVIEW BOULEVARD
For listings, see above

(☕) **Where to stay**
1	Balafon Beach Resort	A2
2	Bamboo Village	B3
3	Dandimayo Apartments	D2
4	Paradise Suites	C4
5	Seaview Gardens	C4
6	Sky Guesthouse	D5

Off map
Lisa's Apartments	D4

(✕) **Where to eat and drink**
7	Buka African Kitchen	B3
8	D'Nubian Seafood Garden	D2
9	Justice Bar & Restaurant	A2
10	Manna Bakery & Café	C3
11	Muna's Bar & Restaurant	B3
12	Poco Loco	A2
13	Spice Hub	D4
14	Swiss Tavern	A7
	The Vineyard	
	(see The Village Mall)	D4

8

135

✗ WHERE TO EAT AND DRINK A row of perhaps half a dozen restaurants runs along the north side of Seaview Boulevard and includes several affordable options specialising in West African cuisine, although as elsewhere, there is a fair turnover with places coming and going each season. Tropic Shopping Centre, The Village and Hendon Court (former Dream Park) malls also boast a few eateries, including a branch of Mosiah's Jamaican (page 145) and The Vineyard, a perennial stand-out for wine lovers. The excellent Manna Café will delight those who can't stand the sight of another Nescafé packet.

Upmarket

✴ **The Vineyard** [134 D4] 1st floor, The Village Mall; **m** 331 1111/2; **e** vineyard.gambia@gmail.com; ⏱ noon–23.00 Mon–Sat, 17.00–23.00 Sun. This owner-managed restaurant has an attractive modern interior with light-wood furnishing, a large-screen TV for sports events, free Wi-Fi & the choice of airy indoor or terrace seating. An interesting international menu focuses on Indian cuisine, complemented by a lengthy cocktail & wine list, with most being sold by the glass. *Mains around £7–9.* $$$

Mid-range

✴ **Poco Loco** [134 A2] Seaview Bd; **m** 274 2500; **w** pocolocogambia.com; **f** pocolocogambia; ⏱ 10.00–late daily. Set on a solid wooden deck at the beach end of Seaview Bd, this brightly coloured dbl-storey beach bar scores highly on ambience & location, & is a popular destination for live music at w/ends. A good cocktail menu is accompanied by an eclectic selection of local & continental seafood & other dishes. There's an upstairs sunset deck plus a beach area with sunbeds. *Mains mostly in the £5–7 range.* $$$

D'Nubian Seafood Garden [134 D2] Bertil Harding Hwy; **m** 770 9622; ⏱ 09.00–01.00 daily. Focused mainly on fresh seafood, served with a choice of 7 tasty sauces, this relatively smart eatery also offers a selection of Gambian dishes. *Mains in the £6–8 range.* $$$

Muna's Bar & Restaurant [134 B3] Seaview Bd; **m** 343 6277, 299 4995; ⏱ 08.00–midnight daily. With seating on the airy terrace or in the sports-bar-like interior (complete with free Wi-Fi & large-screen TV), this is a popular hangout during live football matches. It has an unusually varied menu including seafood, curries, wrapped baguettes & pan-African dishes, spanning the continent from the Cape to Morocco, which can be explored in the Taste of Africa sampler. *Mains in the £4–8 range.* $$

Budget

✴ **Manna Bakery & Café** [134 C3] Hendon Court (Dream Park); **m** 391 8700; ⏱ 07.00–16.00 Mon–Sat. This bakery & patisserie is a fantastic spot for a fresh coffee, b/fast, bagel sandwich, soup, or a fresh loaf of sourdough, & it also serves a tempting selection of other pastries & fresh juices. You can eat inside or on the terrace, & there's free Wi-Fi. $$

Buka African Kitchen [134 B3] Seaview Bd; **m** 744 4676; ⏱ 10.00–02.00 Sun–Thu, 10.00–04.00 Fri/Sat. With long hours that make it a good spot for a last round, this unpretentious Nigerian-owned restaurant also serves a varied selection of dishes from all around West Africa. *Mains £4–7.* $$

Justice Bar & Restaurant [134 A2] Seaview Bd; **m** 278 2901; **f** JusticeBarRestaurant; ⏱ noon–midnight daily. The active & enthusiastic Gambian management has made this one of the better new restaurants in the neighbourhood, with stylish & comfortable terrace seating & a menu of kebabs, burgers, grills & Gambian favourites, plus a full bar. *Mains £4–7.* $$

ENTERTAINMENT AND NIGHTLIFE The former Duplex Club is still an important landmark on Seaview Boulevard (aka the Duplex Strip), but the club is long gone, and you'll find Star Casino there instead. The nicest spot for an outdoor drink is probably beachfront Poco Loco, which faces west to catch the sunset and usually hosts live music over weekends. More sedately, most of the restaurants along Seaview Boulevard have agreeable terraces that stay open until well after midnight.

SHOPPING The country's two largest shopping malls face each other on either side of the Bertil Harding Highway here, with **The Village Mall** [134 D4] to the east and **Tropic Shopping Centre** [134 C4] to the west, plus the smaller **Hendon Court** (aka Dream Park) just to the north. All are home to several trendy clothes and souvenir shops, a few restaurants, and at least one well-stocked supermarket. Xpress Supermarket in The Village has a particularly good selection. Less comprehensive but more convenient for those staying at the far end of Seaview Boulevard is the small **Djembe Mini-Market** [134 A2] near Poco Loco. A bit further north on Bertil Harding Highway, the new **Irie Shop** [134 D1] (m 734 7867; f Irie Shop Gambia) has a particularly good selection of souvenirs and crafts.

ACTIVITIES The main centre of tourist activity in North Kololi is the hotel swimming pools and, of course, the beach in front of Poco Loco, which is far more alluring than its eroded counterpart at the end of the Senegambia Strip. The only bespoke tourist attraction in the area, situated directly opposite The Village, is Dream Park, a family-oriented amusement park that opened in 2007 but looked very closed at the time of writing. Whether it will open again is anybody's guess. **Lamin's Local Tours** [134 A3] (m 341 2338; e laminthebiker@gmail.com; f) operates near Poco Loco on Seaview Boulevard with bikes available at around £5/10 for a half/full day.

THE 'SENEGAMBIA' STRIP

Ubiquitously referred to as Senegambia after the iconic 350-room hotel that dominates its beachfront, the touristic heart of Kololi consists of a J-shaped kilometre of road lined with dozens of restaurants, bars and other tourist facilities. Ironically, however, while this part of Kololi is easily the busiest resort along the Gambian coast, the main beach leaves much to be desired by comparison with most of its counterparts. This is due to tidal erosion, which has been an issue here for decades and the focus of several restoration initiatives, the latest being the construction of a nearly 1km-long rock barrier, laid along the beach here at the end of 2018. This has stemmed the tide for now, with a wide and sandy beach accessible by staircase over the rocks at low tide, and waves lapping at the boulders when it's high. Thus, the sun loungers and umbrellas inside the barrier remain available, or you need only follow the J-curve a few hundred metres west to reach the more pristine beach that runs south from Kololi Beach Club to Bijilo.

GETTING THERE AND AWAY Kololi lies 20km from Banjul International Airport via Yundum and Sukuta, around £20 in a taxi. Coming from elsewhere, for instance Fajara, Serekunda or central Banjul (where transport to Kololi leaves from the station on Rene Blain Street opposite Gamtel House), just ask for 'Senegambia' and you'll be dropped at the junction.

Heading out from Kololi, private taxis can be picked up at the main taxi park on the south side of the Senegambia Strip. However, since these are official tourist taxis, they tend to be quite expensive. A cheaper option is to walk up to Senegambia Junction and pick up a shared or private taxi from Bertil Harding Highway.

WHERE TO STAY

Upmarket

Kololi Beach Resort [138 B6] Off Senegambia Strip; m 713 4203; e bookings@kololi.com; w kololi.com. Set in large, quiet & well-groomed beachfront grounds that incorporate a large swimming-pool area, an adults-only plunge pool, private beaches, bar & restaurant, mini supermarket, book-swap library & golf course, this

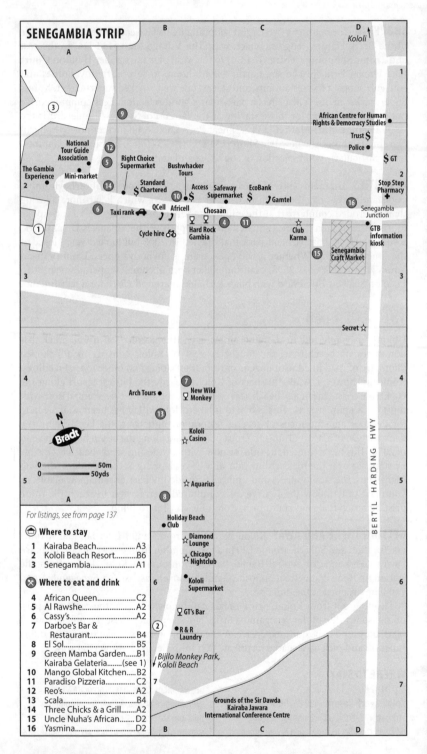

SENEGAMBIA STRIP

Kololi

African Centre for Human
Rights & Democracy Studies ●

Trust $
Police ● $ GT

Stop Step
Pharmacy

National
Tour Guide
Association

Right Choice
Supermarket

Bushwhacker
Tours

The Gambia
Experience ● Mini-market

Standard
$ Chartered

Access
$

Safeway
Supermarket
$

EcoBank
$

♪ Gamtel

Taxi rank 🚗

QCell
♪ ♪

Africell
♪

Chosaan
♀ ♀

Club
Karma ☆

Senegambia
Junction

GTB
information
kiosk

Cycle hire 🚲

Hard Rock
Gambia

Senegambia
Craft Market

Secret ☆

Arch Tours ●

New Wild
♀ Monkey

Kololi
☆ Casino

☆ Aquarius

BERTIL HARDING HWY

Holiday Beach
● Club

☆ Diamond
♀ Lounge

☆ Chicago
Nightclub

● Kololi
Supermarket

♀ GT's Bar

● R & R
Laundry

Bijilo Monkey Park,
↓ *Kololi Beach*

Grounds of the Sir Dawda
Kairaba Jawara
International Conference Centre

N
Bradt

0 _____ 50m
0 _____ 50yds

For listings, see from page 137

🛏 **Where to stay**

1 Kairaba Beach...................A3
2 Kololi Beach Resort...........B6
3 Senegambia.......................A1

❌ **Where to eat and drink**

4 African Queen...................C2
5 Al Rawshe.........................A2
6 Cassy's..............................A2
7 Darboe's Bar &
   Restaurant......................B4
8 El Sol................................B5
9 Green Mamba Garden.....B1
   Kairaba Gelateria........(see 1)
10 Mango Global Kitchen.....B2
11 Paradiso Pizzeria..............C2
12 Reo's................................A2
13 Scala................................B4
14 Three Chicks & a Grill......A2
15 Uncle Nuha's African........D2
16 Yasmina...........................D2

family-owned & -managed club runs primarily as a private resort for its members, but it can also be booked by non-members, & it is possible to turn up at reception & take a room or a villa on the spot if one is available. Accommodation is in large, airy 1- & 2-bedroom villas with modern furnishings, fully fitted kitchen, fan & AC, & private patio or balcony. Other positives are the hands-on management, direct beach access, plentiful monkeys & birdlife & proximity to the many restaurants & bars along the strip. *1-/2-bed villas from £105/night for 2–6 people; low season discounts available.* **$$$$**

米 Kairaba Beach Hotel [138 A3] (160 rooms) Senegambia Strip; ✆ 446 2940–2; m 269 7375, 775 7727; e info@kairabahotel.com; w kairabahotel.com. One of the oldest, classiest & most consistently praised of The Gambia's larger hotels, this 5-star property lies in lush 20ha grounds bordering the Senegambia Hotel & running down to Kololi Beach. Ideal for birdwatchers & sun worshippers alike, it is also well placed for exploring the restaurants & nightlife along the adjoining strip. Built in the Portuguese style, the neat & spacious en-suite rooms, though a little old-fashioned, are bright & well equipped with quality fittings. All rooms come with a twin or queen-size bed, satellite TV, AC, tea-/coffee-maker & a large glass door leading out to a private balcony. Facilities include 6 restaurants & bars, a lovely swimming-pool area, a beauty salon, a gift shop, an excursions desk & the country's only observatory, as well as sports such as darts, table tennis, squash, outdoor chess, lawn games & mountain-bike hire. The Kairaba lacks the flair of some of the boutique hotels listed elsewhere in this book, & rooms come with quite a high price tag, but taken on its own rather corporate terms, it's difficult to fault. *£91/112 standard/deluxe dbl, £150 suite, all rates B&B.* **$$$**

Mid-range

米 Senegambia Hotel [138 A1] (351 rooms) Senegambia Strip; ✆ 446 2717; m 200 0342; e info@senegambiahotel.com; w senegambiahotel.com. The largest hotel in The Gambia, the iconic Senegambia has been a sensibly priced & thoroughly reliable all-round mid-range option since it opened in the early 1980s. Its most attractive feature is the luxuriant 10ha beachfront garden, whose lush tropical vegetation, filled with interesting nooks & crannies, supports plenty of wildlife, including giant monitor lizards, playful green monkeys & an alluring selection of woodland birds (notably the likes of oriole warbler & black-headed gonolek). There is even a special 'vulture feeding' event, which takes place at around 11.00 daily, & attracts dozens (sometimes hundreds) of these large scavenging birds. Other facilities include a pleasant swimming-pool area, a beach bar, a well-stocked gift shop, tailors, a unisex hairdressing salon & several restaurants, as well as tennis, squash, table tennis, volleyball, minigolf & archery. It is close to dozens of bars & restaurants, but there's also a wide range of in-house evening entertainment, including stage shows, African cabaret nights & a weekly BBQ. The rooms are in 2-storey buildings dotted around the gardens, & they all have AC, fan, sat TV, safe, en-suite bath or shower & private balcony or patio. Overall, it has a lot more character than most package hotels, & it's an excellent central choice for birders or families with mixed interests. *From £59/72 sgl/dbl B&B, less out of season.* **$$$**

Budget

Devon Lodge [map, page 84] (8 apts) Off Bertil Harding Hwy; m 707 6017, 773 6750; e devonlodgegambia@ gmail.com; w devonlodgegambia.com; 🇫 devonlodgegambia. Run by an English–Gambian couple, these highly rated self-catering apts come with dbl/twin bed, en-suite shower, well-equipped kitchen, open-plan living area, sat TV & private veranda overlooking the well-tended gardens. There's free Wi-Fi, & the hosts are happy to organise shopping or take-away services. The apts occupy a peaceful location close to Bijilo Forest Park, away from the buzz of the main strip but still within walking distance of the main cluster of restaurants. *£30/night or £200/week.* **$$**

Lisa's Apartments [134 D4] (6 rooms) Kololi; m 249 9996; e info@lisasgambia.com; w lisasgambia.com. All of the rooms at this new Dutch–Gambian establishment tucked away in the Kololi backstreets 600m east of the Tropic Shopping Centre are accessible for those with disabilities, & come with en-suite bath & kitchenette. There's a small vegetable garden & a restaurant is planned. *£28/night or £202/week.* **$$**

Sky Guesthouse [134 D5] (8 rooms) Off Bertil Harding Hwy; m 370 0701; 🇫 SkyGambia. Set back just off the highway between The Village & Senegambia, this is a great budget choice for those wishing to sample the local restaurants & nightlife, less than 1km from the beach. Under active new management, the en-suite rooms are recently renovated & come with ceiling fans, hot water & nets. Good value. *£13/15 dbl with fan/AC or £21/26 for 1-/2-bed apt.* **$**

✖ **WHERE TO EAT AND DRINK** The best part of 50 restaurants are clustered within 5 minutes' walk of Senegambia Junction. Most international cuisines are well represented, and standards are pretty high. The listings below are therefore quite selective, pulling out a few well-established favourites, along with some newer places that offer exceptional value or an unusual menu or ambience. But don't be afraid to explore further – there are plenty of other choices and the healthy competition level tends to weed out any real duds sharpish.

Upmarket

❋ **Reo's** [138 A2] Off Senegambia Strip; m 730 0030; w reosgambia.com; f reosbarandrestaurant; ⏰ 11.00–02.00 daily. This modern bar & restaurant is well known for the quality of its food & has possibly the best burger in The Gambia as well as steaks, seafood, Italian dishes & other favourites. Either sit inside with AC & flatscreen TV for sporting events or under the fan on the balcony outside. They keep long hours so you can linger as late as you like over their sizeable cocktail list. *Most mains in the £5–13 range.* **$$$–$$$$**

❋ **Scala Restaurant** [138 B4] Off Senegambia Strip; m 990 4984; f; ⏰ 18.30–23.00 daily. Established back in the 1980s, this Danish-owned & -managed restaurant has long been highly rated for its ambience, service, quality food & reasonable prices. The emphasis is on continental fine dining & the menu, though not extensive, includes an imaginative selection of fish, seafood & meat dishes. There's also usually live West African music at a comfortable volume. *Mains mostly in the £7–12 range.* **$$$–$$$$**

African Queen Restaurant [138 C2] Senegambia Strip; m 756 9236; ⏰ 08.30–midnight daily. If the pushy waiters touting at the entrance don't put you off, this well-established restaurant is perhaps the pick of a bunch of similar semi-outdoor set-ups lining the southeast side of the strip. Serves a range of seafood, grills & sizzlers, including some superb peri-peri prawns. *Most dishes cost around £6–8, while the house specialities – lobster, tiger prawns, various sizzlers – are around £10–13.* **$$$–$$$$**

❋ **Green Mamba Garden** [138 B1] Off Senegambia Strip; m 778 6818, 774 5594; ⏰ 19.00–23.00 daily. Tucked away on an inauspicious alley running north past the Senegambia Hotel, this lovely garden bar & restaurant has a lively but peaceful atmosphere (at least when the nearby hotel standby generator is standing by), a good cocktail & wine list, & exceptional food. The speciality is the Mongolian grill (allowing you to select from dozens of raw ingredients to make your own fresh stir-fry). *Grill £6.50 for 1 round or £8.50 for as many as you like. It also has a varied selection of à la carte grills in the £7.50–10 range.* **$$$**

Mid-range

Al Rawshe Restaurant [138 A2] Senegambia Strip; m 772 2821; ⏰ noon–midnight daily. This excellent Lebanese restaurant with indoor & outdoor seating places a strong emphasis on seafood. Specials include a grilled 'catch of the day' for 2 (*£11.50*), a Lebanese-style Fri buffet, & a good meze selection. **$$$**

Cassy's Lounge [138 A2] m 288 8000; f cassyslounge; ⏰ 18.00–late Wed–Mon. This stylish new restaurant & rooftop terrace bar has quickly become a new favourite on the Senegambian dining scene, serving a selection of elegantly plated continental & African dishes, plus quality cocktails at the bar. It's under the same ownership as Cassy's Café in The Village shopping center, which is well-loved for coffee & cakes. **$$$**

Darboe's Bar & Restaurant [138 B4] Off Senegambia Strip; m 781 6814, 759 6661; f darboesrestaurant; ⏰ 08.00–02.00 daily. Thanks to its large-screen TVs, this cheerful locally owned eatery is often packed during key Premier League football matches & other major sports events. But the long hours (& free Wi-Fi) ensure that it is also a great spot for English-style b/fast, a lunchtime sandwich or burger, a tasty Gambian dinner dish such as chicken yassa, afra or domada, or a night out watching (occasional) live music.

Mains are around £6, while sizzlers are more like £9. $$$

El Sol [138 B5] Off Senegambia Strip; m 732 0000; w elsolgambia.com; ⏰ 17.00–22.30 daily. Choose between a tastefully decorated AC interior or the veranda to enjoy Mexican classics such as nachos & burritos, as well as burgers, steak, chicken dishes & tapas. There are also sumptuous desserts & an extensive cocktail list – passion-fruit mojito, anyone? *Mains in the £7–9 range, tapas £4–6.* $$$

Mango Global Kitchen [138 B2] Senegambia Strip; m 749 9990; ⏰ 11.00–23.00 daily. The best Indian in Kololi, this long-serving restaurant has an extensive menu that includes curries, tandoor grills & filling biryani dishes. Vegetarians are well catered for here. *Most mains are in the £5–7 range.* $$$

Three Chicks & a Grill [138 A2] Senegambia Strip; m 232 3333; ⏰f 3chicksandagrill; ⏰ 17.00–23.00 daily. Colourful, relaxed café with a lovely, brightly painted patio decked in pretty fairy lights & relaxed bamboo furniture. Friendly staff serve some of the juiciest burgers in the country, as well as delicious wings, freshly cooked fish & steaks. *Mains in the £6–9 range.* $$$

Yasmina [138 D2] Senegambia Strip; m 793 7003; f YasminaRestoBar; ⏰ 09.00–midnight daily. Situated right on Senegambia Junction, this informal terrace restaurant is a bit of a landmark, good for people-watching or football-watching, & there's some lounge singing on the w/ends. The menu is decidedly continental, with a variety of chicken, fish, steak & pasta on offer. *Mains £6–11.* $$$

Paradiso Pizzeria [138 C2] Senegambia Strip; m 777 9333; ⏰ 10.00–23.00 daily. This local joint looks a little shabby from the outside but the food

is excellent, especially the huge choice of different pizzas (cooked while you wait), which you can eat inside or take away. Service is variable & can be quite poor when it is busy, but it's very affordable. *£4–7 for regular pizzas.* $$–$$$

Budget

✳ **Spice Hub** [134 D4] Kololi; m 733 2832, 330 0401; f Spice Hub by Chef Bojang. This new restaurant 150m east of the Tropic Shopping Centre does a delicious & creative assortment of fish, chicken, grills & curries, & it's one of the few places you can try local grain *findo* (fonio), often hailed as an up-and-coming superfood. *Mains £4–6.* $$

Kairaba Gelateria [138 A3] Senegambia Strip; m 790 7860; ⏰ 09.00–midnight daily. Situated just outside the entrance to the eponymous hotel, this very agreeable fan-chilled delicatessen serves freshly brewed coffee, fruit juices, imported ice cream, waffles & pancakes, as well as a selection of savoury-filled paninis. *Paninis around £5, waffles/pancakes £3.* $$

Swiss Tavern [134 A7] Off Senegambia Strip; m 202 2121; f swisstaverngambia; ⏰ 10.00–23.30 daily. Situated on the pretty beach between Kololi Beach Club & Bijilo Forest Park, this modern beachfront resto-bar serves a selection of Gambian & seafood dishes, as well as slightly cheaper sandwiches & snacks, either under the beach bantabas or on the breezy veranda. *Mains around £5.* $$

✳ **Uncle Nuha's African Restaurant** [138 D3] Senegambia Strip; ⏰ 08.00–20.00. The only place on the strip catering to a predominantly Gambian clientele, this sweaty hole-in-the-wall next to the market serves large, carbo-loaded platefuls of whatever local dish(es) they've conjured up that day. No nonsense. No alcohol. Great value. *Mains around £1–3.* $

ENTERTAINMENT AND NIGHTLIFE The Senegambia Strip lies at the epicentre of The Gambia's limited nightlife scene. A handful of dedicated nightspots can be found on the road parallel to the Bertil Harding Highway, including **Diamond Lounge** [138 B6] (f DiamondloungeGambia), **Chicago Nightclub** [138 B6] and **Aquarius** [138 B6] (f aquariuscafe) – one of The Gambia's longest-running clubs. There are also usually a couple of identikit clubs on the first floor of the row of buildings that also includes the African Queen (see opposite) – the names seem to change by the season. Around the corner on the highway, **Secret Night Club** [138 D3] is the one with the gigantic signboard. Between them, they are usually open every night, from sometime in the evening until the early morning or when the last guest leaves. All are pretty much out-and-out pickup joints, frequented by large numbers of prostitutes, bumsters and other potential hangers-on, and theft is also an occasional problem.

For a more wholesome night out, many of the restaurants listed from page 140 (and some that aren't) double as terrace bars, staying open until midnight or later, and it is really just a case of picking whichever one takes your fancy and pulling up a seat. Among the best spots for live music are neighbouring **Chosaan** (next to African Queen; m 774 6808) and **Hard Rock Gambia** [138 B2] (m 730 8224) and then around the corner the **New Wild Monkey** [138 B4] (m 248 4922; f) and **GT's Bar** [138 B6] (m 238 6085; f gts.barrestaurant.5) slightly further down. **Darboe's** (page 140) also occasionally has music. Most of the shows kick off between 20.00 and 22.00, often depending whether it's a weekday or the weekend. Finally, the rather dour **Kololi Casino** [138 B5] is also just here.

OTHER PRACTICALITIES

Banks and foreign exchange Three banks are represented on the main strip with ATMs: **Standard Chartered Bank** [138 B2], **Access Bank** [138 B2] and **EcoBank** [138 C2]. You can also find **GT Bank** [138 D2] and **Trust Bank** [138 D2], both with ATMs on opposite sides of Bertil Harding Highway less than 100m north of Senegambia Junction. In addition, there must be a dozen private **forex bureaux** along the strip and the side road to Kololi Beach Resort, all offering similar rates. It can be worth shopping around, though be warned that it will be difficult to shake off the attentions of any bumster who notices you leaving a forex bureau without having changed any money.

Guided excursions Several agencies offer day trips to sites such as Banjul City, Abuko Nature Reserve and Makasutu Cultural Forest, as well as dolphin-watching trips, 'Roots Excursions' to Albreda, Juffureh and Kunta Kinteh (James) Island, and excursions to most other sites west of Serekunda and Brikama. Established agencies include the upmarket and highly regarded **The Gambia Experience** (w gambia. co.uk), which has an office in the Senegambia Hotel [138 A2], and the more budget-oriented **Arch Tours** [138 B4] (opposite the New Wild Monkey; m 272 9896; w arch-tours.com) and **Bushwhacker Tours** [138 B2] (Senegambia Strip; m 706 2502, 991 2891; w bushwhackertours.com). Trips can also be arranged through the official government-trained guides at the National Tour Guide Association shelter next to the traffic circle in front of the Senegambia Hotel [138 A2].

Health and beauty The best options are the hairdressing and beauty salons in the Kairaba and Senegambia hotels.

Internet Most hotels and restaurants now have Wi-Fi.

Laundry If your hotel can't do your laundry, your best option is **R & R Laundry** [138 B1] next to GT's Bar.

Shopping Neighbouring malls The Village and Tropic Shopping Centre (page 137) both sit 500m north of Senegambia Junction. Both are home to a selection of shops catering mainly to tourists and wealthier locals, and Xpress supermarket in The Village is very well stocked. Several smaller but reasonably well-stocked grocery shops can also be found along the strip, the best being the **Right Choice Supermarket** [138 B2] (m 794 0525; ⊕ 09.00–22.00 daily) next to the Standard Chartered Bank. Others include the **Safeway Supermarket** [138 C2] and an anonymous **mini-market** [138 A2] on the main circle next to the entrance of the Senegambia Hotel.

Situated on the southwest side of Senegambia Junction, the **Senegambia Craft Market** [138 D3] incorporates around 50 stalls selling a wide variety of local and traditional craft items and clothes. Other good handicraft outlets include the gift shops in the Senegambia and Kairaba hotels.

Tourist information The **Gambian Tourist Board** (**GTB**) maintains a kiosk on Senegambia Junction next to the craft market [138 D2], but it seldom seems to be manned.

BIJILO AND SUKUTA

Though it lies only 2km southwest of Kololi (from which it is separated by the small Bijilo Forest Park), low-key Bijilo is strikingly different in feel, with beach activity being centred on a wide sandy shore that is relatively quiet and bumster-free. Once upon a time rather ignored by the growing tourist industry next door, Bijilo today houses several package hotels, most of which lie on or very close to the beach. It's also the proposed future home of The Gambia's first Radisson Blu – a massive US$100 million project with a planned 400 rooms and 60 VIP suites, being built as part of The Gambia's ambition to host an Organisation of Islamic Cooperation summit; President Barrow laid the foundation stone in July 2022.

As it stands, Bijilo represents a kind of best-of-both-worlds scenario, as there's little of the hustle and bustle associated with all the other resorts to its northeast, yet it is literally just a 5-minute taxi ride to the cluster of restaurants and late-night scene at nearby Kololi. Immediately inland of Bijilo, Sukuta is a neighbourhood best known to overland travellers as the site of the legendary Camping Sukuta (page 144).

GETTING THERE AND AWAY Bijilo flanks the Bertil Harding Highway about 2km southwest of Kololi en route to Brusubi Turntable (Junction), the traffic circle and flyover at the four-way junction with Sayerr Jobe Road (to Serekunda), the AU Highway (to Banjul International Airport and Brikama), and Coastal Road (which runs south to Brufut, Tanji, Gunjur and Kartong). The hotels in Bijilo all lie within around 200m of Bertil Harding Highway, so are readily accessible on shared taxis or other public transport between Bakau or Kololi and Brusubi Turntable. Coming to or from the airport, you will need to take a private taxi, which costs around £20.

WHERE TO STAY *Map, page 84*
Exclusive
☀ **Coco Ocean Resort & Spa** (89 rooms) Bertil Harding Hwy, Bijilo; ☎ 446 6500; m 776 0072; e info@cocoocean.com; w cocoocean. com. Arguably the most stylish large hotel in the country, the 5-star Coco Ocean sprawls across expansive & well-tended gardens, complete with some resident monkeys, down to a long, attractive beach decked out with shaded sunbeds. The hotel's whitewashed arches & domes are reminiscent of North Africa or the Swahili Coast, &

accommodation is in a variety of airy & attractive high-ceilinged suites & houses, all of which come with the expected trimmings. The costlier units also have verandas, sitting rooms & private plunge pools. Facilities include 3 restaurants, 3 swimming pools, & an excellent spa. *From £120 B&B, HB available.* $$$$

Upmarket
Seafront Residences (20 rooms) Bijilo Beach, behind the filling station; ☎ 446 3147; m 701

9000; e info@seafront.gm; w seafrontgambia. com. This Mediterranean-style all-apt complex, which opened in 2012, has a large & attractive freeform swimming pool, & is less than 5 mins' walk from Bijilo Beach. Though rather lacking in character, the apts are spacious & modern, & consist of 1 or 2 bedrooms with king-size bed & net, a sitting room with sat TV, a well-equipped modern kitchen & a bathroom with combined tub/ shower. Good value. *From £65/100 1-/2-bedroom apt, all rates B&B.* **$$$**

Mid-range
Kasumai Beach Guest House (6 rooms) Off Senegambia Hwy; m 701 0020; e office@ kasumaibeach.com; w kasumaibeach.com. This Austrian-run guesthouse offers comfortable rooms right on the beach, next to the popular beach bar of the same name. Rooms include Wi-Fi, flatscreen sat TV, AC & free access to sunbeds around the 2 swimming pools. *From £50 dbl B&B.* **$$$**

Lemon Creek Resort (56 rooms) Off Bertil Harding Hwy, Bijilo; m 661 1200; e booking@ lemoncreek.net; w lemoncreek.net. Dutch-owned & -managed, & built in Spanish colonial style, this small hotel slots somewhere between the package & boutique ends of the markets. The sizeable & tastefully decorated rooms are arranged in dbl-storey blocks & all contain a wooden 4-poster queen-size bed with net, fan, AC, sat TV, safe & private balcony. The large grounds are bisected by a small stream, with the swimming-pool area on the opposite side to the rooms. The property leads to a semi-private swimming beach enclosed by natural vegetation & boasting a small but pretty lagoon. Overall, a clear standout in this price range. Good value. *From £53/66 standard/deluxe dbl B&B, with low-season discounts.* **$$$**

Baobab Holiday Resort (42 rooms) Bertil Harding Hwy, Bijilo; m 734 7963, 329 5253; e baobabbookings@hotmail.com; w baobabresort.net. Very popular with Dutch package tourists, this compact & unpretentious resort lies opposite the Coco Ocean, about 10mins' walk from the beach. The neat, clean en-suite rooms, in colourful dbl-storey blocks centred on a welcoming figure-of-8 swimming pool, all come with queen-size bed, Wi-Fi, fan, sat TV, hot shower & private terrace, with optional AC & fridge. There

are also apts with a sitting & dining room. Facilities include a good restaurant & spa. *From £40 dbl B&B.* **$$**

Budget and camping
✳ **Sardinka House** (6 rooms) Off Bertil Harding Hwy, Bijilo; m 211 2235, 786 0005; e sardinkahouse@yahoo.com; ▯ Sardinka Guest House. Run by a long-term resident British couple, this friendly, family-oriented place centres around a pool surrounded by palms & a relaxing bantaba, where you can enjoy some of the coldest drinks in The Gambia, sunbeds, a craft shop & library. All rooms either have, or have access to, fully equipped kitchens, as well as TVs & fans; 2 have AC. There is a solar backup system so you won't notice power cuts. Ask if there are any fishing excursions on during your visit. Excellent value. *£30/35/50 studio/1-bed/3-bed (sleeping up to 6).* **$$**

Shelley's (24 rooms) Off Bertil Harding Hwy; m 990 7040, 254 7385; e shelleysgambia@ outlook.com; w shelleysingambia.com. Close to the Bijilo Medical Centre, this Welsh-run guesthouse is centred on a large swimming pool. The rooms are spotlessly clean & modernly decorated & there are family rooms available, as well as 2 apts. There is a bar/restaurant serving snacks & simple home-cooked meals with a large TV & pool table, as well as a small gym. Good value. *£15 pp B&B.* **$$**

✳ **Camping Sukuta** (18 rooms) 500m north of Sayerr Jobe Rd, Sukuta; ✪ 13.4193, -16.7158; m 991 7786; e campingsukutagambia@yahoo. de; w campingsukuta.com. Something of an overlanders' institution, this German-owned & -managed lodge & campsite in Sukuta has long been the place to stock up, rest up & trade knowledge & experiences with drivers coming in the opposite direction. Efficiency, comfort & friendliness are the bywords of this camp, which lies in well-tended & tidy gardens & has a good book swap & library, a small shop that sells essential vehicle spares & a selection of groceries, a self-catering kitchen, & Wi-Fi (£1/day). The restaurant was only doing b/fast in 2023, but the bar is stocked. Accommodation is clean, well maintained & comes with fan. *£11/14 sgl/dbl, £20 en-suite dbl, £28 house with AC & veranda, £4 pp camping plus £2–3/vehicle.* **$**

✳ **Sea Shells** Senegambia Hwy; m 776 0070, 742 8820; f seashellsgambia; ⏰ 10.30–late Mon–Sat. One of the finest restaurants in The Gambia, this Moroccan-run place serves, as the name implies, fresh local seafood (the house speciality is lobster thermidor) but also fine meat dishes such as chateaubriand. The setting is warm & intimate & service is impeccable & friendly. Additionally, the pastry chef makes exquisite cakes, cheesecakes (including their famous Nutella cheesecake) & some of the best bread in the country. There's also an excellent wine list. *Mains in the £8–12 range, lobster thermidor £20.* $$$$

✳ **Mosiah's Jamaican Bar & Restaurant** Senegambia Hwy; m 537 7701, 288 0328; f mo2gambia; ⏰ 09.00–late daily. About 700m along from Brusubi Turntable as you enter Bijilo, this has rapidly become a well-known address for its take on Jamaican classics with a Gambian touch, plus burgers, salads & excellent fresh juices. They've got 2 locations now; the other is in the Hendon Court (Dream Park) building near Senegambia (page 136). For meat eaters, the goat curry is a must. *Mains £5–7.* $$$

2 Rays Senegambia Hwy; m 995 9696, 750 6725; ⏰ 08.00–late daily. Founded by 2 brothers who both have 20 years' experience working in the restaurant business, this popular address opposite the forest park serves a range of international favourites including fillet steak, meatballs, fajitas, burgers & various pizzas & pastas, plus a varied assortment of cocktails. There's an attached bakery, & they have another location on the Senegambia Strip. *Mains around £6.* $$$

Kasumai Beach Bar & Restaurant Off Senegambia Hwy; m 701 0020; w kasumaibeach.

com; ⏰ 09.00–22.00 daily. Next door to Sunbird Beach Bar, this also offers sunbeds & a restaurant serving continental food, fresh seafood, Gambian dishes & a decent wine list. The gardens are a lovely place to enjoy a drink & free Wi-Fi is provided. There are several events each week including live music on Sun, salsa, & a fire & culture night. A massage service is also available. *Mains around £6.* $$$

✳ **The Blue Kitchen** Sayerr Jobe Rd; m 980 4961; f bluekitchengambia; ⏰ 09.00–23.30 daily. Part of a German NGO where a percentage of all profits are fed back into local community projects, this bar & restaurant serves excellent Gambian & European food in lovely surroundings. Either sit inside the main restaurant/bar area where a huge flat-screen TV broadcasts major sporting events or, for more tranquil surroundings, sit in the gardens backing on to a local woman's vegetable garden, small children's playground & craft shop. *Mains around £4.* $$

✳ **Sunbird Beach Bar & Restaurant** Bijilo Beach; m 990 1914, 777 0127; w sunbirdbeach. com; ⏰ 09.00–late. Another strong contender for The Gambia's best beach bar. Setting this one aside from the competition is the lovely green lawn shaded by palms, running down a slope towards the wide open sands of the beach. There's a choice of seating at tables or sunbeds with thatched umbrellas, & the friendly waiting staff will bring snacks such as sandwiches or European/Gambian mains to your relaxation point of choice. To find it, take the first right heading south from Coco Ocean Hotel on the Senegambia Hwy. *Mains around £5.* $$

WHAT TO SEE AND DO Inland from the beach, Bijilo is a primarily residential area with few sights as such, although MyFarm offers a fascinating insight for anyone interested in local eco-farming techniques and products.

Bijilo Forest Park (m 778 4902; ⏰ 07.00–18.00 daily; entrance D150, children under 12 free) Today protecting roughly 36ha of coastal forest and scrub overlooking the beach running south from Kololi Beach Club, the Bijilo Forest Park, created in 1952 and widely known as the 'Monkey Park', ranks among the best-preserved habitats of its type in the country, yet it lies within easy walking distance of the Senegambia Strip and associated hotels. For most visitors, its main attraction is the opportunity to get close to free-ranging but very habituated populations of three primate species: the widespread and easily seen green monkey, the slightly shyer and more localised red colobus, and the seldom-seen patas monkey. Other mammals include Gambian sun squirrels, which are frequently spotted in the trees, and striped ground squirrels, which you can see on the forest floor. In addition, Bijilo supports one-third of all the butterfly species recorded in the country, a variety of lizards including Nile monitor, agama and brown-flanked skink, and more than 130 bird species, including three types of bee-eater, red-necked falcon, stone partridge and rarities such as Ahanta francolin and western bluebill.

Despite sustained protest from local environmental groups like the Gambia Environmental Alliance (🇫 geagambia), the northern 15ha of the park were controversially de-gazetted in early 2017, and the forest was cleared to make way for a major development – the Sir Dawda Kairaba Jawara International Conference Centre was inaugurated on this former parkland in early 2020. Since then, Green Up Gambia (w greenupgambia.org) has led an admirable restoration and tree-planting campaign in the remaining parkland, but in late 2022 the park once again found itself at the heart of a major development dispute – this time involving the US Embassy, which plans to relocate its Gambian facility in the coming years. The dispute centres on the West Africa Livestock Innovation Centre site, which is set within the reserve, but – according to the Gambian government – is not officially a part of it. The US has promised to provide a new visitors' centre, guide training and other unspecified support to the park, but environmental groups have once again cried foul against this seemingly endless salami-slicing of one of the region's precious few remaining wilderness areas. The US-led technical assessment was ongoing as this guide went to print.

The newly constructed conference centre sits directly between the Senegambia area and the park, so the new entrance to the reserve (⊕ 13.4364, -16.7254) is no longer quite so convenient as it once was – but it is accessible from either the beach or the Bertil Harding Highway, and is still only 1km from Senegambia Junction, reachable on foot. Here, you need to pay the entrance fee and pick up the more-or-less mandatory guide, a service included in the entrance fee, though a tip is expected. From the gate, a network of nature trails, comprising several kilometres of well-marked and maintained footpaths, leads around the reserve. The paths are

FEEDING THE MONKEYS   By Craig Emms and Linda Bartlett

Please do not feed the monkeys at Bijilo or anywhere else. It may seem like a cool thing to do but these are wild animals, no matter how cute they look. Feeding monkeys makes them aggressive towards humans, as they come to expect food. If you don't have any food on you then they may attack purely out of frustration. Males can be very large and have a vicious set of teeth. Also remember that these animals may carry diseases such as rabies. Unfortunately, although tourists have been told these facts for years, some local guides have encouraged them to feed the monkeys. The result of this is that a large troop of green monkeys now travels along the coast from Bijilo every day, calling in at every hotel and house on the way, causing damage and frightening people with their aggressive behaviour. There will come a point in the not-too-distant future when these monkeys will cause so much trouble that they will have to be controlled in some way, either by trapping and relocation, or by simply shooting them. All because a few tourists think it's cute to feed the wild monkeys.

divided into colour-coded circular routes, so that you can choose how far and in what direction you want to walk. Most of it is fairly level, though there are a few steeper parts with rough steps. Another straight path which runs through the forest and scrub near to the beach is known as 'the ornithological path', since it affords excellent opportunities to view many of the park's birds. Overall, Bijilo Forest Park is a wonderful example of how the Gambian coastline once looked and is well worth a visit at any time of the year.

If you are staying outside Kololi, most hotels and operators can easily arrange visits here, or you can just ask a taxi to drop you at the entrance – there will always be taxis waiting outside when you are finished.

MyFarm (Nema Kunku, near Sukuta; ✪ 13.3956, -16.6906; m 712 1212, 378 5025; w africastartup.org; ◼ MyFarmAfricaStartUp) With the motto 'Helping the community to help itself', this 1ha farm was set up by the Norwegian NGO Africa Startup as a training and education centre for young Gambians, offering an 'educational journey from seed to business', learning through play and practical activities. MyFarm aims to demonstrate best practice in horticultural techniques, adding value to local produce and encouraging entrepreneurship. Their guiding principle is environmental protection, showcasing appropriate sustainable alternative technology, and they aim to become self-sustaining through various income-generating activities including the sale of high-quality local produce and beauty products, some of which are available at Timbooktoo bookshop (page 119). Check their website for volunteering opportunities.

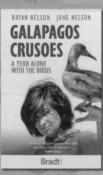

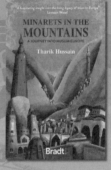
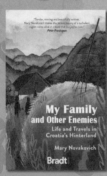

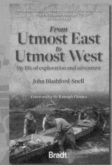

Part Three

THE COASTAL BELT

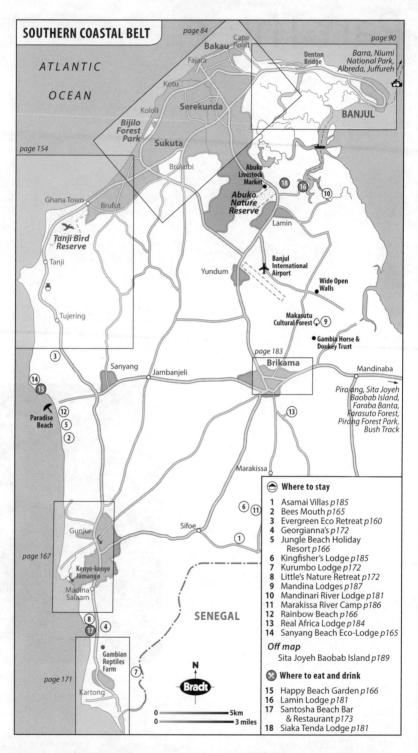

page 84

SOUTHERN COASTAL BELT

page 90

ATLANTIC

OCEAN

page 154

Cape Point

Bakau

Fajara

Denton Bridge

Barra, Niumi National Park, Albreda, Juffureh

Kotu

Serekunda

Kololi

Bijilo Forest Park

Sukuta

BANJUL

Brusubi

Ghana Town

Brufut

Abuko Livestock Market

Abuko Nature Reserve

(18) (16)

(10)

Tanji Bird Reserve

Lamin

Tanji

Banjul International Airport

Wide Open Walls

Tujering

Yundum

Makasutu Cultural Forest (9)

● Gambia Horse & Donkey Trust

(3)

Sanyang

Jambanjeli

page 183

Brikama

Mandinaba

(14)
(15)

Pirang, Sita Joyeh Baobab Island, Faraba Banta, Farasuto Forest, Pirang Forest Park, Bush Track

(12)
(5)
(2)

Paradise Beach

(13)

Marakissa

(6) (11)

Where to stay

1 Asamai Villas *p185*
2 Bees Mouth *p165*
3 Evergreen Eco Retreat *p160*
4 Georgianna's *p172*
5 Jungle Beach Holiday Resort *p166*
6 Kingfisher's Lodge *p185*
7 Kurumbo Lodge *p172*
8 Little's Nature Retreat *p172*
9 Mandina Lodges *p187*
10 Mandinari River Lodge *p181*
11 Marakissa River Camp *p186*
12 Rainbow Beach *p166*
13 Real Africa Lodge *p184*
14 Sanyang Beach Eco-Lodge *p165*

Sifoe

(1)

Gunjur

page 167

Kenye-kenye Jamango

Madina Salaam

(8) (4)
(17)

Off map

Sita Joyeh Baobab Island *p189*

SENEGAL

● Gambian Reptiles Farm

(7)

N

Bradt

Where to eat and drink

15 Happy Beach Garden *p166*
16 Lamin Lodge *p181*
17 Santosha Beach Bar & Restaurant *p173*
18 Siaka Tenda Lodge *p181*

page 171

Kartong

0 ————— 5km
0 ————— 3 miles

The Coastal Belt: An Overview

It's tempting to introduce the Atlantic coastline north and south of Greater Banjul as the very best of The Gambia, or something similarly hyperbolic. True, there are a great many more tourist amenities, of an overall higher standard, packed into the confines of Greater Banjul and Kololi. Conversely, when it comes to free-spirited exploration, nowhere on the coast can offer an adventure comparable to heading upriver into the largely undeveloped and off-the-beaten-track interior. Yet here you can arguably enjoy the best of both worlds.

This is particularly true of the coastline south of Greater Banjul. Coming from the city, it feels refreshingly rustic and unaffected, and you can still find small fishing villages looking entirely organic and at home in the lush nature reserves and swathes of farmland that define the Gambian countryside. Easy to get around, the south is liberally dotted with a collection of low-key and sensibly priced eco-lodges and beach camps, whose down-to-earth ethos is the very antithesis of the packaged hotels of Greater Banjul. Not least, the actual beaches are, for the most part, quite splendid – long swathes of white sand shaded by swaying palms and largely free of unsightly developments.

Even more remote and undeveloped is the northern coastline protected in Niumi National Park. Accessible from Greater Banjul only by ferry or by private boat transfer, this short stretch of coast lies almost entirely on Jinack Island (separated from the mainland by a narrow creek), where a handful of tiny villages nestle alongside a few unabashedly rustic beach camps and one of the finest swimming beaches in the country.

The coastal belt covered in the subsequent chapters also incorporates some inland or riverside sites commonly visited as a day trip out of Greater Banjul. On the North Bank, several riverine locales collectively inscribed as the 'Kunta Kinteh Island and Related Sites' UNESCO World Heritage Site are the goal of the popular Roots excursions from the resorts. On the South Bank, the road to Brikama, the country's second-largest town, offers access to the wonderful Abuko Nature Reserve, Makasutu Cultural Forest and Brikama Craft Market – as well as Banjul International Airport, the point of entry for all fly-in tourists to The Gambia.

HIGHLIGHTS

TANJI BIRD RESERVE The eco-lodge in this community-owned reserve is a favourite of birders. Equally tantalising are day trips to the bird-rich Bijol Islands and a walking trail to Tanji Bridge (page 158).

TANJI This down-to-earth village, among the largest on the south coast, is renowned for its frenetic artisanal fishing beach and fascinating village museum, as well as offering peaceful kayak excursions (page 160).

TUJERING BEACH South of Tanji, this ranks among the country's most beautiful and safest swimming beaches, with the bonus of offering good birding, not to mention tasty food at the locally run beach bars (page 164).

KARTONG BIRD OBSERVATORY Well established as a ringing centre, this excellent facility overlooking a community wetland reserve is the best starting point for exploring a corner of the country famed for throwing up avian rarities and new records (page 175).

ALLAHEIN RIVER It's possible to cross this river to Senegal and visit villages of the Casamance region, at what must be one of the most beautiful border crossings in Africa. Alternatively, pull up a chair for a riverside lunch with an international view (page 175).

GAMBIAN REPTILES FARM At once a rehabilitation, breeding and community education facility, this herpetological centre outside Kartong is a great place to see (and learn about) snakes, tortoises, lizards and crocodiles at close quarters (page 176).

ABUKO NATURE RESERVE The Gambia's largest surviving tract of Upper Guinean Forest supports a wonderful variety of birds (270 species recorded in 1km^2) and small mammals such as monkeys and antelope (page 178).

BRIKAMA CRAFT MARKET For serious handicraft buyers, this well-organised market near Brikama is the best place in the country to pick up quality work at source (page 185).

MAKASUTU CULTURAL FOREST Enjoyable day tours, night extravaganzas and extended stays at the architecturally flamboyant Mandina Lodges are offered at this owner-managed private reserve – the most westerly site to possess a genuinely 'upriver' feel (page 186).

ALBREDA, JUFFUREH AND KUNTA KINTEH (JAMES) ISLAND This trio of slave-trade-related historic sites, collectively inscribed as a UNESCO World Heritage Site, is the target of the popular Roots excursions to the North Bank and Fort James (page 198).

JINACK ISLAND Comprising the entire Atlantic coastline north of the river mouth, budget-friendly Jinack is both the centrepiece of Niumi National Park and the country's ultimate 'desert island fantasy' destination (page 203).

GETTING AROUND

A network of good surfaced roads connects the main towns and villages in this region. The most important of these, both running in a broadly north to south direction, are the South Coast Road from Greater Banjul and Kololi to Kartong via Brusubi Turntable, Tanji, Sanyang and Gunjur, and the Brikama Highway (effectively the start of the South Bank Road) between Serekunda and Brikama via Abuko, Lamin and Banjul International Airport. Connecting these two trunk roads in a broadly west to east direction are the surfaced roads between Brusubi Turntable and Banjul International Airport (newly expanded into a dual carriageway), between Sanyang and Brikama, and between Gunjur and Brikama.

The area is serviced by plenty of gelly-gellys and shared taxis. Coming from Greater Banjul, the main terminus for transport along the South Coast Road is Dippa Kunda Station in Serekunda, though you should also be able to pick up something at Brusubi Turntable, universally known as 'Turntable'. Heading to Brikama and sites en route, transport can be picked up at a station on Mosque Road about 400m south of Serekunda Market, or at Westfield Junction. Day excursions to most sites in the region can also be arranged through hotel activities desks, local tour operators or private guides.

OTHER PRACTICALITIES

Accommodation is plentiful, but it is more spaced out and very different in style from the clustered package hotels that dominate in Greater Banjul. It includes some of the country's finest boutique lodges and hotels, mostly dotted around Brufut, along with a succession of fine beachfront eco-lodges (typically with solar power, borehole water and compost toilets) south of Brufut, and plenty of low-key budget beach and other camps throughout. With the exception of the boutique hotels around Brufut, rooms with air conditioning are a rarity, though the expansion of the power grid means that fans are now considerably more common than they used to be.

Standalone **restaurants** are relatively thin on the ground, since most people tend to eat at their hotel or camp. There are a few **banks** with **ATMs** in Brikama, and on the road back towards Serekunda, as well as at Barra (the North Bank ferry terminus opposite Banjul). There are no banks or ATMs elsewhere north of the river (not in Niumi National Park, Albreda or Juffureh) and the most southerly ATM on the coast is just a few hundred metres south of Brusubi Turntable. Mobile data is typically decent in the towns but can be patchy in between. Many of the better hotels do have Wi-Fi, or can get you connected using a mobile hotspot/router in a pinch.

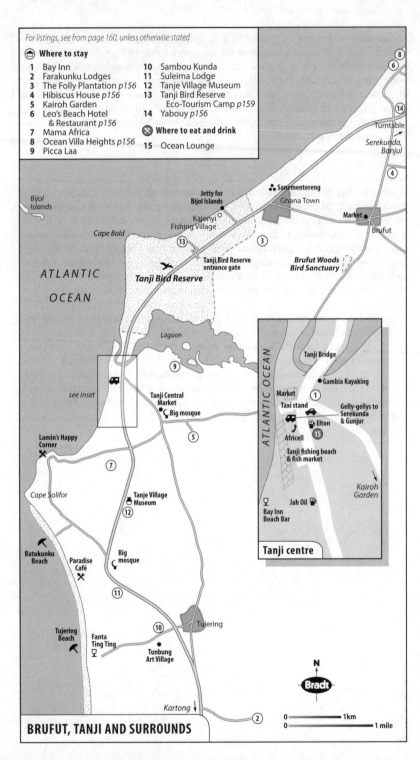

For listings, see from page 160, unless otherwise stated

Where to stay

1 Bay Inn
2 Farakunku Lodges
3 The Folly Plantation *p156*
4 Hibiscus House *p156*
5 Kairoh Garden
6 Leo's Beach Hotel & Restaurant *p156*
7 Mama Africa
8 Ocean Villa Heights *p156*
9 Picca Laa
10 Sambou Kunda
11 Suleima Lodge
12 Tanje Village Museum
13 Tanji Bird Reserve Eco-Tourism Camp *p159*
14 Yabouy *p156*

Where to eat and drink

15 Ocean Lounge

Bijol Islands

Jetty for Bijol Islands

Kajonyi Fishing Village

Sanementereng

Ghana Town

Market

Brufut

Cape Bald

ATLANTIC OCEAN

Tanji Bird Reserve entrance gate

Tanji Bird Reserve

Brufut Woods Bird Sanctuary

Serekunda, Banjul

Turntable

Lagoon

see inset

Tanji Central Market

Big mosque

Lamin's Happy Corner

Cape Solifor

Tanje Village Museum

Batukunku Beach

Paradise Café

Big mosque

Tujering Beach

Fanta Ting Ting

Tunbung Art Village

Tujering

Kartong

Tanji centre

ATLANTIC OCEAN

Tanji Bridge

Gambia Kayaking

Market

Taxi stand

Elton

Gelly-gellys to Serekunda & Gunjur

Africell

Tanji fishing beach & fish market

Kairoh Garden

Bay Inn Beach Bar

Jah Oil

N

Bradt

0 ———— 1km
0 ———— 1 mile

BRUFUT, TANJI AND SURROUNDS

9

Brufut, Tanji and Surrounds

Past Kololi and Bijilo, the Gambian coastline curves in a southwesterly direction for about 8km to Bald Cape, before veering sharply southward to Cape Solifor, the country's most westerly landfall, another 5km further south. Within this relatively short stretch of Atlantic frontage, the coast undergoes a dramatic change in character, as the built-up resorts north of Bijilo give way to the residential suburbia of Brufut and then the more rustic open shoreline and fishing villages typical of the south coast. Further south, Tanji Bird Reserve, which incorporates Bald Cape, is one of the country's most rewarding ornithological sites, and a near-essential day trip for keen birdwatchers. The village of Tanji, on the reserve's southern border, is another popular tourist attraction, thanks to its bustling fishing beach and well-constructed private museum to its south. For those who prefer to base themselves away from the main resorts, the area also boasts a good diversity of accomodation. Though the (ex-Sheraton) Coral Beach Hotel closed its doors and has been up for sale since 2020, there's still plenty of luxury to be found at a couple of sumptuous boutique hotels in Brufut. Alternatively, you can have a more natural experience at the very reasonably priced eco-lodge in Tanji Bird Reserve, or even stay with one of The Gambia's great chefs, Ida Cham.

BRUFUT

This town of around 23,000 people feels somewhat transitional between Greater Banjul and the small villages and wilder beaches that characterise the south coast, coming across like a semi-rusticated southern outpost of the sprawling city with which it intergrades. Traditionally, Brufut is primarily a residential area, and even today it couldn't be described as resort-like in the manner of, say, Kololi or Kotu. But it also houses a few alluring upmarket boutique hotels in the form of Leo's Beach Hotel and Hibiscus House. On the southwestern border of Brufut, the small village of Ghana Town was founded by Ghanaian fishermen, who catch and smoke fish for export to their home country.

GETTING THERE AND AWAY Brufut flanks the main Coastal Road for a distance of about 4km south of Brusubi Turntable (Junction), the landmark traffic circle (and new flyover as of 2023) at the four-way intersection of Coastal Road (to Gunjur), Sayerr Jobe Road (from Serekunda), Bertil Harding Highway (from Kololi and Bijilo), and the AU Highway (from Banjul International Airport and Brikama). Its hotels are all quite well signposted if you are in a private vehicle, but Leo's Beach Hotel and Hibiscus House are both fairly isolated and best reached from the airport (or elsewhere) in a private taxi, which should cost about £20. If you are heading to Brufut Woods, you could catch a shared taxi or gelly-gelly to the central market area of Brufut, and walk from there.

WHERE TO STAY *Map, page 154*

Exclusive/luxury

✴ **Leo's Beach Hotel & Restaurant** (6 rooms) Brufut Heights; m 721 2830; e info@leosgambia. com; w leos.gm. Opened in 2013, this absolutely stunning boutique hotel, owned & managed by a flexible, efficient & enthusiastic Austrian couple, has quickly gained an enviable reputation for its food, service & quality accommodation. Set on a low cliff, it is centred on a large swimming pool in neat gardens that lead to a footpath running down to a beautiful secluded beach. The large en-suite rooms, which combine clean contemporary lines with quality imported fittings & stylish local rosewood furniture & décor, mostly have a sea view & all come with AC, fan, sat TV, minibar, stereo, coffee-making facilities, hot water & even a mobile phone loaded with local numbers for your personal use. A 20kW photovoltaic solar-energy system provides enough electricity to cover all its power demands. An added attraction, well worth the excursion even if you are staying elsewhere, is the breezy poolside restaurant, which specialises in simple but delicious Mediterranean-style seafood. Not cheap, but still excellent value for money. *From £120/138 sgl/dbl B&B.* **$$$$**

Upmarket

✴ **Hibiscus House** (10 rooms) Brufut; m 717 2337, (+44)(0)7787 505384; e info@hibiscushousegambia.com; w hibiscushousegambia.com. The backstreets of Brufut might not seem like the most obvious location for one of The Gambia's top boutique hotels, but it is where you will find Hibiscus House, nestled unobtrusively among low-rise local compounds & fantastically bumpy dirt roads. Set in a mango-shaded compound rattling with birdlife & dominated by a sparkling swimming pool, this hotel is notable for its hands-on & very accommodating British owner-managers, sociable atmosphere & welcoming staff, all of which ensure plenty of repeat business. The spacious, individually styled rooms are simply but tastefully decorated, with twin or queen-size bed, fans & en-suite hot shower, & there are also 2 apts that share a second pool. Although it is 2km from the sea, the hotel has the advantage of a bumster-free village setting away from the main tourist areas. For those who want a break from the in-house pool, the hotel can arrange trusted local taxis to

take you to various isolated beaches further south, as well as expeditions further afield. Facilities include free Wi-Fi, an excellent restaurant & bar, & a lounge with plenty of board games & books. *£85 dbl Garden Room, £115 dbl Casuarina Deluxe room, min stay 3 nights, all rates B&B.* **$$$**

Mid-range

✴ **The Folly Plantation** (8 rooms) Brufut; m 261 6775, (+44)(0)7842 454078; e thefollygambia@gmail.com; w the-folly-gambia.business.site; ⨍ TheFollyGambia. While this affable & animated British-run guesthouse in the sandy streets on the outskirts of Brufut may feel remote, it's ideally placed for exploring village life, the nearby bush & wide empty beaches, all just a 20-min drive from the main coastal resorts. From the highway, take the last left just before the Tanji Bird Reserve begins & continue straight for 900m. The traditional palm leaf-roofed roundhouses are comfortable & tastefully decorated, with solar power, fans & en suites with hot water. The bar attracts local expats & tasty food is on offer, with lovingly prepared Gambian dishes & European favourites. Tours can be arranged with local people & enthusiastic owner Nikki also provides hairdressing services & other beauty treatments. *£60 dbl B&B with cheaper self-catering & budget rooms available.* **$$$**

Ocean Villa Heights (7 rooms) Brufut Heights; m 248 7430, 377 7663; e info@oceanvillaheights. com; w oceanvillaheights.com. Situated upon a clifftop overlooking a deserted beach, Ocean Villa Heights is a British-run boutique hotel complete with an iconic red telephone box at the entrance. Rooms are modern & comfortable, all with AC & en suites with hot water. A restaurant serves both Gambian & European dishes in the £5–8 range. The hotel offers sea fishing, birdwatching & other tours, or you can simply relax on the sun terrace by the pool. *£53 dbl B&B.* **$$$**

Budget

Yabouy (6 rooms) Ocean Rd, Brusubi; m 772 7272, 372 7273, 990 4990; e ida@gambianhomecooking. com; w gambianhomecooking.com; ⨍ gambianhomecooking. As well as running a popular cooking school (see opposite), Ida hosts guests in her beautiful house. The homestay is on the highway heading west towards Tanji & in close proximity to the shops & bars of the Turntable area as well as the beaches of Brufut Heights. The rooms are spotlessly clean, tastefully decorated with African artwork & equipped with fan, nets & Wi-Fi. Outside is a lovely shady courtyard in which to relax. *£28 dbl B&B*. **$$**

✖ WHERE TO EAT AND DRINK   *Map, page 84*

Chosaan   Ocean Rd, Brusubi; m 290 2686. Probably the pick of several roadside bar-restaurants catering to locals, expats & tourists along the road heading west from Brusubi Turntable, not least as it's the only one offering Wi-Fi & live music every night. Food is reasonably priced & the large tiled veranda is a great spot to spend an evening. *Mains around £4–6*. **$$**

OTHER PRACTICALITIES

Banks and foreign exchange There are several banks with ATMs in the area, including **GT Bank** and **EcoBank**, as well as several private **forex bureaux** around the Turntable and the first 100m or so of Ocean Road heading west. Beware that the Turntable garage is a well-known haunt of pickpockets.

Shopping There are several mini-markets catering to expats, tourists and wealthier locals in the immediate vicinity of the Turntable, along with the side-by-side 24-hour **Medicare** and **Stop Step** pharmacies.

WHAT TO SEE AND DO Because Brufut marks the transition between the developed coast north of Bijilo and the more rustic south coast, it makes a useful base for exploring in either direction. The hectic Senegambia Strip, with its dozens of restaurants and nightspots, is only about 6km to the northeast (a 20-minute taxi ride), while Tanji Bird Reserve and fishing beach are only a few kilometres to the south, as are the lovely beaches at Batukunku and Tujering.

Yabouy Cooking School (m 772 7272, 372 7273; e ida@gambianhomecooking. com; w gambianhomecooking.com; 🄵 gambianhomecooking; ⏲ Sep–May) Legendary local Ida Cham (owner of Yabouy guesthouse, see opposite) has created an experience that is, for many, the highlight of their Gambian holiday. A day's cooking with Ida in her Brufut home is not a simple case of spending the day in her kitchen. First off, you'll put on African clothes – brightly patterned shirts for men and dresses and head scarves for women. Next up, you travel together to nearby Tanji market – a sensory overload in itself – where Ida will guide you through the various stalls to buy fish, vegetables and other ingredients. Her emphasis is on healthy choices and she's well versed in catering for vegetarians or those with specific dietary requirements. After returning and preparing the meal as a group, you will eat together communally, Gambian style, and then relax to play local games and share cultural insights. The day lasts from 09.00 until 14.00 and is £55 per person, which includes a transfer to and from your hotel. Ida also arranges a supper club (Come Dine with Ida), where she serves a home-cooked evening meal against a backdrop of kora and storytelling (⏲ 19.00–22.00; £28 pp inc hotel transfer). A new farmstead in Tujering with pick-your-own veg and an art gallery is also in the works.

Brufut Woods Bird Sanctuary (⊕ 13.3750, -16.7549; entry D50) This wedge-shaped community-organised sanctuary, which lies about 2km inland from the Tanji Bird Reserve, is an initiative of the West African Birds Study Association (WABSA), an organisation formed in 1994 by a group of local youths and bird guides dedicated to preserving the country's flora and fauna. Protecting around

1km² of well-preserved coastal woodland immediately south of Brufut, this dry scrubby forest, serviced by a good network of footpaths, is regarded as perhaps the best site for woodland birding this side of Abuko, though species seen here tend to be associated with more open canopies. Among the more interesting birds regularly observed are African pied hornbill, striped kingfisher, green turaco, Vieillot's barbet, swallow-tailed bee-eater, mottled spinetail, red-shouldered cuckoo-shrike, yellow-bellied hyliota, red-bellied paradise flycatcher and western violet-backed sunbird. It is also often a rewarding site for raptors such as lizard buzzard, dark chanting goshawk, Gabar goshawk, African harrier-hawk, long crested eagle, palm-nut vulture and lanner falcon. A local guide nicknamed Doctor Owl is well known for his ability to locate nocturnal species such as Verreaux's eagle-owl, white-faced scops owl and long-tailed nightjar. There is also a new (paid) photo hide here (m 329 6385; w photohidegambia.com).

To get there, catch a shared taxi or other public transport to Brufut, request to be dropped at the central market, then ask for directions to the reserve entrance and ticket office, which is on the west side of the Madiana Road about 800m south of the town centre. All the birding guides based at Kotu Bridge know the site and can guide you there.

Sanementereng (⊕ 13.3885, -16.7676) About 500m north of the Tanji Bird Reserve's northern boundary – and less than 100m from the appropriately cheerful **Smile Gambia Beach Bar** (◼f thesmilebeachbar), where they opened a few neat rooms in 2022 (£14 dbl; $) – lies this sacred site, best visited with a local guide. Located in a clearing in the clifftop, this baobab tree and simple hut attracts Muslims from all over The Gambia in search of good fortune or health. There's a stone at the base of the hut for offerings, while the well at the bottom of the cliff is said to contain special water that can help women overcome infertility.

TANJI BIRD RESERVE

Established in 1993, the 6km² Tanji Bird Reserve (m 981 6799, 206 4997; ⊕ daily; entrance D35 pp) protects most of the 4km coastline between the Ghana Town fishing beach and the mouth of the Tanji (or Karinti) River on its southern border. It incorporates Cape Bald, a lateritic peninsula that resurfaces about 1.5km from the mainland to form the tiny Bijol Islands, the country's only offshore territory, which is also protected within the reserve. Although not exactly historical in a conventional sense, the coast protected by Tanji Bird Reserve was first documented in 1456 by the pioneering Portuguese explorer Luiz de Cadamosto, who encountered dangerous breakers around Cape Bald while sailing between the mouths of the rivers Gambia and Casamance, and also reported the presence of an unnamed river there.

Despite its small area, Tanji Bird Reserve encompasses a wide range of habitat types, including sandy beaches, tidal lagoons, mangrove swamps, barren flats, coastal scrub and dry savannah woodland. More than 260 bird species, including 34 birds of prey, have been recorded, with the greatest diversity being noted in early and late winter, when many Palaearctic passage migrants stop by. Of the rarities, it is worth looking out for white-fronted plover, Audouin's gull and kelp gull on the beach. Other interesting marine birds include ruddy turnstone, slender-billed gull, and half a dozen tern species. Inland you may be lucky and find red-billed quelea or yellow-breasted apalis alongside more typical woodland and grassland species. The Bijol Islands are an important breeding site for several species. A large breeding colony of royal terns can be found on the smaller of the two islands, along with lesser numbers of Caspian tern, grey-headed gull and western reef heron. Up to 700 roosting pelicans are present over June to August, and smaller numbers can be seen throughout the year.

Tanji Reserve is not just good for birds. Green turtles have been known to nest on the Bijol Islands and along the beach on the mainland part of the reserve, especially over June to October. The mammals present here include western red colobus, green and patas monkeys, various genets, African civet, spotted hyena, crested porcupine and bushbuck. There are also snakes such as pythons, cobras and puff adders, though of course you will be extremely lucky (or unlucky, depending on your view) to see any of these. There is also a good selection of butterflies and dragonflies at Tanji. In the sea just off the reserve a number of marine mammals have been spotted, including minke whale, Atlantic hump-backed dolphin and bottlenose dolphin. The extremely rare monk seal was once found here, but has not been observed for at least a decade.

The main activity in the reserve is **bird walks**, which can be undertaken with or without a guide (D500/hour), as you choose. You are free to explore anywhere on foot; an excellent introductory trail leads from the eco-lodge and park headquarters to Tanji Bridge, which crosses the lagoon formed by the Tanji River as it empties into the ocean immediately north of Tanji village. It takes about 45 minutes to walk this, but if you are looking at birds, it might well take 2 or more hours. The other main activity is morning **boat trips** to see the stunning birdlife on the Bijol Islands, which can be arranged through the lodge and cost D900 per person (minimum group size of five). The boat trips run from September to December daily, but only go once weekly over the breeding season of January to August, to avoid overly disturbing the birds. For an in-depth look at the Bijol Islands, see this presentation from Linda Barnett and Craig Emms, authors of the first-ever edition of this guide in 2001: w youtube.com/watch?v=0MUTggPdaD0.

GETTING THERE AND AWAY Tanji Bird Reserve is bisected by the main coastal road between Brufut and Tanji. There are two main access points from this road. The first, coming from the north, is Kajonyi Fishing Village (⊕ 13.3846, -16.7750), the official launch site for boats to the Bijol Islands, which lies about 200m north of the main road along a dirt track signposted to the right, 400m past the Ghana Town junction for Brufut. Less than 1km past this, the main entrance gate and eco-lodge site (about 500m from the main road) are also signposted to the right (⊕ for junction 13.3796, -16.7806).

In a private taxi, either of these access points is around 20–30 minutes' drive from the main coastal resorts further north. Alternatively, the regular gelly-gellys that leave from Dippa Kunda Taxi Park (Bakoteh Junction) for Tanji can drop you at either of the access points by request.

WHERE TO STAY AND EAT   *Map, page 154*

✴ **Tanji Bird Reserve Eco-Tourism Camp** (8 rooms) m 741 0027; e ecocamptanjibirdreserve@ yahoo.com. Opened in 2013, this eco-lodge, set above the beach on a low ridge overlooking a small waterhole that attracts plenty of birds & other wildlife, is an ideal base for budget-conscious nature lovers & birdwatchers seeking an alternative to the package hotels further north. A few management changes means service & standards can be a bit variable, but it has good eco-credentials, being part of a project to help local people derive meaningful income from what was community land before it became a reserve, & profits are split between local communities & the reserve management. The accommodation, in semi-detached bungalows with high-domed roofs designed for natural ventilation, is built with eco-friendly mud bricks & relies solely on solar power (with inverters for storage when there's no sun) & borehole water. The brightly decorated rooms have tiled flooring, fridge, twin beds with wooden net frames, en-suite cold shower, standing fan & private balcony. Day visitors are welcome to make use of the attractive outdoor restaurant, which has seating in summer houses, & serves seafood & Gambian dishes in the £6–7.50 range, though you may want to call first if you're in a hurry. *£24 dbl B&B.* **$$**

TANJI AND AROUND

Immediately south of the bridge across the Tanji River mouth, the main South Coast Road bisects Tanji (also sometimes spelt Tanje or Tanjeh), a busy seafront town of around 15,000 inhabitants that stretches inland for about 1km to a central square flanked by a market and a large mosque. The busiest fishing and fish-smoking centre along the Gambian coast, Tanji makes for a popular day trip out of the coastal resorts further north, though its wide sandy beach – lined with pirogues and strewn with dead fish and offal – is more an extension of the market than it is a viable swimming venue. In addition to offering a fascinating glimpse into the everyday workings of a traditional fishing beach and market, Tanji is the jumping off point for wonderful short kayak excursions up the Tanji River.

GETTING THERE AND AWAY The town is bisected by the main road along the south coast and easily reached by shared taxi or gelly-gelly from Dippa Kunda Taxi Park in Serekunda or Brusubi Turntable south of Bijilo. The fare is less than D50. It is also easy enough to pick up transport on to Gunjur, Kartong and other destinations further south.

 WHERE TO STAY *Map, page 154, unless otherwise stated*
Most people visit Tanji as a day trip, often in conjunction with the neighbouring bird reserve, but there are a handful of affordable lodges scattered in and around town.

Upmarket
⁎ **Evergreen Eco Retreat** [map, page 150] (5 rooms) ✆ 13.2903, -16.7920; m 702 1151, (+44)(0)7954 583517; e evergreengam@gmail. com; w evergreengambia.com. Tucked away in the bush just south of Tujering, Evergreen Eco Retreat lies in a beautiful & meditative garden about 30 mins' walk from the quiet expanse of a deserted beach. There are 4 spacious & tastefully decorated roundhouses complete with king-size beds, wet rooms & porches as well as a luxury house with its own patio, all built using local materials & according to sustainable eco principles. The restaurant serves freshly cooked meals of the day, fusing African & international cuisines, & vegetarians are well catered for. Holistic massage therapies & yoga workshops can be arranged, along with birding guides. Additionally, the lodge supports several local projects including beekeeping & moringa (a tropical tree that provides many nutritional & health benefits) production, & products are available to purchase.

The lodge is signposted on the right-hand side of the highway as you leave Tujering heading southwards. Warmly recommended for anyone seeking a quiet eco-retreat. *£75/85 sgl/dbl roundhouse, £100 for the dbl luxury house, all rates HB.* **$$$**
⁎ **Farakunku Lodges** (4 rooms) ✆ 13.3024, -16.7770; m 726 0669, 706 2725; e heather-moses@farakunku.com; w farakunku.com. Situated inland of the main coastal road near the village of Farakunku, which lies about 7km south of Tanji & 2km past Tujering, this small lodge comes across as a true labour of love, thanks to the enthusiastic & eco-conscious British–Gambian owner-managers, who live on site & are very attuned to the interests & requirements of birdwatchers, their main clientele. The compact but well-tended grounds are alive with birds, as is a sanctuary with bird pool in a separate compound a minute's walk away. The spacious & well-ventilated octagonal lodges have high wooden ceilings, screened windows, tiled floors,

ceiling fan, cane furniture, king-size beds with walk-in nets, a secure lock-up dressing room for cameras & other costly birding gear, & en-suite hot shower. Facilities include a small but welcome plunge pool, bicycle hire & a restaurant serving a set 3-course meal that can cater for pretty much any special culinary requirements with advance notice. An integrated solar system powers the entire site. 3 excellent bird guides are permanently employed at the lodge, which lies in an area of woodland that supports superb avian variety. The lodge can also be used as the base for a full week-long birding package visiting different sites every day, while non-birders are catered for by day excursions to the lovely beaches at nearby Tujering & Batukunku. One of our top recommendations for bird enthusiasts anywhere in The Gambia. Very fair value, too. *£80/93 sgl/ dbl HB.* **$$$**

☀ Mama Africa (8 rooms) ✪ 13.3462, -16.7975; m 745 0730; e info@mama-africa-gambia.org; w mama-africa-gambia.org. Set in a large plot of land 600m off the main road just south of Tanji village, internationally acclaimed Gambian artist Isha Fofana & her German husband have lovingly created this lodge & art centre, where the stylish roundhouses sit in a garden studded with sculpture & carvings. Each house is a work of art in itself & the spacious solar-powered rooms are beautifully decorated & have king-size beds, wet rooms & fans. The restaurant serves Afro–European fusion food with vegetables including chard, beetroot & others not normally grown in The Gambia, plucked straight from the adjacent gardens, which guests are welcome to visit. The cultural centre is full of displays of local art & workshops in a variety of disciplines from batik to botany can be arranged. *£71/88 sgl/dbl B&B.* **$$$**

Suleima Lodge (7 rooms) m 390 5079, 990 5079; e suleimalodge@yahoo.com, bohagan1@ hotmail.com; ⬛ hotelsuleimalodge2014. Situated between the villages of Batakunku & Tujering, this lodge lies in large, forested gardens centred on a 33m-long pool only 10 mins from a quiet beach. Accommodation is in solar-powered suites whose Sahelian-influenced architecture has an earthy, organic feel. The surrounding area is good for birdwatching & fishing, & the lodge also offers several excursions further afield. *£85 dbl, £125 suite, both B&B. HB & FB available.* **$$$**

Budget

☀ Sambou Kunda (4 rooms) ✪ 13.3170, -16.7972; m 753 3097, 753 3085; e samboukunda@gmail.com. Set in a forested area just 10 mins' walk from the beach, this is a new & outstanding-value Gambian–Spanish lodge. Built according to eco principles with compressed earth blocks & local materials, the very large spacious rooms have en-suite wet room & a mezzanine level with an additional bed. Delicious Spanish & African meals are served in the large thatched bantaba for around £5–6. The owners also offer tailor-made trips in The Gambia, Senegal & Conakry in Guinea, specialising in off-the-beaten-track places that most operators don't reach. Profits from tourism help support a local school that teaches solar installation to young women from the surrounding villages, aiming to provide education, generate jobs, train entrepreneurs & empower women. *£24 dbl B&B.* **$$**

Bay Inn (5 rooms) ☎ 441 5255; m 512 4422, 506 2008, 254 8630. The most central option in Tanji is near the bridge & kayak launch, & just opposite Nyanya's Beach Lodge (which was not functioning as of 2023). Rooms are straightforward & modern, with en-suite bath & fan or AC. It's got a large, if somewhat underutilised, roof terrace, with great views over the town & bolong, & a street-facing restaurant serving various grills & an affordable daily dish. They've also got an associated beach bar with some new roundhouse guestrooms about 1km to the south, just on the other side of Tanji's main fishing beach (✪ 13.3525, -16.7996). *£20/26 fan/AC dbl.* **$$**

Picca Laa (10 rooms) ✪ 13.3593, -16.7897; m 319 5352; e book@piccalaa.co.uk; w piccalaa. co.uk. Set in large, forested grounds just 10 mins from the beach, this eco-friendly lodge, managed by Tanji locals, is a great option in this range. Brightly coloured solar-powered roundhouses are simple but clean & come with dbl or twin beds & en-suite bathroom with cold shower, although their eco principles mean there is no AC. Complimentary drinks are offered on arrival, & tasty Gambian evening meals, made using vegetables grown on site, are served for around £7. Birding tours to Tanji & other nearby reserves are offered with local guide Laibo Manneh, late-night excursions to Kololi can be arranged, & bikes can also be hired if you fancy a leisurely cycle along the beach. *£25 pp B&B.* **$$**

Shoestring

Kairoh Garden (24 rooms) ⊕ 13.348333, -16.783783; m 999 3526, 751 6138; e information@kairohgarden.com; w kairohgarden.com; f. Set in the semi-rural backroads east of central Tanji, in massive orchard-like grounds with permaculture gardens teeming with birdlife, this welcoming Dutch–Gambian owner-managed lodge helps to fund the Kairoh Garden Foundation, which supports the education of around 100 disadvantaged local children & creates agricultural opportunities for local women. It is set back about 2km from the beach & consciously chooses to offer its guests an integrated & down-to-earth African village experience rather than a resort-like atmosphere. Accommodation is basic but clean & well ventilated, with a choice of bright en-suite rooms or dingier rooms with shared showers, all with nets & private balconies, but no AC or fan.

Facilities include a restaurant serving set meals for around £6–8, bicycle hire & a relaxed *bantaba* set below mango trees hung with hammocks. Tours can be arranged around The Gambia, & they have a 2nd location in Kuntaur (page 239). They can also put together programmes for professionals such as nurses & teachers to meet their Gambian counterparts working in local communities. *£12/15 pp with shared/en-suite bath, B&B.* **$$**

Tanje Village Museum (9 rooms) m 992 6618, 705 7045; e abdoulie.bayo@yahoo.com; f. The forested grounds of this popular museum provide a tranquil retreat with traditional Mandinka-style roundhouses available in which to stay, providing a unique guesthouse experience. The simple huts with en-suite bathrooms have dbl or twin beds with nets & cold showers. The restaurant serves Gambian & European food as well as the usual bottled drinks. *£10 pp B&B.* **$**

✄ WHERE TO EAT AND DRINK *Map, page 154*

For something informal and affordable in the centre, the restaurant at **Bay Inn** (page 161; **$**) is a good choice. Otherwise, **Ocean Lounge** (m 788 2817, 397 7877; **$$**), despite sitting just steps from Tanji's chaotic main market and road junction, is a much more charming address, with garden seating and a long menu of meat and seafood dishes for £4–6, plus a full bar.

WHAT TO SEE AND DO In addition to the sites listed below, Tanji Bird Reserve (page 158) is easily visited from Tanji, since the entrance gate lies only 3km back along the road to Brufut.

Tanji fishing beach This is the largest of the series of small artisanal fishing centres that stretch along the coast south of Brufut. As such, it is a fascinating place, and particularly suited to photographers with lots of opportunity for action shots (though as always, be respectful – a little chat can go a long way). The first thing you'll notice upon entering this or any other fishing beach will be the sometimes overwhelming smell, followed by the collection of brightly painted wooden pirogues anchored just offshore or pulled up high on to the beach. These local canoes vary in size from small one-man jobs to large boats that have crews of 20 or more, which include shelters for the sailors on longer journeys. You may even see a few boats under construction on the beach, and it is fascinating to see how they are put together using methods that have changed little over generations. Many of the larger boats are not Gambian and are crewed by a whole range of nationalities, from Senegalese right through to people based as far away as Ghana.

Most of the fishing that takes place from these pirogues uses traditional methods. Gill nets are used to catch small quantities of fish, which are then landed on the beach and sold to local traders, who in turn sell them to the coastal communities. Many fish are also sun-dried or smoked in huts by the beach. If you walk around and show an interest, most people will be pleased to show you how the process works. Unfortunately, while smoking is an excellent way to preserve fish, it is also heavy on firewood, with the result that huge areas of coastal forest and scrub around Tanji have been chopped down. The construction of an ice plant to freeze fish has somewhat reduced this demand, but cold storage chains away from the coast remain quite limited.

If you keep your eyes open as you walk along the beach among the pirogues you will see all sorts of discarded marine life, from crabs to the severed heads of hammerhead sharks. Two things that you shouldn't see are dolphins and marine turtles, which are legally protected in The Gambia. There are, and always will be, accidents where these species are caught and drowned in fishing nets, and of course there are also unscrupulous people who will break the law, but on the whole local fishermen do avoid beaching dolphins and turtles.

Boat trips If you are feeling adventurous, you might like to go out on a short trip on a pirogue or even accompany the crew while they are fishing. This will cost you, of course, but fishing is a hard life and not well paid, so the crew will welcome the additional income. There are no fixed prices as hardly any tourists are brave enough to do this, so you will have to negotiate. A trip like this can be very exciting as you crash out through the surf. You may feel a little unsafe in some of the pirogues, which seem to roll about too much or leak in water just a little too fast; don't be overly worried, but do make sure you have a life vest. Remember that these fishermen have to go out every day in these same boats, no matter what the conditions are like, and most of them are very good at what they do. Do remember to watch your camera gear or binoculars, as they are extremely likely to get wet, especially during setting off and landing. We suggest you keep them safely wrapped up in plastic bags during these parts of your trip or, better still, don't take them with you at all. Once salt water gets into your camera or binoculars they corrode very fast and are more or less ruined!

Kayak trips (✇ 13.3599, -16.7968; m 241 1111; e gambiakayakingfishing@ gmail.com; w goddardswatersports.gm; ▮ Gambia Kayaking) From a poorly signposted base directly at the southeast corner of Tanji Bridge, professional outfitter **Goddard's Watersports/Gambia Kayaking** offers highly recommended guided kayak excursions up the Tanji River. Here, you can paddle your way out of Tanji's noisy coastal bustle and disappear into a hushed thicket of mangrove forest, cut through by a series of narrow channels that would be inaccessible to any larger boat. This small river once served as a dump for residents nearby, but has been rehabilitated and protected in partnership with the local community. Birders can spot kingfishers, rollers, pelicans and a variety of other waterbirds.

Trips depart around 07.00 and 15.30 daily (£30 pp; call ahead to book) and last between 3 and 4 hours, including a break at a scenic spot upriver to stretch your legs and have a snack or a drink. Though the excursions are suitable for all levels of expertise, they also have wooden pirogues suitable for small groups who are not interested in kayaking. They can also arrange fishing trips.

Tanje Village Museum (✇ 13.3396, -16.7961; m 992 6618, 705 7045; e abdoulie. bayo@yahoo.com; ☉ 08.00–17.00 daily; entrance D240 with discounts for Gambians & children, inclusive of optional guide) Founded in the 1990s by Abdoulie Bayo, former curator of Banjul's National Museum, the excellent Tanje Village Museum is very popular with tourists and is also used extensively by local school groups for educational purposes. It lies about 1km south of town on the landward side of the main coastal road. It is divided into several parts, most impressively perhaps a life-size replica of a traditional Mandinka compound showing various types of huts and their uses, and the museum also hosts traditional craftspeople such as a blacksmith, weaver and kora player.

There is a building with various displays on Gambian culture and musical instruments, as well as an informative display on the wildlife of The Gambia (the latter put together by Craig Emms and Linda Barnett, the authors of the original Bradt Guide from 2001). The short nature trail through the grounds includes a selection of labelled trees, and a trail guide can be bought with information on the traditional medicinal uses of 30 species. Set aside 45–60 minutes for the full guided tour. At the end of your exploration of the museum you'll find welcome shade in the bantaba, where a selection of cold drinks and food is for sale. The forested museum grounds provide a tranquil retreat and offer unique Mandinka-style roundhouses in which to stay (page 162).

Batukunku Beach Two of the loveliest beaches in The Gambia lie on the coast immediately south of Cape Solifor, the country's most westerly point. Coming from the north, the first and least developed of these is Batukunku, whose wide sandy beach is set in a shallow bay protected by a small rocky peninsula about 1km south of Cape Solifor. To get there, there's a dirt road that makes a 4.5km loop west of the main road out to Cape Solifor and back. From the north, it's reachable from the signposted turn-off towards Mama Africa (✪ 13.3490, -16.7957), hitting the cape after 2km. Stop off here at the aptly named **Lamin's Happy Corner** (✪ 13.3450, -16.8100; m 737 2892) for a cheerful lunch, then follow the road south/southeast back to the main coastal road (✪ 13.3279, -16.8004) at Batukunku village.

Alternatively, it's about 2.5km down the sand to another well-loved beach shack, ✳ **Paradise Cafe** (✪ 13.3230, -16.8041; m 772 4788), where friendly Malang and his crew will prepare simple dishes such as freshly caught fish, chicken and chips or rice for around £5 – ring in advance if you don't want to wait (but did you really come out here to hurry?). The beach here has a reputation for being very safe in terms of both security and swimming.

Tujering Beach About 2km south of Batukunku Beach as the crow flies, the long sandy beach at Tujering is just as beautiful, and also home to a handful of welcoming beach bars serving up cold drinks and the catch of the day. The most reliable of these is probably **Fanta Ting Ting** (✪ 13.3068, -16.8024; m 726 3141), a comfortable and likeable place to sit over a few drinks or a meal (the catch of the day costs around £5; lobster and prawns are pricier). Swimming is normally safe, but check with Fanta's before you take the plunge. You can drive to within about 200m of the beach, after which you need to walk through sandy dunes surrounding a reed-fringed lagoon that often offers rewarding birding. The beach lies about 1.5km west of the main coastal road; to get there drive south past Batukunku for another 2km or so until you reach the village of Tujering, where you need to turn right on to a dirt road at a junction signposted for the Tunbung Art Village and Fanta Ting Ting Beach Bar (✪ 13.3137, -16.7886).

Tunbung Art Village (Tujering; ✪ 13.3099, -16.7897; m 998 2102, 982 7255, 594 9064; e info@tunbungartvillage.gm; w tunbungartvillage.gm; f) The quirky and wonderful Tunbung Art Village is a ragged assembly of skewed huts, wildly painted walls and random sculptures that peer out behind walls and from treetops. It's the creative universe of Etu Ndow, a renowned Gambian artist who sadly died in 2014, but whose memory is kept alive by his nephew Abdoulie. Workshops are available (around £40 for a half-day workshop for two) in screen printing, painting and crafts using natural materials. The studio is in the forested grounds of the family compound and there's a permanent exhibition of Etu's work, as well as a couple of guest rooms.

10

South to Kartong

The least-developed and arguably most attractive part of the Gambian coast runs south from Tanji for about 30km to Kartong and the Allahein River on the border with the Casamance region of Senegal. Starting from the north, there are three main clusters of accommodation in the area. First is Sanyang, which lost many of its hotels to a redevelopment scheme a decade ago but is now home to a growing handful of relaxed beach lodges, and then Gunjur, the largest city in the area, 10km further south. Finally there is Kartong along the Senegalese border, which is a low-key but particularly rewarding destination for nature lovers thanks to its attractive beach and riverine scenery, well-managed reptile park and a cluster of good birdwatching sites.

SANYANG

Located about halfway between Tanji and Gunjur, this junction town of around 13,000 inhabitants lies 3km inland of the long stretch of palm-fringed white sand referred to by Gambian operators as Paradise Beach – and it's easy to see why they call it that. Many of the camps lining Sanyang Beach were bulldozed to the ground in 2013, but the developments they were demolished to make way for never materialised. So, in the years since, a handful of breezy beach camps have recolonised the coast here, and it's as tempting as ever to pull up a chair in paradise.

GETTING THERE AND AWAY Regular gelly-gellys to Sanyang town leave from the Dippa Kunda Taxi Park in Serekunda and cost around D20. There is also plenty of transport connecting Sanyang to other towns along the main road between Brufut and Kartong, as well as along the 13km road east to Brikama, giving quick and easy access to the airport. Irregular shared taxis connect Sanyang town to the beach.

WHERE TO STAY AND EAT *Map, page 150*

✳ **Sanyang Beach Eco-lodge** (15 rooms) How Ba Rd; ✪ 13.2722, -16.8022; m 397 2422, 218 8382, 314 2644; e info@ecolodgehawba.com; w ecolodgehawba.com. At the northern end of the cluster of Sanyang resorts, this new lodge near Sanyang Point feels delightfully remote, with a row of small but neat en-suite rooms facing a wide sweep of beach & an airy resto-bar serving Gambian dishes around £5/plate. Can arrange guided birding & other local excursions. *£16 pp B&B.* **$$**

Bee's Mouth (4 rooms) Paradise Beach; m 239 8101; e beesmouthgambia@ gmail.com; w beesmouthgambia.com; f beesmouthgambia1. Set facing the ocean about 400m south of Jungle Beach, this clutch of atmospheric wooden bungalows & tipi-style standing tents feels a fair bit more organic than the other options on this stretch of beach. The British–Gambian managers ran a B&B in Brighton before opening up here in 2018. The kitchen focuses on produce from their own gardens, & as the name implies, they also make their own honey. £35 dbl. **$$**

Jungle Beach Holiday Resort (10 rooms) m 998 6188, 998 6143. A friendly beach bar & restaurant that escaped the purge of 2013, this resort has a lovely ambience, set in a coconut grove that provides shade for the sunbeds on this idyllic beach. The resto-bar does reasonably priced Gambian & European meals & local musicians put on regular *djembe* performances. Basic rooms are available with nets & fans. £20/£28 sgl/dbl B&B. **$$**

Rainbow Beach (15 rooms) Paradise Beach; m 972 6806, 715 8487; e jjjawla@yahoo.com;

w rainbow.gm. Next door to Jungle Beach, this has a slightly more package-holiday feel. There is a restaurant & beach bar – serving a very nice fish & chips – plus a spa offering massage & beauty treatments. In season, there is traditional wrestling on the beach most Sundays at 16.00. Basic rooms have en-suite bathrooms, nets & fans. £16/19 sgl/ dbl B&B. **$**

Happy Beach Garden m 340 1473, 380 0430. This cheerful garden space dotted with thatched bantabas is a fine place to while away an afternoon with a seafood lunch (around £4) & a cold beer, or to pitch a beachfront tent for the night. **$$**

WHAT TO SEE AND DO Slightly quieter and more easily accessible than both Tanji and Gunjur, Sanyang's fishing village is very picturesque with colourful pirogues lining the beach. It's a popular spot for musicians and many drumming courses and performances are available to see and experience: just ask at any of the beach bars. Sanyang is also a known nesting beach for turtles, and local NGO **Smile For Life** (m 999 5059, 778 8509; w smileforlifethegambia.org; ⨍ smileforlifethegambia) works to safeguard turtle nesting sites in the area, running regular patrols in season (June–November) and relocating nests to their protected hatchery as needed – they have protected more than 12,000 eggs since their founding in 2011. They also do youth and community sensitisation in communities along The Gambia's southern coast. You can join one of their nighttime nesting patrols, or it's also possible to volunteer with them for several weeks at a time; send founders Omar and Mariama a message for details.

The four-day **Sanyang International Cultural Festival** (⨍ Sanyang International Cultural Festival) takes place yearly, usually during the final week of January, with contemporary and traditional music, cultural dance, a tourism fair, African cuisine, kids' games, arts and crafts, and organised tours to historic places and sacred shrines. At the time of writing, it hadn't yet been held post-Covid; it will hopefully be back up and running during the lifespan of this edition. Some of the money generated goes to helping local children and improving school facilities.

GUNJUR AND MADINA SALAAM

Despite being the largest town on the south coast, Gunjur still supports a relatively modest population of around 18,000, most of whom live close to the landlocked town centre, which is notable for its busy market, but is otherwise of limited interest to travellers. About 2km west of the town centre lies the small but vibrant Gunjur artisanal fishing beach and nearby Bolong Fenyo Community Reserve, the latter a good site for birdwatching. A similar distance south of town, tiny Madina Salaam (literally 'Village of Peace'), also known as Gunjur Madina, is the site of a few pleasant but low-key lodges situated on or close to the beach.

GETTING THERE AND AWAY Gelly-gellys to Gunjur go along the coast from Dippa Kunda Taxi Park in Serekunda or inland from Brikama, and cost around D40. However, if you want to stay at any of the lodges around Madina Salaam, you are best off catching a vehicle heading on to Kartong and getting dropped off en route.

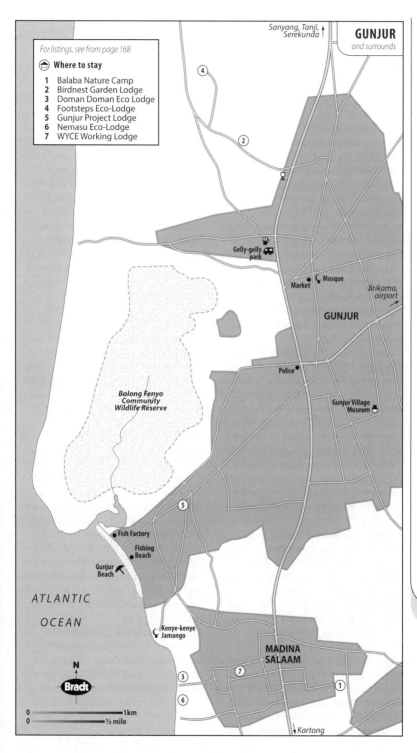

For listings, see from page 168

⊖ **Where to stay**

1 Balaba Nature Camp
2 Birdnest Garden Lodge
3 Doman Doman Eco Lodge
4 Footsteps Eco-Lodge
5 Gunjur Project Lodge
6 Nemasu Eco-Lodge
7 WYCE Working Lodge

Sanyang, Tanji, Serekunda ↑

GUNJUR
and surrounds

Gelly-gelly park

Market ● ⌂ Mosque

GUNJUR

Brikama, airport →

Police ●

Gunjur Village Museum ⌂

Bolong Fenyo Community Wildlife Reserve

● Fish Factory

Fishing Beach

Gunjur Beach ⟋

ATLANTIC

OCEAN

⌂ Kenye-kenye Jamango

MADINA SALAAM

N
Bradt

0 ————————— 1km
0 ————————— ½ mile

Kartong ↓

There is also a fair amount of transport connecting Gunjur to other towns along the south coast.

 WHERE TO STAY AND EAT *Map, page 167*

Mid-range

✱ **Footsteps Eco-Lodge** (9 rooms)
m 770 0125, 773 2060; e holidays@
footstepsinthegambia.com;
w footstepsinthegambia.com. Set on a large
permaculture-based plot tended by the hands-
on British/Norwegian owners & their friendly
& enthusiastic Gambian management & staff,
this perennially popular eco-lodge northwest of
Gunjur runs entirely on solar power & borehole
water, grows fruits & vegetables, & boasts a unique
freshwater swimming pool that relies on natural
filtration as opposed to chemicals. Accommodation
is in brightly painted & airy domed huts with
1 dbl or 2 sgl beds, en-suite shower, odourless
compost toilet & solar fans, & there are also 3
larger 2-bedroom log cabins & a 2-bedroom house
set in the vegetable patch a short distance from
the main gardens. There's plenty of birdlife in the
gardens, & it's about 25 mins' walk to the beach
along a well-defined bush path. The restaurant
serves a selection of tasty light lunches in the £5–7
range, as well as a set 3-course dinner, with all
dishes using fresh homegrown & locally sourced
ingredients. Fishing trips & other excursions can
be arranged. Free airport transfers are included in
stays of 3 days or longer. It lies about 1.5km west
of the main South Coast Rd, about 2km north of
Gunjur, & the junction is clearly signposted. Credit
cards accepted. *Roundhouses £55/80/90 sgl/dbl/
trpl B&B, £90 houses sleeping 4–6, with low-season
discounts.* **$$$**

✱ **Nemasu Eco-Lodge** (18 rooms) m 368
6127, 742 7774; e nemasuecolodge@gmail.com;
w nemasuecolodge.com. Under US–Australian
management, this small & beautifully sited solar-
powered camp is set in a grove of tall swaying
palms right on the beach, well signposted about
1km from Madina Salaam, & has a very peaceful
& relaxing atmosphere. There's a range of
accommodation options, including spacious en-
suite roundhouses, newer bungalows with ocean
views, a secluded Shell House with a monkey
family for neighbours & a private safari tent in the
nearby forest. Meals, mostly fresh fish & seafood,
are in the £4–6 range, & are served in an open-
sided beach restaurant & bar. *Rooms with shared/*

en-suite bathroom £18/27 pp; £36 pp house; all
rates B&B. **$$$**

Birdnest Garden Lodge (5 bungalows) ↘ (Italy)
+39 334 5957519; m 228 8274; e olicz@hotmail.
com; w birdnestgardenlodge.com. Situated about
1km from Footsteps, this shady & peaceful Italian–
Gambian owner-managed boutique retreat
consists of 5 comfortable & tastefully decorated
en-suite dbl bungalows with king-size or twin
beds. There is also a stylish & airy communal
sitting area whose décor & architecture show a
fusion of Mediterranean & African influences, a
mixture also reflected in their menu of Italian (call
ahead for pizza!) & Gambian dishes. It is 25 mins'
walk from the beach, & a variety of excursions can
be arranged. *£36/53 sgl/dbl B&B.* **$$$**

Budget

Balaba Nature Camp (10 rooms) m 991
9012, 781 7476; e balabacamp@icloud.com;
w balabacamp.co.uk; f BalabaCamp. This long-
serving locally run lodge, set in a large compound
in an area of relatively pristine Guinea savannah
woodland near Madina Salaam, is about 700m
from the main coastal road along an unsigned
track that runs inland almost opposite the turn-off
for WYCE. Accommodation, built in the local style,
is in sgl, dbl or twin rooms or round huts, with
mosquito nets & kerosene lamps, using shared
showers & toilets. The surrounding woodland
holds wildlife such as monkeys, monitor lizards &
bushbuck, & a list of birds seen by previous visitors
exceeds 500 species & includes many rarities. A
range of activities is available by request, & the
camp can also run excursions to most sites of
interest within day-tripping distance. Alternatively,
you can walk to the beach, about 25 mins from the
camp, & catch some sun. *£45 FB, with reductions
available for HB.* **$$**

Gunjur Project Lodge (8 rooms) m 314
5757, 992 2674; e info@gunjurproject.com;
w gunjurproject.com. Owned & managed by a
British family involved in several local community
projects, this lodge lies about 2km southwest
of Gunjur close to the fishing beach & affiliated
Bolong Fenyo Community Reserve. It started life
as a base for (mostly British & Dutch) school &

youth groups coming to The Gambia to work on community projects, but ordinary tourists are also welcome, with the option of being involved in these projects if they so choose, or taking community-led workshops in drumming, dancing, kora, batik, cooking & more. The lodge is set in a spacious, neat, solar-powered compound with a small sparkling swimming pool, Wi-Fi & a shaded restaurant serving burgers & filled baguettes in the £3–4 range & a cosmopolitan selection of mains for around £5–6. The tiled rooms are on the small side but bright, airy & spotlessly clean, & come with dbl or twin bed, net, en-suite shower & private balcony, but no fan or AC. It is less than 1km from the beach & Bolong Fenyo. *£45/50/70 sgl/dbl/trpl B&B.* **$$**

WYCE Working Lodge (10 rooms) m 672 7808; e info@wycegambia.org; w wycegambia.org. Operated by the British-based Gambia-registered WYCE (short for Wonder Years Centre of Excellence), this is emphatically a working lodge aimed at volunteers (skilled or unskilled) willing to spend anything from a few days to several months working on local community projects, though passing travellers are also welcome, especially those willing to get involved in their work. The charity is dedicated to working with the Gambian government & local communities to make The Gambia a 'wealthier & healthier place for everyone' through the provision of a first-class education & health-care system, & as such it is involved in the funding & running of a local school & clinic, & other skill-based projects ranging from beekeeping to candle-making. Basic but very clean rooms have twin beds, nets & en-suite shower & flush toilet. Meals are served in a relaxed communal area with an outdoorsy feel & a good stock of books & board games. Rates are inclusive of laundry & all meals. *£40 pp FB, if staying for 7 nights airport transfers inc.* **$$**

Shoestring
Doman Doman Eco Lodge (2 rooms) m 362 3564, 277 7614. This rootsy address sits right on the beach about 500m south of the Kenye-kenye Jamango mosque. The en-suite rooms are in roundhouses that open onto a sandy compound, which is prime real estate for kicking back in a hammock or sitting around the bonfire by night. Manager Lamin is eager to please & can arrange surfboards, drum lessons & good seafood meals. They've also got a few tents for hire. *£13/17 standard/superior dbl, £8 pp in a tent, all rates B&B.* **$**

WHAT TO SEE AND DO

Gunjur Beach Less than 1km west of the Gunjur Project Lodge, this working fishing beach, though neither so chaotic nor so large as its counterpart at Tanji, is a good place to watch colourful pirogues land with the day's catch and distribute them to traders on the shore. There's a Japanese-built ice plant in the small beachfront village, which is also known as Kajabang, and several smoking houses run inland along the main road. Protected by a natural rock reef a few hundred metres offshore, the beach running north from the village is usually fine for swimming (safest, though, to ask first).

Gunjur Village Museum (✪ 13.1659,-16.7532; m 643 6637; e lamin@ gunjurmuseum.com; w gunjurmuseum.com; entrance D100) Clearly signposted from the Gunjur–Brikama road and run by the cheerful and highly knowledgeable Lamin Bojang, this little museum is very much a labour of love, showcasing natural, cultural and historical artefacts from all over The Gambia. Lamin is also a bird and wildlife guide, with a particular interest in medicinal plants, and offers nature walks in the surrounding forest. The museum launched a crowdfunding campaign in 2023 to support rebuilding works after a particularly difficult rainy season destroyed part of the building. It's an admirable project and operates with no outside funding; any donations would be gratefully received.

Bolong Fenyo Community Wildlife Reserve (m 910 2969; e gepadg@yahoo. com; w gepadg.com; ▮ gepadg1; entrance D50, optional guides (who know the birds well) can be hired for around D250) Situated immediately inland of Gunjur Beach, Bolong Fenyo was the first community conservation project established in The Gambia, and was formally gazetted in 2008. Operated by the Gunjur Environmental Protection and Development Group (GEPADG), it extends over 3km² of savannah and wetland habitats, including the eponymous freshwater lagoon and around 400m of coastline, and protects a range of small mammals including bushbuck, red-flanked duiker, red colobus and green monkey, as well as a resident crocodile population. The main attraction is birds, of which around 150 species have been recorded, including osprey, African jacana, black crake, grey-headed kingfisher, red-bellied paradise flycatcher, green crombec, capuchin babbler and many marine birds typical of The Gambia. The entrance gate lies on the north side of the main road between Gunjur Project Lodge and Gunjur Beach. About 5km further north along the beach, the Katima Delta, which comprises a series of bolongs (creeks) that empty into the sea, is also very rich in birdlife, with huge flocks of terns and white-faced whistling ducks.

Kenye-kenye Jamango Located about 3km south of Gunjur Beach (⊕ 13.1455, -16.7755) near Nemasu Eco-Lodge, this sacred pilgrimage site, which attracts Islamic scholars and worshippers from all over West Africa, is also known as the Sand Dune Mosque, perched as it is atop a 10m-high dune overlooking the beach. The site is sacred because of a visit there by El Hadj Umar Tall (c1797–1864), the founder of the short-lived Toucouleur Empire and influential leader of the Tijaniyya Brotherhood that has since become the largest Sufi order in West Africa. Umar Tall's pilgrimage to Mecca between 1828 and 1831 made him famous (and earned him the title El Hadj), and he went on to challenge the political and social order of the old theocracies, replacing them with a new and more militant brand of Islam. His jihads (holy wars) imposed his authority from Senegal to Nigeria and attracted thousands of disciples from all over the region, including the Aku (freed slaves of African origin) of Sierra Leone. He visited what is now The Gambia during the latter part of his life when he had turned to a more peaceful philosophy. He stayed in several places in The Gambia, but at this site near Gunjur longer than anywhere else, praying in the shade of trees and large boulders. Everybody is permitted to visit the sacred grounds, and to view the mosque, but only Muslims can enter the building (an architecturally uninteresting concrete construction).

KARTONG AND SURROUNDS

Reputedly founded more than 450 years ago, the agreeable border village of Kartong (also spelt Kartung) is known throughout the Senegambia region as the site of a sacred pool called Kartong Folonko. The small town's 5,500 inhabitants are known as Kartonkas, and include a small but distinct community of Balanta immigrants from Guinea-Bissau. The compact town centre lies about 1km inland of the Atlantic coastline and 2km north of the Allahein (or Halahin) River, which flows along the border with Senegal. Kartong is one of the country's most rewarding ornithological destinations, with a checklist of more than 385 species – including several recorded nowhere else in the country – and the area's reputation in birdwatching circles has grown hugely since the opening of the Kartong Bird Observatory on the western outskirts of town in 2010. Other attractions include the Kartong Folonko, boat trips on the mangrove-lined Allahein River, Lemonfish Art Gallery and the out-of-town Gambian Reptiles Farm, while the lovely stretch of coast north of town is lined with beach camps and eco-lodges.

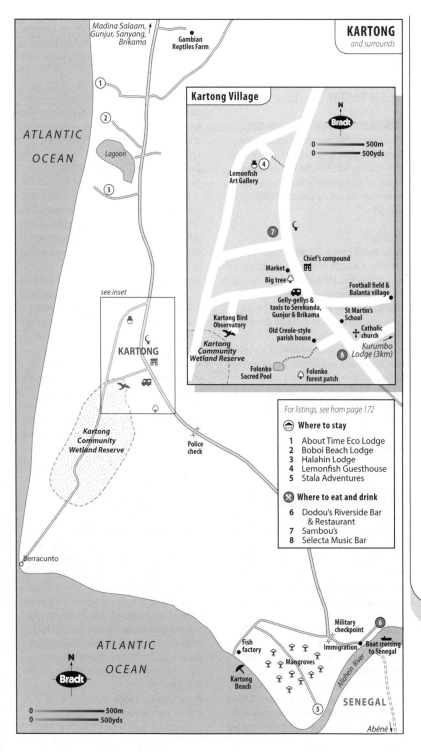

KARTONG
and surrounds

Madina Salaam,
Gunjur, Sanyang,
Brikama

Gambian
Reptiles Farm

ATLANTIC
OCEAN

Lagoon

Kartong Village

N

0 ——— 500m
0 ——— 500yds

Lemonfish
Art Gallery

Chief's compound

Market

Big tree

Football field &
Balanta village

see inset

Gelly-gellys &
taxis to Serekunda,
Gunjur & Brikama

St Martin's
School

Kartong Bird
Observatory

Catholic
church

KARTONG

Old Creole-style
parish house

Kurumbo
Lodge (3km)

Kartong
Community
Wetland Reserve

Folonko
Sacred Pool

Folonko
forest patch

Kartong
Community
Wetland Reserve

Police
check

Berracunto

For listings, see from page 172

⊖ **Where to stay**
1 About Time Eco Lodge
2 Boboi Beach Lodge
3 Halahin Lodge
4 Lemonfish Guesthouse
5 Stala Adventures

⊗ **Where to eat and drink**
6 Dodou's Riverside Bar
   & Restaurant
7 Sambou's
8 Selecta Music Bar

ATLANTIC
OCEAN

N

0 ——— 500m
0 ——— 500yds

Military
checkpoint

Fish
factory

Immigration

Boat crossing
to Senegal

Mangroves

Kartong
Beach

Allahein River

SENEGAL

Abéné

GETTING THERE AND AWAY Occasional gelly-gellys and shared taxis connect Kartong to Serekunda's Dippa Kunda Taxi Park (D60) and the central station in Brikama (D40). If you can't find direct transport, it will be easiest to catch a vehicle to Gunjur and change there.

🏠 WHERE TO STAY   *Map, page 171, unless otherwise stated*

Mid-range

Little's Nature Retreat   [map, page 150] (7 rooms) **e** atthias.fiene@gmx.net. This new German–Gambian lodge sits in an isolated patch of bush about 400m from the beach, offering colourful & comfortable en-suite rooms in roundhouses around the garden. *£31/40 sgl/dbl B&B*. **$$**

Budget

Boboi Beach Lodge   (12 rooms) **m** 777 6737, 394 3888; **e** boboibeachlodgethegambia@gmail. com; **w** boboibeachlodgethegambia.com. Located a few hundred metres west of the main coastal road, this attractive & well-established beach lodge runs down to a sublime beach about 3km north of Kartong & offers the choice of camping (in your own tent), accommodation in a very basic but naturally aerated treehouse (a semi-enclosed stilted platform with a mattress & mosquito net), more spacious beachside bungalow (sleeping up to 4) or 'deluxe' hutted accommodation (a brightly decorated en-suite room with 1 dbl & 1 sgl bed, but no AC or fan). It serves traditional dishes & seafood (£4–6). *£35 deluxe treehouse/roundhouse, £50 bungalow, £15 standard treehouse, £9 pp camping, all rates B&B*. **$$**

Georgianna's   [map, page 150] (5 rooms) **m** 941 9699, 713 9798. Along the main road 4km north of Kartong, this is a popular expat hangout, especially for the weekly Sun roast. The location is convenient, if not particularly atmospheric, & the en-suite rooms facing the garden are tidy & well equipped. They can arrange all kinds of boat trips, including fishing, & excursions to their camp upriver near Bintang. *£17/20 sgl/dbl B&B*. **$$**

Halahin Lodge   (16 rooms) **m** 709 5705, 993 3193; **e** boubajaiteh@yahoo.co.uk; **w** halahin. com. Set in sprawling palm-shaded grounds leading out to one of the most fabulous beaches in The Gambia, this chilled-out beach lodge 2km north of Kartong is named for the river that flows along the Senegalese border. Accommodation is in standalone en-suite huts with 1 dbl & 1 sgl bed,

tiled floor, cane furniture & nets but no fan or AC. A breezy outdoor restaurant serves a varied selection of seafood & other dishes in the £4–6 range. *£22/31 sgl/dbl B&B*. **$$**

Kurumbo Lodge   [map, page 150] (3 rooms) **m** 341 9326; **e** riarugge@gmail.com; **w** kurumbolodge.com. Set about 3km due east of Kartong along the Allahein River, this small Dutch-run outpost has a few rooms in a large house using shared ablutions. The large, leafy gardens lead down to the riverside, from where you can explore by kayak. *£20 dbl B&B*. **$$**

Lemonfish Guesthouse   (4 rooms) **m** 990 0036, 725 1948; **w** lemonfishgambia.nl. This likeable art gallery set on a slope a few mins' walk from the town centre offers limited accommodation using shared bathrooms in airy & brightly decorated twin rooms with nets. The delightful & rather bohemian veranda with nothing but the sound of songbirds for company makes this a wonderful retreat for anyone in search of peace & quiet. Meals are available to residents (around £5), & it also serves chilled beers & sodas. Boat excursions, birdwatching & fishing trips can also be organised & there are occasional African movie nights. It's a bit less active since the Dutch founder passed away in 2022, but remains a recommendable address. *£17 pp B&B*. **$$**

Stala Adventures   (5 rooms) **m** 745 2553; **e** laminleba@gmail.com; **f** stalaadventure. Reached along a tidal track through the mangroves, this small, locally owned lodge lies on the banks of the Allahein about 5km south of the town centre – quite a trek in the midday heat! Once there, the location is lovely, & the staff can arrange boat & birding excursions on the river, plus seafood & other Gambian dishes for around £5 per plate. Accommodation is in clean riverside huts with twin or dbl beds & en-suite shower & toilet, but no AC or fan. It is a community-based venture, with 30% of profits going to a local clinic. *£20 dbl B&B*. **$$**

About Time Eco Lodge   (6 rooms) **m** 716 4739; **e** abouttimelodge@gmail.com; **w** abouttimelodge.org. Set just north of Boboi, this homey British–Gambian lodge has an enviable beachfront location, with several en-suite rooms in

roundhouses scattered around the gardens behind. *From £15 dbl B&B.* **$**

✕ WHERE TO EAT AND DRINK *Map, page 171, unless otherwise stated*

Most of the accommodation listed opposite serves adequate to good food. There are also a few small restaurants and bars in the town centre, with **Sambou's** (**m** 703 0260; **$**) being the pick of the eateries. For a cold beer, look out for **Selecta Music Bar** on the main road south of the market, facing the signposted turnoff to Kurumbo.

❋ Dodou's Riverside Bar & Restaurant **m** 730 7217, 344 6785; ◼ Dodousplace; ◷ 07.00–19.00 daily but stays open later for dinner by request. This restaurant is notable for its stilted wooden deck where you can watch terns & gulls skim the surface of the Allahein River & mangroves on the Senegalese shore opposite. It is owned & managed by a friendly chef who learned his craft at one of the country's top package hotels, & has a varied menu of pizzas, sandwiches, seafood & other mains. Sun is lobster

day, & there is usually a stock of chilled beers & sodas. Given the restaurant's location, unless you've time to kill, it might be wise to call in advance so it has time to assemble ingredients & prepare the dish of your choice. Highly recommended. *Most meals £5–9, lobster £11.* **$$$**

Santosha Beach Bar & Restaurant [map, page 150] **m** 911 9841; ◼ santoshabeachhangout. Well-loved & well-managed beachfront resto-bar near Little's with beach beds & thatched bantabas for shade. *Meals around £5.* **$$**

WHAT TO SEE AND DO Kartong's community tourism association was defunct as of 2023, so there is no longer a central location in town where one can pick up a guide. If you'd like a guide, your best bet is therefore to arrange this through your accommodation.

Kartong Folonko Sacred Pool (⊕ 13.0906, -16.7615) This small, green, forest-fringed crocodile pool in the heart of town has been sacred ever since Kartong was founded, though its renown today is linked partially to a visit by the eminent mid 19th-century marabout El Hadj Umar Tall (page 170). According to the caretakers, the pool is home to around 20 harmless crocodiles, including one albino whose occasional (semi-legendary at this point) emergence from the water is said to bring good fortune to those who witness it. However, our understanding is that the pool's one-time crocodilian inhabitants have mostly relocated to the artificial wetlands created by sand mining west of town, and sightings today are infrequent. Birds, by contrast, are prolific in the substantial forest patch around the pool, which is traditionally protected as a sanctuary and hosts an interesting selection of species including blue-breasted kingfisher, splendid glossy starling, green-headed sunbird and African paradise flycatcher.

In common with several other crocodile pools in West Africa, Folonko is an important fertility shrine and pilgrimage site whose presiding spirit is said to be the daughter of Kachikally in Bakau (page 109). Childless couples or other individuals seeking divine blessings can bring a gift of kola nuts, candles or money to the pool's elderly female caretakers, who will then pray to the crocodiles on their behalf, a rather eerie ritual that sounds midway between a chant and speaking in tongues. And while this practice has clear pagan roots, it seems that most of the pilgrims who visit the site are Muslim, a good example of how traditional beliefs are often integrated into exotic faiths in this part of Africa (and elsewhere, for that matter).

Folonko is still very much an active shrine, attracting far more West African pilgrims (Fridays and Saturdays are the busiest) than it does tourists. Non-pilgrim visitors are nonetheless welcome, provided they take off their shoes before they approach the pool, treat the shrine with respect, and offer the caretakers a small tip (around D100 per person). The unsignposted site is most easily located by following the main road through Kartong south from the market, then turning west opposite the Catholic church, passing an interesting Creole-style building to your right, and following a footpath through the forest for perhaps 100m to the pool.

Lemonfish Art Gallery (m 990 0036, 725 1948; w lemonfishgambia.nl; ⊕ daily) Situated on the northwest outskirts of town, this admirable gallery was launched in 2005 with an exhibition featuring 28 artists from all over West Africa, and it remains one of the best-stocked galleries in the country, with colourful local artworks adorning every spare square inch of wall space. The artists also run workshops. In addition to a fine selection of contemporary African paintings, the gallery also stocks and sells sculptures, jewellery, batiks and fashion items. It is unable to take credit cards, so come with cash if you intend to purchase. Browsers are welcome and the wide veranda is a great spot for a coffee or cold drink.

TURTLE SOS GAMBIA

The beaches of West Africa have long been a nesting ground for turtles, but in 2015, not a single leatherback turtle was reported in The Gambia for the first time in living memory. In fact, all five of the turtle species found here are now endangered, and while there are many natural obstacles to their survival, it's humankind that brings the biggest threat. Aside from hunters, the turtles must contend with fishermen's nets and plastic waste out at sea, as well as scavenging dogs, monitor lizards, cows on the beach and coastal erosion on the shore, fuelled by unchecked sand mining.

Turtle SOS The Gambia (m 364 7687; e tusostg@gmail.com; f) began as a collaboration between Sandele Eco-Retreat in Kartong (which was not accepting guests as of 2023) and a number of local and international partners. Since 2014, the project has set up a re-nesting and hatching centre as well as monitoring turtle activity along a 27km stretch of beach. They also help volunteers to raise awareness in local schools and some of the staff have transitioned from hunters to conservationists.

Landing, a former poacher who is now better known as Papa Turtle, explained how as a teacher he earned just D150 a month – less than £3 – with which he had to support not only his wife and children but also his late brother's family. With turtle eggs fetching upwards of D600, it's easy to see why so many poachers carry out this illegal activity. While hunting, Papa Turtle noticed the decline in the population and soon realised that there would be no turtles left if he continued to poach, so when Turtle SOS approached him to work alongside them, it was an easy choice for him.

If you'd like to get involved, visitors can join Turtle SOS The Gambia's school outreach or beach patrol activities between June and December, including a visit to the secure hatchery where rangers relocate the eggs found laid in insecure locations. The meeting point is still at Sandele (north of Kartong across the main road from the Gambian Reptiles Farm), but make arrangements with Turtle SOS The Gambia directly via Facebook or WhatsApp in advance of your intended visit.

Kartong Festival One of the most prominent festivals in The Gambia has been held in Kartong annually since 2006, usually (but not always) over the first full weekend in February (it was held in April in 2023). The three-day festival takes place in the grounds of St Martin's School and at the nearby football pitch at the southeast end of the village. It is dominated by music and dancing displays, most of them traditional, but it also includes a variety of other events and workshops. For further details, visit their Facebook page (**f** KartongFestival).

Kartong Bird Observatory/Community Wetland Reserve (**m** 700 3147, 733 2225; **e** kartongbirdobservatory@hotmail.com; **w** kartongbirdobservatory. org) The focal point of birding activity on the south coast and only permanent ringing station anywhere in the country, Kartong Bird Observatory was established in 2010 by a team of British birding enthusiasts including resident ringer Colin Cross, who lives on site. It lies on the western edge of town, a couple of minutes' walk from the market, overlooking a large reed-fringed freshwater pool inhabited by an incredible variety of birds. Over 4,000 birds are ringed annually as part of an ongoing international research programme into bird migration.

With more than 385 bird species recorded in the immediate vicinity, Kartong Bird Observatory is one of the most rewarding sites for aquatic birds anywhere in The Gambia. Among the more alluring regulars are African crake, dwarf bittern, greater painted snipe, Allen's gallinule and pygmy goose, with morning being the best time for bird photography and observing rarities. It is also worth being here in the evening, when around 1,000 herons of eight different species come to roost in the reed beds, and there is a chance of four-banded sandgrouse and both long-tailed and standard-winged nightjar. Look out, too, for crocodiles, which are common in the wetlands and grow up to around 4m long. Armitage's skink (page 110) has also been recorded here.

This pool facing the observatory forms part of a proposed, but mostly nominal, Kartong Community Wetland Reserve, which (in theory) extends southward from town across an expanse of reed beds, open pools and other wetland habitats, most of which are a by-product of the extensive industrial sand mining practised in the area several decades ago (artisanal mining still takes place). To explore the wetland further, take the dirt road running south from the observatory towards Berracunto, which effectively doubles as an elevated causeway offering great views to both sides over several permanent and seasonal pools and other wetland areas. Berracunto is another important sacred site (where you'll usually find a drinks-seller under the bantaba) and while it doesn't really reflect this visually, it can be a very good spot for woodland birds and (at dusk) long-tailed nightjar.

Further afield, the Kartong area is a reliable site for the localised black-crowned crane. It also hosts several species rare or absent elsewhere in the country, and has thrown up a number of firsts for The Gambia in recent years. Among the more unusual species recorded here are an American wigeon, brown noddy, Baillon's crake, little crake, Cassin's honeybird, black-crowned sparrow lark, cuckoo finch and Hudsonian whimbrel. Birders are most welcome to visit the observatory to obtain information about recent sightings at Kartong, but they do not offer guides or other services.

Allahein River Beyond Kartong, the surfaced coastal road carries on southwards for about 3km to a T-junction and immigration post where a left turn leads after about 1km to the north bank of the mangrove-lined Allahein River, which also forms the border with Senegal. Serviced by Dodou's Riverside Bar & Restaurant (page 173), this is an excellent place to chill out over a meal or drink, and is also the recognised base for organising boat trips on the river, which usually take in Pelican Island and a nearby oyster factory but can also be tailored towards fishing. The river is rewarding for birds, with various pelicans, kingfishers, gulls, terns and waders likely to be seen. Expect to pay around £12–15 for one or two passengers, up to £25–30 for groups of five to eight. Similar trips can also be arranged through Stala Adventures (page 172) for a minimum of around £16.50 for up to five passengers.

Kartong Beach Turn right at the T-junction mentioned on page 175 and after 800m you will emerge at Kartong Beach, about 1km north of the mouth of the Allahein River. More of a working beach than a swimming beach (be mindful of currents), there is a small hamlet and fishing centre here. The beach running southeast towards the river mouth is well worth exploring, whether you are a keen birder or want to sunbathe in a quiet spot. Good birds sometimes seen include white-fronted plover and great-spotted cuckoo.

Gambian Reptiles Farm (m 700 4672; e paziaud.luc@gmail.com; ⊕ 08.30–17.30 daily; entrance D300 pp) On the east side of the main coastal road about 3km north of Kartong, this sanctuary is the brainchild of Frenchman Luc Paziaud, a long-time resident of The Gambia. It provides sanctuary to a wide variety of injured

A TASTE OF CASAMANCE

Kartong is home to The Gambia's southernmost – and by far most scenic – border crossing, at the Allahein River. Here, motorised canoes putter back and forth across the mangrove-lined waters that mark the division between The Gambia to the north and Senegal's Casamance region to the south.

Note, however, that this crossing is staffed only by Gambian, and not Senegalese, immigration authorities. This poses a few complications for travellers wishing to travel extensively in Senegal. These are usually – assuming your nationality does not require an entry visa for Senegal – solved by making the trip to the Séléti border post for an entry stamp and perhaps a bit of finger-wagging from Senegalese authorities. But for local trips exiting and re-entering The Gambia at Kartong, it's possible to take a dip into Casamance for an afternoon or a couple of days to visit the picturesque and popular village of Abéné, 10km south of the river.

Once on the Senegalese side, there are a handful of 4x4s and moto-taxis waiting to take people onwards to Abéné. The sandy jungle track passes through the tiny village of Niafourang before dropping you off in remote and Rastafied Abéné, where there are numerous guesthouses, but no ATMs (dalasis are not widely accepted, but can be changed into the CFA francs used in Senegal at some of the shops along the main road).

To spend the night in Abéné there are many options, but we recommend you head straight for the **Little Baobab** (£15 dbl B&B; **$**). Founded by Simon Fenton, author of the second edition of this guide, and his wife Khady Mane, it has en-suite roundhouses with composting toilets and lovingly tended gardens set in a quiet stretch of forests and fields at the edge of town. Simon was tragically killed in a car accident in 2017, but Khady and their two sons are still rolling out the red carpet for visitors. No online booking; contact Khady directly via WhatsApp at m (+221) 77 066 9497.

or problem reptiles (in particular venomous snakes that enter houses and need to be removed), most of which are released into the wild when an opportunity presents itself. It doubles as a breeding centre for endangered species and as an educational facility. Indeed, the few thousand Gambian schoolchildren who visit annually are taught that reptiles are not all bad. Most snakes, for instance, are harmless to humans, but help control the numbers of agricultural pests. And crocodiles, by targeting slower and weaker fish as prey, play an important role in curbing the spread of piscine diseases, leading to greater population stability among the riverine fish that form a vital source of protein in the Gambian diet.

For tourists, the farm is so unusual and interesting that it is well worth a visit, even if you can't stand snakes (in which case you might want to think of it as therapeutic). The 45-minute tours are led by well-informed guides who will gladly tell you everything you ever wanted to know about snakes but were too scared to ask. In the process, you'll get to see giant monitor lizards, the sluggish Bell's hinged tortoise, chameleons and other lizards, plus a collection of snakes that includes pythons, puff adders and spitting cobras. Unlike most reptile parks in Africa, this is not a tourist trap but a labour of dedication and love, and the income generated by visits helps cover running costs. More adventurously, Luc can also arrange nocturnal river trips to count crocodiles (another facet of his work) for around £45 per person.

11

Inland to Brikama
and Pirang

The second-largest town in The Gambia, Brikama lies some 15km inland of the Atlantic coastline at Sanyang, and 20km south of the urban conglomerate comprising Banjul, Serekunda and the main coastal resorts. A bustling but somewhat nondescript market town flanking the main South Bank Road to Basse, it rivals Serekunda's Westfield Junction as the main route focus in the coastal hinterland, and feels somewhat transitional in character between the urbanised coast and the underdeveloped country further upriver – a mood epitomised by the down-to-earth livestock market at Abuko and close-to-source handicraft market outside Brikama.

As towns go, Brikama is nothing to shout about. But it does lie at the heart of an area bristling with wildlife-viewing opportunities, all within easy day-tripping distance of the coastal resorts. Foremost among these is Abuko Nature Reserve, the country's largest extant patch of true closed-canopy forest, alive with monkeys, small antelope and colourful forest birds. Other prominent birdwatching sites include community-run forest reserves at Farasuto and Bonto-Pirang, the riverine woodland at Marakissa, the shrimp ponds outside Pirang and the mangrove-lined creeks around Lamin Lodge. Last but not least, Makasutu Cultural Forest is not only home to the creek-side Mandina Lodges, a superlative upmarket eco-retreat, but also offers day tours that provide a fascinating introduction both to the culture and wildlife of the coastal hinterland.

ABUKO LIVESTOCK MARKET

The small town of Abuko, which straddles the busy Brikama Road around 6km south of Westfield Junction, is the site of one of the country's best-known and busiest livestock markets (◈ 13.3993, -16.6520). It is arguably worth a visit at any time of year, but it becomes a chaotic regional focal point during the build-up to Tobaski, as Eid al-Adha is known in The Gambia. Tobaski commemorates the willingness of Abraham to follow a divine instruction to sacrifice his son Ishmael on a mountainside, and it is customary for every family to slaughter a ram. One-third of this ram is eaten by the family, one-third given away to relatives and one-third given to the poor. Over the weeks prior to the festival, breeders and herdsmen from all over the country descend on the market, and the place overflows with rams and people bargaining for them. The market is on your right just before the Abuko Nature Reserve heading towards Brikama, and there is plenty of transport to Abuko from Serekunda and Brikama. Tobaski coincides with the end of the annual Hajj (pilgrimage) to Mecca – see page 76 for predicted dates.

ABUKO NATURE RESERVE

Situated on the Brikama Road less than 30 minutes' drive from the northern beach resorts, Abuko Nature Reserve (◔ 06.30–18.00 daily; entrance D35) is a popular goal for day trips out of Greater Banjul, particularly with birdwatchers. Extending over a mere 1km², it is the oldest sanctuary in the country, initially set aside in 1916 as a catchment area providing fresh water to Banjul, then gazetted as a nature reserve under the supervision of Eddie Brewer, first director of the Wildlife Department of The Gambia, in 1968, and extended to its present size in 1978. The most important habitat in Abuko is the rare remnant patch of pristine gallery forest that hems in the small Lamin River and a few associated pools. This is one of the most northerly projections of the Upper Guinean Forest that extends along much of coastal West Africa from the Casamance region of Senegal to western Ghana. Away from the river, the vegetation thins out to become Guinea savannah, which is not as rare as the gallery forest, but still supports plenty of wildlife.

Abuko contains a quite remarkable biodiversity for a reserve of its size, with many thousands of species of fungi, plants, trees, insects and other invertebrates living in and beneath the tall leafy forest canopy. Around 50 mammal species have been recorded, most visibly green monkey, red colobus, bushbuck and Maxwell's duiker. It also supports a varied selection of birds, with some 270 species recorded, and it is perhaps the best site this close to Banjul for forest specialists such as turacos, greenbuls and hornbills. Hides help you to get close to the animals, which are very used to humans and relatively easy to see – indeed, the monkeys in particular virtually ignore human visitors as they go about their daily routines. The least edifying aspect of the reserve is the so-called animal orphanage, a rundown zoo-like set-up that houses a few miserable monkeys and spotted hyenas.

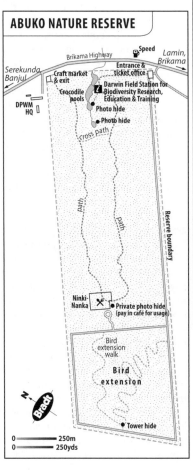

GETTING THERE AND AWAY Abuko Nature Reserve is clearly signposted on the southwest side of the Brikama Road about 7km southeast of Westfield Junction and 1km past the town of Abuko. Public transport running between Serekunda and Brikama can drop you at the entrance. Alternatively, tourist taxis from Kotu, Kololi and the other beach resorts should cost around £18, and standard taxis are even cheaper. In addition, organised excursions to Abuko are offered by most hotels and tour operators in the Greater Banjul region.

AROUND THE RESERVE The ticket office and entrance gate lie at the reserve's southeastern corner, alongside the Brikama Road. In addition to paying the entrance fee here, you have the option of picking up a bird guide for about D300, depending on how long you spend here. You can also rent a pair of binoculars for D50–100. Entering the woods, you may encounter someone raising money to 'support the reserve' – you can safely ignore this forest flimflammer. From the gate, a reasonably well-maintained 200m footpath leads through tall gallery forest and across a bridge to the first of Abuko's pools. A quiet vigil here is likely to yield sightings of green monkey, red colobus, bushbuck, Maxwell's duiker, crocodile and Nile monitor, along with water-associated birds such as black-headed night heron, squacco heron, African jacana, African darter and giant kingfisher.

Just past this, on the right, the **Darwin Field Station for Biodiversity Research, Education and Training** (page 186) houses a display about the wildlife in Abuko, while the area around the toilet often yields the localised Ahanta francolin. The centre's upper storey affords a good view of the main crocodile pool, which supports a wonderful variety of birds, including hamerkop, black crake and various herons, kingfishers and birds of prey. At the end of the dry season (March and April), these pools constitute the only fresh water for kilometres around, and thus act as a magnet for larger birds including spoonbills, storks, ospreys and even the odd pelican. As evening turns to night, there is a fantastic display consisting of hundreds of straw-coloured fruit bats that drop by for a drink after leaving their daytime roost at nearby Lamin, but you need special permission to stay on and wait for this.

From the Darwin Field Station, the footpath continues westward through the gallery forest, passing a couple of photo hides in various states of (dis)repair. Among the more conspicuous forest species resident here are such beauties as violet turaco, bearded barbet, common wattle-eye and red-bellied paradise flycatcher. Less easy to observe are several Upper Guinean forest species at the extreme northern edge of their distribution, among them white-spotted flufftail, green turaco and western bluebill, while other birds uncommon elsewhere in the country include African goshawk, leaflove, grey-headed bristlebill, yellow-breasted apalis, oriole warbler, collared sunbird, yellow-bill, red-shouldered cuckoo-shrike and green hylia. Heading further east, the forest thins out and you find yourself walking through Guinea savannah with an open canopy allowing you to see the sky.

The footpath then leads to the so-called **animal orphanage**, which was originally established as a refuge for animals that had been orphaned, injured or kept illegally as pets. In its early days, it provided sanctuary to The Gambia's only lions, as well as the orphaned or confiscated chimpanzees that were later released into the River Gambia National Park. Today, the most interesting inhabitants of the orphanage are a few listless spotted hyenas, which – like many of the other inmates – were born in captivity and seem destined to die there. The rather cheerless atmosphere is alleviated slightly by the **Ninki-Nanka Restaurant**, serving chilled drinks and snacks, plus a couple of Gambian plates if desired. This is also where birders can pay to use a small tin hide overlooking a freshwater pool that's too small to hold many waterbirds, but does tend to attract a steady stream of thirsty forest birds, from turacos and kingfishers to smaller weavers and finches. There was no water in the pool when we visited in 2023 – contact caretaker Green (m 502 3798) to get the current status.

Beyond the orphanage, the bird extension walk loops through more savannah to a **tower hide** where you can stand above the level of the treetops. This is a very pleasant walk that takes you through woodland, scrub and open areas. Because of the winding nature of the path, you feel as though you have walked through a much larger area than you actually have. Rejoining the main footpath at the orphanage leads you through more savannah until you reach the gallery forest again. The path then takes you to the exit of the reserve – rather annoyingly this dumps you out alongside the busy Brikama Road 600m from where you entered the forest. There is supposed to be a footpath about halfway along connecting the two sides and taking you back to the first footpath and the entrance via the education centre, but it was unusably overgrown in 2023.

LAMIN

Situated on the Brikama Road about 9km southeast of Serekunda, Lamin is a moderately sized town remarkable only for the large colony of straw-coloured fruit bats that inhabits the mango trees behind the mosque on the main road. It is also the junction town for Lamin Lodge, a very enjoyable stilted restaurant on the verge of Tanbi Wetland Reserve (page 102), about 8km southwest of Banjul. Lamin Lodge is a good place to arrange boat trips into the reserve, which is one of the country's most important coastal wetlands (indeed, there's long been talk of designating it as a national park) and home to an immense variety of birds, along with substantial populations of the hefty marsh mongoose and the secretive West African manatee. Nearby Mandinari is also a good place to learn to play the *akonting* (page 25).

GETTING THERE AND AWAY Lamin lies along the main road between Serekunda and Brikama, and there is plenty of transport there from both towns. Lamin Lodge is 2km east of town, off any transport route, so you must either hire a taxi or walk. Another possibility, popular with birders and fishing enthusiasts, is to come by boat from Denton Bridge (page 102) at the northern end of the Tanbi Wetland Reserve close to Banjul.

 WHERE TO STAY AND EAT *Map, page 150*

✳ **Mandinari River Lodge** (6 rooms)
⊕ 13.3813, -16.6021; m 339 4555, 742 6521;
e mandinari@hotmail.co.uk; w mrlgambia.com.
Set alongside mangrove-lined creeks in the village of Mandinari, 6km from Lamin on a newly surfaced road, this eco-lodge & restaurant is centred on a little pool area with a small restaurant/bar & BBQ. Bright & airy roundhouses are nicely decorated in earthy hues, & come with en-suite shower, small kitchenette & garden terrace with hammocks leading down to a swimming area in the bolong. There are 2 bird hides right on the grounds, or the owners can organise boat & fishing trips & birdwatching excursions in the nearby Tanbi Wetlands (& further afield), as well as visits to Mandinari village to gain an insight into local life. Free airport transfers included with 2-night stay. *£35 dbl B&B.* **$$**
Lamin Lodge ⊕ 13.3936, -16.6243; m 778 4058, 349 9146; ☑ laminlodge; ⊕ 07.00–19.00 daily (dinners by advance request only). This

venerable & wonderfully rickety stilted 3-storey construction is owned & managed by the same people as Janjanbureh Camp (page 249). It's a great place to enjoy a relaxed lunch in the company of the birds, green monkeys & other wildlife that inhabits the surrounding creeks & mangroves. It serves a good selection of seafood & meat dishes, as well as chilled beers & sodas. It can also arrange dugout trips into the mangroves for a reasonable rate, as well as trips further afield to Abuko Nature Reserve, Janjanbureh or the North Bank combination of Juffureh & James Island. There are a variety of other businesses at the car park; Lamin Lodge sits all the way down the wooden walkway. *Mains mostly in the £4–5.50 range.* **$$**
Siaka Tenda Lodge ⊕ 13.3983, -16.6358; m 725 8044, 507 9663. This newly opened hangout signposted 1km off the road to Lamin Lodge sits between mangroves & rice fields & is another local option for lunch & a trip into the mangroves or to see locals harvesting oysters nearby. **$**

YUNDUM

About 6km southwest of Lamin and 15km from Serekunda, the village of Yundum lies close to the junction of the Brikama Road and the newer Bertil Harding

Highway running northwest to Brusubi Turntable (for the south coast and Kololi), which was being expanded to a dual carriageway in 2023. It is best known as the site of Banjul International Airport, which is the only facility of its type in the country and carries up to a million passengers annually. Established during World War II as a military airfield, it is where Franklin D Roosevelt became the first serving US president to set foot on African soil during a refuelling stop en route to the Casablanca Conference with his British counterpart Winston Churchill in January 1943. The modern airport, designed by the Senegalese architect Pierre Goudiaby, opened in 1997 and underwent significant rehabilitation works in 2021. If you're in need, there are several ATMs here that tend to be reasonably reliable. The only other points of interest in Yundum are a small but high-quality fruit market by the side of the road, and the adjacent National Bee-keepers Association, which sells an assortment of cheap but very tasty locally produced honey and items made of natural beeswax, including decorative candles.

If you're heading to the airport and need a stopover, the **Woodpecker Resort** (❧ 447 3680; m 349 0811, 990 8781; e reservation.woodpecker.gm@gmail.com; w woodpeckerresortgambia.com; £33/40 sgl/dbl; **$$**) is a decent option, with clean rooms offering free Wi-Fi and a restaurant serving fast-food options in the £5–7 range. There's a pool (D100 for non-residents), darts, table tennis and a widescreen TV, and they offer free airport transfers.

BRIKAMA

The administrative headquarters of the West Coast Region, bustling Brikama, though scarcely a metropolis with a population of 80,000, is the second-largest town in The Gambia (a statistic that will give travellers heading upriver some notice of what to expect in terms of urban development). Brikama lies about 22km south of Serekunda, and here the Brikama Road becomes the South Bank Road, turning east towards Soma and Basse and bypassing Brikama's compact town centre 1km to its south. It is a busy little town, with some historical pedigree, though it has little to show for it unless perhaps you count the small and low-key old town, which runs south from the central market towards the old mosque. Brikama is of interest to travellers primarily for its superb and well-priced craft market, located right at the beginning of town as you arrive from Yundum. It is also the main springboard for gelly-gellys and shared taxis heading upriver along the South Bank, and the closest town to a few more rural tourist sites, notably Makasutu Cultural Forest, Marakissa River Camp, and the Pirang Forest Reserve and shrimp pools.

HISTORY According to oral tradition, Brikama was founded in the 13th century by a group of 40 Mandinka exiles from present-day Mali, and its first ruler was one Mansa Kolley. It is said that the site was chosen because it fulfilled a prophecy that the migrants should only settle when they came across a large santang tree (a type of mahogany) whose boughs were hung with the remains of an antelope eaten by a leopard. The town was twice destroyed in local conflicts (in 1854 and 1874), but in both cases it soon recovered.

Today it is well known as the home of one of The Gambia's most famous musical dynasties. This is the Konte family of *jalis* (praise singers) and kora players. The dynasty includes Burama Konte, a well-known composer who was active in the late 19th and early 20th centuries. His son Alhaji Bai Konte (1920–83) became the first solo kora player to tour the USA when he played at the 1973 Newport

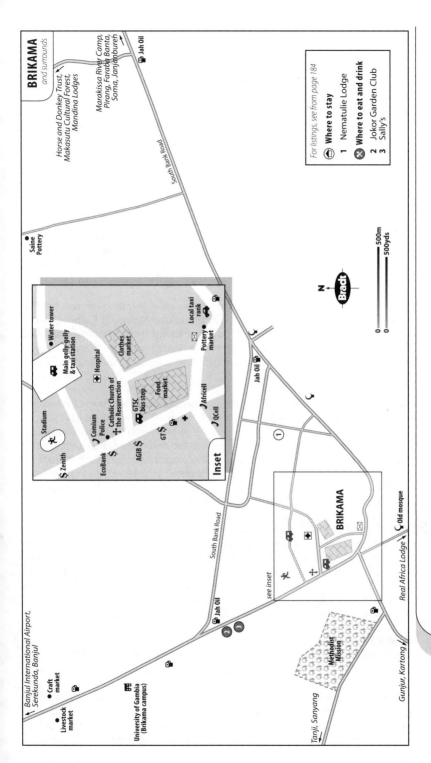

BRIKAMA
and surrounds

*Marakissa River Camp,
Pirang, Faraba Banta,
Soma, Janjanbureh*

*Horse and Donkey Trust,
Makasutu Cultural Forest,
Mandina Lodges*

For listings, see from page 184

Where to stay
1 Nematulie Lodge

Where to eat and drink
2 Jokor Garden Club
3 Sally's

Saine
Pottery

South Bank Road

N

Bradt

0 ___ 500m
0 ___ 500yds

Inset

Stadium

Water tower

Main gelly-gelly
& taxi station

Hospital

Zenith

Comium
Police

Catholic Church of
the Resurrection

Clothes
market

EcoBank

AGIB

GT

GTSC
bus stop

Food
market

Local taxi
rank

Pottery
market

Africell

QCell

Jah Oil

Jah Oil

Jah Oil

1

South Bank Road

see inset

BRIKAMA

Old mosque

Real Africa Lodge

Gunjur, Kartong

2 3

Jah Oil

Banjul International Airport,
Serekunda, Banjul

Craft
market

Livestock
market

University of Gambia
(Brikama campus)

Methodist
Mission

Tanji, Sanyang

Jazz Festival, and several of Alhaji's sons went on to have successful music careers, including Dembo Konte (d2014) (often in collaboration with Senegalese musician Kausu Kuyateh) and Malamini Jobarteh (d2013), both of whom toured regularly and released several international albums. Today, the family business remains secure: several of Alhaji Bai Konte's grandchildren are still recording music, including Jali Bakary Konteh, Mafu Conteh, Pa Bobo Jobarteh, Dawda Jobarteh and, until recently, Tatadindin Jobarteh (d2021). Ask someone to guide you to Jali Kunda ('the place of the jalis') in Brikama if you'd like to explore this tradition further.

GETTING THERE AND AWAY Traffic permitting, Brikama is only about 20 minutes' drive from Serekunda and 30 minutes from Banjul, though it is often longer than that, and certainly takes a bit longer in the regular gelly-gellys and shared taxis that cover both routes for less than D80. Direct roads and regular public transport also link Brikama to Sanyang 13km to the west, and Gunjur 19km to the southwest. For travel upriver, the main station in central Brikama is the best place to pick up gelly-gellys and shared taxis heading to the likes of Tendaba, Soma, Janjanbureh and Basse, or to the Casamance (Senegal) border at Jiboro.

WHERE TO STAY The most popular places to stay in the Brikama area are the exclusive **Mandina Lodges** (page 187) in the nearby Makasutu Cultural Forest, and more moderately priced **Marakissa River Camp** (page 186) south of town. Otherwise, options in Brikama itself are slim indeed. If you're camping, you might try asking the friendly caretaker at the Methodist Mission if you can overnight in their green compound.

Real Africa Lodge [map, page 150] ✪ 13.2519, -16.6340; m 250 4880; e realafrica696@gmail. com; f. Set 3km south of Brikama market (towards Dimbaya) in the suburban village of Manduar, the simple rooms in duplex roundhouses in a small garden here are nothing fancy, but a significant step up from Nematulie Lodge. *£11/22 sgl/dbl B&B.* **$$**

Nematulie Lodge [map, page 183] (30 rooms) ✪ 13.2768, -16.6427; m 788 1394, 340 7682. This reasonably central & acceptable cheapie is just about the only offering in town, sitting in a large compound in the back roads northeast of the market. Accommodation is in small round huts with sgl or dbl bed, net, en-suite shower & toilet but no fan. No food. *£10 dbl.* **$**

WHERE TO EAT AND DRINK *Map, page 183*
There is no shortage of **street food** on offer in and around the central market and bus station, as well as a few undistinguished sit-down eateries. The best-known nightspot is the **Jokor Garden Club** ($), a lively bar and erratic eatery that hosts occasional live music concerts on the road towards the market near the junction with the South Bank Road. Another couple of blocks towards the market, **Sally's** ($) claims to be open 24/7, serving chicken and chips, curries and the like.

OTHER PRACTICALITIES
Banking and foreign exchange There are several banks with ATMs, notably EcoBank, AGIB and GT Bank, all on the road west of the market.

Shopping Though not touristy in the slightest, the **central market** in Brikama is one of the largest in the country and a good place to buy groceries, clothes and most other day-to-day items. There is also a small **pottery market** in the town centre, and the **main craft market** out of town along the Serekunda Road.

Hidden away in the backstreets of Brikama, **Saine Pottery** (⊕ 13.2921, -16.6302; w 718 0626; m sainepottery.com; ⨍ Saine Gallery Gambia) first opened in 1980, when Edrissa Saine started working the local red-earth clay. He passed away in 2016, but his wife Fatoumatta Mendy and their children and grandchildren carry on his tradition. The creations here run the gamut from cookpots to decorative vases and busts, and they offer full-day potting workshops for those who want to try their hand at the wheel.

AROUND BRIKAMA

Brikama craft and livestock markets
Now situated about 2km from the town centre on the east side of the Serekunda Road, this once legendarily chaotic craft market now offers a relatively sedate and orderly buying experience. It is one of the best places in the country to buy crafts in general, and woodcarvings in particular, since its 80-odd stalls cater more to retailers than to tourists, and it is the source of many of the handicraft items sold at inflated prices in the more touristy markets on the coast. Indeed, Brikama is a noted centre for carvers (who produce their best workmanship in the shape of masks or gazelle groups) and you can watch them at work while you browse. For all that, a lot of the stall owners are quite pushy, and it is easy to get sucked in and buy everything in sight, or to get completely fed up with the hassle and give up before buying anything. Whatever else, try to be both firm and polite with the vendors, telling them you are just looking for the moment, and to maintain a sense of humour at all times. It can be worth the hassle if you find that piece that you really want. Opposite the craft market is a small livestock market that can be quite interesting to wander around when it's busy, and where you are unlikely to receive much hassle – unless of course you are thinking of buying a goat or cow!

Marakissa
Situated in a well-wooded area about 4km north of the Senegalese border at Darsilami, the village of Marakissa lies about 6km south of Brikama along a tarmac road serviced by a regular trickle of bush taxis. It is a popular spot with birdwatchers owing to its proximity to the Allahein River (the same one that forms the border with Senegal near Kartong), which lies about 1km south of town and is home to the long-established Marakissa River Camp. The two key birding sites here are the camp itself, which lies 1km south of Marakissa village, sandwiched between a bend in the river and the west side of the road running to the border, and the bridge across the river about 300m further south. The well-wooded section of river flowing past the camp is a good site for giant kingfisher, white-breasted cuckoo-shrike and greater, lesser and spotted honeyguide, while the marshier areas and paddy fields that flank the bridge frequently host large numbers of waterfowl and waders, as well as African jacana, black crake and painted snipe. The camp can also arrange affordable canoe trips along a stretch of river where osprey, long-crested eagle and red-necked falcon are often seen. For non-birders, the area is home to plenty of crocs and giant monitor lizards.

 Where to stay and eat Map, page 150

Asamai Villas (6 rooms) ⊕ 13.1769, -16.6819; m 788 2817; ⨍. On the back road between Darsilami (3km) and the Gunjur Hwy at Sifoe (2km), this new lodge sits in a forest patch just off the Allahein. Opened in mid-2023, the modern bungalows have large canopy beds, the restaurant does pizzas, pastas & African plates for around £5,

& there's even a swimming pool. *£56 dbl B&B.* **$$$**

Kingfisher's Lodge (8 rooms) ⊕ 13.1942, -16.6563; m 982 4290, 789 3006, 358 9761; ⨍ Marakissa kingfishers lodge. Situated by the river about 400m off the main road, this very friendly lodge has a tranquil bush feel.

Solar-powered roundhouses come with dbl bed, en-suite bathroom, separate living area & beautiful garden, & welcoming host Fatou can cook Gambian & European dishes for around £6. A couple of canoes are available to hire (D250/hr) & there's an on-site guide with a good knowledge of local flora & fauna who can take you hiking in more remote areas (D300/hr). *£14 pp B&B.* **$$**

Marakissa River Camp (12 rooms) ✪ 13.1937, -16.6544; **m** 777 9487, 990 5852; **e** marakissa@planet.nl; **w** marakissarivercamp.nl. Boasting a lovely remote riverfront location about 1km south of Marakissa village, this simple, tranquil & well-managed Dutch-owned camp feels a world away from the hectic coastal resorts to its northwest. Accommodation is in round thatched huts with twin beds, nets, en-suite showers & 24hr solar power, while the restaurant serves decent food on a stilted wooden terrace overlooking the river. With 2ha of natural grounds, it's a popular location for birders & guides are available. There are also canoes for hire. Day visitors are welcome. A far more agreeable budget option to staying in Brikama. *£12 pp B&B.* **$$**

Makasutu cultural forest (**m** 721 7743, 791 4670, 303 1407; **w** mandinalodges.com/makasutu-forest) An exemplary ecotourism project, Makasutu Cultural Forest is set alongside the beautiful mangrove-lined Mandina Creek about 5km northeast of Brikama. It is best known perhaps as the site of the exclusive and architecturally innovative Mandina Lodges, but it also offers a selection of worthwhile activities that ensure it's a regular goal for day trips from the coastal resorts. Managed in collaboration with the surrounding communities, the reserve was established in 1993 by two well-travelled British enthusiasts, James English and Lawrence Williams, fulfilling a local legend that two white men would save the forest and make it famous (something they learned after the forest opened). It first opened to clients seven years later, since when it has won many awards, including the National Order of The ambia in 2012. 'Makasutu' means 'sacred and deep forest' in the local Mandinka language, and the reserve encompasses around 10km^2 of riparian forest, savannah and mangroves, and supports plenty of wildlife – most conspicuously around 200 very habituated Guinea baboons, but also various smaller primates, antelope and carnivores, and aquatic creatures such as crocodile and the occasional West African manatee. The marine and terrestrial birdlife is stunning too.

Makasutu Cultural Forest is highly regarded within The Gambia, not just because of the wildlife found there, but also because it is such a successful blend of different facets. It provides steady employment to more than 100 local people in an area that had seldom seen many visitors in the past: not only workers such as gardeners, drivers, cooks and guides, but also the woodcarvers who utilise the site to sell their wares, and the musicians and dancers who entertain the guests. Visitors, meanwhile, are rewarded with an experience they will long remember and carry home in their hearts. A programme to encourage school visits enables Gambian children to learn about their environment in a fun and positive way. Makasutu, in a nutshell, embodies all that is good about genuine ecotourism.

Getting there and away Coming from the coast or airport, Makasutu (as well as the Horse and Donkey Trust) is clearly signposted on the left side of the main South Bank Road about 2.5km past central Brikama. The reception for day visitors lies about 3km along this road, and it is another 1km from there to Mandina Lodges and the arena for the Night Extravaganza (page 188). Overnight stays are usually booked inclusive of transfers from the airport (or wherever you are staying either side). Day trips can be arranged through any local tour operator, with the main specialist being The Gambia Experience (page 52). Plenty of public transport runs from Brikama past the junction, but not along the last 3–4km to the reception and lodges.

⌂ **Where to stay and eat** *Map, page 150*

✳ **Mandina Lodges** (9 rooms) ☎ UK +44 (0)1489 866939; e mandina@gambia.co.uk; w mandinalodges.com. One of the most inspired & exclusive lodges in the country, Mandina Lodges is spaciously laid out on the south bank of the creek for which it is named. The common area features a large jungle-shaded swimming pool, the imaginative architecture & décor of the tall thatch-roofed dining area & bar, the fine international cuisine, & the wide wooden deck overlooking a mangrove-lined stretch of creek teeming with birdlife. The solar-powered accommodation is all fantastic, & you have the choice of a pagoda-like floating river lodge, a thatch-topped stilted river lodge, newly built garden lodge or a dbl-storey jungle lodge set a little inland. All rooms come with a framed & netted super king-size bed, high-quality fittings, safe, huge windows offering 180-degree views, balcony, fan & en-suite toilet (composting in the floating/stilted lodges) & hot shower. All guests have personal guides, who can take them on canoe trips through the mangroves (where there's a good chance of encountering rarities such as white-backed night heron & African finfoot), relaxed walks through the forest, or a range of other activities including fishing & birdwatching. Optional sunset cruises & fishing excursions are extra. The lodge restaurant serves a range of well-presented Gambian dishes, & dinner can be taken alfresco either at one of the tented wooden dining areas or in your lodge. Most people love Mandina Lodges' peaceful bush atmosphere,

Intended to give the villages of the 85km² Ballabu Conservation Project (a buffer zone to Makasutu) a makeover, transforming them into the subject of a street-art ecotourism circuit, Wide Open Walls is the brainchild of Makasutu's Lawrence Williams and Njogu Touray. The project saw aerosol-brandishing street artists from at least a dozen different countries make their mark on a handful of local villages with a total of around 400 vibrant spray-paint creations. Some have now started to fade, but there are plans for more artworks to go up during the lifespan of this edition. The most accessible of these funkily decorated villages is **Galoya** (◈ 13.3299, -16.6164). Though it's not formally developed for tourism, anyone can drop in and visit, either in isolation or as an add-on visit to Makasutu; just be prepared to make a donation of around D100, payable to the village. Or contact Njogou if you'd like to know more: m 992 8371; e njogutouray2@gmail.com.

If you want to sleep near here you can go to **Wunderland Lodge** (◈ 13.3162, -16.5996; m 368 9112, 784 2450; w wunderlandlodge.com; £25 dbl; **$$**), which has well-kept roundhouses in a lovely isolated spot on the bolong, 2.5km southeast of Galoya in Kubuneh, the next village over.

plentiful birdlife & wide range of outdoor activities – but the lack of AC or Wi-Fi, & remote location, mean it isn't for everybody. Bookings are made directly through The Gambia Experience (page 52). *From £200 dbl HB.* **$$$$$**

What to see and do The highly worthwhile and enjoyable **day tours** of Makasutu start at around 07.30 (or slightly later if you prefer) in an open clearing below a giant baobab alongside a tall termite hill. You then set out on foot through lush creek-side vegetation encompassing palm forest, mangroves, savannah and dense forest, looking for baboons, birds and other wildlife, before taking to the water in dugout canoes, then returning to land for another short walk. A Gambian buffet-style lunch is followed by traditional Jola music and dancing. Other cultural interactions include a visit to a local marabout and watching a palm tapper at work. The best numbers for booking day trips are m 721 7743, 791 4670, 303 1407, and the cost is around D1,200 per person.

Since 2014, Makasutu has held the Night Extravaganza every two to three weeks in high season, which starts at 18.00 (when thousands of egrets fly past on the way to their nocturnal roost) in a riverside arena set beneath the stars below a four-storey viewing platform. The extravaganza includes a buffet dinner, kora and djembe music, and a climactic performance of traditional masked dancers and fire-breathers. The extravaganzas can be booked through the same number as the day tours and cost around D1,700 per person.

Gambia Horse and Donkey Trust (m 991 2781, 371 214, 970 2004; w gambiahorseanddonkey.org.uk; ⊕ 09.00–17.00 daily) Opened in spring 2017, this is a sister facility to the long-serving institution in Sambel Kunda (page 244). As it's upcountry, here the trust carries out a variety of veterinary, educational and community development measures, including offering mobile veterinary clinics and emergency care, provisioning destitute families with donkeys and training to successfully care for them, and running educational courses for both young learners and Gambian veterinary students.

The warm and welcoming staff and volunteers offer informal tours of the centre, where you will meet the whole cast of horses, donkeys, dogs and even camels they are attending to. There's usually plenty of work to be done, so you can often lend a hand if you're so inclined. (They are also always seeking volunteers with veterinary experience – see their website for details.) The centre is clearly signposted on the left side of the South Bank Road heading east out of Brikama, from where it's 2.5km north along the same track leading to Makasutu.

PIRANG AND FARABA BANTA

The villages of Pirang and Faraba Banta (sometimes written Faraba Bantang), situated less than 2km apart some 12km east of Brikama, are about the furthest inland one would normally go from any of the coastal resorts in day-tripping mode. Pirang is known as the site of a pair of massive silk cotton trees that reputedly once formed part of its fortifications. The larger of the two, standing 43m high and a similar distance around, is claimed to be the tallest tree in West Africa, and even if this is untrue, it is nevertheless a quite magnificent specimen.

Previously unremarkable Faraba Banta will soon be nothing of the sort, with the scheduled 2023 inauguration of a brand new central campus for the University of The Gambia, the first of its kind, set on 80ha of land at the west end of the village. Otherwise, the area is of interest mainly to birdwatchers, who have the choice of exploring several worthwhile sites, notably Farasuto Forest near Koloro, Pirang Forest near Bonto, Pirang Pools north of Pirang, and the so-called Bush Track running south from Faraba Banta.

GETTING THERE AND AWAY Pirang lies along the main South Bank Road and is serviced by regular bush taxis from Brikama, 12km to its west. To explore the surrounding birding sites, however, you'll either need to charter a taxi from the coast, or else be prepared for a bit of walking and/or hopping around on local transport or donkey- or horse-cart. Directions to the individual sites are given under their respective headings.

WHERE TO STAY *Map, page 150*

Most people visit as a day trip from the coast, but there's now accommodation just 1km away from the Farasuto Forest at **Sita Joyeh Baobab Island** (m 267 2595, 346 5987; w sitajoyeh.gm; f sitajoyeh; £22 dbl; **$$**), situated on a tiny islet in the nearby bolong. Rooms here are in duplex rondavels with shaded first-floor observation decks, and they can arrange a variety of activities on land and water. Otherwise, the nearest accommodation is about 10km east in Tumani Tenda and Kafuta (page 214).

AROUND PIRANG The following sites are described in the sequence you reach them coming from Brikama or the coast.

Farasuto Forest Community Nature Reserve (⊕ 13.2977, -16.5652; m 707 3623; e mamadou.w.jallow@farasuto.org, mamadouwj@yahoo.co.uk; w farasuto. org) Situated 2km northeast of the South Bank Road where it bisects the village of Kuloro, Farasuto Forest is a 3ha relict patch of closed-canopy forest a short distance inland of the River Gambia. Originally left uncleared by local villagers for use as a ceremonial circumcision site, it was set aside as a community reserve in 2008 at the behest of the Kuloro Bird Club, which comprises around 30 locally based bird guides. Though quite small, Farasuto supports an incredibly diverse birdlife.

Around 100 species have been recorded within the forest, and another 200 from the immediate vicinity. It matches Abuko as a site for forest interior specialists, with 11 such species recorded, including Ahanta francolin, green turaco, spotted honeyguide, grey-headed bristlebill and green hylia, and (alongside Pirang) is the only place in The Gambia where the secretive African wood owl can be somewhat reliably observed. Other birds characteristic of Farasuto are violet turaco, sulphur-breasted bush-shrike and several types of greenbul and sunbird. Early morning is the best time to visit to do the very small site justice.

To get to Farasuto, you must first head to the village of Kuloro, which straddles the South Bank Road 8km east of Brikama and 4km west of Pirang (any gelly-gelly headed between these towns can drop you there). The junction for the reserve is on the left coming from Brikama, and although it is no longer signposted, anybody can point you in the right direction. From the junction, a dirt feeder road runs northeast for 2km, passing through the village then open fields to the entrance gate, which may or may not be manned.

Pirang Forest Park (⊕ 13.2816, -16.5531; m 988 7198, 207 6134; w projectwildgambia.com/pirang-bonto-forest; entrance D50, guides around D300) The centrepiece of the Pirang-Bonto Ecotourism Community Project, the 64ha Pirang Forest Park protects The Gambia's second-largest remaining block of moist closed-canopy forest (the largest being Abuko). With a canopy extending to 35m above the ground, Pirang Forest supports more than 200 bird and 80 butterfly species, along with substantial but skittish populations of red colobus, green and patas monkey. It has long been known to birders as the main Gambian site for white-spotted flufftail and wood owl (with the latter also now regularly recorded at nearby Farasuto). Other good forest birds include Ahanta francolin, red-thighed sparrowhawk, green turaco, swamp greenbul, green crombec and western bluebill. It is the only Gambian site for Puvel's illadopsis.

Situated to the north of the South Bank Road near the village of Bonto, Pirang Forest Park is very accessible but unsignposted and quite difficult to locate. Coming from the coast, you need to follow the South Bank Road for 10km past Brikama until you reach Bonto Junction (⊕ 13.2779, -16.5571) about 2km before Pirang village. At the junction, there is a small sign pointing left towards Bonto village; follow this, then after 500m turn right, then after another 300m (after passing a church to your right), left again. The small reception building lies about 150m down this road, and here you can pay the entrance fee, as well as arrange a guide (optional but recommended). Try to time your visit for during the week, as the main path through the forest joins the villages of Pirang and Bonto and there are always plenty of kids at weekends who hassle visitors.

Pirang Pools (⊕ 13.2753, -16.5256; m 237 8831, 261 6716, 262 4835; entrance D50) Extending over about 1km² between Pirang village and the South Bank of the River Gambia, this area formerly hosted about 70 artificial pools that were the site of a shrimp farm but have now been drained (although periodically they do hold water). It is generally listed as the most reliable site in The Gambia for the regal black-crowned crane, but sightings of this unmistakable tall bird have been infrequent for a number of years (although there was a confirmed sighting in 2017 by a local guide). There are also usually good numbers of spoonbills, egrets, kingfishers, waders and other waterbirds, including spur-winged goose and white-faced whistling duck, especially during the wet season. It is possible to see yellow-crowned bishop in the sedges, and crested lark and plain-backed pipit along the bunds. Raptors such as long-crested eagle, western banded snake-eagle and osprey are common during the dry season. The most southerly former pools lie about 600m northeast of the main square in Pirang and can easily be reached from there on foot.

Faraba Banta Bush Track This informal 3km trail running south from the South Bank Road through an area of relatively open savannah is known as a good site for greyish eagle-owl, a sub-Sahelian endemic recently split from the more widespread spotted eagle-owl. Other good birds associated with the trail are the semi-nocturnal Temminck's and bronze-winged courser, and a host of raptors including ten eagle and snake-eagle species, lizard and grasshopper buzzard, and various goshawks. The track starts in Faraba Banta on the south side of the South Bank Road, almost opposite the signpost for Faraba Kairaba (⊕ 13.2483, -16.5248). You are free to explore independently, but if you want a guide (you will need one to stand a chance of seeing the eagle-owl) and one doesn't find you, then ask around for Abdoulaye, who lives close to the start of the track. If you keep walking, you'll wind up in Jiboro after 10km.

12

Niumi and the North Coast

Lightly populated by comparison with its southern counterpart, the coastal portion of the North Bank Region comprises around 13km of bona fide coastline, running up to the Senegalese border from the port of Barra, as well as a long stretch of river frontage running south from Barra towards the venerable port of Albreda. Historically, the north coast and its hinterland formed the Kingdom of Niumi, a centralised Mandinka state that was founded during or before the 15th century, and grew wealthy on the back of the slave trade that dominated the lower river economy into the early 19th century. Today, the old kingdom, which ran inland from the coast as far as Jurunku Bolong, is split into two administrative districts: Lower and Upper Niumi. It also shares its name with Niumi National Park, which protects the coastline north of Barra, an area dominated by Jinack Island, a narrow sandy sliver separated from the mainland by the Niji Bolong in the north and mangroves in the south.

Niumi is relatively undeveloped in terms of tourist accommodation, which is limited to a handful of budget lodges on Jinack Island and around Albreda. Indeed, most tourists who explore the area do so on one of the full-day 'Roots Tours' offered by hotels and operators in the resorts around Banjul. These popular tours focus on the village of Juffureh, which *Roots* author Alex Haley claimed as his ancestral home, and on nearby Albreda and Kunta Kinteh (formerly James) Island, which together host five of the seven structures inscribed in 2003 as the 'Kunta Kinteh Island and Related Sites' UNESCO World Heritage Site (the other two being Fort Bullen in Barra and the Six-Gun Battery in Banjul). The highlights of Niumi can also be explored independently, crossing from Banjul using the Barra Ferry and picking up road transport from there.

BARRA AND SURROUNDS

Occupying a westerly prominence on the north side of the 3km-wide strait where the River Gambia empties into the open sea, Barra, with a population of 5,500 (or 15,000 including neighbouring Essau), is the principal town and main transport hub of the northern coastal hinterland. The town is surprisingly bustling for its size, and the chockablock market area around the ferry and bus terminals is perpetually crammed and particularly hectic (and home to a few shady bumster types who habitually try to involve themselves in any transaction involving a tourist). The name Barra is the Portuguese for a port entrance, or a sandbank that forms at the entrance to an estuary, referring to the narrowing of the River Gambia at its mouth, and in pre-colonial times it was widely used by Europeans as a synonym for all of Niumi. The only attraction of note in Barra is Fort Bullen, which forms part of the UNESCO World Heritage Site taking in Kunta Kinteh Island and surrounds.

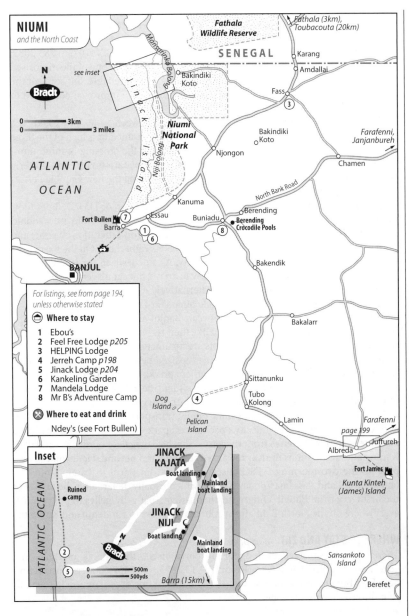

NIUMI
and the North Coast

see inset

Bradt

| 0 | 3km |
| 0 | 3 miles |

ATLANTIC

OCEAN

Fathala
Wildlife Reserve

SENEGAL

Fathala (3km),
Toubacouta (20km)

Karang

Amdallai

Bakindiki
Koto

Fass

Bakindiki
Koto

Njongon

Niumi
National
Park

Kanuma

Farafenni,
Janjanbureh

Chamen

North Bank Road

Fort Bullen
Barra

Essau

Buniadu

Berending

Berending
Crocodile Pools

BANJUL

Bakendik

Bakalarr

For listings, see from page 194,
unless otherwise stated

Where to stay

1 Ebou's
2 Feel Free Lodge *p205*
3 HELPING Lodge
4 Jerreh Camp *p198*
5 Jinack Lodge *p204*
6 Kankeling Garden
7 Mandela Lodge
8 Mr B's Adventure Camp

Where to eat and drink

Ndey's (see Fort Bullen)

Sittanunku

Dog
Island

Pelican
Island

Tubo
Kolong

Lamin

Farafenni
page 199

Albreda

Juffureh

Fort James

Kunta Kinteh
(James) Island

Inset

JINACK
KAJATA

Boat landing

Mainland
boat landing

ATLANTIC OCEAN

Ruined
camp

JINACK
NIJI

Boat landing

Mainland
boat landing

Bradt

| 0 | 500m |
| 0 | 500yds |

Barra (15km)

Sansankoto
Island

Berefet

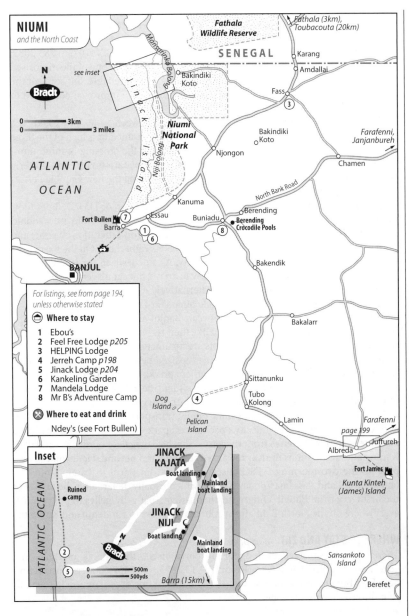

GETTING THERE AND AWAY Barra sits at the mouth of the Gambia River, on the north shore directly opposite Banjul, and the Banjul–Barra ferry is the westernmost river crossing in the country. The recent spate of bridge-building seen upriver has yet to reach here – and in fairness, the 3km strait between Banjul and Barra represents a significantly larger project than any of the upcountry bridges. Though the Barrow government has repeatedly promised that a bridge *is* in fact coming, this is several years off at minimum. (A bypass bridge about 15km upriver between Sittanunku and Bonto has also been proposed – either way, it'll be a while.)

So until then, you'll be on a boat. From Banjul, Barra is serviced both by a public ferry and by regular private pirogues. The only option for vehicles is the official ferry run by **Gambia Ferry Services** (℡ 422 3729/9932/4107; m 783 3083; w ferries.gm; ⓕ GPA Ferries), while foot passengers can take one of the motorised pirogues. The official ferry service has long been quite unreliable, but some of the boats have been replaced and the service is on the whole improved compared to several years back.

The ferries run every day, very roughly hourly between 07.00 and 23.00. The speed and efficiency of your trip is still somewhat determined by which of the three ferries you end up on, though. (Allow 35 minutes for the crossing at minimum.) The *Kunta Kinteh* is the best boat, while the *Kanilai* and *Johe* are smaller and slower – track which one you're getting and when it's arriving using the new Gambia Ferries App (Android only).

The fare as of early 2023 is D170/800 per motorcycle/car, or D35/D60 per foot/bicycle passenger. (Also D50 per goat/sheep and D150 per head of cattle, should you be herding.) The ferry leaves Banjul from the jetty on Liberation Avenue, and both drivers and foot passengers can buy their tickets right there. On the Barra side, tickets are also sold at the entrance to the jetty. As a pedestrian (or with a bicycle/moto), you can typically get on the first ferry to arrive, but car drivers can be subject to long queues and a significant wait. Alternatively, you can purchase a 'priority ticket' which allows you to skip the vehicle queue for D1,500.

The passenger pirogues that run between Banjul and Barra are effectively the waterborne equivalent of bush taxis, and like their terrestrial counterparts, are often uncomfortable and overloaded. Incidents are fortunately rare, but not unheard of – seven people drowned when their pirogue capsized here in 2013. If you do decide to risk it, try to avoid stormy or windy weather and ask for a life jacket. The pirogue fare is D50 per passenger, plus about D10 on either side to be carried from the shore to the boat (as most locals do, to keep their clothes dry!).

Back on land, Barra is an important public transport hub for the north coast, and road transport departs the city's packed taxi park – opposite the police station a couple of hundred metres from the jetty – for the Senegalese border at Amdallai/Karang and destinations upriver towards Farafenni and beyond. Here you can also pick up the two morning GTSC buses that run from Barra to Lamin Koto (for Janjanbureh) and Passamas/Foday Kunda, which usually depart after the arrival of the first ferry from Banjul. Otherwise, there are regular gelly-gellys to pretty much everywhere on the North Bank, from Albreda and Fass to Farafenni and Kuntaur.

🏠 **WHERE TO STAY AND EAT** *Map, page 193*

There's a real shortage of lodging in Barra itself, though, as of 2023, the government-linked **DK Jawara Resort** (✪ 13.4875, -16.5467) under construction near Fort Bullen means there should soon be at least one decent option in town, in roundhouses facing the water.

HELPING Lodge (14 rooms) Fass; m 994 5174, 360 7148; e helping-lodge@helpingcharity.org. uk; w helpingcharity.org.uk. Run by UK-based charity HELPING (Help for Education & Local Projects IN Gambia), this new guesthouse is in a peaceful location just south of Fass, which is great for birding. The en-suite rooms are spacious & scrupulously clean, with hot showers & Wi-Fi.

Transfers from the South Bank & excursions to the sights on the North Bank can be arranged. All profits go towards providing free education for local children & supplies for the local clinic. *£22 dbl B&B.* **$$**
Ebou's Essau; ✪ 13.4807, -16.5309; m 938 3251. This sleepy lodge is hidden away on a backstreet behind the market in Essau, about

2km east of the ferry terminal. Rooms are in a cluster of roundhouses set around an often-empty swimming pool. *£12 dbl.* **$**

Kankeling Garden (3 rooms) Essau; ✆ 13.4741,-16.5273; m 247 6168; e shumbaarts@gmail.com; f kankeling. Situated on a small riverfront promontory east of Essau, 'Kankeling' means 'as one' in Mandinka, & the idea behind the garden was to create a space for both locals & visitors to enjoy the country's music & culture. Their 3-bed bungalow is set among plenty of fruit trees, but facilities are fairly basic, with compost toilet & water collected from a nearby tap by donkey cart. *Rooms £20/night, camping £8 pp.* **$**

Mandela Lodge Barra; ✆ 13.4864, -16.5446; m 390 1620. This unsignposted guesthouse is an acceptable fallback about 200m from the Barra

ferry terminal, should you not be able to make it across for the night. Rooms in the newer building are considerably more pleasant. *£9 dbl.* **$**

Mr. B's Adventure Camp Buniadu; m 711 2240; e b.adventurecamps@gmail.com; f mrb. adventure. Set 9km east of Barra in Buniadu village at the turnoff for Albreda, this happy hippy hangout has a handful of simple huts in a green compound (with plenty of space for vehicle parking). The cheerful owner can arrange all trips in the area in his old-school multicoloured Land Rover, or take you to their satellite camp on Jinack Island. *£9 dbl.* **$**

Ndey's Options are limited at this unmarked resto-bar next to Fort Bullen, but there's a little garden to sit in & usually a cheap daily dish, plus a cold beer if you're lucky. **$**

OTHER PRACTICALITIES There are now two ATMs in Barra, from Trust Bank and Access Bank. The next ATMs on the North Bank are all the way in Farafenni.

AROUND BARRA

Fort Bullen Museum (🕘 08.00–18.00 Mon–Sat; entrance D100) Standing sentinel on Barra Point a few hundred metres west of the ferry jetty, Fort Bullen was the only such structure built on the West African coast with the express purpose of helping eradicate the slave trade. It was constructed on the so-called 'Ceded Mile' granted to the British by King Burungai Sonko of Niumi in 1826, in exchange for an annual subsidy of £100 following negotiations conducted by Sir Charles Bullen, the commander of HMS *Maidstone*. Initially, the fort consisted of little more than the two cannons Bullen took ashore to Barra Point to complement the gun battery at Banjul by covering the northern half of the 3km-wide strait between the two.

Development of the site was stalled when Burungai Sonko tried to revoke the Ceded Mile treaty, a decision that led to the Barra War of August 1831 to January 1832, in which the French stepped in to assist the British against Sonko's forces. The present fort, a rectangular laterite structure with a 1,200m² floor area, tall battlements and a circular bastion in each corner, was built over 1833–34, and its three-gun battery allowed the British to have full control over which ships could enter or leave the river mouth. As a result, the Royal Navy was able to seize more than 1,600 ships and free at least 150,000 captives between then and 1870. During this time, Fort Bullen came under attack only once, when a small force of British troops and civilians had tried to arrest some people in the nearby town of Essau but was fought off with the loss of several lives. The survivors of the force retreated to Fort Bullen, only to abandon it for four months until the following year when the fighting was over.

At the beginning of World War II, the Senegalese government sided with the Vichy government in France. This left the British colony surrounded by a potentially hostile enemy, so they modernised the fort and brought in more weapons, namely a four-inch Vickers machine gun (which is still there today) and a 12-pounder. After the war, the fort was again abandoned until it was declared a National Monument in the 1970s. It was renovated in 1996 for the Roots Homecoming Festival (page 26). In 2003, it was inscribed as part of the 'Kunta Kinteh Island and Related Sites'

UNESCO World Heritage Site. A small museum dedicated to the abolition of the slave trade opened here in 2013, but as of 2023 the exhibits were all stacked up in a storage room due to damage in the exhibition space – you can still have a look and the guides do their best, but it's difficult to engage with much of the collection.

Berending crocodile pools (⊕ 13.4834, -16.4640) This small village 10km east of Barra is the site of several pools linked by a shallow watercourse and surrounded by a small but beautiful patch of forest. The pool is known for its population of crocodiles, which are mostly fairly small and seem to be quite shy, though reputedly they do sometimes emerge towards dusk. It is said that when the Mandinka of

SIDE TRIP TO SENEGAL: FATHALA AND TOUBACOUTA

A quick dip over The Gambia's northern border into Senegal is an increasingly popular part of the Gambian tourism circuit, so much so that some attractions on the Senegalese side of the border now get a majority of their clientele from across the line. Senegal is visa free for more than 100 nationalities, including all EU/EEA states, UK, USA and Canada (but note you may be asked for proof of yellow fever vaccination on either side of the border).

Most popular among these excursions is the **Fathala Wildlife Reserve** (w fathala.com), whose entrance gate sits less than 6km north of the border crossing at Amdallai/Karang. The reserve consists of 6,000ha of densely wooded Sudano-Guinean savannah, and a 2,000ha fenced area at the core of the reserve where the animals reside. As the reserve matures, plans exist to eventually fence the remaining 4,000ha. In the main reserve you'll find southern and eastern African transplants like zebra, giraffe and rhino, as well as local antelopes and primates. And though the presence of introduced exotic species means that the game viewing here may not be the most authentic, it is no less atmospheric or exciting for it, and still represents one of the best game-viewing experiences in Senegambia.

Although the rhino, giraffe, buffalo and zebras might steal the show, the real rarity here is the critically endangered western giant eland (*Taurotragus derbianus derbianus*), which was the first animal to be translocated here when the reserve was initially developed back in 2006. Also known as the Derby eland, it's the largest antelope on earth, weighing up to 1,000kg and standing nearly 2m high. Its coat is striated with narrow white bands, its enormous furry dewlap swings freely under its chin, its intimidating spiral horns can themselves be over a metre long, and there are fewer than 200 of them anywhere in the world – this is one of a very small handful of places you can see them in a semi-wild habitat. You're also sure to encounter more common antelope like red-flanked duiker (*Cephalophus rufilatus*), bohor reedbuck (*Redunca redunca*), roan antelope (*Hippotragus equinus*) and waterbuck (*Kobus ellipsiprymnus*), along with primates like Temminck's red colobus (*Procolobus badius temminckii*) and the pig family's most iconic member, *Phacochoerus africanus*, better known as the common warthog.

There is also a separate enclosure here home to several lions, and visitors can take a guided walk alongside these famous felines. These walks have become something of a fixture on the Senegambian tourist trail, and while they're undoubtedly exhilarating and sure to get your heart pumping one way or the other, the domesticity of the lions isn't everyone's cup of tea. Entering the enclosure, you walk through the bush holding a wooden staff, while your guides

Berending first arrived in the area, they prayed regularly at the pools, but the practice has dropped away slightly now that most locals follow more orthodox strains of Islam. The two main reasons for praying appear to be for a good harvest and to increase fertility for women who have trouble conceiving. Those who pray at the poolside normally bring fish for the crocodiles but won't swim there. Even if you don't see the crocs, it is a great site for birds, with turacos and robin-chats calling from the lush foliage, broad-billed rollers perched higher in the canopy, and jacanas, crakes and kingfishers active around the reedy shore.

Berending lies on the main North Bank Road about 10km east of the Barra Ferry Terminal and 1km past the junction for Albreda (and Mr. B's, page 195).

wield a nice bit of donkey meat on a spike. The lions here aren't from the wild, but have been bred in South Africa, and as such haven't had the wilderness experience necessary to recognise prey in the same way as a wild lion would; regardless, the meat keeps their attention a lot better than you and your camera do. The walk has plenty of time for photo ops and even a chance to pet the lions. Some criticise the walks as rather exploitative and zoo-like, and that's a decision you'll have to make on your own, but the rangers are professional, the lions are well cared for and it's an undoubtedly thrilling experience to be in their company.

Most tour operators on the Gambian coast can easily arrange a trip to Fathala, and while it's possible to visit as a (long) day trip from the coastal resorts, if possible you should rather take advantage of the chance to enjoy a **night in the reserve**, watching the comings and goings at the lighted waterhole just in front of the restaurant and pool, and sleeping in the top-notch luxury safari tents (**$$$$$**), each with canopy beds, outdoor shower and private terrace. Or continue to nearby Toubacouta, where there's plenty of more affordable accommodation.

A straight shot 17km north past Fathala, the chronically sleepy Mandinka town of **Toubacouta** is the biggest tourist centre in the Sine-Saloum Delta, but still feels remarkably village-like, consisting of a tangled clutch of dirt roads and twisting footpaths splayed along the mangrove-lined shores of the Saloum River to the west. It serves as a jumping-off point for pirogue or kayak trips around the myriad creeks and islands of the delta and any of the guesthouses here can arrange trips throughout the estuary. Popular destinations include the Île aux Coquillages, where baobabs grow directly out of the millions of oyster shells that form the island, the Île aux Oiseaux, where up to 40,000 pairs of royal terns have been known to nest, and the traditional fishing village on Île Sipo.

The waters off Toubacouta are also one of the best places in the delta to see and experience bioluminescence, the milky glow aroused in marine plankton, known as dinoflagellates, when they're disturbed. Take a dip by night to see the surreal, swirling, sparkling trails of light that follow each of your limbs through the water, and soak up the meditative stillness of nighttime in the delta.

Toubacouta has an excellent range of accommodation catering to all budgets. **Les Palétuviers** (w lespaletuviers.com; **$$$$$**) is the most luxurious spot in town, with gorgeous green grounds and superbly stylish rooms, including a baobab treehouse and offshore floating suite. **Keur Saloum** (w keursaloum.com; **$$$**) is a more traditional resort, and there are several warm & welcoming family-style guesthouses like **Keur Niaye** (w keur-niaye-maison-dhote.com; **$$$**), **Keur Thierry** (w keurthierry.com; **$$**) and **Keur Youssou** (w keuryoussou.com; **$**).

12

Inexpensive bush taxis run there regularly from Barra. The pools lie a few hundred metres from the main road, and can be reached by following a sandy track that leads off to the right just before an immense kapok tree.

Fass Situated 2.5km south of the border with Senegal at Amdallai/Karang and 16km north of Barra, this small town is known for its large, colourful and lively Wednesday *lumo* (market), frequented by both Gambians and Senegalese. If you are in the area, it is worth a visit – there are plenty of bush taxis from Barra, especially on market days. Helping Lodge (page 194) is also here.

ALBREDA, JUFFUREH AND SURROUNDS

Huddled so close together that it's difficult to tell where one ends and the other begins, the historic twin villages of Albreda and Juffureh (also known as Albadarr and Gillifree, or other variants thereof) sit on the North Bank of the River Gambia about 25km upriver of Barra and Banjul. Together with nearby Kunta Kinteh Island, 3km across the water, these villages played a pivotal role in the slave trade that dominated the economy of the lower River Gambia from the late 15th to the early 19th centuries. At various times, the Portuguese, British and French all maintained trading posts in the vicinity, while Kunta Kinteh Island was revived as a strategic British naval base in the abolition era. Today, the area is the focal point of a UNESCO World Heritage Site whose seven components include Fort James on Kunta Kinteh Island and four separate buildings in and around Albreda. Juffureh, meanwhile, leapt to international prominence in 1976 with the publication of Alex Haley's *Roots* (page 201), which claimed it as the place where his ancestor Kunta Kinteh was captured by slave traders. All in all, it's a fascinating area, contrasting with the south coast resorts in almost every conceivable way, and well worth visiting, whether you do so independently or as part of a tour.

GETTING THERE AND AWAY The overwhelming majority of visitors to Albreda, Juffureh and Kunta Kinteh Island join one of the organised Roots Tours offered by most south-coast hotels and ground operators. This is certainly the easiest option, but the area is also accessible to independent travellers who are prepared to put up with the vagaries associated with the ferry from Banjul to Barra (page 96). From Barra it's about 35km by road, first following the surfaced main North Bank Road east for 9km as far as Buniadu, then turning right on to a newly surfaced road that heads southwards through Bakendik and veers eastward at Tubo Kolong before entering Albreda. (If approaching from the east, the new surfaced road continues another 30km past Albreda, rejoining the North Bank Road at a well-marked junction in Kuntair.) The route from Barra is covered by a few shared taxis and gelly-gellys, which take under an hour and cost D60, while private taxis should cost around D1,500 but incur a good 2 or 3 hours of waiting time. It's also possible to arrange boat excursions to James Island and Albreda from Lamin Lodge, Tumani Tenda and Bintang on the South Bank.

 WHERE TO STAY AND EAT *Map, opposite, unless otherwise stated*

✳ **Jerreh Camp** [map, page 193] (22 rooms) Sittanunku; m 711 4769, 393 3412; e jerrehcampgambia@gmail.com; f Jerreh1997. With a delightfully isolated location down a signposted sandy track 4.5km west of the Albreda road at Sittanunku, this is one of the most scenic guesthouses on the north coast. The rooms are nothing to shout about, but all are neat & comfortable enough. There's no mains power: with less than 5 rooms occupied, the generator is on

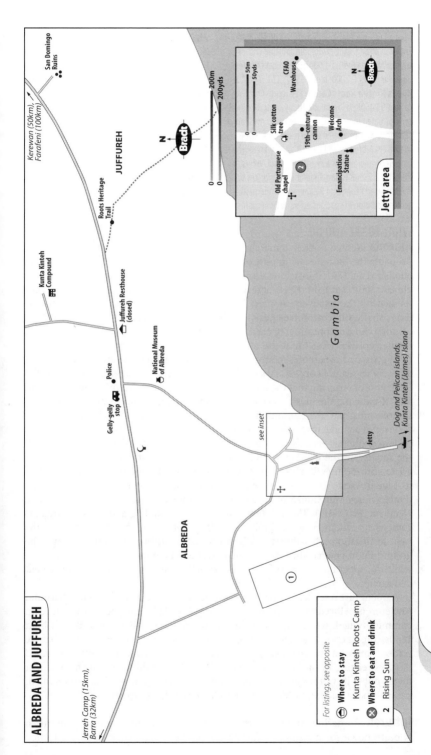

ALBREDA AND JUFFUREH

Jerreh Camp (15km),
Barra (32km)

Kerewan (50km),
Farafeni (100km)

San Domingo
Ruins

JUFFUREH

Roots Heritage
Trail

Kunta Kinteh
Compound

Juffureh Resthouse
(closed)

Gelly-gelly
stop

Police

National Museum
of Albreda

ALBREDA

see inset

Jetty

Dog and Pelican islands,
Kunta Kinteh (James) Island

G a m b i a

N

0   200m
0   200yds

Jetty area

Old Portuguese
chapel

Silk cotton
tree

19th-century
cannon

Welcome
Arch

CFAO
Warehouse

Emancipation
Statue

N

0   50m
0   50yds

For listings, see opposite

Where to stay

① 1 Kunta Kinteh Roots Camp

Where to eat and drink

✕ 2 Rising Sun

from 19.00–midnight; with more, it's on all night. They can arrange sunset/dolphin spotting cruises & trips to Albreda (both D1,000 pp), or boat transfers from Banjul for D5,000. Meals £5–7. *£13.50 dbl.* **$**
Kunta Kinteh Roots Camp (34 rooms) m 790 4782, 991 4508; e kuntakintehrootscamp7@gmail. com. Situated in green riverside grounds, this long-serving & well-managed camp is the only game in town in Albreda – so luckily it's a good one. The garden compound has a swimming pool, views to the jetty & James Island, food at similar prices to the affiliated Rising Sun Restaurant, & adequate accommodation in spacious en-suite twin rooms

with nets & roof fan, or dbl rooms with standing fan. Good value. *All rooms £13.50.* **$**
Rising Sun Restaurant m 790 4782; ⊕ 07.30–17.00 daily. Situated on the main square behind Albreda Jetty, this friendly open-sided restaurant is an agreeable spot for a tasty, sensibly priced drink or meal, with on-the-ball staff used to pulling out the stops for tour groups. Sandwiches & snacks are available, along with a varied selection of fish, chicken & steak dishes. Portions are generous & a full selection of cold soft drinks & alcoholic drinks is available. *Meals around £5.50, snacks £2–3.* **$$**

WHAT TO SEE AND DO

Albreda Rented to French merchants by the King of Niumi in 1681, Albreda was probably the busiest slaving post on the River Gambia until the trade was legally abolished in 1807. Most tour groups arrive at the Albreda Jetty, which extends almost 300m into the river, and leads to the main square via a short footpath flanked by the relatively modern **Welcome Arch** and **Emancipation Statue**. A large, shady **silk cotton tree** lies at the heart of the square, and below it is a 19th-century **cannon**, presumably used by the British to bar slaving ships from sailing further upriver. Here (or at the road entrance to town), independent visitors will be approached by a representative of the **Juffureh–Albreda Youth Society** (m 705 4419; w jaysgambia.org; f jaysyouths), which was established in 1993 with the dual aims of ensuring that the local community benefits collectively from tourism, and of reducing the hassle to visitors presented by pushy guides and children. All visitors must pay the community fee (D200 pp), which includes the (optional) services of a guide, who will expect a fair tip.

Two buildings inscribed as part of the UNESCO World Heritage Site flank the square. To the left, behind the Rising Sun Restaurant, the substantial ruin of a late 15th-century **Portuguese chapel** is probably the oldest extant structure of its type in West Africa. To the right, reached via a 50m footpath, is the timeworn double-storey **warehouse** once occupied by the Compagnie Française d'Afrique Occidentale (CFAO). The link between the CFAO Building and the slave trade is somewhat tenuous, as it was probably built in 1847, more than a decade after the twin fortifications at Bathurst and Barra closed the river to unwanted traffic. The ground floor, entered through an open arcade, served as a shop and warehouse, while the upper floor comprised the residential quarters of the CFAO management and agents.

A 500m dirt track leads from the right side of the main square to the **National Museum of Albreda** (w ncac.gm; ⊕ 08.00–17.00 daily; entrance fee included in community fee), which is housed in the Maurel Frères Building, a British-built 1840s construction that later served as a warehouse of the eponymous Lebanese trader. Small but harrowing, this well-organised museum has several detailed displays relating to the slave trade out of West Africa and to the harsh treatment meted out to its victims after their arrival in the Americas. It also has a room full of paraphernalia relating to Alex Haley and the *Roots* phenomenon.

Juffureh Bordering Albreda to the east, the tiny Mandinka village of Juffureh is best known for housing the family compound associated with Kunta Kinteh of *Roots* fame (see below). In fact, there is some dispute among historians as to whether Juffureh could have been the place where Kunta Kinteh actually lived. This is because the village is only 1km from the former slaving emporium of Albreda, whose traders would usually have sourced captives from further afield than what was practically their own doorstep. Whatever the truth, the family still lives and welcomes visitors at the **Kunta Kinteh Compound** (⊕ 13.3385, -16.3814; m 772 1233; ⊕ daily; visitors are expected to make a small donation), where they will tell you the oral history of the village and the story of Kunta Kinteh, and pull out a stash of old clippings relating to Alex Haley's visit. Given the tourist traffic the Kunta Kinteh Compound has experienced over the years, it feels very much like a village homestead, displaying few, if any, trappings of the wealth one might expect. Indeed, it isn't even signposted: to get there from the main road, you need to head north at the junction opposite the (defunct as of 2023) Juffureh Resthouse, then turn right after 150m, and enter the first compound to the left. Ghanaian YouTuber Wode Maya visited in 2019 and produced an informative video of his time with the family: w youtube.com/watch?v=ULtR1JfSRJw.

ALEX HALEY, JUFFUREH AND THE *ROOTS* SAGA

Juffureh achieved global fame in the wake of the 1976 publication of Alex Haley's *Roots*, which purported to trace the author's ancestry back to this otherwise unremarkable village. The hero of Haley's story was his ancestor Toby, a slave bought by a Virginian plantation owner called John Waller. According to Haley, Toby had started life as Kunta Kinteh, born to an Islamic Mandinka family in Juffureh, before being captured by slavers as a small boy and then shipped to America on a longboat, where he spent weeks confined below deck with little food or water. Renamed by Waller, Toby passed on the details of his childhood capture to his sons, who in turn recounted them to their sons and so on, allowing Haley to trace his ancestry back to Kunta Kinteh and Juffureh.

A massive critical and public success, *Roots* sold more than a million copies in its first seven months, spending 22 weeks at the top of *The New York Times* bestseller list, and it earned its author the 1977 Pulitzer Prize. The television series that followed was nominated for 37 Emmy Awards, winning nine, and attracted 130 million viewers in the US alone. It also brought tourism to Juffureh in a big way. At the peak of its popularity, the village was visited by 80% of tourists to The Gambia, and even today it remains something of a pilgrimage site for US visitors boasting some African ancestry.

In 1993, Alex Haley suffered a fatal heart attack, 17 years after the publication of *Roots*. Within a year of his death, his private papers had exposed much of the *Roots* saga to be invention. It transpired that Toby had been living in America for at least five years before Kunta Kinteh was supposedly shipped there from Juffureh, and that he died almost a decade before the birth of the 'daughter' that supposedly linked his lineage to Haley's. Despite the exposure, however, the Roots Tour to Juffureh and environs remains one of the most popular excursions from the resorts that line the coast south of Banjul. And rightly so. True, there is little doubt that Haley consciously fabricated the genealogical link between himself, Toby and Kunta Kinteh. But there is no denying the deep symbolic truth underlying the *Roots* saga, nor the horrific trade in human lives that formed its inspiration.

Back on the main road, 600m east of the new mosque and main junction, a signposted arch to the right marks the start of the **Roots Heritage Trail** (❂ 13.3375, -16.3789), a short nature walk that leads to the waterfront and which is intended as a place of quiet contemplation. Another 350m east from here along the main road, and also to the right, a short footpath leads to the brooding **San Domingo Ruins** (❂ 13.3383, -16.3754), set in an overgrown clearing alongside a massive baobab tree. One of the earliest European trade stations founded in West Africa, San Domingo dates to the late 15th century, when it supported a small mercantile community of Portuguese settlers and people of Luso-African descent, who acted as hosts and middlemen to visiting ships. In its prime, the settlement comprised a few large buildings, including one 'of two storeys with courses of mortar running through the laterite rock, plaster tinted pink, a yellow brick arch over one window as well as four rectangular windows beneath a wooden lintel', set in large gardens with a freshwater well. All that remains today is the ruin of one double-storey house, which may or may not be the one described above.

Kunta Kinteh (James) Island Renamed in honour of Kunta Kinteh in 2011, this small rocky outcrop in the River Gambia, 3km to the southeast of Albreda, was formerly called James Island and is still most widely referred to by that name. It was one of the first landfalls made by the 1456 expedition led by Portuguese sailor Luiz de Cadamosto, who named it St Andrew Island after a shipmate they buried on the island. The first fort was built there by Latvians in 1651, only to be seized ten years later by the theatrically named Royal Adventurers of England, who renamed the island in honour of James, Duke of York. Ideally placed to provide strategic defence for English interests along the river and as a staging post for the shipment of enslaved people, James Island and Fort James were captured by the French then recaptured by the English several times over subsequent decades.

The location of James Island ensured a clear passage downriver for whichever power controlled it at the time. Hence it was subject to frequent attacks. In 1719, a group of Welsh pirates overran Fort James and carried off all the goods and slaves. It was attacked less successfully in 1768 by a regiment of 500 Niumi men. In 1779, the French seized the island one last time, without firing a shot, and destroyed the fort. In 1816, British naval Captain Alexander Grant, who was responsible for the British presence in Banjul, also entered into an agreement with the King of Niumi, allowing the British Royal Navy to reoccupy the abandoned fort in exchange for an annual payment of 300 iron bars. Later, however, the British claimed that the king reneged on the deal, so they abandoned their plans for James Island and withdrew, concentrating their future efforts on Banjul. The island was abandoned altogether in 1829.

Almost 200 years later, the extensive ruins of Fort James, centrepiece of a UNESCO World Heritage Site, form the most important relict of the slave trade in this part of The Gambia. Despite its ruinous state, the fort is a poignant site. What remains of the thick stone walls are held together by bulbous baobab roots and scampered across by rats and lizards. The base of the dungeon, in which up to 140 enslaved people were once impounded, also survives. A few cannons line the shore, while the beaches are littered by beads, once the main form of currency in this part of Africa. The island is not sinking, as is often stated, but it does require regular maintenance to remedy erosion caused by wave action. However, the eroded shores in fact consist of artificial embankments, built of earth and rock and supported by piled stakes that were created to extend a natural area so small it barely allowed room for anything other than the fort.

Most if not all Roots Tours include a boat trip to James Island. It can also be visited independently by boat from Albreda. This will cost around D1,000 per boat for a party of up to five, and can be arranged with any of the official guides, or at the tourist info point on the main square. The D200 community fee charged to all visitors also covers your trip to the island. An hour is more than enough time to see everything the island has to offer.

Dog and Pelican islands (✪ Dog: 13.3646, -16.5090; Pelican: 13.3596, -16.4939) These two small islands lie in the River Gambia, just off Dog Island Point. Dog Island, supposedly named after the dog-like barking of the baboons that once inhabited it, was colonised by the British in 1661, who renamed it Charles Island and built a fort on it. However, because the island was vulnerable to attack at low tide, when it is possible to walk to it from the mainland (though we have not tried this yet), the fort was abandoned in 1666. The rock that constitutes the island was used to construct both the early fortifications in Banjul and those on James Island. Today there is no sign of Charles Fort. It is possible to hire a boat (from Barra or Jerreh Camp, for example) to take you to the island, but take good care as the landing can be rocky!

NIUMI NATIONAL PARK

Effectively a southern extension of Senegal's vast Parc National de Delta du Saloum, the 50km² Niumi National Park is one of the finest and most accessible of The Gambia's protected areas, less than an hour's journey from Banjul, but also one of the most underpublicised. Established in 1986, the park incorporates most of the Gambian coastline north of Barra Point. The dominant feature of the park, with its northern tip nudging into Senegal, is narrow, isolated Jinack Island, which is separated from the mainland by the Niji Bolong in the north and shallow mangrove beds (crossable on foot in places when the tide is low) in the south. Jinack is also sometimes known as Paradise or Coconut Island, in reference to the 10km arc of unspoilt sandy beaches along a western coastline whose gradual decline makes for unusually calm swimming conditions. Opposite Jinack, the mainland part of Niumi comprises a large chunk of bush and woodland savannah stretching north from the village of Kanuma, as well as the magnificent Masarinko Bolong and the escarpment above it.

> ### GREEN JINACK
>
> Jinack is also (in)famous throughout The Gambia for its expansive marijuana plantations. These are still illegal in The Gambia, but tolerated here for a variety of reasons, one being a series of horrible curses and misfortunes that supposedly befell the last authorities that came to the island to prosecute the growers. Thus, as the story goes, no authority dares set foot on the island today, and the waving fields of weed would seem to confirm this. Remember well, though, that this spiritual protection ends at the island's shores – it would be inviting trouble to carry any of the local produce back to the mainland. (Or to the Senegalese corner of the island, where there's still growing going on, but also a few forestry agents who may like to see your documents if they suspect you've wandered over from The Gambia – no word on whether the curse applies to them!)

Jinack Island protects a fair amount of wildlife, and it can be very rewarding for birdwatchers. The main attraction for most visitors, however, is the beach, which is serviced by just a couple of small camps – quite gloriously underdeveloped by comparison with most of its counterparts south of the River Gambia. Here, the thunder of traffic and the inanities of bumsters are a distant memory, along with most modern facilities of any kind. In fact, the entire island, populated as it is by a scattering of fishermen, farmers and their families, offers a rewarding, tranquil and unaffected glimpse into rural Gambian life. It's particularly suited to keen walkers, whose enjoyment will be enhanced by the absence of motor vehicles on Jinack, and the friendly, welcoming vibe exuded by the villagers.

GETTING THERE AND AWAY Most visitors to the two main beach lodges arrange a boat transfer from Banjul or elsewhere on the south coast when they make a booking. This will cost D3,500 per boat (max ten passengers) one-way and takes around an hour. If you prefer to make your own way there from Barra, bush taxis (D75) run to two mainland drop-off points just across the bolong from Jinack Niji and Jinack Kajata. The villages are only about 500m apart, so it's not particularly important which one you get dropped at. (A private hire for this trip will cost around D1,500 one-way.) Once at the waterfront, it's about D50 per person for the boat crossing. It's less than 30 minutes walking from Niji or Kajata to either of the ocean-side lodges. The road approaches may be impassable during the rains, but are usually fine in the dry season.

It's also possible to walk or (motor)cycle up the beach at low tide. Ask for Black Cow Crossing (✪ 13.4895, -16.5435) in Barra, where kids will pole you back and forth across the shallow southern end of the Niji Bolong on a small pontoon for a few dalasi. From here, its 9km straight up the beach to the two lodges.

Finally, you can also get a boat from Jinack Kajata to Bakindiki Koto on the mainland, where there's a small, yet-to-be-named lodge (m 702 7812) and a decently graded 10km road to Fass.

ORIENTATION Jinack Island lies mostly within The Gambia, but the northern part also stretches across the border into Senegal. The small population lives almost entirely in the north, in four villages, of which two lie on the Gambian side. These are Jinack Niji and the more northerly and moderately larger Jinack Kajata, which lie only 500m apart on the island's eastern shore. Both of the accommodation options face the Atlantic, about 1.5km west of the two villages.

 WHERE TO STAY AND EAT *Map, page 193*
Jinack and Feel Free lodges sit 150m apart along the oceanfront west of the villages. Mr. B's Adventure Camp also has a small satellite camp on the east side of Jinack Island facing the Niji Bolong – make arrangements to stay here via their main camp in Buniadu (page 195). Smile Inn (m 297 1131) restaurant does Gambian meals in Jinack Kajata.

⁕ **Jinack Lodge** (5 rooms) m (+44)(0)7979 751751 (UK), 368 8230, 938 4716, 777 8935; e info@jinacklodge.com; w jinack-lodge.com. Set in sprawling acacia-shaded grounds leading down to an idyllic beach, this friendly British–Gambian venture offers accommodation in colourful solar-powered cottages with a dbl/twin bed, net, outdoor seating & en-suite cold shower & toilet. There are no fans or AC, but the rooms have good natural ventilation. The large common area has a well-stocked bar & restaurant serving daily set menus with meals around £5–6. It is a lovely place to chill in a hammock or take advantage of the many relaxed walking opportunities in the vicinity,

& to try your hand at their telescope. They can also arrange day trips to most points of interest in & around Banjul. *£21 dbl, HB & FB available.* **$$**

☀ **Feel Free Lodge** (7 rooms) m +44 (0)7966 510276 (UK), 345 7547, 343 0994; e feelfreelodge@outlook.com; w feelfreegambia. com; . Overlooking a beautiful sweep of beach, this eco-friendly lodge offers colourful en-suite dbls set in an idyllic garden in the sand, with an open-sided restaurant & bar serving Gambian meals & cold beers. The staff can also organise trips to nearby Niumi National Park, plus visits to Jinack village & its school. Beachside BBQs & evening dance shows are also offered. *£14/20 sgl/ dbl B&B.* **$**

WHAT TO SEE AND DO For most visitors, the main attraction of Niumi is the **beach** on Jinack, but it is also possible to walk for miles on the island, with the sea on one side and the lush greenness of the bush on the other, accompanied only by small birds wading along the tide's edge or the silhouette of an osprey soaring overhead. Thanks to the Niji Bolong, which separates the island from the mainland, it has never been seriously developed, so it retains a fair variety of wildlife. Indeed, leopard tracks were a common sight here until relatively recently – though these have largely disappeared in the last two decades. There are still numerous warthogs, however, as well as some of the country's largest crocodiles living in the Niji Bolong.

A British bird-ringing group has studied the birdlife here for several years, resulting in a species list that is phenomenal. Especially prevalent are large numbers of Palaearctic migrants that overwinter in the rich coastal scrub or feed themselves up before travelling further south. At Buniadu Point near the north end of the island, there are several **lagoons** and a large sand spit that is submerged only at high tide. Here you will find hundreds of gulls, terns and waders, with perhaps a few pelicans or even a greater flamingo. Birds of prey are well represented with dozens of overwintering ospreys along the bolongs and the coast, as well as African fish eagle, shikra, Gabar goshawk, African harrier-hawk and even the massive martial eagle. Uncommon birds recorded here include white-fronted plover, bar-breasted firefinch and European scops owl. The paths running through the interior pass through woodland, shrub and submerged paddies alive with the likes of Senegal coucal, bearded barbet, yellow-crowned gonolek, black-crowned tchagra and various rollers, widows and finches.

Another highlight of a visit to Jinack has to be the possibility of **encountering dolphins**, especially around December and January. Bottlenose dolphins can sometimes be seen on the boat trip between Barra and Jinack, cavorting and playing in the waves. A large group of Atlantic hump-backed dolphins also occasionally swims only 100m or so from the shore, giving anyone on the beach an excellent view. This last species is a real speciality as it is found only along the coast of West Africa. There appears to be a group of 20 or so dolphins that spend part of their time off Jinack and the rest of it further north in the Delta du Saloum.

Part Four

UPRIVER GAMBIA

Upriver Gambia: An Overview

The River Gambia is the fourth-longest waterway in West Africa at 1,100km. It rises in the moist and mountainous Fouta Djalon region of Guinea (a watershed that also forms the source of the rivers Senegal and Niger), then flows through Senegal's vast Niokolo-Koba National Park before finally crossing into The Gambia some 300km inland of its mouth as the crow flies, or 450km upstream as the crocodile swims. As it continues its sedate journey towards the Atlantic, this perennial ribbon of greenery and rich source of protein forms the very lifeblood of the Gambian interior. It is also the watery spine that dictates the outline of a serpentine country whose parallel northern and southern borders seldom stray more than 25km from the river's banks as they mimic its worming course.

Below the Barrakunda Falls just on the Senegal side of the border (which is really a small rapids at best), the river is flat and sluggish, registering a total altitude drop of around 20m after it crosses into The Gambia. It widens as it approaches the Atlantic, and becomes increasingly saline and tidal past Kuntaur, about 180km from the estuary. Until 2019, not a single bridge spanned the Gambian stretch of the river, but there are now three: at Soma/Farafenni, Basse Santa Su and Fatoto. The river remains navigable upstream all the way to the Senegalese border, though no scheduled passenger boats take advantage of this asset. Instead, all traffic inland must follow one of two parallel land routes, the so-called South Bank and North Bank roads, which both follow a similarly twisting path between the river on one side and the Senegalese border on the other. Though the vast majority of vehicles now use the new bridges, there are still a few vehicle ferries plying their way back and forth across the river at places like Kau-ur, Janjanbureh and Bansang.

In travel terms, 'Upriver Gambia' embraces anywhere and everywhere significantly inland of Brikama – something like 95% of the country's total surface area. Yet such is the imbalance between coastal and inland tourist development that any excursion upriver should be undertaken in a spirit of adventure and flexibility. True, roads through the interior have registered massive improvements, with the South Bank and North Bank roads now surfaced all the way upcountry to their meeting point at Fatoto. And upriver residents happily report significant improvements in the provision of water and power in recent years, too, along with an increasingly good mobile data network, but in most other respects, travel here is a throwback to the backwater West Africa of years past – you're not in Kombo anymore, Toto!

So throw whatever ideas you may have had about The Gambia as 'Africa light' out the window: travel conditions upriver are no different to, and in some cases more rugged than, those of many countries considered much more difficult to travel in than The Gambia. Accommodation tends to be quite rudimentary and rundown, the culinary variety is extremely limited, car breakdowns are commonplace and the best-laid plans are frequently upset by a general aura of unhurried nonchalance.

For all that, upriver travel offers plenty of rewards, particularly to those willing to engage with West Africa on its own laid-back terms. The humdrum small towns and charming traditional villages of the interior stand in organic contrast to the artificiality of the coastal resorts, and the region also has much to offer in terms of wildlife viewing. And while travel conditions might be on the rough side, Upriver Gambia could hardly be friendlier or safer. If the prospect of independent travel seems daunting, it is easy enough to book on to a guided one- or two-night excursion to the likes of Tendaba Camp, Bintang Bolong or the Chimp Rehabilitation Project (CRP) in River Gambia National Park. More adventurously, you could rent a self-drive vehicle, or make use of the extensive bus and gelly-gelly network, to travel all the way inland to Basse Santa Su. Either way, no visit to The Gambia would seem complete without an excursion into its rustic interior.

HIGHLIGHTS

TUMANI TENDA This simple but well-run ecotourism camp, only an hour's drive inland from the coastal resorts, offers good birdwatching along with an interesting set of cultural activities (page 213).

BINTANG BOLONG Probably the most characterful goal for a budget overnight trip upriver is the stilted lodge with saltwater swimming pool set among the mangroves, or indulgance in a little bush luxury at Abca's Creek (page 215).

TENDABA CAMP The largest upriver camp, Tendaba is a birdwatcher's paradise and the best base for canoe trips into the vast Bao Bolong Wetland Reserve, home to several rare and eagerly sought species (page 219).

KIANG WEST NATIONAL PARK The country's largest terrestrial reserve protects a little-visited tract of savannah and riverine woodland rich in monkeys, antelope and birds (page 221).

KERR BATCH STONE CIRCLES The less impressive but more off-the-beaten-track of the country's two ancient UNESCO-inscribed stone circle sites is famed for its unique lyre-stone and an adventure to reach (page 234).

WASSU STONE CIRCLES The most accessible and famous archaeological site in The Gambia, UNESCO-inscribed Wassu comprises 200 megaliths arranged into 11 stone circles (page 239).

RIVER GAMBIA NATIONAL PARK The top mammal-viewing destination in the interior is home to a renowned Chimp Rehabilitation Project (and excellent clifftop camp). Monkeys and birds are also prolific on boat trips to the islands (page 240).

JANJANBUREH This small but historic town, set on a forested island in the middle of the River Gambia, is a popular chill-out venue and aspiring ecotourism hub (page 244).

KUNKILLING FOREST PARK Monkeys and forest birds are the main attractions of this small community-managed park upriver of Janjanbureh (page 253).

BASSE SANTA SU The most remote and least Westernised of Gambian towns has an attractive riverside setting and compellingly traditional feel (page 256).

GETTING AROUND

The River Gambia divides the interior into two halves, which are generally referred to as the North Bank and South Bank, and are connected by three new bridges at Soma/Farafenni, Basse Santa Su and Fatoto. Both banks are serviced by one main road running inland from the coast in a broadly easterly direction almost as far as the eastern border with Senegal. Both are now surfaced in their entirety. The South Bank Road runs from Serekunda and Brikama through Soma to Basse Santa Su (with surfaced feeder roads running north to Tendaba and Janjanbureh), and finally ending at Koina. The North Bank Road starts at Barra, opposite Banjul, and runs through Farafenni and Lamin Koto (on the riverbank opposite Janjanbureh), continuing until it meets the South Bank Road at Fatoto. The main north–south road, the so-called Trans-Gambia Highway, is an important through route between northern and southern Senegal, taking in the Senegambia Bridge and passing through the towns of Farafenni and Soma.

The best road transport is the GTSC bus service that covers the main roads through the North and South Bank, leaving mainly in the morning. The South Bank service runs several times daily between Serekunda and Basse Santa Su via Brikama, Soma and Janjanbureh, while the North Bank service runs two buses in each direction daily between Barra and either Lamin Koto or Passamas/Foday Kunda. In addition, almost all routes are plied by regular private passenger vehicles known as bush taxis or gelly-gellys. These are slightly more expensive than the GTSC buses, and much less comfortable, but they operate far longer hours.

Since 2019, the sometimes days-long queues to cross the river are largely a thing of the past, and Banjul–Barra is now the only major river crossing point that remains unbridged. So while waits of several hours to cross with a vehicle are still commonplace there (pedestrians and motorcycles get through much more quickly), crossing the river, and getting around the country more broadly, has never been easier. Unless you're really getting off the beaten track, the only ferry service you are likely to use is the short crossing between Janjanbureh and Lamin Koto.

Considering that the River Gambia is navigable all the way to the eastern border with Senegal, it is surprising that the few tours to the interior are mostly road-based. However, one operator that does specialise in bespoke water-based expeditions all the way upriver is **FairPlay Gambia** (w fairplaygambia.com) – see page 252.

OTHER PRACTICALITIES

Upriver travel conditions can come as a shock. Whereas facilities at the coast tend to approximate Western standards (albeit with a touch of Africa at the edges), travel inland is emphatically a back-to-basics experience. There are, for instance, only a small handful of ATMs in the entire region (in Farafenni, Soma and Basse), and foreign-exchange facilities generally consist of the nearest Mauritanian-run general store (which, admittedly, usually works pretty well!). The mobile data network is massively improved, but it can still sometimes go out for hours, or occasionally days, at a time.

Until recently, no upcountry town had access to permanent grid electricity. While this is changing fast, and most upriver towns of a certain size are now connected, this is by no means universal and many smaller settlements are still left out. To find out if your hotel is on the grid, just ask if they have power from NAWEC (pronounced 'na-weck' – the National Water and Electricity Company).

And for those who still do *not* have NAWEC power, managing a business – particularly one catering to visitors – remains as complicated as ever. Low visitor numbers can make it impossible to afford the running costs of a generator or the installation costs of a solar system, which means limited or no access to fans or AC (read: long, hot, sticky nights), limited availability of chilled drinks, poor quality of lighting in rooms and restaurants and a reduced standard and variety of food (which cannot be frozen or refrigerated). For some, this simplicity is part of the charm of upriver travel, enhancing the rusticity of the riverside camps and their sense of removal from the coastal resorts. But fair to say it will not appeal to everybody!

13

Inland to Soma and Farafenni

The most significant north–south road through The Gambia is the 25km strip of well-maintained asphalt that connects the Senegalese border posts at Kerr Ayib and Sénoba. Often referred to as the Trans-Gambia Highway, this interlude along the RN4 between the Senegalese towns of Kaolack and Ziguinchor is probably the busiest road in the Gambian interior. And despite its modest length, it is punctuated by two significant towns in the form of Farafenni and Soma, set on either side of the 2019 Senegambia Bridge. This chapter covers both the Trans-Gambia Highway and the area to its west, running inland from Brikama and Albreda, and incorporating the larger part of the North Bank, West Coast and Lower River regions.

As the closest part of the interior to the coastal resorts, the area featured in this chapter is ideal for those seeking a short escape upriver. The most popular goal for

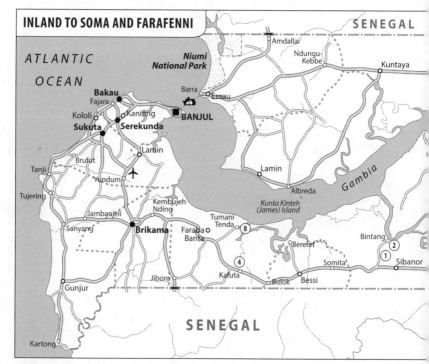

tourists is probably Tendaba Camp, a sprawling riverside lodge bordering two of the country's most important conservation areas, namely Kiang West National Park and Baobolong Wetland Reserve. There are also less well-known riverside camps at Tumani Tenda and Bintang Bolong. The North Bank town of Farafenni and its South Bank counterpart of Soma are, respectively, the largest and third-largest Gambian towns inland of Brikama, and have decent facilities, but are of limited interest other than as places to break a journey.

THE ROAD EAST TO KALAGI

Kalagi lies 100km east of Brikama along the South Bank Road, immediately before it crosses the Bintang Bolong, a wide tributary of the River Gambia that also marks the border between the Western and Lower River regions. The surfaced road connecting Brikama to Kalagi runs through a mosaic of tropical wooded habitats, and provides a springboard to several diversions, most of which (ie: the camps at Tumani Tenda and Bintang Bolong) are associated with the River Gambia to the north. The road between Brikama and Kalagi also offers access to the ex-president Jammeh's home village of Kanilai on the southern border with Senegal.

TUMANI TENDA The Jola village of Tumani Tenda lies on the west bank of the wide mangrove-lined Kafuta Bolong, which merges with the River Gambia about 6km downstream. It is a relatively modern village, having been founded in the 1960s by immigrants from Senegal's Casamance region, and takes its name from a peanut picker called Tumani who once lived there, while Tenda means riverbank. Living here is a strongly Islamic and sustainability-oriented community of 300 individuals

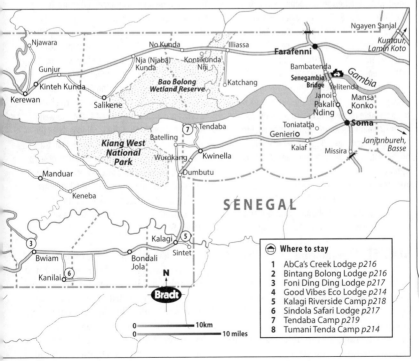

Where to stay
1 AbCa's Creek Lodge *p216*
2 Bintang Bolong Lodge *p216*
3 Foni Ding Ding Lodge *p217*
4 Good Vibes Eco Lodge *p214*
5 Kalagi Riverside Camp *p218*
6 Sindola Safari Lodge *p217*
7 Tendaba Camp *p219*
8 Tumani Tenda Camp *p214*

13

split between seven families, which owns around 140ha of land planted with a rich diversity of crops and indigenous plants. In 1999, the village became the site of The Gambia's first ecotourism project, following the construction of a creek-side camp that continues to fund a variety of community projects.

Tumani Tenda is well known to birdwatchers as the best site in The Gambia for observing the brown-necked parrot, a large, handsome and noisy bird that roosts in the mangroves and usually flies across the Kafuta Bolong at around 08.00 and 17.00 en route to and from its feeding grounds. Other birds frequently seen in the area include long-crested eagle, stone partridge, long-tailed nightjar, six species of kingfisher, grey-headed bush-shrike and a selection of waders, herons and other waterbirds. Plenty of interesting and quite affordable activities are offered, including bird walks, boat trips to a bird-rich island on the Kafuta Bolong, tie-dye batik workshops, soap- and salt-making, fishing, oyster collection, farming tours, community forest tours and much more besides (check the website w tumanitenda. co.uk for more details). Visitors are asked to dress modestly in keeping with the local Islamic sensibility.

Getting there and away Tumani Tenda lies 2.5km northeast of the South Bank Road, along a dirt road signposted to the left about 20km east of Brikama and 2km before the village of Kafuta. Most operators based in and around the coastal resorts can arrange a transfer there. Alternatively, any bush taxi heading to Kafuta (D40) or further east can drop you at the junction, from where it is less than 30 minutes' walk to the camp.

 Where to stay and eat *Map, page 212*

Good Vibes Eco Lodge (3 rooms) ✛ 13.2072, -16.4656; m 236 5912; e goodvibesecolodge@ yahoo.com; **f**. Though it's only about 1km from Tumani Tenda Camp across the bolong, this Rastafied hippie haven actually sits in Kafuta village, about 7km away by road. Tucked away in an organic garden behind the village football pitch & about 700m north of the South Bank Road, the 3 en-suite rooms here are simple & tidy, & the welcoming proprietors can arrange boat trips & guided tours of the village. Vegetarian meals on request, or use the guest kitchen. *£8/9.50/11 sgl/dbl/trpl.* **$**

Tumani Tenda Camp (13 rooms) ✛ 13.2166, -16.4683; m 791 5080, 990 3662; e tumanitenda@hotmail.com; w tumanitenda. co.uk. Formerly known as Kachokorr Camp,

this well-organised rustic creek-side camp is the focal point of the ecotourism project & all activities can be arranged here, both for day or overnight visitors. The rooms were undergoing a top-to-bottom renovation as of 2023, & the active management was arranging rooms for visitors in the village in the interim. An attractive open-sided restaurant/bar next to the creek serves decent local meals for around £4/plate, as well as a limited selection of drinks. Alongside all the typical excursions, including birding & boat trips, you can make soap & go oyster collecting, or see a traditional Jola drum & dance performance. Every family in the community has at least 1 member working at the camp, ensuring that they have at least 1 monthly salary coming in. Good value. *£7 pp B&B.* **$**

BEREFET Also known as Brefet, this mixed Mandinka and Jola village of fewer than 400 people stands on the south bank of the Brefet Bolong, a wide creek separated from the River Gambia by the sprawling Sansankoto Island. Berefet lies almost exactly due south of and less than 10km from Kunta Kinteh Island and the North Bank village of Albreda (page 198), and it boasts a similar historical pedigree to them both. The first European trading post was established here in 1664 by a group of British traders known as the 'Gambia Adventurers'. Attacked and plundered by rival French traders from Albreda in 1724, Berefet remained dormant for decades prior to 1779, when the Royal Africa Company built a new trading post that would be operated by a succession of individuals prior to being destroyed by the French again in 1820.

Before 1820, the only Africans known to visit the area freely were palm-oil tappers from Casamance in Senegal. Soon after that, however, a Jola village was established alongside the stone ruins, which provided a useful source of building material. The Jola were later joined by Mandinka settlers. The village has moved twice since its establishment, as the water from the wells became too salty, and all that remains of the old trading post is a pile of rubble that appears to be the corner of a slave house.

Wildlife in the vicinity includes green monkey, patas monkey, bushbuck, warthog and the usual wealth of birds, including a population of brown-necked parrots that fly across the bolong in the mornings and evenings, giving another good reason to visit. The rare Campbell's mona monkey has long been rumoured to be present, but it's been years since this was reliably confirmed.

Though the village has a beautiful setting right on the banks of the Brefet Bolong, all accommodation had ceased functioning as of our visit in 2023; head here as a day trip, or ask to see the alkalo if you'd like to arrange a night's stay in a local home. Or 8km east as the crow flies in Jakoi Sibirik, find the new Barracuda Lodge (⊕ n 13.2685, -16.3025; m 7295812; w barracudalodge.com), which opened in late 2023 under the same management as Georgianna's in Kartong (page 172) with ten en-suite rooms (**$**), a boat dock and a swimming pool.

Getting there and away Berefet (⊕ 13.2434, -16.3802) lies 6km north of the main South Bank Road along a dirt road signposted to the left at Bessi, about 35km east of Brikama.

BINTANG BOLONG The largest of the many tributaries that feed the River Gambia, Bintang Bolong rises in southern Senegal and enters The Gambia immediately east of Kalagi (page 218) before meandering westwards for another 50km to its confluence with the main river at Bintang Point. The mangrove-lined creek shares its name with the village of Bintang, which lies on its west bank about 10km upstream of the confluence and supports a population of around 700. Bintang is best known today as the home of the stilted Bintang Bolong Lodge, one of the longest-serving and most popular upriver camps in The Gambia, situated only 55km from Brikama by road, yet a world away from the coastal resorts in spirit.

Modest though Bintang might be today, its importance as a mercantile port in the earliest days of Luso-African trade is well documented (sometimes under the name Vintang). In 1665, the British explorer Richard Jobson noted that the Royal Africa Company maintained a trade agent there 'chiefly for elephant tusks, wax, honey, etc', and in the early 1680s, the Portuguese explorer Francisco de Lemos Coelho described Bintang as 'the best village on the river, having much trade in hides, as well as wax, ivory and slaves', while the French priest Michel La Courbe noted that it was 'rather a large town...located on the slope of a hill, with many trees and several Portuguese style houses...built of earth and covered with palm fronds as large as table cloths'. So far as we are aware, no traces of this long period of European settlement and trade remain, though the hillside location mentioned by La Courbe indicates the site is unchanged.

Getting there and away Bintang (⊕ 13.2497, -16.2113) is connected to the main South Bank Road by a surfaced 6km feeder road running north from the tiny village of Killy (which lies about 2km west of the much larger village of Sibanor).

Coming from the coast, it's a straightforward 80–90km drive that shouldn't take more than 90 minutes, and organised day and overnight excursions can be arranged through any tour operator. Using public transport, two gelly-gellys run daily from Brikama directly to Bintang (D70), leaving at 10.00 and 15.00. Alternatively, you can pick up one of the more regular vehicles to Sibanor, ask to be dropped at Killy, then take one of the small vehicles that shuttle regularly on to Bintang. Sometimes the lodge's own transport can pick you up if you book in advance.

Where to stay and eat   *Map, page 212*

✴ **AbCa's Creek Lodge** (40 rooms) ✆ 13.2279, -16.2232; m 799 4413/9; e abcagambia@hotmail.com; w abcascreeklodge.com. With a feeling of Tarzan's jungle hideaway, this Dutch–Gambian-run lodge has a stunning creekside location just 5 mins south of Bintang. Funkily decorated en-suite rooms (in 3 categories) are carved from the bush, overlooking the beautifully manicured grounds & dense mangroves beyond. The stylish open-air restaurant serves meals for £5–10 using fish caught from the creek & vegetables grown in the garden, & there's a fantastic range of activities on offer, including kayak & boat trips through the mangroves, bike & walking tours, cooking lessons, dance & drum workshops & visits to the local village & historical sites. They also offer day trips to Albreda & Kunta Kinteh Island (page 198). Sitting here as the sun rises & the dawn mist evaporates, while monkeys leap from the trees, is just magical. *£38/44 standard sgl/dbl, £56/62 sgl/dbl dlx river view, all rates B&B.* **$$**

Bintang Bolong Lodge (18 rooms) ✆ 13.2491, -16.2111; m 704 3081, 992 9362; e reception@ bintang-bolong.com, solodsaman@gmail.com; w bintang-bolong.com; f Bintang Bolong Lodge (Gambia). One of the longest-serving upriver lodges, & slightly deteriorated since its heyday, this place still has a beautiful mangrove setting & winning rusticity that compensate for the rather basic amenities. Most of the complex is stilted, with raised wooden walkways connecting the main dining area & the rooms, which have 1 dbl & 1 sgl bed, a small en-suite shower & private deck overlooking the water for waterside & VIP rooms. In the early evening, power is drawn from a large generator that also lights up parts of the nearby village. The large & comfortable restaurant/bar serves Gambian & European meals in the £4–6 range, along with chilled wine, beer & soft drinks. On the nearby riverbank is a small saltwater swimming pool & a hill (a rare thing in The Gambia) that gives a great view over the lodge, the mangroves & the bolong. The lodge arranges boat trips into the surrounding mangroves & further afield to Kunta Kinteh Island, as well as various foot & jeep excursions (check the website for full details). If there are enough guests, dancers & musicians from the village will provide entertainment in the evenings. *£20/22/30 inland/waterside/VIP dbl B&B.* **$$**

BWIAM (✆ 13.2300, -16.0794) Located between the South Bank Road and Bintang Bolong 15km east of Sibanor, Bwiam is one of the larger towns in the interior, with a population of around 4,000 and a bustling market that makes few concessions to tourism. The town has one rather spurious claim to fame in the form of the so-called *karelo* (cooking pot) that protrudes about 50cm above the ground among a stand of white-flowered silk-cotton trees, just outside of town. There are lots of local tall tales regarding the karelo: one states that this pot is impossible to move. Another more colourful legend claims it has magical powers that make it swivel to point in the direction of an attack – a story probably explained by the fact that the karelo is the base for an artillery piece, although no-one seems to know why or when it was placed there.

Getting there and away Non-express GTSC buses between Serekunda and Soma all stop at Bwiam, but it is probably more efficient to get a bush taxi or gelly-gelly from Brikama (D70).

Where to stay and eat *Map, page 212*

Foni Ding Ding Lodge (20 rooms) **m** 313 9333, 620 3254, 700 1964; **e** bwiamlodge@ gmail.com; **w** bwiamlodge.weebly.com. Also known as Bwiam Lodge, this community-owned guesthouse, signposted 400m from the main road, is affiliated to the Ding Ding Bantaba organisation, which helps fight child poverty as well as providing training & employment to local adults. Accommodation is in reasonable en-suite rooms with fans, nets & cane chairs. It caters mainly to volunteer groups, & while the staff can theoretically arrange birding, fishing, canoeing & cultural excursions, give plenty of notice – they are unlikely to be prepared for drop-in visitors. *Around £7 dbl.* **$**

KANILAI (⊕ 13.1685, -16.0099) Abutting the Senegalese border about 12km southeast of Bwiam, Kanilai was a rather obscure and unremarkable Jola village prior to the rise to power of its most famous son, former president Yahya Jammeh, in office from 1994 to 2017. During his tenure, the town benefitted from no shortage of presidential largesse, with new street lights, asphalt roads and reliable electricity – all amenities the neighbouring villages could only dream of – plus a presidential palace, tourist hotel, wrestling arena and game park.

Since 2017 and Jammeh's flight to exile in Equatorial Guinea, however, the town has seen its fortunes fade. The presidential palace now garrisons troops, the grand mosque at the village entrance stands weed-choked and incomplete, and the once-grand festivals held here have not been seen for years. The tourist hotel and expansive presidential farms have been repossessed.

Indeed, the tension in Kanilai is palpable. In contrast to the 'Gambia has decided' slogans still visible all over the country from the 2016–17 election crisis, the graffiti in Kanilai unsurprisingly takes a different stance, with messages spray-painted along the trafficless main road both defiant and anxious – 'we trust Jammeh' and 'is Gambia sinking?'.

As of 2023, the village is still home to several contingents of Gambian soldiers as well as ECOMIG (ECOWAS Mission in The Gambia) troops – another development that has been much to the local population's chagrin. Therefore, you ought to exercise serious discretion when using a camera in Kanilai, or you're likely to end up explaining yourself to any number of men in uniform with time on their hands.

All that being said, the tourist lodge here is under new management and in surprisingly good nick, and it could still make for a useful base for exploring the sites between Brikama and Soma, provided that you have your own vehicle.

Getting there and away Kanilai lies about 80km east of Brikama and less than 2 hours' drive from the coastal resorts. Coming from the west, it is connected to the South Bank Road by a surfaced 8km feeder road – getting rather pot-holed as of 2023 – signposted about 4km east of Bwiam. Using public transport, if you cannot pick up a direct bush taxi in Brikama (D80), take one to Bwiam and change vehicles there.

Where to stay and eat *Map, page 212*

Sindola Safari Lodge (40 rooms) ⊕ 13.1725, -16.0062; **m** 222 4530, 794 4333, 533 3837; **e** reservations.sindola@gmail.com; ✕ SindolaL. Formerly owned by ex-president Jammeh, this resort seemed likely to go to rack & ruin after his deposition, but has unexpectedly kept up its standards under new management. The large, shady grounds are carefully kept, & set at the northeastern end of Kanilai: make a left at the gates of the presidential palace & continue 150m. Accommodation is unusually comfortable for this far upriver, even if the semi-detached roundhouses with TV, AC & en-suite shower are a little dated by now. Facilities include a large pool & poolside restaurant serving meals in the £5–7 range, a children's playground, & tennis, volleyball & basketball courts. It may fill up if there's a conference on, otherwise you're likely to have the place to yourself. Good value. *£28/34 sgl/dbl B&B.* **$$**

What to see and do There are still Jola-style wrestling competitions held from time to time (you'll have to ask around), or the hotel can arrange performances by local Jola cultural groups. Kanilai also lies within an hour's drive of Bintang Bolong, Kiang West and Tendaba.

Kanilai game park (⏲ 07.00–20.00 daily; entrance (inc guide) D350 pp) The only permanent attraction in Kanilai is this rather lamentable artificial 10km² reserve, which protects an area of former Guinea savannah once used for farming and for foraging livestock. When it opened as Jammeh's private safari park a couple of decades back, caged residents included lion, rhino and giraffe translocated from South Africa, but these have all long since died or escaped. Remaining wildlife includes some caged hyena and crocodiles, and several semi-free-ranging species not indigenous to The Gambia, including zebra, wildebeest and eland. There are also naturally occurring troops of patas and green monkey, scrub hare, honey badger and squirrels, together with a good mix of birds including helmeted guineafowl. You can contact supervisor Malang Saidy directly (m 372 4197), but in practice it's better to arrange visits through the reception at Sindola Safari Lodge. You will need your own vehicle to drive around.

KALAGI (✦ 13.2470, -15.8361) This town of around 1,000 inhabitants flanks the South Bank Road some 30km east of Bwiam on the west side of the Bintang Bolong, which also forms the boundary between the West Coast and Lower River regions. The town itself is nothing special, but the adjacent stretch of creek is of interest for the extensive replanted mangroves on the opposite bank, the product of a community project established in 2011, and it also supports a fair selection of wading birds. Kalagi could be a pleasant spot for a boat trip on the bolong, or to break up the trip between the coast and points further east, but the village guesthouse was non-functional in mid-2023.

Getting there and away Although GTSC buses between Serekunda and Soma stop at Kalagi, it is probably more convenient to use a gelly-gelly or bush taxi from Brikama (D100).

Where to stay and eat *Map, page 212*

Kalagi Riverside Camp (8 rooms) ✦ 13.2512, -15.8313; m 909 5215. This camp, with a scenic location on the south side of the main road immediately before the bridge across Bintang Bolong, was non-functional pending much-needed renovations as of mid-2023. You can send the owner a WhatsApp message for the current status. With notice, they may still be able to arrange a boat trip on the bolong for you.

TENDABA, KIANG WEST AND BAO BOLONG

Although any one of them can be visited independently of the others, Tendaba Camp, Kiang West and Bao Bolong are conveniently clustered together alongside the River Gambia, about 100km upriver of its mouth, and are best treated as a single multi-faceted attraction. The main focal point for tourists, set in the riverside village of Tendaba some 25km north of Kalagi, is Tendaba Camp, which was established in the 1970s by a roving Swedish sea captain, but has long been under local management. Tendaba is probably the most famous and frequented camp in the Gambian interior, and particularly popular with birdwatchers thanks to the diversity of habitats and species concentrated in the vicinity. Though the camp probably still trades a bit on its reputation and location as much as anything else, significant renovations were underway as of early 2023, and the newly remodelled rooms look set to breathe some life into this upriver stalwart.

Although the agricultural land around Tendaba offers some excellent birding opportunities, the most popular activity here is boat trips into the mangrove-lined channels of the vast Bao Bolong Wetland Reserve, a birdwatching magnet that lies on the facing North Bank but is far more accessible by water than from the landward side. Less commonly visited but equally alluring is Kiang West National Park, which flanks Tendaba immediately to the east. Kiang West is the largest terrestrial protected area in The Gambia, and the last confirmed sanctuary to the roan antelope, as well as being an important refuge for several species of raptor and other large savannah birds. It's also the best remaining leopard habitat in The Gambia, but their continued presence here is uncertain and irregular at best. For planning purposes, one night at Tendaba Camp is just about sufficient to fit in a boat trip into Bao Bolong and some local exploration by foot, but a minimum of two nights is advised if you also want to take a game drive into Kiang West.

GETTING THERE AND AWAY Tendaba Camp is in the village of the same name, around 6km north of the junction town of Kwinella, which lies on the South Bank Road about 115km east of Brikama. The road from the coast to Tendaba is fully surfaced, so it shouldn't take much more than 2 hours to cover in a private vehicle. It is also easily reached by private taxi, and every driver knows where it is. Alternatively, you can catch a GTSC bus from Serekunda or a bush taxi from Brikama and ask to be dropped off at Kwinella (D120), though you may need to walk or hitch the last 6km from there.

Many people visit Kiang West National Park on an organised excursion out of Tendaba Camp, but it is also possible to drive there yourself (page 222).

🏠 **WHERE TO STAY AND EAT** *Map, page 212*

In addition to Tendaba Camp, it is normally permitted to camp at the headquarters of Kiang West, 2km west of Dumbutu, for a small fee. It is also worth noting that Sindola Lodge (page 217) in Kanilai, though it lacks the riverside location of Tendaba Camp, offers superior accommodation, and would be a perfectly feasible base from which to explore this trio of attractions, being less than 60km away on a good surfaced road.

Tendaba Camp (45 rooms) m 319 0533, 325 2851; e tendabacampmail@yahoo.com; w tendabacampthegambia.com. This sprawling & well-established camp lies in the heart of the small village of Tendaba, right on the South Bank of the River Gambia. It offers a wide variety of accommodation, much of which has benefitted from a 2022–23 programme of renovations – so ask to see a couple of options. Standard rooms come with en-suite bath & fan, & deluxe come with AC. There's now mains electricity, & other facilities include a swimming pool, a restaurant serving decent buffet lunches & dinners for D400 & a neat little bar – where they put on performances if busy – perched alongside the river beach & sunbeds. Activities include guided or unguided bird walks in the surrounding area, boat trips into the Bao Bolong Wetland Reserve (parties of up to 4 pay D1,500, any additional person is D350 extra) & guided jeep safaris into Kiang West (D4,000 for up to 8 people then D500 per additional person, exclusive of park entrance fees). *£10 pp en-suite dbl, £24 dbl with AC, £27 VIP dbl, all rates B&B.* **$$**

13

EXCURSIONS AND ACTIVITIES

Birdwatching around Tendaba There are some excellent birdwatching areas within easy walking distance of Tendaba Camp. Wooded areas immediately around the village support the likes of bearded barbet, Bruce's green pigeon and pygmy sunbird, while the mangrove-lined riverfront is home to various kingfishers and water-associated birds. A particularly worthwhile site is the airfield, which lies about 1km back along, and on the east side of, the feeder road from Kwinella. Terrestrial and woodland species to look out for here include Abyssinian ground hornbill, bateleur, African hawk eagle, four-banded sandgrouse, white-throated bee-eater and the highly endangered brown-necked parrot. The airfield is bordered by a large shallow lake that often supports pink-backed and great white pelican, and a variety of plovers, waders and storks (including the striking but seldom-seen saddle-billed stork). You can explore on your own, but there are usually also a few birding guides based loosely at the camp who will gladly take you around the area for a small fee.

Bao Bolong Wetland Reserve The normal goal for boat trips out of Tendaba is the Bao Bolong Wetland Reserve, which lies on the opposite side of the river some 2km from the camp. Bao Bolong is the largest of The Gambia's six protected areas, covering 220km^2, and it was designated as a Ramsar Wetland of International Importance in 1996. It is named after the 140km-long Bao Bolong, which rises near Ferlo in Senegal and empties into the River Gambia about 5km upstream of Tendaba. A number of smaller bolongs flow through the reserve into the main river, and they support some of the country's tallest mangrove forests, because the lower salinity this far upriver exerts a lower osmotic pressure on the trees. The reserve is a very important natural resource for surrounding communities. The mangroves act as a nursery for huge numbers of spawning fish, which form an important source of protein in the local diet. Some of the reserve is also used to grow rice, and thatching, building and fencing materials are harvested from within its boundaries.

Boat trips The twice-daily boat excursions into Bao Bolong offered by Tendaba Camp are highly recommended to anybody who fancies a quiet, peaceful trip into the mangroves. The boats follow the labyrinthine Kisi and Tunku bolongs, which are lined with tall mangroves, home to hermit crabs and mudskipper fish, and offer a good opportunity to see interesting mangrove, wetland and other bird species. It is probably the best place in the country to look for African finfoot, a medium-sized waterbird that likes to skulk among the mangrove roots. Also likely to be seen are white-backed night heron, goliath heron (the world's largest heron), hamerkop, martial eagle, blue-breasted kingfisher and mouse-coloured sunbird. Somewhat less frequent are rarities such as white-crested tiger heron, Allen's gallinule, Pel's fishing owl, African swallow-tailed kite, brown-necked parrot, little green woodpecker and African blue flycatcher. Dolphins might stray this far upstream in the dry season, when the water is most saline, while hippos occasionally make an appearance during the rains. Coming by boat, you are unlikely to see any of the other large mammals associated with the reserve, the list of which includes spotted hyena, side-striped jackal, red river hog, West African manatee, sitatunga, and African clawless otter.

From the North Bank While the vast majority of visitors to Bao Bolong come by boat from Tendaba Camp, the reserve can also be approached from the North Bank Road. The laterite road leading south from Kontikunda Niji (⊕ 13.5648, -15.7933) is probably the best option if you have a vehicle or have hired a cart, as this follows the base of the escarpment to the west of Bao Bolong, and is good for wildlife. In addition, dirt tracks lead south into the reserve from the villages of Salikene (⊕ 13.4853, -15.9642), Njaba Kunda (⊕ 13.5580, -15.9139) and Katchang (⊕ 13.5064, -15.7531). These tracks are often impassable to vehicles, so you may have to walk or hire a horse- or donkey-cart from one of the villages.

To sleep near here, stay at the admirable **Morgan Kunda Lodge** (⊕ 13.5744, -15.7467; w morgankunda.com) in Jajari. This new community-focused address is connected to the Morgan Clark Foundation (w morganclarkfoundation.org) and revenue goes to projects supporting education and maternal health in upcountry The Gambia. The lodge is oriented towards birders and has its own shaded viewing platform, along with a local bird list downloadable from their website. Guests are hosted on an all-inclusive basis for £70/110 single/double (minus drinks, 2-night minimum; **$$$$**).

Kiang West National Park (m 623 2581; ◷ 08.00–18.00 daily; entrance D35 pp; guide fee D100 per party per hour) Situated 5km downstream of Tendaba, Kiang West National Park is the largest terrestrial reserve in The Gambia, extending across 110km² of dry woodland savannah interspersed with relict forest patches, baobab stands and raffia palm swamp. Established in 1987, it protects an area that has suffered relatively little from human activity, and is probably the country's best remaining example of wilderness, as well as being an important refuge for wildlife. The park incorporates about 12km of river frontage, and associated habitats such as mangrove-lined creeks, salt pans and tidal flats. Its other outstanding geographic feature is a tall laterite escarpment that indicates the past course of the river, and affords some marvellous riverine views and wildlife watching. The best time to visit is towards the end of the dry season, when the vegetation is sparser and you have a

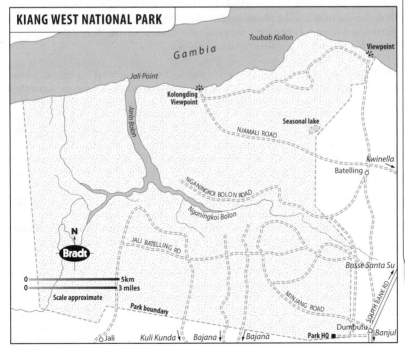

13

far better chance of seeing mammals. However, a visit at any time of the year is sure to produce something of interest.

Fauna Kiang West supports a rich and varied fauna, but seeing most large mammals requires a bit of luck and effort. Most conspicuous are the park's primates, which include Guinea baboon, green monkey, patas monkey and red colobus, along with the nocturnal Senegal bushbaby. Other quite common species include scrub hare, crested porcupine, warthog, roan antelope, bushbuck and duiker. Kiang West hosts the country's most varied selection of terrestrial carnivores, including banded and marsh mongoose, serval, side-striped jackal, caracal, spotted hyena and leopard (though these are now likely to be locally extinct), but with the exception of mongooses, these creatures are all very shy and good at remaining hidden from watching eyes. The River Gambia is home to West African manatee, African clawless otter and bottlenose dolphin, none of which is seen regularly by visitors. Swampy areas also reputedly provide refuge to the sitatunga, an elusive aquatic antelope about the size of a bushbuck. The river here is usually too saline to support hippo, but the West African crocodile is fairly common.

Kiang West is a superb birding site, with more than 300 species – around half the Gambian total – recorded to date. This includes at least 20 large raptors, notably osprey, African fish eagle, martial eagle, long-crested eagle and the colourful bateleur (the last-named has been adopted as the park's official symbol). You also have a good chance of coming across the Abyssinian ground hornbill, a massive and rather prehistoric-looking bird usually seen stalking about in open country in pairs or small parties. Other Gambian birds that have their stronghold in Kiang West include white-rumped swift, red-winged pytilia, brown-rumped bunting and brown-necked parrot. For more dedicated birders, it is worth searching among the 'little brown jobs' for the plaintive cisticola, which is very local in the more open parts of woodland. Other localised passerines associated with Kiang West include sun lark and chestnut-crowned sparrow-weaver.

Getting there and away The easiest way to visit Kiang West is with one of the affordable jeep safaris offered by Tendaba Camp (page 219; £55 for up to 8 people). If you have your own 4x4, the park can also be visited independently, using a few possible approaches. The better of these from most points of view is the same route used by jeep safaris from Tendaba Camp, which starts on the surfaced feeder road from Kwinella on the South Bank Road. Some 1.2km north of the South Bank Road at Kwinella, or 4.5km south of Tendaba, turn onto a dirt road running to the west and follow it to the village of Batelling (⊕ 13.4098, -15.8433). The village is the most reliable place to pay your entrance fees and arrange a guide (it is also of minor interest for a quartet of rusting cannons set in a copse opposite the mosque, the only relict of European fortifications built in the 18th century).

Recent reports indicate that road conditions are best on the 4.5km road between Wurokang (2.5km west of Kwinella on the South Bank Road) and Batelling when approaching from the south. From Batelling it is another 3km north to the entrance gate (⊕ 13.4361, -15.8506), which is marked by a disused concrete block on the right.

The other approach is from the village of Dumbutu, on the South Bank Road about 6km west of Kwinella, coming from the coast. From Dumbutu, an unsurfaced 2km road runs west to the park headquarters (⊕ 13.3478, -15.8506) and what is nominally the main entrance gate. The gate here is frequently untended, however, so you may end up waiting a while to locate somebody to collect your entrance fee and arrange your guide. In addition, it is a long way from the headquarters to the river, and the internal roads are often in poor condition.

Game drives The main game-drive circuit lies to the north of Batelling and can be covered in about 2 hours as a round trip from Tendaba Camp, though birdwatchers in particular will surely want to dedicate at least half a day to it. Wildlife tends to be most active and conspicuous in the first 2 hours after sunrise and last hour before sunset. Ordinarily, we would recommend trying to be there as early in the morning as possible, but given that the park gates only open at 08.00 and you are bound to lose time sorting out paperwork at Batelling or the park headquarters, late afternoon is probably the better option.

Three specific sites of interest lie close to the entrance gate 3km north of Batelling. The first is a palm-fringed seasonal lake (✪ 13.4392, -15.8478) overlooked by a low laterite cliff and accessed via a 500m track that branches northeast immediately past the entrance gate. When the lake holds water, it supports plenty of birds and often attracts baboon and warthog. It is also sometimes visited by the handsome roan antelope towards the end of the rainy season.

Better known is Toubab Kollon ('White Man's Well'; ✪ 13.4487, -15.8470), which lies on a flat but pretty stretch of mangrove-lined riverbank 2km north of the entrance gate. The site of a long-gone Portuguese trade outpost, Toubab Kollon is also thought to be the most easterly landfall made by the Italian navigator Luiz de Cadamosto when he led the first recorded expedition up the River Gambia on behalf of the Portuguese throne in 1455. At that time, the area was the residence of a Mandinka king called Battimansa, with whom Cadamosto entered into some petty trade. Toubab Kollon now hosts a crumbling picnic site with a view over dense woodland alive with birds but not all that great for mammal-spotting.

Finally, about 3km further west, there is the Kolongding Viewpoint (✪ 13.4375, -15.8689), which can be reached along a signposted sandy track branching west from the road between the entrance gate and Toubab Kollon. Kolongding is set atop a 20m-high, west-facing laterite cliff overlooking a series of shallow pools along the bank of the River Gambia. Wait here quietly either early in the morning or in the hour or so before it gets dark, and you're almost certain to see some wildlife action below.

SOMA AND SURROUNDS

Soma is a busy crossroads town situated where the Trans-Gambia Highway intersects the main South Bank Road around 145km east of Brikama. Despite being the third-largest town in the Gambian interior, supporting a population of around 12,000, it is a rather dusty and amorphous place, possessing all the charm of an overgrown truck stop, and little that might be of interest to travellers except perhaps the large market. Facilities include a couple of small lodges, and it is a good place to buy food, drink and fuel, and to get those punctured tyres repaired. It is also the major public transport hub along the South Bank Road between Brikama and Basse. A few old colonial buildings still stand at Mansa Konko (Mandinka for 'King's Hill'), the former administrative capital about 1.5km north of the modern town centre, while the Soma Wetland, immediately west of town, is the closest place to the coast where the eagerly sought Egyptian plover is regular.

GETTING THERE AND AWAY Coming from the coast or from Basse, the best way to get to Soma is by GTSC bus. A handful of such buses (regular and express) run

Inland to Soma and Farafenni. SOMA AND SURROUNDS

13

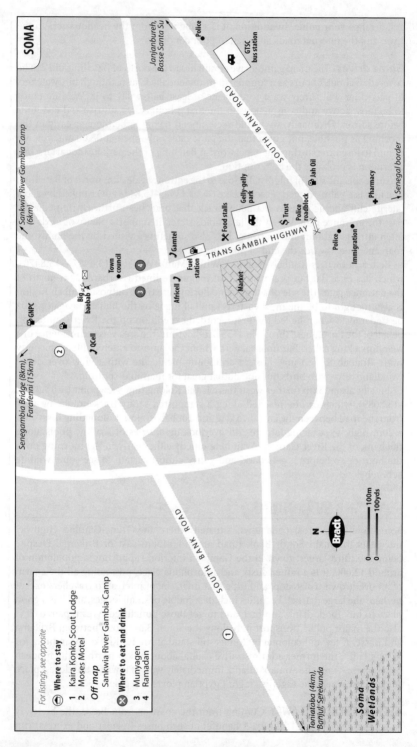

SOMA

Janjanbureh,
Basse Santa Su

Police

GTSC
bus station

Sankwia River Gambia Camp
(6km)

SOUTH BANK ROAD

Senegal border

Jah Oil

Pharmacy

Gelly-gelly
park

Food stalls

Senegal border

Trust

Police
roadblock

Gamtel

Town
council

Fuel
station

TRANS GAMBIA HIGHWAY

Police

Immigration

Africell

Market

Big
baobab

GNPC

QCell

Senegambia Bridge (8km),
Farafenni (15km)

SOUTH BANK ROAD

N

Bradt

0   100m
0   100yds

Toniataba (4km),
Banjul, Serekunda

Soma
Wetlands

For listings, see opposite

Where to stay
1 Kaira Konko Scout Lodge
2 Moses Motel
Off map
Sankwia River Gambia Camp

Where to eat and drink
3 Munyagen
4 Ramadan

daily in both directions between Kanifing (Serekunda) and Basse, leaving between 06.00 and noon, and stopping at the GTSC station in Soma, which lies a few hundred metres east along the South Bank Road just before the police station. All these buses also stop at Brikama, Janjanbureh and Bansang. The express buses are quicker and much more comfortable, but are unfortunately almost always full when passing through Soma, and there were no GTSC buses originating their journeys in Soma at the time of writing.

If the GTSC bus timetables don't suit, plenty of bush taxis and gelly-gellys connect Soma to Serekunda, Brikama, Janjanbureh, Basse and most other towns and villages along the South Bank Road, with fares all under D180. They are less comfortable than the GTSC buses, but operate to more flexible hours.

On the Trans-Gambia Highway, bush taxis run north across the Senegambia Bridge to Farafenni (D100) and south to Sénoba on the border with the Casamance region of Senegal, only 7km away. If continuing across either border from here, you will most likely need to change vehicles at the border. Cars pay D200 to cross the bridge. Most bush taxis and gelly-gellys leave from the main bus station opposite the market.

 WHERE TO STAY *Map, opposite*
Generally speaking, there are more and better lodging options in Farafenni than Soma, so consider a quick trip over the bridge if you're not taken with any of the options below.

Budget
Sankwia River Gambia Camp (3 rooms) ⊕ 13.4920, -15.5080; m 754 9491. Set in an isolated spot on the river 6km northeast of central Soma, this new community-run guesthouse opened in early 2023 & offers tidy en-suite rooms in quiet natural surroundings – one of a very few options in the immediate Soma/Farafenni area to do so. There is mains electricity for the fans in the rooms. Meals are available on request & the bar stocks cold drinks but no alcohol; it's acceptable to bring your own. *£15 pp B&B.* **$$**
Kaira Konko Scout Lodge (12 rooms) m 665 5474, 205 9552, 383 9538; e info@kairakonko. com, kintehlamin200@yahoo.com; w kairakonko. com. This agreeable Scout-affiliated set-up is situated in a neat concrete compound along the Brikama Rd about 1km west of the main crossroads & a few hundred metres from the Soma Wetland.

The main building has a few small but airy & clean twin rooms with tiled floor, net & fan, using either shared or en-suite ablutions. Some new AC rooms were under construction in early 2023, & there are also a couple of VIP rooms in a separate building. The self-catering kitchen has a fridge for guest use. Meals on request. *£8/11 pp fan/AC room; £25 pp FB.* **$**

Shoestring
Moses Motel (10 rooms) m 706 9255. Situated on the northwest side of the main junction, this long-serving guesthouse has a useful central location. Rooms in the front building surrounding the leafy courtyard are quite grubby & worn, but the newly built rooms at the back are categorically nicer. All are en suite, but the layout & quality vary so ask to see a couple before committing. *£6/12 fan/AC dbl.* **$**

✕ **WHERE TO EAT AND DRINK** *Map, opposite*
Munyagen Restaurant m 215 5151, 537 2901. Just opposite Ramadan, this has a nice covered terrace from which to watch the street life in the evening over a plate of benachin. **$**
Ramadan Restaurant m 778 2997; ⊕ 08.00– midnight daily. The pick of a few local eateries lining the main road running south towards the market, this serves a rotating menu of Gambian favourites like yassa & domoda, plus a few classics like omelette & chips or chicken & rice. *Around £2.50/plate.* **$**

OTHER PRACTICALITIES

Banking and foreign exchange The **Trust Bank** opposite the **market** has the only ATM in town. Your best bet for changing money is one of the many Mauritanian-run general stores along the main roads.

EXCURSIONS AND ACTIVITIES

Birdwatching around Soma The South Bank Road immediately west of town lies on a 1km-long causeway flanked by the Soma Wetlands, which can offer rewarding birdwatching at any time of year, and is rated one of the best sites in the country for Egyptian plover during the wet season (July to November). Also worth investigating are the rice paddies that lie alongside the Trans-Gambia Highway past Janoi, about 7km north of Soma and 2km before reaching the Senegambia Bridge. It is a good site for waders, plovers, yellow-billed stork, a variety of raptors and winding cisticola.

Toniataba (⊕ 13.4369, -15.5784) The village of Toniataba, about 4km west of Soma as the crow flies, is the site of one of the oldest traditional buildings in The Gambia, a *murubungu* (roundhouse) with a circumference of around 60m. According to local tradition, the house was originally built around 180 years ago by a marabout called Jimbiti Fatty, who is now buried underneath the floor. The marabout who lives there today – reputedly the seventh in the line – is still regarded to be one of the most important in the Senegambian region, and the house is probably the only surviving example of this type of building. Visitors are welcome, but be aware that you may only view the murubungu from the outside, photography is forbidden, and you will be expected to donate something to the building's upkeep (we were asked the dalasi equivalent of around £165, but settled at a less preposterous figure of around £2). To get there from Soma, follow the South Bank Road out west for 4km, then turn right at the AFET sign and you will reach Toniataba after another 2km.

FARAFENNI

The North Bank counterpart to Soma, Farafenni lies astride the Trans-Gambian Highway about 6km north of the Senegambia Bridge. It is the most populous upriver urban centre in The Gambia, supporting around 30,000 inhabitants, and the fifth-largest town countrywide. It is also the most important crossroads north of the river, with a strategic location that attracts plenty of traders from Senegal, Guinea and Mauritania to its weekly *lumo* (market), which is held on the northern outskirts of town every Sunday. Though Farafenni is not at all orientated towards tourists, it has above-average facilities, including most of the ATMs anywhere upriver of Brikama, the APRC General Hospital (one of the country's largest) and a scattering of fuel stations, hotels and local eateries.

GETTING THERE AND AWAY Farafenni lies about 110km east of Barra (the North Bank ferry terminus opposite Banjul) and a similar distance west of Lamin Koto (the North Bank ferry terminus opposite Janjanbureh). The road between Barra and Lamin Koto is surfaced in its entirety, and driving non-stop in a private vehicle you can reach Farafenni in well under 2 hours coming in either direction.

Heading east from Barra, the road crosses the Koular Bolong at Kerewan after about 50km. Kerewan (population c5,000) is the only major settlement along this

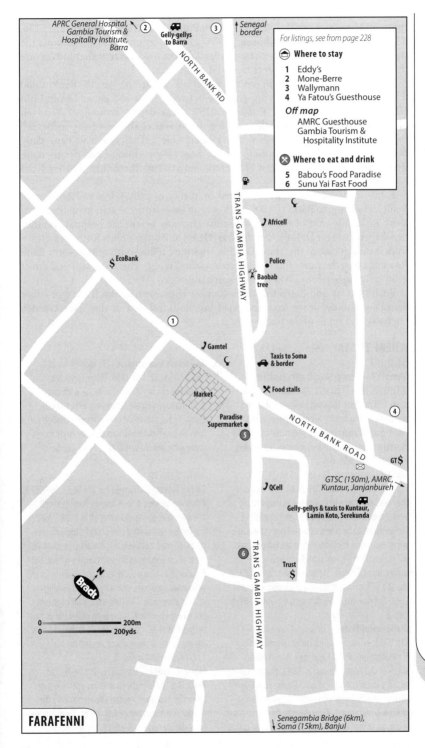

APRC General Hospital, Gambia Tourism & Hospitality Institute, Barra

Gelly-gellys to Barra

NORTH BANK RD

Senegal border

For listings, see from page 228

Where to stay
1 Eddy's
2 Mone-Berre
3 Wallymann
4 Ya Fatou's Guesthouse

Off map
AMRC Guesthouse
Gambia Tourism & Hospitality Institute

Where to eat and drink
5 Babou's Food Paradise
6 Sunu Yai Fast Food

TRANS GAMBIA HIGHWAY

Africell

EcoBank

Police

Baobab tree

Gamtel

Taxis to Soma & border

Market

Food stalls

Paradise Supermarket

NORTH BANK ROAD

GT

GTSC (150m), AMRC, Kuntaur, Janjanbureh

QCell

Gelly-gellys & taxis to Kuntaur, Lamin Koto, Serekunda

Trust

TRANS GAMBIA HIGHWAY

N

0 ____ 200m
0 ____ 200yds

FARAFENNI

Senegambia Bridge (6km), Soma (15km), Banjul

route, and here you can sleep at the **Dembo Fula Clinic Guesthouse** (m 256 5176, 623 8784) or **Lourdes Guesthouse** (m 939 2740). Continuing east, you cross the Bao Bolong after 90km, from where you can take the road less travelled and explore the Bao Bolong Wetland Reserve from the north (page 220).

Two GTSC buses run in either direction along the North Bank Road daily, passing through Farafenni en route between Barra and either Lamin Koto (D170) or Passamas/Foday Kunda (D275); these depart around 07.00 in all directions (though they usually wait for the arrival of the first ferry in Barra), passing through Farafenni 2–4 hours later. One GTSC bus also runs daily between Farafenni and Kanifing via the Senegambia Bridge and South Bank Road, departing at 06.30 from Farafenni, and starting the return journey from Kanifing at 13.00 (D200).

Farafenni is, of course, also serviced by plenty of gelly-gellys and bush taxis. Vehicles heading to Barra (D150) and Kerewan leave from the station on the North Bank Road just west of the Trans-Gambia Highway before the hospital. Vehicles heading to Kuntaur (D110), Lamin Koto (D150) and other points further east leave from a station east of the Trans-Gambia Highway, 100m south of the North Bank Road just past the post office. This second station is also where you will find direct gelly-gellys to Serekunda via the Senegambia Bridge.

Bush taxis up and down the Trans-Gambia Highway to Soma (D100) or either Senegalese border leave from the main junction, just east of the Trans-Gambia Highway and south of the police station.

 WHERE TO STAY *Map, page 227*

Budget

Gambia Tourism & Hospitality Institute (GTHI) (3 rooms) m 951 9986. At the edge of town 1.5km along the road towards Barra, this tourism training facility is out of the way, but clean, quiet & characterless, much like its equally pleasant counterpart in Janjanbureh (page 249). *£12/20 sgl/dbl B&B.* **$$**

AMRC Guesthouse (11 rooms) ✪ 13.5717, -15.5883; m 738 3700, 799 2037. This was long the cleanest option in town, & was undergoing a total renovation in early 2023, so hopefully it can continue to be relied upon for high standards when complete. It's hidden on a backstreet east of Farafenni's main junction & just before the University of Gambia/Medical Research Council. Use the GPS co-ordinates or ask around – as they say in The Gambia, a person with a mouth is never lost. **$**

Wallymann Hotel (22 rooms) m 330 0303, 710 0133; e wallymannhotelgm@gmail.com; ☐ Wallymann Hotel Farafenni. About 600m north of the turnoff towards Barra, this new hotel sits in a large compound with 2 rows of modern tiled rooms facing a somewhat scraggly central garden & restaurant. Arguably the best address in town, all things considered. *£11/14 fan/AC dbl.* **$**

Ya Fatou's Guesthouse (12 rooms) m 753 3420, 506 5717, 717 7459. Clean, quiet & as central as can be, it's hard to argue with this well-managed locale for an easy, if not exactly characterful, overnight in Farafenni – though you'll have to go elsewhere for food. Suite-style rooms come with hot shower & AC. *£14 AC dbl.* **$**

Shoestring

Eddy's Hotel (30 rooms) m 204 0682, 767 6073. This long-serving & well-known hotel (so well known it had no signboard at all in 2023 – look out for the red-walled compound), tucked away on a side road between the market & EcoBank, is centred on a shady courtyard planted with mango & palm trees that double as daytime roosts for the yellow-winged bats which fly around picking off insects after dusk. The rooms are a bit rundown, but all are en suite & come with either dbl or twin beds & fan or AC. Gambian meals & chilled beers are available, & there is a protected car park. *£11/14 dbl with fan/AC.* **$**

Mone-Berre (12 rooms) m 399 7499, 228 7440. This is a friendly shoestring option & more colourful than many of the above, but only the AC rooms are recommended – those with fan are exceedingly rundown. *£8/11 fan/AC dbl.* **$**

✖ WHERE TO EAT AND DRINK Map, page 227

The central junction is home to dozens of stalls serving anything from Senegalese-style *café touba* to black-eyed (*niebe*) bean sandwiches, quick-and-easy omelettes, fried fattayeh dumplings and slow-grilled *afra* BBQ – all washed down with a cooling *wanjo* hibiscus drink. It really explodes to life every evening, when trying to choose in the dark can be somewhat overwhelming. If you'd like something a bit calmer, try one of the following:

Babou's Food Paradise m 292 2191; ⏰ 08.00–late daily. Head up above the supermarket for fast foods like pizzas, brochettes & shawarma. No alcohol. *From £2.* $

Sunu Yai Fast Food m 762 7043, 995 5524; ⏰ 07.00–22.00 Mon–Sat. The pick of the local eateries that line the main road, this place is well known for its chicken, served roasted, grilled or yassa-style. No alcohol. *Mains around £3.* $

OTHER PRACTICALITIES

Banking and foreign exchange Several banks are dotted around town, two of which have ATMs: **EcoBank**, a few doors down from Eddy's Hotel, and **GT Bank**, 200m east of the main junction towards Lamin Koto. This is also perhaps the easiest place in the country to change CFA francs into dalasi – with all the traffic from Senegal, many places quote prices in either currency side-by-side; ask in any Mauritanian-run shop.

Shopping The **central market** is one of the busiest in the country, though not at all geared towards craft shopping. The **Paradise Supermarket** (under Babou's) on the main road next to the market is well stocked with packaged goods.

14

Janjanbureh and Central River Region

Running both north and south from the River Gambia to the respective borders with Senegal, the Central River Region (CRR) starts about 20km upstream of the Senegambia Bridge between Soma and Farafenni and continues eastward for another 100km or so inland to the border with the Upper River Region. As with the rest of the country, the River Gambia is the dominant geographic feature

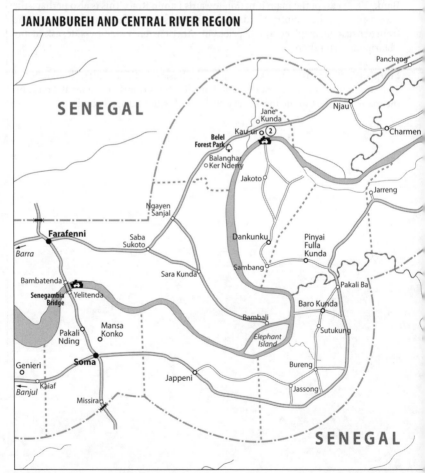

JANJANBUREH AND CENTRAL RIVER REGION

SENEGAL

Panchang

Njau

Jane Kunda

Kau-ur ②

Charmen

Belel Forest Park

Balanghar
Ker Nderry

Jakoto

Jarreng

Ngayen Sanjal

Farafenni

Saba Sukoto

Dankunku

Pinyai Fulla Kunda

Barra

Sambang

Sara Kunda

Pakali Ba

Bambatenda

Senegambia Bridge

Yelitenda

Baro Kunda

Bambali

Mansa Konko

Elephant Island

Sutukung

Pakali Nding

Genieri

Soma

Bureng

Banjul

Kaiaf

Jappeni

Jassong

Missira

SENEGAL

of CRR, and the main tourist focus. However, since salt water from the Atlantic Ocean only intrudes upstream as far as Kau-ur (with some seasonal variation), the riverbanks of CRR are lined not with mangroves but with an altogether more biodiverse and visually appealing mosaic of riparian woodland, gallery forest and freshwater swamp.

The low-key administrative capital of CRR is the old trading town of Janjanbureh, which lies on the north shore of MacCarthy Island about 270km upriver of Banjul. An agreeable and characterful small town, it is studded with timeworn old buildings, and the surrounding riparian woodland offers some good birding and monkey-watching opportunities. Janjanbureh is also the busiest tourist focus in the Gambian interior, serviced by close to a dozen budget camps and guesthouses, and offering good opportunities to get out on the river. Several worthwhile and reasonably accessible birding sites lie to the east of Janjanbureh, among them a well-known bee-eater colony near Bansang and the underrated Kunkilling Forest Park.

The two most compelling attractions in CRR both lie downriver from Janjanbureh. For wildlife lovers, River Gambia National Park, which protects a wide island-

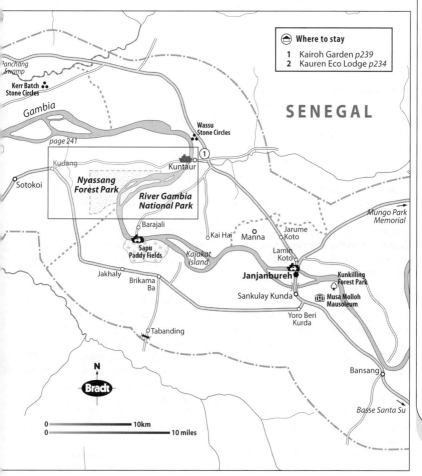

studded stretch of jungle-fringed river, is best known for the orphaned chimp communities established on three of its islands, but it also supports hippos and a good variety of monkeys and birds. What's more, the clifftop tented camp operated here by the Chimp Rehabilitation Project easily ranks as the most alluring lodging anywhere upriver of Makasutu. Different altogether are the mysterious medieval stone circles that scatter the North Bank between Farafenni and Janjanbureh. The most famous of these megaliths can be found at Wassu and Kerr Batch, both of which are easily accessible and form part of the Stone Circles of Senegambia UNESCO World Heritage Site.

THE SOUTH BANK FROM SOMA TO JANJANBUREH

The surfaced 130km road connecting Soma to Janjanbureh can be covered comfortably in under 2 hours. There is little of great interest here apart from a few forest parks and bolongs that sit astride the road, though it might be worth considering a stop at one or two of the places mentioned below. This is also the best route if you are driving from the coast to the Chimp Rehabilitation Project Camp in River Gambia National Park (page 243); the junction is on the north side of the road at Kudang, around 80km from Soma and 20km past Jarreng. Using public transport, all GTSC buses between Serekunda and Basse stop at Soma and Janjanbureh, but for villages in between you are better off using gelly-gellys or bush taxis.

PAKALI BA This small village lies on the west side of the bridge across the Sofaniama Bolong, a large creek that forms the border between the Lower River and Central River regions some 45km east of Soma. The wetlands emanating from the bolong can be rewarding for birds, with marabou stork and black-crowned crane among the more interesting species recorded.

JARRENG Situated about 14km northeast of Pakali Ba, this small village is well known for its market, which deals mainly in furniture made from cane and raffia. Some real bargains can be had here, though transporting a cane bed-base on the plane home might be difficult. Still, even if you're not buying, it's very interesting to watch a craftsperson at work and to see how the furniture is made. From the village it is only 2km north to the River Gambia; here you can hire a pirogue and boatman to explore around Pappa Island, where there is a chance of spotting hippos (but always keep a safe distance).

SAPU PADDY FIELDS Running north of the South Bank Road between Jakhaly and Brikama Ba, starting some 35km east of Jarreng, an extensive area of freshwater swamp has been converted to paddy fields using a tidal irrigation system. Two agricultural schemes here collectively support almost 70 villages and more than 30,000 families. The area is also regarded as one of *the* birding hotspots in CRR, thanks to a rich mixture of habitats that also includes agricultural land and riverine forest. The area is good for sandpipers and other waders, and interesting species recorded include Pel's fishing owl, pygmy goose, collared pratincole, black coucal, African finfoot and white-backed vulture. About 800m north of Brikama Ba, a copse of mahogany trees on the left side of the Saruja Road (just after a small church) is a reliable roost for the outsized Verreaux's eagle-owl.

There are several road approaches to the paddy fields, the most convenient being the track that branches north from the village of Madina Umfally (✪ 13.5435,

-14.9588) about halfway between Jakhaly and Brikama Ba. You should reach the most southerly rice fields about 500m along this track, at a T-junction from where a 10km loop road leads past several patches of marsh and forest before returning to the same point. You can also cross to the North Bank here: head north through the paddy fields until reaching the ferry landing (⊕ 13.5760, -14.9436) near the village of Wali Kunda. Here, the *Niani* vehicle ferry connects across to Barajali (page 254).

If you are interested to learn more about the agricultural schemes, visit the Sapu Agricultural Station, which lies 3km along a side road signposted to the north about 2km east of Brikama Ba. Using public transport, any vehicle headed between Soma and Janjanbureh can drop you at Brikama Ba, from where you can either walk to the paddy fields, or travel in style on a hired horse- or donkey-cart.

THE NORTH BANK FROM FARAFENNI TO JANJANBUREH

The 120km of surfaced road between Farafenni and Lamin Koto (the North Bank village opposite Janjanbureh) can be driven comfortably in under 2 hours. Though travel times are similar, this stretch of North Bank Road offers a lot more of interest to travellers than its southern counterpart, namely easy access to the UNESCO-inscribed ancient stone circle sites at Kerr Batch and Wassu (pages 234 and 239), and the opportunity to explore River Gambia National Park by boat from Kuntaur. As with the South Bank Road, the best option for travelling directly between Farafenni and Lamin Koto is the GTSC bus, but plenty of bush taxis also run along the road and can be used to hop between other towns.

ELEPHANT ISLAND Almost 5km long and 2.5km wide, the largest island along the River Gambia lies in a transitional area at the farthest point upriver affected by saline water from the Atlantic. Its name dates back at least to the 16th century, when the Portuguese geographer João de Barros noted that roughly halfway upriver to Kuntaur was a landmass 'which our men call the Island of Elephants on account of all the elephants there'. It is also depicted as the Ille Oliphante on a French map dated to 1623. Sadly, the last individual elephant recorded anywhere in The Gambia was shot in the 1920s, but the shallow waters around the island do support the river's most westerly resident hippo population, amounting to around 100 individuals. Also resident are crocodiles and green monkeys, and the plentiful birdlife includes black-crowned crane.

To get to Elephant Island from the main North Bank Road, turn south at either Saba Sukoto or Ngayen Sanjal, from where two newly surfaced roads meet at Sara Kunda and continue a further 12km to the remote village of Bambali, on the forested riverbank facing the island. Occasional bush taxis run from Farafenni to Bambali, and the 35km trip is much easier since the 2022 completion of the road. Bambali isn't set up for tourist activities but the *alkalo* (chief) should be able to arrange lodging in a village compound. Possible trips include a long walk along the river, or an early-morning or late-afternoon pirogue trip to see the hippos. It's also possible to be taken out at night by a local hunter who will try his best to spot hyena, warthog or even crocodile for you.

KAU-UR The small town of Kau-ur (also spelt Kaur), about 40km east of Farafenni, and connected to it by regular bush taxis, is one of two points where the North Bank Road comes close to skirting the River Gambia. It is quite an old town, first documented in 1625 under the name Caur, the 'port of palm trees', by André

Donelha, a Luso-African trader from Cape Verde. Today it's a rather ramshackle market town set against a fetching pair of small hills, and is a somewhat important centre for the groundnut trade – there are several warehouses and a port serving sizeable barges used to export the nuts. The *Niamina* vehicle ferry also crosses towards the South Bank village of Jakoto from here.

A few points of interest lie alongside the road west of Kau-ur. The first of these coming from Farafenni is Belel Forest Park, which sits on the south side of the road about 5km west of Kau-ur. Belel protects probably the best example of Sudanian savannah woodland anywhere on the North Bank, comprising a rich mixture of small trees and bushes with the occasional huge baobab tree dotted among them. Birdlife is phenomenal and includes Savile's bustard, black-headed plover, white-faced scops owl, striped kingfisher and various rollers, bee-eaters, parrots and starlings. The chestnut-crowned sparrow-weaver was first added to the Gambian list in 1994 based on a sighting here. Unfortunately, the future of this forest is murky: the last decade has seen a number of farm fields cut into the heart of the forest, as well as the founding of a religious pilgrimage site and associated village, Arafat, on a riverfront hilltop on the far side of the woods, with an access road cutting straight through.

Continuing along, the first easily found stone circle coming from Farafenni lies about 2km before Kau-ur. Local folklore has it that this stone circle was formed by a wedding party that was turned to stone. To get there, look for the signposted track to Genge Wolof School; follow it north until you pass two little hamlets. The small stone circle lies beneath a tree about 100m past the second hamlet and about 75m east of the track. Back on the main road, about 1km before Kau-ur, the small near-perennial Kau-ur Swamp often hosts a good selection of birds, including little bittern, greater painted snipe, malachite kingfisher, purple swamphen and sometimes even Egyptian plover.

 Where to stay and eat *Map, page 230*

Kauren Eco Lodge (2 rooms) ✪ 13.7019, -15.3228; m 322 9421, 717 1286. Also known as Kauren River Camp, this sleepy outpost at the edge of town is built on a high point overlooking the river & boasts panoramic views & a couple of well-built, comfortable rooms using solar power. Meals can be arranged for around £5/plate, & camping is possible. BYOB – & booze is a rare commodity in Kau-ur, so shop early. Unsignposted, but easy to find with GPS. Call ahead. *£17 pp B&B.* **$$**

NIANIJA BOLONG AND PANCHANG SWAMP Heading east from Kau-ur, the North Bank Road draws close to the Nianija Bolong near Njau (15km past Kau-ur; see opposite), and runs roughly parallel to it for another 25km or so, giving access to a handful of birding sites connected to the bolong and its surrounding wetlands. There's a waterhole just south of the road at Njau, plus a short western tributary of the bolong continuing southeast from here, and a further 10km to the east lies the Panchang Swamp (next to its eponymous village). This permanent wetland is another extension of the Nianija Bolong and is centred around a large perennial pool that often hosts a rich birdlife, including a variety of herons and egrets, African jacana, Egyptian plover, Allen's gallinule and a resident population of African pygmy goose. Another 15km east, the road crosses the bolong at Nyanga Bantang, where similar birds can be spotted.

KERR BATCH STONE CIRCLES (🕐 08.00–18.00 daily; entrance D100) One of four UNESCO-inscribed stone circle sites in Senegambia, Kerr Batch, also known as Singhu Demba, is the most important of around 50 such megalithic sites that flank

Along the North Bank Road, 15km east of Kau-ur, sits Njau – the hometown of activist Isatou Ceesay. She's been profiled by the BBC, Deutsche Welle and others, gone on speaking tours in the USA, and is even the subject of a 2015 children's book, *One Plastic Bag: Isatou Ceesay and the Recycling Women of The Gambia*.

And she's garnered all of this attention for the simple act of picking up some old plastic bags that were littering the town. She picked them up, washed them, and started weaving, making cool and colourful tote bags, handbags and backpacks, and selling them at local markets and *lumos*. Despite initial scepticism from the neighbours and village elders, her project soon began to attract other women in Njau who wanted to participate, and they even ran out of waste plastic in Njau and had to go and collect rubbish from nearby villages!

Today, the organisation has grown into the Women's Initiative Gambia (WIG; m 268 6796, 325 3435; e womensinitiativegambia@gmail.com, isatouceesay2002@gmail.com; w womensinitiativegambia.org), and is active far beyond Njau in a variety of entrepreneurship, empowerment and sustainable development schemes organised by and for Gambian women, from agroforestry to natural soap and sustainable briquette production. Visitors to Njau can visit the WIG workshops and see the plastic processing techniques, as well as purchase some of the final products. There are no guesthouses in Njau, but WIG can arrange homestays in the village with local families.

The WIG also works with the **Gambia Cotton Trail** (w gambiacottontrail. com; contact Footsteps Eco-Lodge in Gunjur, page 168) which works to revitalise local cotton production and create uniquely Gambian cotton products and artwork for sale. Many of these pieces are created in Njau, where WIG members process, spin and decorate the cotton into a variety of tapestry and textile art.

the Nianija Bolong as it winds for 30km from the Senegalese border towards its confluence with the River Gambia. It consists of nine stone circles containing a total of 161 individual megaliths, the tallest of which is around 2.5m high and 1m in diameter. It is best known as the site of the country's only lyre-stone, a tall Y-shaped megalith that was broken in the early 20th century and rather clumsily repaired with concrete by the Anglo-Gambian Stone Circle Expedition of 1965. The symbolic purpose of this unusual megalith is a matter for conjecture, but local legends state that it is where two close relatives that died simultaneously were buried.

Kerr Batch is theoretically open from 08.00 to 18.00 daily, though in practice one senses it is more a case of it being open whenever the caretaker is around. The entrance fee includes access to a small museum renovated in 2021, which provides useful background to Kerr Batch and the other Senegambian stone circles, as well as displays relating to contemporary local cultures.

Getting there and away Kerr Batch (⊕ 13.7543, -15.0682) lies 7.5km from the main North Bank Road and is reached by a sandy dirt road signposted to the south at the largish village of Nyanga Bantang, about 40km east of Kau-ur. On public transport, bush taxis run to Nyanga Bantang from Kau-ur, Kuntaur and Lamin

Koto, but from there you must either walk or hire a horse- or donkey-cart (or perhaps a moto-taxi). The best time to be in Nyanga Bantang is Sunday, when the busy *lumo* (market) attracts plenty of traditionally attired Fula women.

KUNTAUR Set on an attractive stretch of the North Bank surrounded by paddy fields, Kuntaur lies about 2km south of the main North Bank Road some 25km past Nyanga Bantang and about 20km before Lamin Koto. Kuntaur is quite a significant

ABSOLUTELY RAMMED – A TRIP TO THE WASSU LUMO

by Dave Adams of FairPlay Gambia (w fairplaygambia.com)

I've always loved a market, so when my wife Fatou asked me to accompany her to the weekly *lumo* to buy a ram, I jumped at the chance.

Lumos, as they are known all across upriver Gambia and parts of Senegal, draw people from the surrounding villages and neighbouring countries, buying and selling all manner of products from magical potions to mobile phones. The closest lumo to where we live in Lamin Koto is at Wassu, home of the famous stone circles.

It's usually a quiet town but this morning a mass of improvised stalls lined the street in front of the shops, with some of them so close to the road that the throng of customers left just a single lane for traffic. Beeping trucks, cars and motorbikes competed for the space with bicycles and horse or donkey carts, while people and animals filled the gaps in between. The market was evening busier than usual, as the Islamic festival of Eid-Al-Adha (Tobaski) was fast approaching. It's a time when Muslims buy new clothes, good food and, most importantly, a sacrificial ram.

Fatou set off at pace, weaving through the chaos and I tried to follow. We turned off the highway and down a small side street with bedsheets strung across the road above us, shielding the glare of the sun and keeping the place cool. Colour is everywhere. From the beautifully dressed women, the stalls selling African cloth, the dazzling displays of soap and cosmetics to gleaming golden jewellery, every shade of every colour that exists in this world is to be found here – sometimes all on one person.

Before we had gone far, the pungent, musky smell of livestock assaulted our senses. We turned the corner and there were rams in all directions. There were trucks full of rams, rams on top of vehicles, people walking rams on ropes, people dragging reluctant ones by their horns, rams on the back of bicycles and even one old man carrying one on his shoulders in the same way you might carry a small child.

We walked towards the *daral*, the enclosed area that serves as a shop floor, and watched the rams. They were so tightly packed together that they had merged into one huge flock. The sellers are mostly Wallenkos, the nomadic Fula people who move with their livestock and their families from place to place seeking pasture and water as the seasons change. They wear long robes and headscarves wrapped desert-style covering all but their eyes. They all carry sticks, but within the *daral* they are without their cutlasses, which are said to be so sharp that they use them to shave.

'Something like that one,' Fatou says, pointing at a stout, clean-looking ram. 'It's a Gambian variety. They're shorter but they have more meat than the Senegalese breeds.'

We enter the *daral* with Fatou leading the way, pushing past rams and people alike. We stop as she feels the flanks of a small Gambian variety and asks the price.

town by upriver standards, supporting a population of around 2,500. It's something of a minor hub for travellers, offering easy access to the Wassu Stone Circles (page 239) barely 3km away, and is also the usual springboard for visits to River Gambia National Park a few kilometres upriver.

Often transcribed as Cantor, Cantoar or Kantora, Kuntaur is a settlement of some antiquity. Its existence was documented in 1456 by the Portuguese explorer Diogo Gomes, the first European to sail this far upriver, who saw it as the most important

'7,000 dalasi,' the seller said, so Fatou gripped it by the horns and examined it for any scars or injuries that would disqualify it from Tobaski duties. She nodded approvingly and after a short discussion agreed with the man on 6,000 dalasi. I took the rope and led Rambo, as I had by now named him, through the crowds and back towards the minibus stand.

It started well. Rambo trotted happily along behind me, as if pleased to be away from the noise and dust of the crowded *daral*. It was only when I stopped to wait as Fatou disappeared round the corner in search of something to cook that my problems started.

Barely had Fatou left when I met an old friend from Janjanbureh. As we greeted one another, I failed to notice that Rambo had taken the chance to find his own lunch. By the time I heard the complaints of the nearby trader, Rambo was nose deep in a bucket of tomatoes and licking his lips. I pulled sharply on the rope and he slid a short distance towards me. I pulled again, but he'd planted all four feet on the floor and refused to budge. I slapped him across the rump and pulled again. Nothing.

Still optimistic despite the increasingly amused looks from all around, I went behind him and with a combined lift and push motion, tried to move him forward. Still nothing. His front feet stayed exactly where they were and he seemed ready to do a forward roll before he'd walk one inch.

By now, red-faced and sweating, I was losing patience. I gripped his front legs together and tried to pull him on his hind ones as I'd seen the Wallenkos do. At first it seemed to work. Rambo looked at me surprised as we shuffled a few steps forward before he stretched his legs out behind him, ending up flat on his belly.

Before the scene could deteriorate further, Fatou reappeared wearing a bag of vegetables on her head. Whether it was the vegetables or her commanding presence I'll never know, but she grabbed Rambo by one gnarly horn and he allowed himself to be walked to the highway and soon after onto a vehicle. An hour later, Rambo was happily installed at our compound, chewing at the lemongrass while I tried to clean the dirt and sheep hair off my jeans.

I grew quite attached to Rambo over the few weeks leading up to Tobaski, so when the day came, I made an excuse to go out while he met his maker. I consoled myself with the fact that he'd lived a happy, healthy life of roaming in the bush as nature intended, far from the cruelty of the industrial farming system that supplies meat to Europe. Well…that and the fact that he was delicious on a plate of spicy Jollof rice. Sorry Rambo.

A longer version of this article is available to read at w resonate.travel/a-visit-to-a-weekly-provincial-market-in-gambia.

market port in the region, with significant commercial links to the then-mysterious gold-trading emporium of Timbuktu (in present-day Mali) and the associated trans-Saharan caravan route to Morocco. Kuntaur also appears in the early 16th-century writings of Duarte Pacheco Pereira as a cluster of four towns, the largest of which supported around 4,000 people and was the site of an important Mandinka livestock market.

Then as now, Kuntaur was the last upriver port accessible to ocean-going cargo boats, and a row of rundown riverfront warehouses recalls its long-past colonial-era prosperity. Today, the maritime traffic consists mostly of tiny passenger boats ferrying traders and tourists back and forth across the river towards Sambel Kunda or the River Gambia National Park; but depending on the season, the quayside still sees a fair few groundnut barges docking here, loading up the crop before their long, slow journey to the coast.

Getting there and away The main transport hub is the junction village of Wassu, which straddles the main North Bank Road about 2km north of Kuntaur. Gelly-gellys to Wassu from Farafenni cost around D100 and those from Lamin Koto cost D50. If you are headed to the Wassu Stone Circles, it's no more than 10 minutes' walk from the taxi park and clearly signposted. To get to Kuntaur, you could walk from Wassu in around 30 minutes, or else charter a donkey-cart for around D60.

Many of the camps at Janjanbureh organise day excursions to Wassu, and it is also possible to travel between Kuntaur and Janjanbureh by boat via River Gambia National Park (page 240).

THE STONE CIRCLES OF SENEGAMBIA

The rivers Gambia and Sine-Saloum (in Senegal) form the southern and northern boundaries of a region scattered with some 30,000 carved stelae arranged into neat circles at several hundred individual megalithic sites. These ancient stone circles, each one reminiscent of a miniaturised Stonehenge, form one of Africa's most enigmatic and intriguing archaeological relicts. And though seldom visited and little known to the outside world, they received an overdue boost when four of the most important individual fields – Wassu and Kerr Batch in The Gambia, Siné Ngayène and Wanar in Senegal – were inscribed as a UNESCO World Heritage Site in 2006.

The stelae of Senegal and The Gambia were hand-carved from iron-rich lateritic stones. Most take a simple cuboid or cylindrical shape, but there are also a few impressive lyre-shaped examples, and some are capped with knob-like protrusions that resemble battery terminals. The stones were cut from quarries close to the sites and set vertically into pre-dug pits. Most stones are fairly small, ranging from only 0.75m, but some are much larger at 3m tall.

The number of stones in each circle varies from ten to 24 and the diameter varies from 4m to 7m. Within each stone circle is a slightly domed rise, usually constructed of sand, though a few mounds are topped with lateritic pebbles, presumably to stop erosion. A common feature of many circles is a line of pillars set away on the eastern side. At some sites there are large groups of circles, at others there is only a single circle, while at others still there are no circles at all, only single pillars.

The discovery of large numbers of skeletons buried below some circles, as well as tools, pottery and miscellaneous ornaments, suggests that these sites are essentially vast funerary complexes. Some of the stone circles seem to mark a mass grave containing bodies thrown chaotically into a pit, perhaps after a battle or an

Note that the right-hand turning towards Kuntaur as you exit Wassu is unsignposted – look out for a signboard from the agricultural ministry and then continue 2km through a set of rice paddies.

Where to stay and eat *Map, page 230*

Kairoh Garden (20 rooms) m 751 6138; e kairohgarden@gmail.com; w kairohgarden. com. The only accommodation in Kuntaur is provided by this unpretentious harbour-front affiliate of its namesake in Tanji. Accommodation ranges from trim new en-suite rooms built in 2023 to basic rooms with nets & common showers. An open-sided restaurant with a great view of the river serves decent meals in the £3–6 range, & beer can be fetched from down the road on request. There are 2 boats for guests to use, & fishing trips (D2,000, plus D500 pp), excursions to Baboon Island (D1,500/2,000/2,500 for 1–3/4–6/6+ passengers), or boat transfers to Janjanbureh (D7,000) can be organised. *£8/10 pp room with shared/en-suite bath, B&B.* **$$**

What to see and do In addition to being the closest town to Wassu, Kuntaur is the easiest base for day trips around Baboon Island in River Gambia National Park. These can be arranged through Kairoh Garden or any of the boats around the riverfront warehouses, and will cost around D1,500–2,500 per party, excluding park entrance fees (page 240).

Wassu Stone Circles (⊕ 13.6913, -14.8736; m 374 5772; ⏲ 08.00–18.00 daily; entrance D100) The best-known and most frequently visited of the four sites that

epidemic disease. In other sites it looks as though people were buried alive as sacrifices. Generally the bodies are poorly adorned, often with only a bracelet for decoration and a weapon, usually a spear, laid beside the body. Sometimes there are also some pottery vessels found by the bodies, usually turned upside-down.

Local oral traditions relating to the erection of the circles are bizarrely inconsistent. While some assert that the stones were set in place at the beginning of time by the gods, others regard them as burial markers left by an ancient race of kings and/or giants, and others still believe they are the petrified remains of disgraced people. Many people also claim that the circles are the home to spirits, whether benign or evil. However, one point on which all oral traditions do concur is that the megaliths have no cultural link with the region's present-day Islamic inhabitants. And this much tallies with the archaeological evidence, which indicates that the stone circles are mostly around 1,000 to 1,500 years old.

But archaeological evidence is also curiously inconclusive about the origin of the megaliths. If they are simply funerary markers, then why do the buried human remains found beneath some circles seem to predate their gravestones by several centuries? What happened to the prosperous and well-organised people responsible for erecting the stone circles over several centuries? Were the constructors, as some archaeologists speculate, associated with the royal city of Cantor, which the Arab chronicler El-Bakri reported as lying somewhere south of the medieval empire of Ghana in AD1067? And is it significant that, while no similar memorials exist elsewhere in West Africa, the southern highlands of Ethiopia, at the opposite end of the Sahel, are studded with megalithic grave markers of a similar size and vintage? We may never know, but part of the fascination of these ancient monuments is the sense of speculation they arouse.

comprise the Stone Circles of Senegambia UNESCO World Heritage Site is Wassu, which boasts the greatest concentration of megaliths anywhere in the country. Altogether, around 200 megaliths – the tallest being about 3m high – are arranged into 11 circles here. In addition, the quarry some 200m east of the main site, where the stones were carved, contains several megaliths that broke in transit or before they had been completed. There's also a well laid-out (albeit rather dusty) museum where an array of models, photographs, paintings and other interpretative material help to bring the history of the stone circles to life. The fenced-off site lies about 500m east of the main North Bank Road, perhaps 10 minutes' walk and clearly signposted from the junction village of Wassu (which holds its *lumo* every Monday).

If you're keen to stay close to the stone circles, **Reliable Guesthouse** (m 371 7475, 587 3202; from £10 dbl; **$**) sits in a landscaped compound a couple of hundred metres away, between the site and the main road, offering basic but new en-suite rooms. There is also the new **Kaima Sala Eco-Lodge** (m 310 3112, 990 2140; e kaimasala@gambia.dk, nacogambia@yahoo.co.uk; **$**), offering accommodation in a set of spacious en-suite roundhouses. The lodge sits adjacent to a lush patch of forest 3.5km east of Wassu, just off the North Bank Road in Kuntaur Fula Kunda.

RIVER GAMBIA NATIONAL PARK

The winding stretch of the River Gambia between Kuntaur and MacCarthy Island has a compelling tropical character, lined as it is with a lush belt of jungle-like riparian forest that evokes the steamy Congo Basin rather than the Sahel. Its centrepiece is the 6km² River Gambia National Park (RGNP; entry D150), which was gazetted in 1978 to protect Baboon Island and four smaller islets, as well as an adjacent stretch of riverbank a few kilometres upriver of Kuntaur.

The most publicised attraction of RGNP is the chimpanzees that have been introduced to three of its islands by the Chimpanzee Rehabilitation Project (CRP; page 243), which also operates an excellent tented camp (page 242) opposite Baboon Island in the South Bank's Nyassang Forest Park, a state-owned classified forest jointly managed in collaboration with several local communities. Revenue raised by tourist visits to the CRP goes primarily towards the care and welfare of the chimpanzees, though a percentage is used to help fund government conservation programmes and community development projects.

In addition to chimpanzees, RGNP supports healthy populations of several naturally occurring primates, most conspicuously green monkey, Guinea baboon and red colobus (researchers recorded almost 600 of the latter near the park in 2019 and launched a commendable community conservation project as a result – see page 244), along with a few-dozen hippos, plenty of crocodiles and monitor lizards, warthogs and manatees, and several small antelope and nocturnal carnivore species. The birdlife is fantastic, too: the handsome palmnut vulture, African fish eagle and osprey all nest along the river, the secretive African finfoot inhabits shaded stretches of riverbank, and it's one of the best places in the country to see forest-associated hornbills, barbets, shrikes, turacos and parrots.

Tourists are forbidden from setting foot on the islands protected within RGNP. This is partly due to the potential danger posed by chimps, who can be quite aggressive toward human intruders. It is also to protect the health of the chimps, which are highly susceptible to human-borne diseases. However, the islands and their inhabitants can be viewed from a boat, ideally with the CRP, which has exclusive access to the smaller channel between Baboon Island and its tented camp. You can also arrange your visit with other boats, ie: those originating in Kuntaur

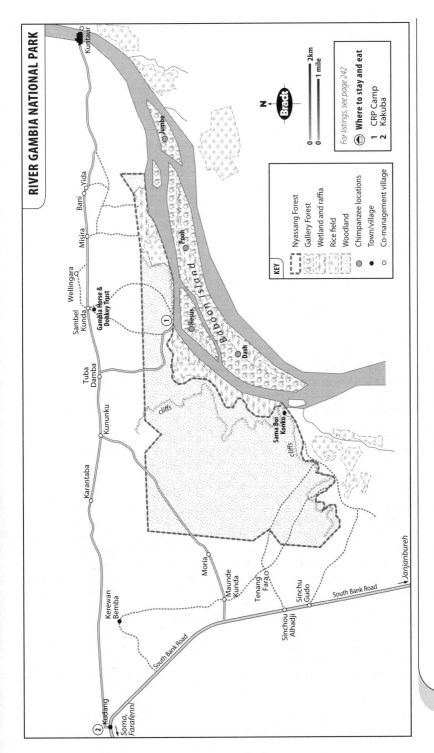

RIVER GAMBIA NATIONAL PARK

KEY

- Nyassang Forest
- Gallery Forest
- Wetland and raffia
- Rice field
- Woodland
- Chimpanzee locations
- Town/village
- Co-management village

For listings, see page 242

Where to stay and eat
1 CRP Camp
2 Kakuba

0 — 2km
0 — 1 mile

N

Bradt

Kuntaur
Jumbo
Yida
Bani
Misira
Wellingara
Sambel Kunda
Gambia Horse & Donkey Trust
Tuba Damba
Kununku
Karantaba
Hesus
Pooh
Dash
Baboon Island
cliffs
Sama Boi Konto
cliffs
Moria
Maunde Kunda
Tenang Farao
Sinchu Gudo
Sinchou Alhadji
South Bank Road
Kerewan Bemba
Kudang
Soma, Farafenni
South Bank Road
→ Janjanbureh

or Janjanbureh, but these are restricted to the main public channel. Either way, it is mandatory to be accompanied by a CRP guide (to whom the entry fee is paid) on any boat trip running through the park.

A NOTE ON ORIENTATION RGNP protects part of an inverted 'S' bend where this typically west-flowing river runs in a broadly northerly direction for about 50km. Furthermore, since the stretch of river that flows around Baboon Island is the central part of the inverted 'S', it actually flows in an easterly direction for around 10km. Rather confusingly, this means that the channel running past what is widely referred to as the South Bank (and past the CRP Camp) lies to the north and west of Baboon Island, while the one running past the nominal North Bank actually flows south and east of the island. Although we draw readers' attention to this apparent paradox, we have opted to stick to the conventional designation of North Bank and South Bank in this section; to do otherwise would be even more confusing.

GETTING THERE AND AWAY The closest town to RGNP and normal springboard for visits is Kuntaur, which lies on the North Bank and is readily accessible from the coast by public transport. Kuntaur lies about 20 minutes by boat from the park boundary, and visitors staying overnight at CRP Camp are usually met by prior arrangement at the mooring beach next to Kairoh Garden between noon and 13.00. If you are self-driving, you can leave the vehicle overnight in the grounds of Kairoh Garden for D50/night. It's equally possible to visit as a day trip by boat from Janjanbureh for £80–100. The round trip takes around 6 hours and can be arranged through FairPlay Gambia (page 252) or most lodgings in town.

Though the CRP Camp is usually accessed by boat from the North Bank, it actually lies on the opposite side of the river and is thus accessible by following the surfaced South Bank Road east to Kudang (about 80km past Soma), where you turn left on to a good laterite road. Bank on up to 4 hours from Serekunda to the CRP Camp.

 WHERE TO STAY AND EAT *Map, page 241*

✴ **CRP Camp** (4 tents, 1 room) m 787 8827, 353 3337; e baboonislands@gmail.com; 🅵 ChimpanzeeRehabilitationProjectCrpIn TheGambia; ⏰ Sat & Sun nights. Consisting of just 4 stilted tents set on a tall laterite cliff on the South Bank of the river facing Baboon Island, this is the closest Gambian equivalent to the upmarket bush camps of eastern & southern Africa. It is also the only truly tourist-class facility inland of AbCa's Creek Lodge in Bintang Bolong, & must rank as the premier goal for a short upriver excursion from the coast. The tents are all set on wooden platforms that look over the canopy to the river, offering great in-house birding (& occasionally primate viewing), as well as good natural ventilation. They come with twin beds protected by solid mosquito nets, a sink at the back, a separate outdoor shower, & plenty of interesting nocturnal animal calls. 2 compost toilets are each shared between 2 of the tents. 1 basic guest room is also available in low season. The other component of the camp is the

Waterhouse, which doubles as a dining room, bar, boat jetty & indoor & outdoor sitting area. Though quite pricey for The Gambia, it is very good value. The camp has historically also been open Thu & Fri nights, but at the the time of writing is only open Sat & Sun nights; it may well return to the original schedule at some point, so it's worth checking. No charging facilities – bring your power bank. Cash only. *£150/250 sgl/dbl, inc all meals, an afternoon boat trip to look for chimpanzees & other wildlife & a morning nature walk. £15 transfer from Kuntaur.* **$$$$$**

Kakuba Hotel m 770 1333; e bmceesay@ gmail.com; 🅵 Kakuba Garden Hotel. Situated in Kudang (10km west of Sambel Kunda), where you have to turn off the South Bank Rd to reach the park, this convenient hotel is a welcome new option on the South Bank. Rooms are modern with AC, & there's even a swimming pool – a real rarity this far upcountry! *£17/27 en-suite sgl/dbl B&B.* **$$**

ACTIVITIES

Boat trips The highlight of a visit to RGNP is likely to be the 2-hour afternoon boat trips operated by the CRP. These leave at 16.00, a good time to view chimps and other wildlife, and more often than not they yield good close-up sightings of chimps in particular, and excellent photographic opportunities. Other wildlife likely to be seen from the boats includes hippo, green monkey, red colobus, and a good range of forest and aquatic birds. The boat trips are included in the room rate for CRP Camp.

With advance notice, the CRP can also arrange boat trips for day visitors out of Kuntaur between 16.00 and 18.00. These cost £25 per person for parties of four to eight, exclusive of park fees (with an optional lunch for an additional £10 per person).

CHIMPANZEE REHABILITATION PROJECT

The Gambia's Chimpanzee Rehabilitation Project (CRP) has its roots in the animal orphanage established by Eddie Brewer, then the Director of Forestry, and his daughter Stella at Abuko Nature Reserve in 1968. The first orphaned chimpanzee was taken in there in 1969, and by 1974 they had several, most of them illegally captured and/or orphaned individuals confiscated from traffickers for the international pet trade. These chimps probably originated from Guinea, as there was no trade in these charismatic apes out of Senegal at the time, and they had long been extinct in the wild in The Gambia.

In 1974, Stella decided to release the orphaned chimps into a valley fed by a perennial natural spring in Senegal's Niokolo-Koba National Park. Unfortunately, however, a conflict developed between chimps released by Stella and a wild community living in the same territory. As a result, the survivors, numbering around seven individuals, were relocated to an island in RGNP in early 1979. At around the same time, another group of five orphaned chimps, under the care of the American primatologist Janis Carter, was relocated from Abuko to Baboon Island, followed by a small group from Holland.

In all, over a 25-year period, some 51 chimps were released on to the islands, in many cases after having undergone a retraining course to teach them to forage for wild food, build nests, etc. Many of the chimps went on to breed successfully, and there is now a population of 142 individuals – including a surviving handful of the chimps released originally – split between four communities across three of the islands. The rehabilitated animals are quite well adapted to wild living, though the shortage of suitable foraging on the confines of the islands means that their diet needs to be supplemented by fruits and other food sourced from nearby villages.

The primary focus of the CRP today remains the welfare of its chimps, but it also oversees tourism to RGNP, and runs an environmental education programme to raise general awareness about conservation in the surrounding villages. CRP founder Stella Brewer Marsden, awarded an OBE for her work for animal welfare, died in January 2008, aged only 56, and is buried at the CRP Camp, close to the base of the trail up the cliff to the standing tents. Her long-time co-director Janis Carter remains CRP project director, and is also very active in chimpanzee conservation in neighbouring Senegal and Guinea. Her extraordinary story was profiled in the 2021 HBO documentary *Lucy, The Human Chimp*.

14

A cheaper option for day visitors – around D240–300 per party – is to take a private boat from Kuntaur. Be warned, however, that the channel between Baboon Island and the South Bank, which usually offers the best chimp viewing, is reserved exclusively for CRP boats. That said, you are still quite likely to see chimps from the channel facing the North Bank, as well as hippos, monkeys and a good variety of birds. This rate excludes park fees, which must be paid whichever channel your boat uses.

Another possible boat trip from CRP Camp, usually done in the morning, runs a short way downstream to Sama Boi Konko (Elephant Cliff), said to be the place where the last lonely elephant in The Gambia fell to his death after seeing his reflection in the water below. You can walk to the top of the cliff, which offers stunning views over the river and islands. This boat trip is not included in the overnight rate, but costs an extra D1,500 per boat.

Guided walks The CRP Camp offers an optional free morning walk on the escarpment flanking the standing tents. This affords good views over the canopy, which is home to red colobus and green monkey, as well as to colourful forest birds such as bearded barbet and violet turaco. By prior arrangement, and weather permitting, it also offers optional night walks, which come with a good chance of seeing bushbabies, owls, giant fruit bats, and possibly also nocturnal predators such as genet.

Red Colobus Project Founded after the encouraging results of a 2019 survey revealed a better-than-expected population of nearly 600 red colobus in the area, this new community conservation initiative (m 268 5843, 505 8204; f C4RCproject) has its headquarters on the South Bank, just south of Missera village (⊕ 13.6620, -14.9416) and 1.5km east of Sambel Kunda.

Visitors here can take a half-day (£30 pp) or whole-day (£48 pp) guided tour, starting at 07.00 with a 3-hour tracking walk in the forest, where red colobus, green monkey and Guinea baboons are likely to be spotted. Half-day tours conclude with a cold drink and a presentation on the project back at headquarters, while the full-day tours continue on to lunch, a local school and a tree nursery. Prices are lower for groups larger than four. They also have two en-suite rooms in a new roundhouse at the forested HQ compound, and some tents to accommodate guests overnight (£22 pp B&B). Visits here can easily be combined with seeing the rest of RGNP.

Gambia Horse and Donkey Trust (w gambiahorseanddonkey.org.uk) Founded in 2002 by the late Stella Brewer Marsden and her sister Heather Armstrong, the Gambia Horse and Donkey Trust (GHDT) is based in the village of Sambel Kunda (⊕ 13.6643, -14.9584), one of more than ten villages that belong to the co-management committee of Nyassang Forest Park. In addition to training paravets, harness makers and farriers, the GHDT sponsors local students and provides resources to schools in the area, as well as educating locals to treat their working equines properly, thus improving farming productivity and the welfare of the animals. Formerly affiliated to the CRP, the trust can be visited on foot or by donkey-cart from the tourist camp, and it also welcomes suitable volunteers. They now have an equally impressive second centre downriver in Makasutu (page 188).

JANJANBUREH AND SURROUNDS

Founded by the British in 1823, the port of Janjanbureh (also spelt Janjangbureh), administrative capital of CRR, stands on the North Bank of the 20km² MacCarthy

Island about 200km inland of Banjul as the crow flies. Officially known as Georgetown (after King George IV) until 1995, it is still often referred to by that name, or as Makati (a corruption of MacCarthy). A busy and thriving commercial centre throughout the colonial era, it is now quite a sleepy laid-back place with a population of some 4,000-odd souls and an economy so stagnant you might well find yourself wondering whether it's a public holiday, irrespective of which day of the week you happen to visit. A shrinking few relics of the town's early days line the picturesque waterfront, and the lushly wooded island is home to plenty of monkeys and birds, but otherwise it is long on atmosphere and rather shorter on conventional tourist sights. Nevertheless, a few energetic local operators are keen to see the town develop as an ecotourism hub and are working hard towards that goal. As such, Janjanbureh, together with the facing stretch of the North Bank, hosts by far the biggest concentration of lodges and eateries in the Gambian interior, most of which fall firmly into the cheap and cheerful category.

HISTORY Not much is known about the early history of MacCarthy Island, though oral tradition states that it was referred to by locals as Janjanbureh after its first settlers, two brothers named Janjang and Bureh. The island first appears on European maps in the late 17th century under the name Lemaine, probably a corruption of the common Gambian men's name Lamin (indeed, the facing North Bank settlement is still called Lamin Koto), and it is almost certainly the place referred to as 'Lame' by the Cape Verdean trader André Donelha in 1625.

The 17th-century settlement in the vicinity of Janjanbureh was Jongkaa Kunda, which stood more-or-less where Lamin Koto does today. Though it lay beyond the reach of ocean-going boats, Jongkaa Kunda evidently played an intermittent role in the slave trade, serving as a periodic trading station to passing European and Luso-African traders, who used the island opposite to hold freshly acquired captives before transporting them further downriver.

In 1785, Richard Bradley purchased Lemaine Island from the King of Niani (the main fiefdom on the facing North Bank) on behalf of the British Crown for around £580. The idea was to convert the island into a small colony for convicts and other 'undesirables' who would have been dumped in the Americas prior to the 1776 War of Independence, but were currently filling up the gaols of England. This plan never came to fruition, however, as the conditions on Lemaine were ultimately deemed unsuitable for Europeans – perhaps unsurprising, given that Bradley himself died in the process of making his acquisition. After the Crown mounted another abortive effort to establish a penal colony in 1786 – this time in what is now southern Namibia, where the land was found to be uninhabitable – some of the 200 inmates originally destined for what would have been the first colonial outpost on the River Gambia were instead bundled onto the First Fleet, arriving in Australia in January 1778. As a result, the island reverted to the King of Niani, and by 1810 it had become the site of a settlement called Morokunda, founded by Islamic Mandinka refugees fleeing conflict on the mainland.

Modern Georgetown/Janjanbureh started to take shape in 1823, when Captain Alexander Grant leased Lemaine Island from the King of Niani on behalf of the British Crown to create a settlement for people freed from enslavement. In the same year, the mud Fort George (named after King George IV) was erected by the British, probably close to the present-day site of the Armitage School, and the Reverend John Morgan acquired a plot of land to start a Wesleyan Mission (now the Methodist Church). Lemaine Island was renamed in honour of Sir Charles MacCarthy, an ardent anti-slavery campaigner who by then also served as

14

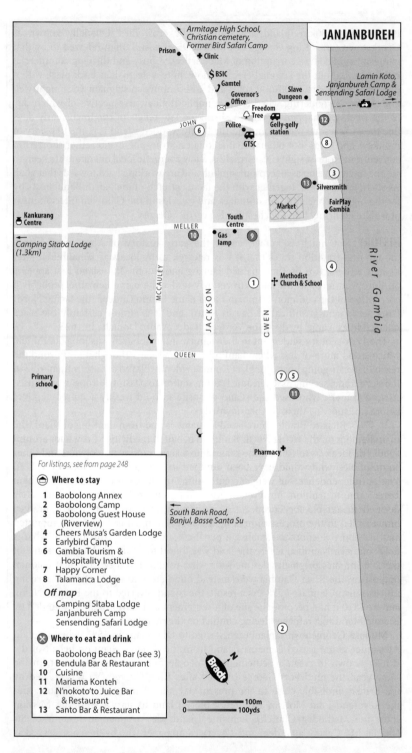

JANJANBUREH

Armitage High School,
Christian cemetery,
Former Bird Safari Camp

Prison

+ Clinic

$ BSIC
Gamtel

Governor's
Office

Slave
Dungeon

Lamin Koto,
Janjanbureh Camp &
Sensending Safari Lodge

Freedom
Tree

JOHN
6

Police

Gelly-gelly
station

12

GTSC

8

3

13 Silversmith

Market

FairPlay
Gambia

Kankurang
Centre

MELLER
10

Youth
Centre

Camping Sitaba Lodge
(1.3km)

Gas
lamp

9

River Gambia

4

MCCAULEY

1

Methodist
Church & School

JACKSON

CWEN

QUEEN

Primary
school

7 5

11

Pharmacy

South Bank Road,
Banjul, Basse Santa Su

For listings, see from page 248

Where to stay

1   Baobolong Annex
2   Baobolong Camp
3   Baobolong Guest House
    (Riverview)
4   Cheers Musa's Garden Lodge
5   Earlybird Camp
6   Gambia Tourism &
    Hospitality Institute
7   Happy Corner
8   Talamanca Lodge

Off map
    Camping Sitaba Lodge
    Janjanbureh Camp
    Sensending Safari Lodge

Where to eat and drink

    Baobolong Beach Bar (see 3)
9   Bendula Bar & Restaurant
10 Cuisine
11 Mariama Konteh
12 N'nokoto'to Juice Bar
    & Restaurant
13 Santo Bar & Restaurant

2

N

0   100m
0   100yds

Governor of Sierra Leone. In 1827, Fort George was relocated close to the present-day commissioner's headquarters, and the subsidiary Fort Campbell was erected on the east side of MacCarthy Island.

The first group of 200 people freed from enslavement, mostly Creoles originating from Sierra Leone, Nigeria or Ghana, arrived at Georgetown in 1832. Three years later the Reverend William Fox opened the Wesleyan (now Methodist) School to educate and evangelise the liberated Creole immigrants. By 1837, however, almost half of the settlers at Georgetown had perished, mostly from tropical diseases such as malaria. The town's population was later boosted by an influx of refugees from the Soninke–Marabout Wars in the 1860s, and counted 1,263 residents as of 1871. Small as it may have been, however, this remote British military outpost on MacCarthy Island is pretty much the sole reason why The Gambia exists today – almost certainly, the river would otherwise have been ceded to the French during territorial negotiations with the British held in 1876.

British administrative reorganisations in the second half of the 19th century saw Georgetown's politico-military importance decline, and the population had fallen to 797 by 1901. But it remained an important trading centre, and the city began to grow again in the early 20th century. The roads were widened in 1905, a post office was opened and a money order system introduced in 1909, and a proper wharf was built in 1917. Over the course of the 1920s, the Bank of British West Africa opened its Georgetown agency, the prestigious Armitage School was established outside town, and a (short-lived) floating bridge was constructed to connect MacCarthy Island to Sankulay Kunda on the South Bank. Georgetown was gazetted as the district and provincial headquarters in 1930, and it remained the second most important administrative centre (and second-largest town in The Gambia in both cases after Bathurst/Banjul) throughout the rest of the colonial era. Post independence, however, Janjanbureh (as the town was renamed in 1995) has again suffered a sharp economic decline, largely owing to its remote location and, until 2010, the absence of a bridge connecting it to either river bank. Though it remains the administrative capital of CRR, Janjanbureh today no longer ranks among the country's 20 largest towns, and the widely expressed hope that its economy would be kick-started following the construction of the bridge to Sankulay Kunda has yet to materialise.

GETTING THERE AND AWAY The 2010 bridge linking the South Bank village of Sankulay Kunda to MacCarthy Island now makes it possible to drive to Janjanbureh directly from anywhere on the South Bank without the delay associated with a ferry crossing. By contrast, there is no bridge connecting Janjanbureh to Lamin Koto on the North Bank; only a motor ferry, which runs between 08.00 and 18.30, costs around D100/50 per car/motorcycle and takes around 5 minutes in either direction. Smaller private boats also ferry passengers between Janjanbureh and Lamin Koto for D10 from roughly 06.00 to 21.30; a private crossing costs D100.

By road, Janjanbureh lies around 275km east of Serekunda, 125km from Soma and 75km west of Basse. The best way to travel to Janjanbureh from any of these towns is with the handful of GTSC buses that leave Serekunda for Basse and vice versa every morning. Leaving Janjanbureh, they stop in front of the police station; you should aim to be there before 08.00 for buses headed towards Serekunda and before 09.00 for buses heading to Basse. The fare is around D200 to Serekunda (or D300 for the express bus) and about D80 to Basse. If it doesn't work out with the GTSC bus, gelly-gellys and bush taxis for all these destinations are slightly costlier and run from the roadside near the Freedom Tree throughout the day.

On the North Bank, one GTSC bus runs daily between Barra and Lamin Koto (the ferry terminal opposite Janjanbureh) via Farafenni, Kau-ur and Wassu. It leaves Barra around 08.00 (depending on what time the first ferries arrive from Banjul) and Lamin Koto at 07.00, and takes around 8 hours in either direction because of the many stops. The GTSC bus to/from Passamas (departing at 07.00 in either direction daily) also stops in Lamin Koto. Additionally, gelly-gellys and bush taxis serve most towns along this route, leaving Lamin Koto from right next to the ferry slipway, and for once these may be quicker than the GTSC bus.

There are no scheduled passenger services, but it is also possible to travel between the coast and Janjanbureh by river with a chartered vessel. FairPlay Gambia (page 252) offers private trips on the *Fula Princess* boat sleeping up to four. A five-day/four-night trip between Janjanbureh and Bintang costs £1,980/2,040/2,100/2,160 for 1/2/3/4 passengers FB.

 WHERE TO STAY *Map, page 246*
Janjanbureh offers a choice of many camps and lodges, but none that rise much above the budget category. Assuming it's not out on a trip, the *Fula Princess* is Janjanbureh's most atmospheric sleep by far, bobbing in the river while anchored offshore (✳£220 B&B, up to 4 guests; book through FairPlay Gambia, page 252).

Budget

Baobolong Camp (20 rooms) m 686 5199, 764 8844, 761 8784; e basirusinyan@yahoo.com; f. Popular with tour operators, this long-serving & relatively well-managed camp has a rather bizarre location on the eastern edge of town, within view of the riverside but separated from it by an overgrown field. The en-suite rooms vary greatly from newly remodelled to getting long in the tooth – ask to see a few. Most are small but clean & come with a fan. Meals £4–6. For large groups entertainment is laid on with local dancers & there is a resident fortune teller. *£20/25/35 sgl/dbl/trpl.* **$$**

Baobolong Guest House (Riverview) (7 rooms) m 764 8844, 334 0196; f. This lodge has an unbeatable central location & the small en-suite rooms all come with dbl bed & fan. Rooms look right out onto the riverfront bar, which does meals around £6 & usually closes up relatively early. *£19/24 sgl/dbl B&B.* **$$**

Earlybird Camp (6 rooms) m 513 5809, 761 9248. This small camp is set in a pleasant green compound tucked away along a footpath down to the riverbank. Rooms are in a newly built block, & most come with fan & en-suite toilet/shower. Meals can be prepared by request (£5), & they can organise boat trips along the river to see hippos. It's one of the more agreeable central options but feels a touch overpriced. *£16 pp B&B.* **$$**

Happy Corner (8 rooms) m 785 3539. As befitting the name, this is a friendly new option, centrally located on Owen Rd & offering simple & tidy en-suite rooms in a small garden compound, with meals on request. *£14/19 sgl/dbl with fan, £19/22 sgl/dbl with AC, all B&B.* **$$**

Sensending Safari Lodge (18 rooms) m 342 1243, 733 4408, 691 1935; e sensendinglodge@ gmail.com, ljobarteh32@yahoo.com. Situated right next to Janjanbureh Camp, this riverside lodge has brighter rooms than its neighbour but less jungly grounds. The choice is between large, thatched round huts or less attractive tin-roofed square rooms, all with 1 dbl & 1 sgl bed, nets, standing fan & en-suite shower. Fans can be run off the generator overnight. Lunch & dinner available for around £5. *£13 pp B&B.* **$$**

✳ **Cheers Musa's Garden Lodge** (5 rooms, 3 under construction) m 786 7828. This little lodge really has its *pieds dans l'eau*, taking better advantage of its riverfront locale than all others in town. The en-suite fan rooms are new & trim, & the waterside resto-bar (meals on request around £4) drops off right into the water. Friendly proprietor Musa can arrange all local activities. *£13/18 sgl/dbl B&B.* **$**

Baobolong Annex (22 rooms) m 731 5093, 738 6152. Owned by the same family as Baobolong Camp but managed separately, this central lodge has a convenient but bland location in a large walled compound on the landward side of Owen Rd. All rooms are en suite; newer rooms are smarter & come with AC, while the older ones have fans but are a bit musty. It serves a good set b/fast & dinner for £4 & £6 respectively. *£11/14 pp for rooms with fan/AC.* **$**

Camping Sitaba Lodge ⊕ 13.5266, -14.7699; **m** 396 4405, +44 7393 207 835 (UK); **w** campingsitabalodge.com; ◙ campingsitabalodge. In an isolated riverside locale on the south side of MacCarthy Island, about 2km from central Janjanbureh, the simple rooms in this garden compound come in a few different configurations, but all are en-suite with ceiling fans & mosquito nets. They can arrange all the usual boat trips & local hikes. Meals available with advance notice. *From £15 dbl B&B.* **$**

Gambia Tourism & Hospitality Institute (GTHI) (3 rooms) **m** 711 0112, 782 3850, 222 2031. Though it's got a rather indifferent location a couple of streets away from the river, the handful of AC rooms at this quiet tourism training centre are the best in town if you're after comfort rather than character. *£12/20 sgl/dbl B&B.* **$**

Janjanbureh Camp (34 rooms) **m** 778 4058, 990 0231. Situated on a forested stretch of the North Bank opposite Janjanbureh town, this pleasant but rather lackadaisically managed lodge boasts lush jungle-like gardens running down to the river & spacious but slightly tired thatched en-suite huts with large beds & nets. There is no power (or generator), which means no AC or fan, but the rooms are quite well ventilated, & lighting is by kerosene lamp & candle. Wildlife is plentiful, particularly from a troupe of resident green monkeys & birds. Meals on request for around £4, with buffets for larger groups. It lies a few hundred metres east of the ferry slipway at Lamin Koto, or you can charter a boat from town for D150. Good value. *£10/14 pp B&B/HB.* **$**

Shoestring

Talamanca Lodge (4 rooms) **m** 722 4674, 992 1100. This simple owner-managed lodge along the river has quite small but acceptably clean en-suite rooms with dbl bed, fan & net. There were new rooms under construction in 2023. *£7 pp.* **$**

✕ **WHERE TO EAT AND DRINK** *Map, page 246*

All the guesthouses listed above can do meals on request, but there is also no shortage of restaurants and bars in Janjanbureh. Note though, that what's available on any given day is largely dependent on the fluctuating offerings available in the city's small market. Most restaurants serve the usual menu of Gambian staples; if you're after something in particular, it's often best to drop in a few hours ahead of time and place your order in advance. Aside from the below, **Mariama Konteh** and **Cuisine Restaurant** (both **$**) also serve the usuals. For meat lovers, given enough notice, local balanta woman Jonsaba will prepare delicious warthog pepper soup; call to arrange delivery (**m** 205 2896). Other options include the following.

✳ **Baobolong Beach Bar** ⊕ 07.00–late. The top sundowner spot in Janjanbureh, this unpretentious bar has a comfortable riverfront deck from where (if the government ever moves the disused ferry parked out front) you can watch the Lamin Koto ferry plough back & forth & other smaller boats slip past, kids doing somersaults from the jetty, & loads of birds – from hornbills to herons – flying over the river. **$$**

✳ **Bendula Bar & Restaurant** **m** 331 9967, 788 8420; ⊕ 07.00–midnight daily. This well-run & well-loved stalwart on Owen Rd is probably the most popular meeting point in town. Grab a seat in the ficus-shaded courtyard & dip into the reliable stock of chilled beers, or order from a varied menu

including fish & chips or chicken yassa & rice. *Around £4/plate.* **$$**

N'nokoto'to Juice Bar & Restaurant **m** 744 4234, 249 6763. The former CFAO warehouse was knocked down to make room for this new riverfront restaurant, opened in 2023. *Around £4/plate.* **$$**

Santo Bar & Restaurant **m** 204 9211. On an open-sided first-floor terrace across the road from Baobolong Beach Bar, this breezy new spot spearheaded by local guide Yusupha serves a menu of Gambian staples & simple b/fasts, & has a full bar. *Around £4/plate.* **$$**

14

Counteracting the steady stream of guides and tour operators from the coast that bring tourists but give little to the local community, Destination Janjanbureh (m 528 9822, 353 0132; ⨍ DestinationJanjanburehGMB) is a local initiative that aims to provide employment in Janjanbureh. They train and license local residents to become guides specialising in the history, culture, nature and people of the island. Any income generated goes directly back into the local community and helps to support development initiatives. Destination Janjanbureh can also arrange tours to local sites as well as meetings with local families and opportunities to experience life in the region. Half- and full-day excursions (inc lunch) can be arranged, and activities include city tours of Janjanbureh (£25 for up to 5 participants), donkey-cart tours to neighbouring villages (£14), palm wine-tapping or cooking lessons (£5 pp) and cultural performances such as the Jamba Jabally Kankurang masquerade, drumming, kora and the Kanyelang women's group, with prices negotiable based on group size. Guided hikes to Kunkilling Forest Park are available (£20), along with day-long kayak (£20) or boat trips around the island (£40), or excursions to River Gambia National Park (£85). Finally, for a truly fascinating and local experience, Destination Janjanbureh can arrange homestays either in the town or at a local village.

OTHER PRACTICALITIES

Banking and foreign exchange There is now a BSIC bank in Janjanbureh, but no ATM. The larger Mauritanian shops are usually willing to change money, including pounds sterling, euros or CFA francs. The usual money transfer services like Western Union and Moneygram are also available in town.

Internet The local mobile data connection is spotty but usually good enough for the basics. Several guesthouses theoretically offer Wi-Fi, but you may need to ask them to top up their mobile router (potentially against a small fee).

Shopping The best shop in town is actually across the river in Lamin Koto: look for Alieu's Supermarket on the west side of the ferry landing. In Janjanbureh itself, there are a number of small boutiques (often Mauritanian-run), as well as the city **market**, which stocks a limited range of fresh and packaged foodstuffs – be sure to come in the morning if you've got serious shopping to do. Otherwise, a better selection is available at Bansang, about 20km to the southeast.

For handicrafts and souvenirs, FairPlay Gambia (page 252) can take you to some local pottery and silversmithing workshops, or you can drop in on third-generation silversmith Papa Cham (m 508 9443) himself and watch him crank up his traditional bellows and forge opposite the Baobolong Beach Bar. Don't be afraid to bargain.

ACTIVITIES AND EXCURSIONS In addition to the attractions discussed below, Janjanbureh is a useful base from which to visit Wassu Stone Circles on the North Bank (page 239), and it is also possible to take a boat out for a rewarding day trip to River Gambia National Park (page 240) from here.

Around town The last few years have taken a significant toll on Janjanbureh's historical buildings. Several of the town's landmark buildings either fell down from lack of maintenance or were knocked down and replaced with modern structures. The best known among what remains is the so-called **Slave Dungeon**. Found next to the ferry landing, this dank subterranean storeroom is touted as having slave-trade associations according to the local oral history, though it in fact only dates to the late 19th century, built as part of a warehouse constructed by the mercantile Maurel & Prom Company. However, it is possible that the same site was used as a camp and assembly point by slave traders in the 16th and 17th centuries. Today the dismal storeroom is adorned with recently added chains and flickering candles to enhance its supposedly sinister mood.

Another landmark with tenuous slave trade associations is the **Freedom Tree**, which was planted in front of the police station to replace the 'original' in 2002, and has become the subject of a legend very similar to the one associated with the Freedom Flag at Albreda. Be warned that local guides are adept at guilt-tripping tourists by showing them this trio of spurious sites and then angling for money. More cheerfully, look out for local musician and Janjanbureh institution, Taka Titi, who will set up his drums and chant the town's history to you as he pounds out a beat.

Continuing up Owen Road from the Freedom Tree and police station, the town's last intact Creole-style wooden house – originally built by the Jones family, one of the 200 liberated slaves brought to MacCarthy Island in 1832 – sadly collapsed entirely in 2022; the ruins are still visible in a splintered heap. The plain rectangular **Methodist Church**, which lies a block further east, is claimed to be the denomination's oldest church in sub-Saharan Africa, having been inaugurated by the Reverend William Fox in 1835 at a site chosen as a Wesleyan Mission 11 years earlier. On the western edge of town, the **Armitage High School** was established as the country's only boarding school in 1927, catering mainly to the progeny of district chiefs, and many of its alumni went on to achieve prominent government positions in the post-independence era. And finally, a contender for the country's most underwhelming historical site is the **'last gas lamp'** on the corner of Jackson and Meller streets – a relic of a gas lighting system installed in 1905, it is basically just a headless pedestal dwarfed by a 10m-tall concrete pylon right alongside it!

At the southern edge of town, the **Kankurang Centre** (m 393 5396; entrance D100, sporadically enforced photography fee D100) is a museum set in a large roundhouse showcasing the masquerade traditions of The Gambia's different regions and ethnic groups. The exhibits are well researched and thorough, offering anthropological insights likely to enlighten seasoned travellers and first-timers alike. And if you're here in January, the **Janjanbureh Kankurang Festival** f, held annually in the second half of the month, is a parade of traditional masks, masquerade and music that is not to be missed.

Kayaking from Janjanbureh

Janjanbureh's position, splayed across the banks of a mid-river island, means it's well-positioned for adventures on the water, and some local operators have started taking advantage of this by offering kayak rental. Newbies can paddle down to the end of the island on a short guided jaunt, while for those with a bit more experience (and/or ambition!), the river is your oyster, and trips to Basse, River Gambia National Park and beyond can all be arranged. Contact FairPlay Gambia (page 252) or Destination Janjanbureh (see opposite) for details.

Birding on MacCarthy Island

Janjanbureh and surrounds offer some superb and undemanding birding opportunities. Indeed, it is possible to see a good selection

Aiming to make use of The Gambia's greatest, yet woefully under-utilised asset, while providing training and employment opportunities for local youth, this social enterprise (m 233 4176; e dave@fairplaygambia. com; w fairplaygambia.com) specialises in upriver ecotourism. Based in Janjanbureh, they work alongside Destination Janjanbureh (page 250) to offer boat trips, birding, kayaking, hiking and more. A variety of kayak excursions are possible, from a half-day wildlife spotting adventure (£30 pp) to larger expeditions downriver to Kuntaur and River Gambia National Park (from £75 pp day trip/£190 pp for a 3-day excursion), or starting out upriver in Basse (page 256) for a four-day paddle with overnight stays in local villages or bush camping (£380 pp).

If you'd rather move along the river under steam other than your own, their custom-built cruising pirogue, the *Fula Princess* (sleeps 4), tours the length of the country – usually over four nights between Bintang and Janjanbureh – with its experienced and friendly crew. Here, you'll spend days puttering up or down the river spotting dolphins and other wildlife, and be treated to excellent meals from the talented crew working the galley. Nights are spent anchored mid-river under the stars, with mattresses and mosquito nets on the top deck or in one of two double cabins downstairs. The full four-night cruises (£2,160 for 4 passengers) make stops at Tendaba, Bao Bolong and River Gambia National Park, among others, but a variety of shorter itineraries (from £540 for 4 passengers/1 night) are also available: see w fairplaygambia.com/sample-itineraries.

They are also developing an admirable network of hiking paths and itineraries through the villages surrounding Janjanbureh, and can arrange specialist excursions for fishers, twitchers, cyclists and more.

of forest and aquatic species from the ferry jetty (or the nearby Baobolong Beach Bar) or in the grounds of Janjanbureh Camp on the North Bank opposite town. But the best bird walk on the island is the rough road that leads west from the town centre, past the prison, then passes through a mosaic of woodland, grassland and cultivation, before it reaches the site of the abandoned Bird Safari Camp after 3km, where the surrounding riparian forest is particularly rewarding. An astonishing seven species of owl (including Verreaux's eagle-owl and the rare Pel's fishing owl) have been recorded in this compact area, along with the likes of violet turaco, Bruce's green pigeon, blue-breasted kingfisher, yellow-throated leaflove, grey-headed bush-shrike, Wilson's indigo-bird and oriole warbler. The (increasingly unstable!) jetty at the former Bird Safari Camp hosts a resident swamp flycatcher, and it's a good place to scan the facing riverbank for the beautiful shining blue kingfisher. You are also likely to see green monkey and possibly red colobus in the vicinity.

If you'd like some further inspiration on walks in the area, hiking enthusiast Gernot Henn has collaborated with Destination Janjanbureh (page 250) to develop and map six trails around Janjanbureh, which can be seen here: w gernothenn. wixsite.com/english/trails.

Lamin Koto Stone Circle Situated about 1.5km from the North Bank ferry terminus at Lamin Koto, this stone circle stands under a large tree on the east side of the main surfaced road to Farafenni. It doesn't compare with the more impressive megalithic sites at Wassu and Kerr Batch (pages 239 and 234), but it is a lot more accessible from Janjanbureh to those with limited time to explore upriver.

Mungo Park Memorial Mungo Park was a Scottish explorer who lived on the North Bank near Karantaba Tenda in 1795 while he learned several local languages in preparation for a trip into the interior to seek the source of the River Niger. He set off with just a few donkeys and servants for company, and had a fascinating journey but failed in his primary goal. When eventually he returned to Britain, he wrote a book entitled *Travels in the Interior of Africa*, which was an instant bestseller. In 1801, Park returned to The Gambia and set off again to look for the river's source, this time with a large force of army deserters. Neither he nor any of his men returned alive.

A tall memorial pillar (⊕ 13.5438, -14.5669), partially renovated in 2023, commemorates the spot from which he set out on his last, ill-fated expedition, about 1.8km from Karantaba Tenda and 30km northeast of Janjanbureh. Bush taxis connect Lamin Koto (on the North Bank opposite Janjanbureh) to Karantaba Tenda and cost less than D60. Once there, anybody will be able to guide you to the pillar, which is within walking distance of the village.

Musa Molloh Mausoleum Musa Molloh Balde was a renowned resistance leader, remembered for his prowess both as a warrior and as a skilful diplomat. In 1884, he became the hereditary ruler of the Fulladu Empire, which ran south from the River Gambia into parts of what are now Senegal, Guinea-Conakry and Guinea-Bissau. After double-crossing the French, he and his followers sought British protection, settling at Kesereh Kunda on the South Bank near Janjanbureh. Tensions flared between Musa Molloh and the colonial government in 1919; he was exiled to Sierra Leone and only allowed to return in 1923, stripped of all his traditional powers. He died and was buried in Kesereh Kunda eight years later. Today his tomb is in a modern but semi-derelict building, and probably only of interest to hardcore history aficionados. It sits about 2km off the South Bank Road, turning north at Boraba village, 1.5km east of the Janjanbureh turnoff.

Kunkilling Forest Park Situated on the South Bank of the river near the eastern tip of MacCarthy Island, some 5km upstream of Janjanbureh, Kunkilling Forest Park (entry D100) has been set aside by four small villages (including Kesereh Kunda) to protect 2km² of forest- and palm-lined riverfront. Run through by four short eco-trails (none longer than 1km), the forest is home to five primate species, including red colobus, along with warthog, banded mongoose, bushbuck, Gambian sun squirrel, hippopotamus and West African manatee. Mammal viewing is erratic but the birding is outstanding, with more than 150 species recorded. The big special is Adamawa turtle dove, which is common here but scarce elsewhere in The Gambia. Other good birds include Pel's fishing owl, red-footed falcon, marsh owl, Beaudouin's snake-eagle, African finfoot, Senegal parrot, shining-blue kingfisher and lead-coloured flycatcher. Visitors are encouraged to walk at dusk and dawn, when the wildlife is most active. There was a government-linked guesthouse (⊕ 13.5210, -14.7072) under construction here at the time of writing, but it's unclear when it might open. The incomplete roundhouses sit riverside, 2.5km past the turnoff at Kesereh Kunda.

The guesthouses and guides in Janjanbureh can arrange visits here, or you can call dedicated forestry guide Haruna Kandeh (m 723 0271), who will set up your transport and accompany you there. The best way to head to the park is by boat, which takes about an hour in either direction, allowing for a few birding stops, and costs around D3,000 per party for the round trip, inclusive of 2–3 hours' waiting time while you explore the forest. FairPlay Gambia (page 252) is a good option to arrange this. By road, you can get to the entrance near Kesereh Kunda in 30–45 minutes. If you don't have your own car, expect to pay around D1,500 for a taxi or D900 for a motorcycle carrying one person only. In addition, there is an entrance fee of D150 per person, and the guide will expect a similar tip. Note that while Haruna the forestry guide knows the forest's attractions well, he has no pretensions to being a specialist birding guide – but can arrange one if so required. The best time to visit is early morning (leaving Janjanbureh at around 06.00) or later afternoon (leaving at around 15.30).

Kajakat Island About 5km long and up to 2km wide, this large island lies in the middle of the River Gambia about 6km downstream of MacCarthy Island and a similar distance upstream of the eastern boundary of River Gambia National Park. Also known as Kai Hai (the name of the nearest North Bank village), the island is said locally to be haunted by various spirits, including a man-eating dragon-like creature that might well reflect a folk memory of an outsized killer crocodile. As a result of its taboo status, the island remains uninhabited, and the cover of dense natural forest is largely intact. Hippos and crocodiles are resident in the surrounding waters, and the island itself supports a similar selection of forest and aquatic birds to the nearby national park, including a large flock of knob-billed ducks that sometimes roost off the south side.

From MacCarthy Island it is easy to take a boat trip to Kajakat. This can be arranged with any local guide or more reliably perhaps with most of the lodges, including Janjanbureh or Baobolong Camp. Expect to pay around D2,400–3,000 per party to rent a boat for a 2–3-hour round trip. With private transport, it would also be possible to visit the island from Kai Hai, which lies about 2km from the riverbank and is the site of several megalithic circles. If you are in the area, a more esoteric national monument is the birthplace of Sir Dawda Kairaba Jawara, the first president of independent The Gambia, at the village of Barajali about 8km west of Kai Hai. There is also a ferry to the South Bank here, crossing over to the Sapu Paddy Fields (page 232) near the village of Wali Kunda.

BANSANG

Perched on the South Bank of the River Gambia between a few attractive small hills and rice paddies about 15km southeast of Janjanbureh, Bansang is a significantly larger and less moribund town, boasting a population of around 7,500, a bustling market, and the country's largest inland hospital. For all that, it is a mostly unremarkable place, with the only point of local interest being a well-established colony of dashing red-throated bee-eaters that nests in a nearby quarry, in a mud bank overlooking a small pool that also hosts plenty of nesting weavers, bishops and other small passerines in breeding season.

GETTING THERE AND AWAY Bansang lies about 15km from Janjanbureh, immediately north of the South Bank Road heading east towards Basse. Several bush taxis run back and forth between the two daily for around D40 per head, and a hand-pulled ferry connects across the river to Bush Town, from where vehicles link to villages on the North Bank. If you are heading to the quarry where the bee-eaters nest (✪ 13.4371, -14.6657), continue along the Basse Road for about 600m past the main feeder road into Bansang, then after crossing a small rise take the first track to your right, which leads to the nesting site after another 500m.

WHERE TO STAY AND EAT Most people who visit Bansang for the bee-eater colony do so either as a day trip from Janjanbureh or en route to Basse. However, there is an excellent new lodge and a couple of adequate cheapies in town if you wish to stay in Bansang.

✳ **Riverside Lodge** (22 rooms) m 720 3000, 514 0200; e riversidelodgebansang@gmail.com; f Riverside Lodge and Garden. In a quiet riverfront compound full of banana & baobab trees on the outskirts of Bansang, this new solar-powered lodge offers the highest-standard accommodation in the area, & the trim en-suite rooms come with canopy beds, nets & ceiling fans, & some have AC. Birders can set up shop under the shady waterside gazebos overlooking the wooded banks. Meals around £5. *£20/27 fan/AC dbl B&B.* **$$**

Bintou's Paradise Hotel (16 rooms) m 755 2465, 999 8990. Boasting a breezy riverside location in the town centre, this hotel displays quite a contrast between the genuinely attractive & characterful deck overlooking a forested stretch of river, & the dark, warren-like interior. The tiled en-suite rooms are quite spacious & acceptably clean. Meals around £5. *£7 pp fan room, £16 AC dbl.* **$**

Margie's Lodge (12 rooms) m 733 7272, 212 3766. Large & slightly wonky but decently kept suite-style AC rooms in a surprisingly cosy compound in central Bansang. *£12/17 dbl/VIP.* **$**

Basse and Upper River Region

Basse Santa Su, more normally abbreviated to Basse, is set on the South Bank of the River Gambia about 370km inland of Banjul by road. The administrative capital of the Upper River Region (population 282,600), it is also the largest Gambian town east of Farafenni, and boasts a hustle and bustle (and selection of services) that belies its relatively modest population of 20,000. Back when river transport

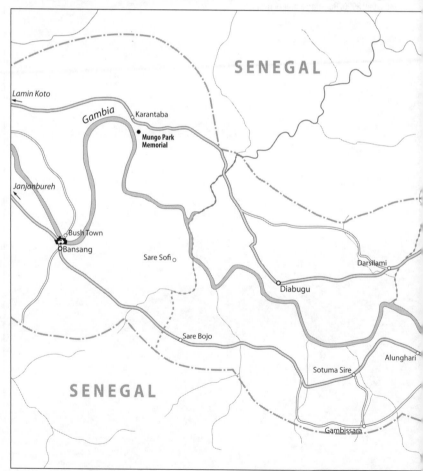

was easier than road, Basse was a port of some significance, as witnessed by the clutch of decaying Victorian buildings that dot its small, timeworn waterfront. And while it still serves as a transport depot for the local peanut and, to a lesser extent, cotton trade, Basse these days is above all a market town. Indeed, the sprawl of narrow streets that comprises the town centre comes across as one vast chaotic bazaar, spilling over with shops and stalls laden with all manner of imported goods and local wares. A massive fire razed much of Basse's central market in early 2020, but a new two-storey market building with some 250 shops was inaugurated here in 2022, and the commercial streets surrounding it are as busy as ever.

Basse has a strikingly different character from any other Gambian town, thanks to its isolation from the coast and strong cross-border trade links, not only with Senegal, which encloses it on three sides, but also to a lesser extent with Guinea, Mali and Mauritania. From a visitor's perspective, it feels far less Westernised than any other comparably sized Gambian town – traditional smocks and straw hats are still very much *de rigueur* here – yet it also has a rather cosmopolitan atmosphere, albeit one that mainly reflects its diversity of West African influences. True, Basse

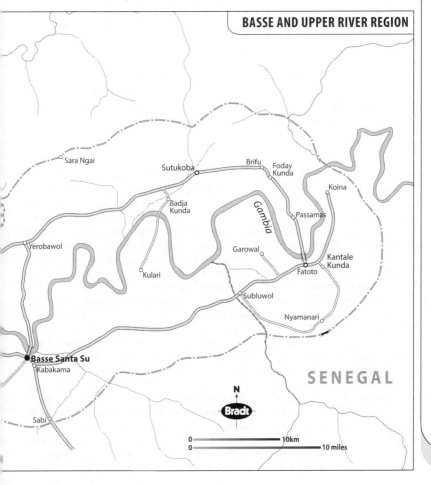

BASSE AND UPPER RIVER REGION

lacks for overt tourist attractions, but for those whose travels in the region are otherwise confined to coastal Gambia, a visit to this busy, noisy, thriving and emphatically African town will be a genuine eye-opener.

Though Basse is refreshingly free of bumsters and touts, a visit there is also without many of the comforts found elsewhere in the country. The town's roads are dusty, pot-holed and uncomfortably narrow, public services such as electricity and running water can be erratic, and all but a couple of hotels and restaurants are fairly rudimentary. Happily, while Basse still feels quite remote from the coast and the 'rest' of The Gambia, the 2021 inauguration of a new bridge over the Gambia River means you can now reach the city from the North and South banks, on surfaced roads the whole way through.

Away from the urban hustle of Basse, the Upper River Region exudes an aura of peace and timeless traditionalism. True, most houses are now roofed with corrugated iron rather than thatch, children attend government-run schools and misshapen satellite dishes reach for the skies in the remotest of villages, but, despite this, many aspects of day-to-day life have changed little in hundreds of years. Women work out in the fields and cook food over open wood fires. Men still go out to hunt with ancient guns, or sit and chat beneath the bantaba. And of course the river continues its timeless meandering, noticeably narrowing as you continue east to the country's end.

Because few toubabs set foot in the area, people tend to be extremely welcoming of and curious about visitors, though English as a spoken language is less common than elsewhere. As is the case with its administrative capital, the Upper River Region is short on bespoke tourist attractions, but it can be very rewarding to those who want to experience a slice of Africa that remains largely undistorted by the trappings of the tourist industry.

GETTING THERE AND AWAY

Basse is about 370km inland of the coast by road. Coming from Banjul or Serekunda, the South Bank Road via Brikama and Soma is fully surfaced and should take about 6 hours in a decent private vehicle. If you're north of the river, Basse is 315km of similarly surfaced road inland from Barra, and has been connected to the North Bank since 2021 by the 250m Samba Juma Bridge, named for a particularly kind-hearted boatman from the city. (While the South Bank is the more heavily trafficked route, birders should note that the North Bank of the Upper River Region is considered the best place to seek the localised sun lark and rufous-tailed scrub robin.)

Using public transport, your most comfortable option is the handful of GTSC buses that run in either direction between Kanifing (Serekunda) and Basse daily, stopping en route at Soma and Janjanbureh. The buses all leave between 06.00 and noon, with the best option being the air-conditioned express service that leaves at 06.30 in either direction. Tickets cost around D300/500 for a regular/air-conditioned bus and the trip usually takes 7–8 hours, depending on the frequency and duration of stops. The express service is a bit more expensive but also an hour or two quicker – very much money well spent. If the GTSC buses are full, or you need to travel in the afternoon, regular gelly-gellys and shared taxis connect Basse to Janjanbureh, Soma, Serekunda and elsewhere on the South Bank for a similar cost, but the vehicles are more uncomfortable and less reliable.

On the North Bank, you could take the daily GTSC bus from Barra to Foday Kunda/Passamas (departs Barra at 09.00; D275) and jump off at Yerobawol junction, from where it's 14km to Basse.

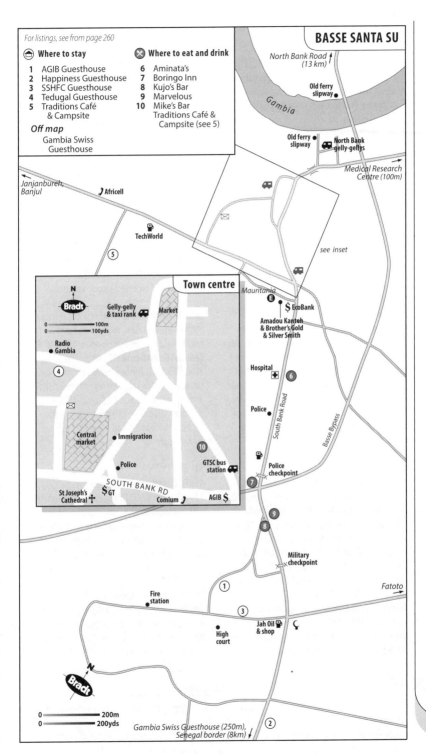

For listings, see from page 260

Where to stay
1 AGIB Guesthouse
2 Happiness Guesthouse
3 SSHFC Guesthouse
4 Tedugal Guesthouse
5 Traditions Café
   & Campsite

Off map
   Gambia Swiss
   Guesthouse

Where to eat and drink
6 Aminata's
7 Boringo Inn
8 Kujo's Bar
9 Marvelous
10 Mike's Bar
   Traditions Café &
   Campsite (see 5)

BASSE SANTA SU

North Bank Road (13 km)

Old ferry slipway

Gambia

Old ferry slipway

North Bank
gelly-gellys

*Medical Research
Centre (100m)*

*Janjanbureh,
Banjul*

Africell

TechWorld

(5)

see inset

Town centre

N

Bradt

Gelly-gelly
& taxi rank

Market

0 ———— 100m
0 ———— 100yds

Radio
Gambia

(4)

Central
market

Immigration

Police

SOUTH BANK RD

St Joseph's
Cathedral   GT

Comium

AGIB

Mauritania

EcoBank

Amadou Kanteh
& Brother's Gold
& Silver Smith

Hospital   (6)

Police

South Bank Road

Basse Bypass

(10)

GTSC bus
station

Police checkpoint

(7)

(9)

(8)

Military
checkpoint

Fatoto

Fire
station

(1)

(3)

Jah Oil
& shop

High
court

Bradt

0 ———— 200m
0 ———— 200yds

*Gambia Swiss Guesthouse (250m),
Senegal border (8km)*

(2)

Basse and Upper River Region   GETTING THERE AND AWAY

15

ORIENTATION

Basse is quite a spaced-out town. The town centre and market area form a compact warren of busy roads lined with all manner of workshops, boutiques and eateries, as well as the main gelly-gelly park and GTSC bus station. The riverfront and former ferry jetty (now a gelly-gelly park serving local villages on the North Bank) lie about 150m further north, and are reached by crossing a small bridge adjacent to the main gelly-gelly park.

About 1km southeast of the town centre, and separated from it by a quickly shrinking open area, the relatively smart suburb of Basse Mansajang is the site of most of the city's hotels, several administrative buildings and the junction for roads running east to Fatoto/Koina and south to Sabi, eastern Gambia's primary border crossing into Senegal.

 ## WHERE TO STAY   *Map, page 259*

Accommodation options in Basse have improved in recent years, but there's still nothing catering specifically to tourists. Local landmark Basse Guesthouse stopped accepting visitors in 2023 pending major (and majorly needed) renovations.

MID-RANGE

Happiness Guesthouse (12 rooms) m 744 8663, 341 0555. This new guesthouse at the edge of Mansajang sits in a rather austere compound, but offers far & away the best accommodation in town. Rooms are sharp & modern with AC, sat TV, Wi-Fi & hot water. There's a good restaurant attached with meals around £4, but no alcohol (OK to bring your own, though). *£17 en-suite dbl.* **$**

BUDGET

AGIB Guesthouse (30 rooms) m 336 1888, 368 2391. Set in a shadeless concrete compound in Mansajang, this Islamic bank-owned hotel is something of a study in soullessness, but offers spacious tiled dbl rooms with AC, Wi-Fi, fridge & sat TV. No alcohol & no restaurant, but meals can be prepared by arrangement. *£9/12 dbl with shared bath/en suite, £20 VIP with 2 dbl rooms & sitting room.* **$**
Gambia Swiss Guesthouse (24 rooms) m 276 9509, 710 9388, 311 9816; e swisslodgegambia@ yahoo.com. Set 300m past Happiness Guesthouse on the road to Sabi, this new guesthouse in a

spaced-out compound is rather out of the way, but has simple & clean rooms with fan or AC. No restaurant. *£8/11 en-suite room with fan/AC.* **$**
Tedugal Guesthouse (12 rooms) m 326 2062, 763 9465. The best option in central Basse, this bright yellow multi-storey compound sits just opposite Radio Gambia, about 250m from the main garage. The tidy rooms come with AC, but there's no food on site. *£11/13 shared bath/en-suite.* **$**

SHOESTRING

SSHFC Guesthouse (19 rooms) m 520 2330, 733 9338, 994 3797. This guesthouse associated with the social security administration in Mansajang lies in agreeably shady grounds; the en-suite rooms (with AC/fan & fridge) are decent but starting to show their age. *£8/room.* **$**

CAMPING

Traditions Café & Campsite m 955 5487. Situated about 200m south of the Serekunda Rd, this family-run café (see opposite) has space for campers to erect their own tent in the small banana garden. *Negotiable £4/tent or so.*

 ## WHERE TO EAT AND DRINK   *Map, page 259*

In addition to the sit-down eateries listed opposite, Basse is pretty good for inexpensive street food, a local speciality being tangy *ful* sandwiches made with fresh *tapalapa* rolls – try the stall in front of Aminata's. Most restaurants in

Basse do not serve alcohol. To slake your well-earned thirst, **Kujo's Bar** (m 764 8510) in Mansajang has a nice vibe and garden setting, while **Mike's Bar** is more central but feels a bit post-apocalyptic. Try **Boringo Inn** for DJs and dancing on Saturday nights.

Traditions Café & Campsite m 955 5487. More a friendly family compound than anything else, this long-serving address can whip up a selection of local & international dishes, but these must be ordered at least an hour or 2 in advance. They can also arrange boat trips on the river for around D1,000/hr or introduce you to a traditional healer who will eagerly prove his credentials. *Dishes around £4.* $$

Aminata's Restaurant m 795 2150, 228 3616; ⏰ 12.00–midnight Mon–Sat. Tucked away behind a shop opposite the hospital, this popular eatery serves a budget-beating selection of 3–4 tasty local dishes. Great value. *Around £1.50–3/plate at lunch & dinner.* $

Marvelous Restaurant m 705 4811, 595 4523; ⏰ 08.00–midnight daily. Across from Kojo's Bar on the way to Mansajang, this place does good Gambian plates & keeps long hours. *£3/plate.* $

OTHER PRACTICALITIES

BANKING AND FOREIGN EXCHANGE Basse is home to The Gambia's only ATMs east of Farafenni/Soma. They can be found at **GT Bank**, **AGIB** and **EcoBank**, all near the central market. Several of the private **forex bureaux** dotted around town seem unwilling to change any foreign currency into dalasi, so ask around at the larger general shops. Many of these, particularly the Mauritanian-run ones, will change money at reasonable rates.

INTERNET There is good cellular network in Basse and several hotels offering Wi-Fi.

SHOPPING Though the **central market** doesn't cater specifically to tourists, quite a few local handicrafts are on offer, generally at cheaper prices than you'll get on the coast. For serious batik-buyers, ask **Traditions Café** about local tie-and-dye artists. And for jewellery, **Amadou Kanteh & Brother's Gold & Silver Smith** (m 383 8593, 392 2229) make quality bracelets and other pieces and are happy to show you the process; follow the signs for the Honorary Consul of Mauritania (m 727 300, 725 2323) to find them.

Though the trade has diminished in recent decades, Upper River is traditionally a cotton-growing region and **The Gambia Cotton Trail** (w gambiacottontrail. com) is working to revitalise local cotton production and create uniquely Gambian cotton products and artwork for sale. With mandatory advance co-ordination (contact Footsteps Eco-Lodge in Gunjur, page 168), you can tour the production and processing sites, and buy some cotton of your own.

ACTIVITIES AND EXCURSIONS

AROUND TOWN The town itself lacks any obvious tourist focus other than the sprawling market, which is great fun to explore, as are the surrounding side roads. That aside, the main attraction is the riverfront, renowned in ornithological circles as the most reliable Gambian site for the localised Egyptian plover or crocodile bird. This distinctive and eagerly sought wader is often seen picking along the muddy riverfront between the new bridge and the old ferry jetty, with sightings being most regular in the early morning between September and December, but unusual from March to May.

15

> ## KAYAK
>
> One of the most unique ways to explore the upper Gambia River is by kayak. **FairPlay Gambia** (page 252) offers a customisable multi-day paddling itinerary, starting in Basse and covering the 110km downriver to Janjanbureh over three days on the water, overnighting in tents or local houses in the tiny riverbank villages of Diabugu Tendala and Sami Karantaba. Here, you'll be given a warm welcome and a privileged peek into a totally untouristed side of The Gambia few outsiders ever get to see. Or you can just keep paddling until you reach River Gambia National Park! More information at w fairplaygambia.com/kayaking.

The set of paddy fields east of the new bridge border the Prufu Swamp/Prufu Bolong just beyond. This is a seasonal marshland that is also recognised as an Important Bird Area, and home to a small breeding colony of red-throated bee-eater. It's easily accessible by foot along the road past the Medical Research Council towards Dampha Kunda.

Also worth a look, and difficult to miss on account of its incessant chirruping, is the colony of Gambian epauletted fruit bats that roosts in the hospital grounds about 300m along the road towards Mansajang. These rank among the largest bats found on the African mainland, with a 1m-long wingspan, and are most impressive at dusk, when columns of several dozen can be seen flapping heavy-winged over the town centre and the hotels in Mansajang.

RIVER TRIPS The best way to see wildlife around Basse is to charter one of the small private passenger boats docked next to the former ferry jetty to take you further along the river. The opening of the bridge, however, has meant that there are fewer boats to be found – and fewer still with motors – so you've got only a few hand-paddled aluminium boats to choose from here.

Out on the water, you should see plenty of green monkeys in the riverine forest, and might also encounter a few outsized monitor lizards. And the birding can be superb, not only improving the odds of your seeing an Egyptian plover, but also offering a good chance of several species that appear to be less common further west, notably a trio of stunning bee-eaters – northern carmine, red-throated and little green – that breed in the mud banks. Even if birding isn't your thing, it is a peaceful and enjoyable river trip, one that could be extended downriver towards another boat crossing point at Kanube (10km west of Basse along the South Bank Road), or upriver as far as Tambasansang (10km away past Dampha Kunda) – hippos are often encountered here, though this is obviously not guaranteed.

Rates are flexible, but expect to pay at least D500–600 per party per hour. Teacher Lamarana Jallow (m 747 3730, 310 4252; e jallowlama65@gmail.com) has a boat, or if you don't feel like negotiating directly, Traditions Café (page 260) can set you up with a boat trip for a fixed rate. For birders, afternoon is probably the best time to do the trip, ideally departing at around 16.00. If you are thinking of boating as far as Tambasansang or Kanube, an earlier start is recommended.

SOTUMA SERE Flanking the main South Bank Road about 12km west of Basse, the village of Sotuma Sere is known locally for its small pottery industry. The products made here are characterised by their earthen colour and white enamel patterns, and include some relatively original and unusual items, including enamelled candlesticks. The potters are easy to find as you will see a batch of various pots placed next to the road, and there are also a couple of roadside kilns.

The village is also known as the birthplace of *jeli* and international kora player Alhaji 'Papa' Bunka Susso, who named one of his albums (available for streaming online) after the village. There was a government-linked guesthouse (✪ 13.3261, -14.3154) under construction here at the time of writing, but it's unclear when it might open. The incomplete roundhouses sit riverside, 3km north of the main road, following a turnoff at the connected village of Sotuma Samba.

If you're headed back to the coast from here, keep your eyes out for **Mankamang Kunda**, 15km west of Sotuma Sire. This is President Barrow's home village, and now houses a large presidential home and a tall green-and-grey mosque built in 2021; both are visible to the south of the South Bank Road.

FATOTO Set in a relatively hilly area about 40km past Basse, the scattered port of Fatoto is the most inland riverine settlement in The Gambia and the meeting point for the North Bank and South Bank roads. The Gambia's two parallel transport arteries come together at a new 170m-long bridge here, completed in 2021. Despite the new infrastructure, Fatoto (population 2,000 or so) still feels like more of an overgrown village than a small town and, other than an immigration post, has no tourist facilities to speak of.

Nevertheless, birdwatchers might want to drive through from Basse, since it offers an opportunity to see several species rare elsewhere in The Gambia, including Adamawa turtle dove, northern carmine bee-eater, and African swallow-tailed kite, the last-named a dainty tern-like bird of prey that hovers effortlessly overhead while it hunts for insects. Otherwise, the main reason you'd be likely to visit Fatoto is for the sense of completion associated with travelling all the way across the country, in which case you may as well aim to do so on a Sunday, when it livens up slightly for the weekly market. A few inexpensive bush taxis run between Basse and Fatoto daily (more on Sundays) for around D50.

Fatoto is also the gateway to The Gambia's easternmost border crossing at Nyamanari. From the main junction at the entrance to Fatoto, it's 12km on a reasonable laterite road to the Gambian border village of Nyamanari (immigration post at ✪ 13.3310, -13.8665), and a further 2km to the Senegalese RN6 road. Senegalese immigration sits to the east along this road at the entrance to Manda (✪ 13.3301, -13.8382). There are occasional bush taxis between Fatoto, Nyamanari and Manda, particularly for Manda's weekly market on Tuesdays.

Thanks to the new roads, it's now also possible to make a loop all the way around the Upper River Region (and therefore the whole country) on surfaced roads. To get back to the coast from here along the North Bank, GTSC buses to Barra depart from Passamas (over the bridge, 5km from Fatoto) daily at 06.30 (D275). The nearest accommodation (indeed the only 'official' accommodation upriver of Basse, as best we can tell) is also on the North Bank Road; this nameless cluster of very basic roundhouses (**$**) sits in the village of **Sutukoba**, 22km from Fatoto.

KOINA The surfaced road finally runs out at this small Sarahule settlement 10km past Fatoto and known throughout the country as the eastern half of a catchy cartographical couplet describing The Gambia as running 'from Kartong to Koina'. Otherwise, there's little to detain you here, particularly since the aptly named 'A Nice Restaurant in Koina' seemed to have closed up shop, and as best we can tell there's also no official accommodation in town.

SARE NGAI The Monday *lumo* (market) at this small village on the Senegalese border 25km north of Basse is one of the best in the Upper River Region. It stocks many products that cannot be found in Basse market and is particularly known for its beautiful cloth. Even if you're not buying, the livestock section is well worth spending some time at. Look for transport at the gelly-gelly park near the former ferry jetty in Basse.

Appendix 1

LANGUAGE

English is the official language. Most people around the coast and other tourist areas speak it to some degree, and many are very fluent. As a rule, however, the further you go upriver, the fewer people speak English. This is where learning a few words in a local language will come in handy. The trouble comes in deciding which language to learn, since several are in everyday use. Mandinka makes most sense as a plurality of the population is Mandinka. But Wolof, Jola or Fula are also commonly spoken, and it's a great icebreaker when you can greet people in their own language so we have also added the commonest greetings. It feels good to know that someone has gone to the trouble of learning a few phrases in your language and just a few words will open many doors.

Note that the foreign words given below are spelt phonetically, ie: as they are pronounced.

UNIVERSAL GREETING The importance of greetings in The Gambia cannot be overemphasised. Everybody greets one another, either verbally or through handshakes, and this can sometimes take several minutes. It's just another manifestation of the friendliness of the Gambian people. Even people who are too far away to talk or to shake hands will clasp their own hands above their head to greet you at a distance. The universal greeting is in Arabic because most of the population are Muslims. The greeting is: *As-Salaam-Alaikum* ('Peace be upon you'), to which the response is: *Wa-Alaikum-Salaam* ('And upon you, too').

BASIC MANDINKA WORDS AND PHRASES

Good morning	*Esama*
Good afternoon	*Etinyang*
Good evening	*Ewulara*
How are you?	*Kori tanante?* (response: *Tanante*, which means 'I am fine')
How is your family?	*Sumoole?* (response: *Ebebeje*, which means 'they are fine')
How is your wife/husband?	*Ila muso/kemo le?* (response: *Ebebeje*)
How are your children?	*Ding ding olule?* (response: *Ebebeje*)
How is your work?	*Do kwo be nadi?* (response is normally: *Domanding, domanding*, which means 'slowly, slowly')
No	*Hani*
Yes	*Haa*
Thank you	*Abaraca*
Thank you very much	*Abaraca bake*

Good	*Abetiata*
Very good	*Abetiata bake*
Water	*Jio*
What is your name?	*Etondi?*
My name is...	*Nto mu...le ti*
Where do you come from?	*Ebota minto le?*
I come from...	*Nbota...le*
How much (money)?	*Jelu lemu?*
Where is...?	*...le?*
White man	*Toubab*
Black man or child	*Mofingo*
Go away!	*Acha!*

WOLOF GREETINGS

Good morning	*Naka subasi*
Good afternoon	*Naka bekeck*
Good evening	*Naka ngosi*
How are you?	*Naka nga def?* (response: *Jamarek*, which means 'I am/they are fine')
How is your family?	*Naka wa kerrgi?* (response: *Jamarek*)
Thank you	*Jere jef*

JOLA GREETINGS

How are you?	*Kassumay?* (response: *Kassumay kep*, which means 'I am fine')
How are you?	*Katabo?* (response: *Kocobo*, which means 'I am fine')

FULA GREETINGS

How are you?	*Nambata?* (response: *Jamtan*, which means 'I am fine')

SERER GREETINGS

How are you?	*Nafio?* (response: *Memehen* or *Jamarek*, which means 'I am fine')

MANDINKA NUMBERS

1	*kiling*	21, 22, etc	*muwang ning kiling* (literally twenty and one), *muwang ning fula*, etc
2	*fula*		
3	*saba*		
4	*nani*		
5	*lulu*	30	*tang-saba*
6	*woro*	40	*tang-nani*
7	*worowula*	50	*tang-lulu*
8	*sei*	60	*tang-woro*
9	*kononto*	70	*tang-worowula*
10	*tang*	80	*tang-sei*
11, 12, etc	*tang ning kiling* (literally ten and one), *tang ning fula*, etc	90	*tang-kononto*
		100	*keme*
		1,000	*wili kiling*
20	*muwang*		

Appendix 2

GLOSSARY

Here follows a glossary of terms and names used in this book and/or in The Gambia itself.

AC	air conditioning
adobe	mud building
afra	grilled meat
alkalo	chief of village
APRC	Alliance for Patriotic Reorientation and Construction (ruling party under President Jammeh 1996–2017)
attaya	bitter green tea
ba	big (often forms part of place names)
balafon	traditional xylophone
bantaba	covered meeting place in centre of village (or in lodge/hotel gardens). It is the origin of the word 'banter'.
baobab	large, distinctive trees
Barrow, Adama	President of The Gambia since 2017
Bathurst	colonial-era name for Banjul
Baye Fall	Gambian and Senegalese disciples of a Sufi Islamic sect founded by Ibrahima Fall, himself a follower of Amadou Bamba, who protested against French colonialism
benachin	red, tangy, sometimes very spicy, rice dish cooked with vegetables and/or meat
bengula	meeting place
bissap (aka wanjo)	sweet drink
bolong (or bolon)	creek
bumsters	young guys who make their living on the fringes of the tourist industry, often through harassment
bush taxi	minibus or larger vehicle used as public transport
butut	cent-like subdivision of dalasi
café touba	spiced sweet coffee
cowry	small white shell used as currency in pre-colonial times
dalasi	local unit of currency
djembe	traditional drum
domoda	stew made with groundnut sauce
DSTV	South African multi-channel satellite television service
endemic	unique to a specific area
en suite	room with private toilet and shower attached
exotic	not indigenous, eg: pine plantations

forest	wooded area with closed canopy
forex bureau	bureau de change
Fula	pastoralist ethnic group living across West Africa
Gamou	Islamic gathering involving a night of praying and chanting with a *marabout*
gelly-gelly	as bush taxi
griot	oral historians and praise singers of the ancient West African empires that tell the histories of families at ceremonies. They are known as *jeli* in Mandinka.
gris-gris	protective talisman worn around the body (pronounced 'gree-gree'. Usually a piece of Arabic scroll wrapped and sewn up in leather. Also known as *juju* or *amulets*.
GTSC	Gambian Transport Service Corporation, a private bus service
guesthouse	cheap local hotel
harmattan	dry dusty wind blowing across West Africa from the Sahara in the dry season
indigenous	occurring in a place naturally
insh'allah	'God willing' in Arabic and an all-round useful phrase ('Will you give me money?' 'Tomorrow, insh'allah')
Jammeh, Yahya	President of The Gambia 1994–2017
Jawara, Sir Dawda	Prime Minister then President of The Gambia from independence in 1962 until 1994
Jola	predominant ethnic group in southern Gambian and the lower Casamance region in Senegal
Julbrew	local lager-like beer
July 22 Coup	Bloodless 1994 coup in which Yahya Jammeh overthrew President Jawara
kankurang	mystical masked creature that accompanies boys during Mandinka initiation ceremonies, or terrorises villages as a form of social control, depending upon your view
kola nuts	bitter and mildly narcotic nuts chewed throughout West Africa
kora	traditional harp-like instrument
Koriteh	local name for Eid al-Fitr, the feast marking the end of Ramadan
koumpo	Jola dancer covered in green reeds that becomes possessed by a spirit and spins out of control
Lamin	name commonly given to first-born sons
lorry	term used occasionally for any large passenger vehicle
lumo	weekly market
mamapara	masked stilted dancer from the Mandinka tribe, known as *chakaba* in Wolof
marabout	Islamic mystic leader
Mbalax	percussive Senegalese pop music, using *sabar* and *tama* drums, popularised internationally by Senegalese singer, Youssou N'Dour
murubungu	mud house
nding	small (often forms part of place names)
nyankotan	basic rice dish
panga	local equivalent of a machete

plassas	greens-based stew thickened with peanut butter
PPP	People's Progressive Party (ruling party under first President Jawara)
Ramadan	the holy month of Islam, commemorating when the Koran was revealed to Muhammad, during which fasting takes place from dawn till dusk
riparian woodland	strip of forest or lush woodland following a watercourse, often rich in fig trees
riverine woodland	as riparian woodland
sabar	traditional drum
Sahel	dry savannah belt dividing the forested coast of West Africa from the Sahara
savannah	grassland with some trees
Serahuli	ethnic group with historic links to the Mali Empire (also called Soninke)
Serer	ethnic group whose main population centre is in northern Senegal and The Gambia
seyfo	district chief
shared taxi	form of public transport carrying a full quota of passengers between two fixed places
shawarma	Lebanese-style take-away comprising grilled meat and salad in pita bread
station	as taxi park
superkanja	okra soup
surfaced road	road sealed with asphalt or similar
tapalapa	Gambian-style baguette
taxi park	terminus for shared taxis and gelly-gellys
Tobaski	also called Eid al-Adha, this commemorates Abraham's readiness to sacrifice his son on God's command and the last-minute substitution of a ram. Every Islamic family that has the means will purchase a ram, of which they eat one third, give one third to their friends and donate the final third to the poor.
toubab	non-derogatory term for white person or Westerner – falsely said to derive from boys asking colonials for 'two bob' coins
town taxi	charter taxi, as in Europe (but not metered) used for a 'town trip'
West Sudanese	architectural style using mud and wood typical of mosques of the Sahel
Wolof	dominant ethnic group on the coast north of the River Gambia
woodland	wooded area lacking closed canopy
yassa	onion-lemon marinade, eaten with chicken or fish

Appendix 3

FURTHER INFORMATION

BOOKS

Food Until Ida Cham (page 157) writes her Gambian cookbook, probably the best guide to the cuisine of the region is from Senegalese chef Pierre Thiam. Not simply a cookbook, but a full-colour exploration of Senegal's culinary culture – equally at home on the coffee table as in the kitchen. Two volumes, *Senegal: Modern Senegalese Recipes from the source to the bowl* (2015) and *Yolele! Recipes from the Heart of Senegal* (2008) are available from Lake Isle Press.

History and culture

Faal, Dawda *A History of The Gambia – AD1000 to 1965* Edward Francis Small Printing Press, 1997. This is quite a detailed and easy-to-find local publication relating the history of the country and dealing with it from the perspective of a West African.

Haley, Alex *Roots: The Saga of an American Family* Doubleday, 1976. Many of the specifics have been discredited since Haley's death, but this Pulitzer-winning tome, set partly in The Gambia, still provides a highly readable novelistic introduction to the slave trade and the impact on its victims.

M'Bai, Pa Nderry *The Gambia: The Untold Dictator Yahya Jammeh's Story* iUniverse, 2012. Written by a highly regarded Gambian investigative journalist now living in the USA, this is probably the most balanced available account of the achievements, failings and peculiarities of President Yahya Jammeh.

Meagher, Allen (Editor) *Historic Sites of The Gambia – An Official Guide to the Monuments and Sites of The Gambia* National Council for Arts and Culture and International, 1998. This is an excellent little book that is very readable and contains lots of information not only on historic sites but also on the culture of the country.

Park, Mungo *Travels in the Interior of Africa* 1858. The extraordinary account of Scottish explorer Mungo Park's journey from The Gambia as he traced the course of the Niger, during which he encountered African despots, was taken captive by a Moorish chief and robbed and stripped naked by Fulani bandits.

Sonko-Godwin, Patience *Ethnic Groups of the Senegambia: A Brief History* Sunrise Publishers, 1985. Widely available in the country, this provides a useful and quite readable overview of the country's main cultural groups.

Thomas, Hugh *The Slave Trade: History of the Atlantic Slave Trade, 1440–1870* Phoenix, 2006. Weighing in at a daunting 900 pages, this is probably the most authoritative recent history of the trade that trafficked an estimated 10 million Africans into a life of bondage in the Americas between the 15th and 19th centuries.

Language There are a few Wolof- and Mandinka-language dictionaries and primers available on Amazon, but to get started, an eminently worthwhile resource is the Live Lingua Project (**w** livelingua.com/peace-corps-language-courses.php), which offers a free archive of downloadable Peace Corps language lessons including Wolof, Jola, Fula, Mandinka and others.

Natural history

Barlow, Clive, Wacher, Tim and Disley, Tony *A Field Guide to Birds of The Gambia and Senegal* Christopher Helm Publishers, 2nd edition, 2005. This out-of-print book used to be *the* field guide to the birds of The Gambia and Senegal. It has been supplanted as first choice by the same publisher's more recent Borrow and Demey guide listed below. Still, it is a very good book, and can safely be recommended as a supplementary field guide to anybody sufficiently dedicated to carry two.

Barnett, Linda, Emms, Craig and Santoni, Christina *The Herpetofauna of Abuko Nature Reserve, The Gambia* Bulletin of the British Herpetological Society, No 77 Autumn, 2001. This short paper covers all the amphibians and reptiles that have been found in this species-rich nature reserve.

Borrow, Nik and Demey, Roy *Helm Field Guide to the Birds of Senegal and The Gambia* Christopher Helm Publishers, 2012. This superb field guide is well laid out, with informative text, good illustrations and detailed distribution maps, and very up-to-date and thorough both for The Gambia and Senegal. A must for all birdwatchers.

Borrow, Nik and Demey, Roy *Helm Field Guide to the Birds of Western Africa* Christopher Helm Publishers, 2004. To the same high standard as the same authors' guide to Senegal and The Gambia, this is less useful to those sticking to these two countries, but a better bet for those travelling more widely in the region.

Edberg, Etienne *A Naturalist's Guide to The Gambia* J G Sanders, 1982 (English edition). Original edition in Swedish. Although quite dated now, this is still the best of the guides available for naturalists who are visiting The Gambia. It includes an introduction to the country, places to visit and a section on common animals and plants. This is a gem of a book with some very good black-and-white illustrations. Worth getting hold of.

Gosney, Dave *Finding Birds in The Gambia* Easybirder, 2011. Useful and compact guide to some of the most popular birding sites in the country, with handy hand-drawn maps too.

Kasper, Phyllis *Some Common Flora of The Gambia* Stiftung Walderhaltung in Afrika, 1999. This is a very useful illustrated guide to the common plants found throughout the country.

Kingdon, Jonathan *The Kingdon Guide to African Mammals* Academic Press, 1997. This is undoubtedly the best and most thorough field guide on terrestrial African mammals, but not really aimed at a casual one-off visitor. All the known land species are covered with the most up-to-date classification. Colour illustrations throughout and easy to use.

Kingdon, Jonathan *The Kingdon Pocket Guide to African Mammals* Princeton Pocket Guides, 2005. This condensed version of the full guide listed above will be sufficient for most visitors, and it is far cheaper and more portable.

Larsen, Torben *Butterflies of West Africa – Origins, Natural History, Diversity, Conservation* Apollo Books, 2005. A monumental achievement by the author, who has spent many years amassing a great deal of data for the region. If you're into butterflies, and aren't put off by the hefty price tag, this will be a must.

Penney, David *Common Spiders and Other Arachnids of The Gambia* Siri Scientific Press, 2009. One for specialists, this enjoyable field guide to the country's spiders, harvestmen, ticks, scorpions and allies has 170 photos.

Penney, David *Field Guide to Butterflies of The Gambia, West Africa* Siri Scientific Press, 2009. Though only 80 pages long, this is a useful field guide to the country's rich variety of butterflies, and illustrated with 230 photographs.

Penney, David *Field Guide to Wildlife of The Gambia* Siri Scientific Press, 2nd edition, 2012. This is a very portable and current paperback primer to the country's wildlife, with plenty of details on invertebrates and plants, but also some useful information on larger species (though coverage of birds is limited). Almost 800 pictures are packed into its 160 pages.

Travelogues

Fenton, Simon *Squirting Milk at Chameleons* (Eye Books, 2015) and *Chasing Hornbills* (Eye Books, 2016). In turn amusing and harrowing, these easy-to-read memoirs by the late updater of the second edition of this guide offer a fascinating insight into life among the Jola people in a village near the Senegal–Gambia border.

Long, Rosemary *Under the Baobab tree* (Eric Dobby Publishing, 1993) and *Together under the Baobab tree* (Eric Dobby Publishing, 1994). Collections of newspaper articles by a Glaswegian journalist who married a Gambian and attempted to set up a beach bar some years ago, although little seems to have changed.

WEBSITES

w **cloudbirders.com** Excellent source for comprehensive user-submitted birding reports.

w **fatbirder.com** Twitchers should visit Fatbirder for news on the latest bird sightings.

w **gov.uk/foreign-travel-advice/gambia** Up-to-date travel and safety advice from the UK Foreign Office.

w **travel.state.gov/content/passports/en/country/the-gambia.html** Up-to-date travel and safety advice from the US State Department.

w **visitthegambia.gm** Official website of the Gambia Tourism Board.

f **The Gambia Tourism Forum** Active Facebook community discussing tourism in The Gambia, inclusive of newcomers and old hands.

f **WATravellers** West Africa Travellers is a Facebook community discussing travel in West Africa more broadly.

Index

Entries in **bold** indicate main entries; those in *italics* indicate maps

INDEX OF ADVERTISERS